GLENN ROBINSON

Lebanon's Predicament

LEBANON'S PREDICAMENT

SAMIR KHALAF

New York COLUMBIA UNIVERSITY PRESS *1987*

Library of Congress Cataloging-in-Publication Data
Khalaf, Samir.
Lebanon's predicament.

Bibliography: p.
Includes index.
1. Lebanon—Politics and government. 2. Lebanon—
Social conditions. I. Title.
DS87.K395 1987   303.4'095692   86-17175
ISBN 0-231-06378-4

Columbia University Press
New York   Guildford, Surrey
Copyright © 1987 Columbia University Press
All rights reserved

Printed in the United States of America

This book is Smyth-sewn.

This Is Roseanne's Book

Contents

                     in Jeopardy**   *261*

                         Notes   *293*

                     Bibliography   *299*

                         Index   *319*

Preface

IN MUCH OF MY TEACHING and research, during the past two decades, I have had an abiding interest in documenting processes of continuity and change in some of the institutional arrangements of Lebanese society. Initially, the effort took the form of limited case studies of family firms, voluntary associations, and labor unions but gradually extended to involve explorations of political leadership, transformation of urban neighborhoods, and the nature and consequences of civil violence in a pluralistic and fragmented political culture.

I have also had the opportunity of being involved at the national and municipal levels in efforts, modest as they are, of reconstruction, urban planning and community development. In both spheres—the scholarly and the applied—I became poignantly aware of an underlying tension between some of the distinctive sociocultural attributes of Lebanese society and its inability to transform itself into a more orderly, just and edifying entity. Lebanon, as it were, is gripped by the horns of a nagging predicament: the very forces that *enable* the Lebanese at the micro and communal level and from which they derive much of their social and psychic supports, *disable* them at the macro and national level by eroding their civic consciousness and symbols of national identity. The formation and deformation of Lebanon, as it were, are rooted in the same forces. The recurrence of violence is, after all, one indication that the Lebanese have not as yet developed the appropriate political formula that allows them to live in both worlds, so to speak, by retaining and reconciling both forms of loyalties.

The essays in this volume, albeit in different ways, are all efforts at elucidating the nature and manifestations of such a predicament. Where possible, attempts are also made to suggest alternative options to resolve or mitigate some of its adverse consequences.

During the earlier period of my research, I did not find it necessary to draw any theoretical inferences or challenge existing conceptual models.

I also had no intentions (or pretensions) of ever bringing the studies together in a single volume. An anthology of one's own work—eight of the twelve chapters are revisions and updated versions of earlier essays published elsewhere—must always run the risk of violating norms of intellectual modesty.

Two circumstances prompted me to entertain such a risk. One is conceptual; the other situational. After the initial upsurge in comparative studies of modernization, the field witnessed a decline during the mid- and late seventies. The past few years, however, have seen a resurgence of interest and a revival of some of the earlier polemics. Scholars are, once again, invoking the old issues as to whether there is any unidirectionality in the process of modernization and to what extent is it possible to justify the idea of a singular path or end to that process. Some, in pursuant to the suggestion of Cyril Black (1967:49), are beginning to foresee a possible "universalization of function but not of institutions." If one accepts this sensible and realistic view, then it is appropriate to ask whether anything meaningful or enlightening can be added about modernization other than the exploration of specific and concrete situations. The Lebanese instance, precisely because it departs so sharply from some of the persisting paradigms and the experience of other countries, offers such a vivid situation.

Second, Lebanon's protracted civil disorder, by far the worst in the country's history, provides a living test of its diminished potential to cope with persisting crises or to obscure any more sources of discordance as it had done on earlier occasions.

On both counts one can make persuasive claims for carrying on such an undertaking. The inconsistency and often inadequacy of the theory, along with the growing vulnerability and agony of Lebanon, renders the inquiry both timely and meaningful. Within this context it is pertinent to probe into the nature of the dialectics between tradition and modernity. Under what circumstances, it is asked, do some of the persisting sociocultural patterns and values reinforce and when do they undermine processes of social change and development?

If the interplay between "tradition" and "modernity" is seen as a dialectical and not as a dichotomous relationship, as it is perceived here, then it is necessary to provide evidence to substantiate such a dualistic interplay. As such, by focusing on concrete institutional arrangements, it can be shown how so-called "traditional" agencies such as family firms, family associations, patronage, and urban neighborhoods have been able to absorb and generate change. Conversely, attempts are also made to show how seemingly "secular" and "civic" instruments of social change, such as labor unions, political parties, civil bureaucracies, and rational policy programs and schemes are obstructed and distorted by the incursion of primordial and parochial sentiments and loyalties.

The chapters are not as disparate a medley as they appear. They have all been selected because they either converge on or substantiate a few of the conceptual dilemmas posed in the theoretical chapter. For example, chapters 2 and 3 set a historical perspective to highlight Lebanon's fragmented political culture. Together they show how earlier episodes of violence had reinforced segmental and parochial loyalties, and hence failed to bring about the desired transformations in society.

Chapters 4, 5, and 6 focus on the political system to demonstrate how the survival of primordialism accounts for much of the deficiency in civility Lebanon has always suffered from and how it continues to shape the clientelistic character of political recruitment and succession. Various forms of patronage are elucidated in an effort to identify their manifestations and consequences.

Chapters 7 and 8 carry the analysis into the spheres of industrial development and voluntary associations. Here, as well, empirical evidence is provided to show how under certain sociocultural circumstances, kinship networks and family loyalty may exert a supportive rather than subversive influence on industrial growth. Perhaps unique to Lebanon, the family has also been effective, through the formation of kinship-based voluntary associations, in meeting certain vital benevolent and welfare needs and functions.

In chapters 9 and 10 the exploration is extended further into the area of public policy and planning. Through concrete case studies of the Lebanese Family Planning Association, and Lebanon's checkered experience with urban planning legislation, efforts are made to underscore the problematic and often ambivalent character of the interplay between sociocultural values and public policy. In the former, indigenous local traditions have been relatively effective in legitimating and supporting family planning programs in a largely unreceptive sociocultural and political setting. In the latter, they have often obstructed the little public efforts made to institutionalize urban planning schemes and zoning ordinances.

Finally, the book ends with two dismaying and daunting portraits of some of the consequences of a decade of civil unrest. One provides, in a rather impassioned tone, an account of the general mood of demoralization of public life, erosion of civility, and the breakdown in the most elementary social ties that normally hold a society together. The other depicts the seamy and disquieting transformations (or deformations) Ras-Beirut—the once open, liberal, and heterogeneous urban district—is currently undergoing.

Despite the general unifying themes interspersing the essays, one cannot ignore the distinct differences underlying their scope and tone. This is inevitable and not altogether an unwelcome feature. The essays span, after all, a period of fifteen years and were written under strikingly different sociopolitical and intellectual milieux. It is more judicious and authentic, under the circumstances, not to efface or doctor such differences. Except for an occasional polishing up of rough syntax and transition and some editing to avoid redundancy, they are presented here in their original form. Where possible and feasible, the essays were updated to incorporate new evidence.

Acknowledgment

A NY FORM OF WRITING is always an expression of one's life experience and what one has learned from others. Bearing witness to Lebanon's relentless agony over the past decade must be, like other encounters with darkness, a momentous and transforming experience. One is never the same again.

When a man's world begins collapsing on all sides, his perceptions of that world and the circumstances exacerbating its disintegration are bound to be dramatically altered. Hannah Arendt in *Men in Dark Times* suggests that "life comes fully into its own only among those who are, in wordly terms, the insulted and injured." Like countless other Lebanese I continue to be violated and injured by the harrowing events which disfigure and dismember Lebanon.

In acknowledging the impact of the war, I also wish to be absolved if, at times, I appear to have violated the strictures of my academic discipline, particularly those which emplore us to maintain dispassion and value neutrality. Such lapses, which occasionally appear in the final two essays are, I trust, forgivable and legitimate misdemeanors when compared to all the havoc and anguish generated by the war.

Since the essays in this book span the best part of my active career, the intellectual debts I have accumulated are too numerous to be justly acknowledged here. I have learned so much from so many that any recognition of some is bound to be arbitrary and partial. I wish, nonetheless, to express my gratitude to those who directly helped in bringing this book about, or those who offered critical comments to earlier drafts and versions along the way: Cyril Black, Marvin Bressler, Charles Issawi, John Mack, Anne Meyer, Edward Said, Michael Simpson, Walter Wallace, and Bayly Winder. My brother Nadim, as an economist, has not always been very sympathetic to the concerns of sociologists. He has been, nonetheless, a querying and interested reader over the years. Two departed mentors and friends of old—Morroe Berger of Princeton and

A. J. Meyer of Harvard—were always unfledging and selfless in their support and encouragement. I wish they were still around to appreciate this modest tribute.

As a research and graduate assistant, Rima Qulaylat Barraj worked diligently, often under trying circumstances, in preparing earlier drafts. She helped in proofreading, editing, and bibliographic entries.

I was privileged to be awarded a Fulbright Fellowship during 1984–85 when much of the final preparation of the book was done while enjoying a sabbatical leave at Princeton University. I am grateful to the Council for International Exchange of Scholars and the Program in Near Eastern Studies and the Sociology Department at Princeton for their generous support and assistance. I also wish to express my appreciation to Mary Bosoian of the American University of Beirut and Kerry O'Donnell of Princeton for their skill in typing and retyping drafts of the manuscripts. Kate Wittenberg of Columbia University Press was extremely helpful in editing and expediting publication of the manuscript.

I did not need the trauma of an ugly war to draw me closer to my family. But it did. My wife, Roseanne, was always willing to listen. She helped in transforming my often convoluted sentences into more readable prose. She never ceased to encourage and inspire when I was dispirited. In still more blissful ways, graced by the buoyant presence of George and Ramzi, she elevated our home into a sobering haven in an otherwise cruel and menacing world. For all this, and much more, this book is lovingly dedicated to her.

Lebanon's Predicament

CHAPTER ONE

On the Dialectics of
Tradition and Modernity

A shortcut is the longest distance between two points.
—Charles Issawi, *Issawi's Law of Social Motion*

MUCH OF THE LITERATURE on comparative modernization
and social change during the past two to three decades has been
dominated by two overriding intellectual traditions or paradigms: the so-
called "developmentalist" and "dependency" models. This ongoing controversy between the two schools is clearly more than just a benign academic debate. It has recently assumed an acute rivalry over the scope and
future direction of Third World studies in general; with all the ethical
and political implications such a controversy is bound to invite (see, for
example, Smith 1985).

Conceptually, the two schools have already gone through successive
redirections and reformulations in efforts to extend the scope and validity
of their underlying perspectives. Both are ambitious, all embracing paradigms, with elaborate analytical schemes and research tools, intended to
establish general frameworks for comparative historical analysis. Though
they claim different parentage (e.g., structural-functionalism for developmentalists and Marxism for dependency theorists), both are rooted in
the classic debate between the romantics and rationalists in the wake of
the French and Industrial Revolutions. Both continue to attract converts
from virtually all the social sciences and humanistic disciplines. More significant, perhaps, both have espoused particular strategies for socioeconomic mobilization and political development.

On the whole, developmentalists consistent with their neoevolutionary
premises, particularly in their writings during the 1950s and 1960s, advanced a unilinear pattern of social change. This is most apparent in the
works of Daniel Lerner (1964), Rostow (1960), among many others.

Even in Lerner's preface to the 1964 edition of his widely read *Passing of Traditional Society*, he continued to propound his overly ethnocentric thesis: "The 'Western model' is only historically Western; sociologically it is global . . . the same basic model reappears in virtually all modernizing societies of all continents of the world, regardless of variations of color, race or creed . . . and that what the West is, the Middle East is seeking to become" (Lerner 1964:viii-ix).

Developmentalists also held a polarized and dichotomous view of the interplay between tradition and modernity and, hence, anticipated the erosion of traditional norms and institutions by the inevitable forces of secularization. If and when traditions persisted, they are seen as inimical to change or, at best, treated as useless and nostalgic survivals.

Leaning heavily on Marxist modes of analysis, the dependency model gained dominance during the 1970s by challenging some of the basic premises of developmentalism. Despite the variety of views often subsumed under this perspective, it is held together by one underlying proposition; namely, that to understand the major forces of change in the Third World, i.e., the "periphery," one must see them ultimately as a by-product of the power of economic imperialism generated by the capitalist "core" or "center" of the international "world system." Virtually all the problems besetting developing societies—poverty, unbalanced growth, political instability, the ideological weakness of the ruling elite, the personal and flimsy character of political parties and coalitions, the absence of class loyalties, and the deficiency of civil and national ties—are linked to changes in the international economic system sustained by the forces of capitalist imperialism. In short, problems of underdevelopment, indeed the misery of much of the Third World, do not derive from traditional resistance to modernity, as developmentalists were inclined to believe, but from the forces of modernity itself. (For an elaboration of these and other prominent views of dependency theorists, see the following: Wallerstein 1974 and 1980; Chilcote 1981; Cardoso and Faletto 1979; Wiarda 1985).

Despite the striking differences between them, the two schools hold, essentially, similar views regarding the nature of the interplay between tradition and modernity. Both assume an inherently conflicting relationship between them. While proponents of developmentalism blame traditional loyalties and institutions for obstructing processes of social change and modernization, dependency theorists warn instead of the "brutalization" and "victimization" of traditional orders by the forces of modernization. "When peasants are dispossessed of their land and herded into urban slums; when traditional artisans find their means of livelihood destroyed; when old patterns of power that provided at least some security are removed and the nuclear family is left to determine its fate as best as it may—then one may indeed expect conflict. But it is modernity, not tradition, that is the origin of the struggle" (Smith 1985:551).

There is no need here to elaborate on the charges leveled against both perspectives. This has been convincingly and amply done by a score of other writers.[1] It is sufficient to repeat that they are not the global models they are often claimed to be. To be more explicit, they are inadequate in helping us understand the nature of the interplay between tradition and modernity in Lebanon. Indeed, they actually distort the socio-historical reality of the country. For at no point in the recent history of Lebanon have the processes of change been so total and all-embracing that they swept aside all the vestiges of its traditional past. Nor have traditional values and institutions been so immobile and obstructive as to pose insurmountable barriers to modernity or to require that they be rendered inoperative by encapsulating or neutralizing their "polluting" impact. Likewise, as will become clear from subsequent discussions, the persistence of communal conflict, protracted political instability, and the absence of class and civic loyalties that continue to plague Lebanon cannot be exclusively attributed to imbalances generated by the world system.

Such misreading is not as benign or innocuous as often assumed. It has done more than generate a large measure of distortion of Lebanon's sociohistorical realities. It has also led to some costly misadventures in schemes for socioeconomic planning and strategies for political development. To this day, planners in Lebanon, like elsewhere in developing countries, continue to receive inconsistent advice. At times, in the name of secularization and rational planning, they are asked to erode, bypass, contain or even devalue their traditional loyalties. At others, particularly when planners become mindful of the commercial or political value of some of the rustic and colorful features of their folklore and popular culture, they are implored to preserve their threatened natural and cultural heritage lest they be exploited or despoiled by foreign capitalists and multinational firms. The very devalued institutions and loyalties become coveted and prized attributes. Little wonder that traditional loyalties are either denigrated or idealized but rarely treated for what they actually are.

The moral to be extracted from these and other critical reassessments of the extensive literature on comparative modernization is plain and clear. We need to disavow ourselves of the conceptual and ideological tyranny of such models. "When the compulsion to theorize is so strong," admonishes Hirschman, "it often induces mindlessness." (Hirschman 1970:329). And we have been a bit too mindless in our efforts to impose such models on inappropriate instances. If we are to employ the indispensable Weberian ideal-typical contrast between "traditional" and "modern," then, in the words of Reinhard Bendix, we should "deideologize" these constructs in such a way as not to impart "a spurious, deductive simplicity to the transition from one to the other" (Bendix 1967:318).

We clearly need an alternative approach for the analysis of the interplay between tradition and modernity in Lebanon. For neither in their antecedents, nor in their patterns and consequences do processes of development and social change in Lebanon comply with the central assumptions and premises of "developmentalism" or "dependency" theory. To repeat, we need an approach that recognizes the possibility in certain contexts of the continuing coexistence and mutual reinforcement of tradition and modernity, and one that makes for greater opportunities for congruence and overlapping whereby tradition and modernity are allowed to infiltrate and transform each other. It is in this sense that the interplay between tradition and modernity is conceived more as a dialectical than a dichotomous relationship.

The purpose of this introductory chapter is to provide further theoretical and empirical evidence in favor of such a dialectical approach. First, the case for the dialectical character of tradition and modernity will be elaborated. Second, an attempt is made to disclose the nature of adaptive modernization and the type of agencies or institutions most effective in bringing it about.

The Case for Dialectics: Sustained Change and Social Cohesion

The case for a dialectical approach requires little in way of theoretical justification. There is no need, in fact, for elaborate models or complex reformulations of earlier conceptual schemes. A score of writers—often proponents of "developmentalism" or "dependency" theory, and others who may not subscribe to such labels—have already introduced concepts or distinctions that can be appropriately employed in analyzing structural and institutional changes without the moral premises and ethnocentric biases inherent in some of the earlier formulations.[2]

The distinction that John Lewis (1969) makes between "adaptive" and "inverse" modernization is one such instance. The "adaptive" type usually involves the gradual, unplanned, and spontaneous proliferation of roles and the progressive development from single, undifferentiated, premodern institutions to more complex, specialized and differentiated ones. Since many of the premodern social institutions and relationships are "carried over"—particularly those that help shape the attitudes of individuals—social cohesion is maintained during the unsettling period of social change.

"Inverse" modernization, on the other hand, occurs "where the gradual processes of change are bypassed and specialized organizational forms are directly transferred to new nations under the guidance of a revolutionary or modernizing elite" (Lewis 1969:6). In some respects this involves the "inversion" of those processes of development that underlie adaptive modernization. The often impetuous revolutionary elites of new nations, according to Lewis, are not only bent on a disruptive and rapid course of modernization, but have consciously repudiated the premodern social relationships that might help sustain minimal social cohesion. In this way, "they exacerbate disorder and destroy potential support: they thereby sow the seeds of their own destruction. Left unchecked, these difficulties would produce extreme social upheaval and a new revolutionary situation" (Lewis 1969:10).

William Friedland (1969) underscores the same emphasis on role and institutional proliferation and adaptiveness of the sociocultural system as crucial elements in the analysis of modernization. What makes a society "adaptive," he argues, "is its willingness or ability to shift institutional emphasis to confront new situations . . . one that can make minor institutions more capable of confronting problems, or that is willing to tolerate inventions of new ways" (Friedland 1969:40).

In analyzing processes of agricultural and ecological change in Indonesia, Clifford Geertz borrows the interesting concept of "involution" from the American anthropologist Alexander Goldenweiser, who devised it to describe

those cultural patterns which, after having reached what would seem to be a definitive form, nonetheless fail either to stabilize or transform themselves into a new pattern but rather continue to develop by becoming internally more complicated. . . . What we have here is pattern plus continued development. The pattern precludes the use of another unit or units, but it is not inimical to play within the unit or units. The inevitable result is progressive complication, a variety within uniformity, virtuosity within monotony. This is involution. A parallel instance . . . is provided by what is called ornateness in art, as in the late Gothic. The basic forms of art have reached finality, the structural features are fixed beyond variation, inventive originality is exhausted. Still development goes on. Being hemmed in on all sides by a crystallized pattern, it takes the function of elaborateness. Expansive creativeness having dried up at the source, a special kind of virtuosity takes its place. (Geertz 1968:81)

Involution in the case of Indonesia was highly functional because it enabled the society to "evade, adjust, absorb, and adapt but not really change" (Geertz 1968:103). Since the particular Javanese village Geertz explored was shaped by forces over which it had little control and since it was denied the means for actively reconstructing itself, it "clung to the husks of selected established institutions and limbered them internally in such a way as to permit greater flexibility, a freer play of social relationships within a generally stereotyped framework. . . . The quality of everyday existence in a fully involuted Javanese village is comparable to that in the other formless human community, the American suburb: a richness of social surfaces and a monotonous poverty of social substance" (Geertz 1968:103).

Involution in Lebanon, particularly as the process manifests itself in family firms, family associations and the internal adaptability of other parochial and communal voluntary associations, assumes a slightly different pattern. In most instances the outer form, the social surface of these organizations, has remained fundamentally the same while their inner substance managed to undergo appreciable differentiation and development. The concept, nonetheless, is relevant and useful precisely because it recognizes the possibility of internal differentiation, variety, development and a certain measure of "virtuosity" while cultural patterns retain their definitive and crystallized form. Outward fixity and inner dynamism, in other words, coexist and reinforce one another.

Dankwart Rustow and Robert Ward (1964) identify the quality of "reinforcing dualism" to explain Japan's classic and perhaps most dramatic instance of the systematic and purposeful exploitation of traditional institutions for the achievement of modernizing goals. They provide ample evidence to falsify the conventional thesis by showing that the role of traditional attitudes and institutions in the modernizing process has often been more "symbiotic than antagonistic" (Rustow and Ward 1964:445). Similar instances of "reinforcing dualism" are evident in the economic field. The maintenance of small traditionally organized units of production alongside the most modern factories seems to have contributed to the rapid and effective economic development of Japan. The obvious conclusion Rustow and Ward draw from this is clear: "Many elements of the traditional society could be converted into supports for the process of political modernization. The result was added impetus of a sort conducive to modernization" (Rustow and Ward 1964:445).

S. N. Eisenstadt's concept of "patrimonialism," particularly as it relates to the persistence of patron-client networks, feudal and semifeudal survivals, and other personalistic loyalties and associations, can also be judiciously applied to explore concrete instances of the reinforcing character of the interplay between traditional and modern forms in Lebanon (for further details, see Eisenstadt 1973). According to Eisenstadt, such a perspective discloses the inadequacies of some of the basic premises of the earlier theories of modernization on at least four counts: "first by showing that many of these societies and states did not develop in the direction of certain modern nation-states; second, by demonstrating that these regimes did not necessarily constitute a temporary "transitional" phase along an inevitable path to this type of modernity; third, by indicating that there was nevertheless some internal "logic" in their development, and last by emphasizing that part, at least, of this logic or pattern could be understood from some aspects of the traditions of these societies and derived from them" (Eisenstadt 1974:241).

As will be shown in subsequent chapters, several of the most widespread institutional and structural arrangements in Lebanon—ranging from patronage, to family firms, family associations, and other communal and parochial voluntary associations—may all be seen as forms of patrimonialism that have been effective, at least at the local and subnational level, in mobilizing resources, accommodating to change and providing a measure of social and psychic reinforcement.

Two other relatively obscure but equally telling examples of the dialectics we have in mind may also be cited. To document the adaptation of traditional Islamic movements to modern conditions, Ernest Gellner provides an insightful analysis of two rather paradoxical but successful instances of so-called "post-traditional" forms in Islam: the Ismailis of the

Shi'a; and the Murids, a Sufi brotherhood in the Senegal (Gellner 1973). The former operates conceptually outside the bonds of Sunni orthodoxy, the latter claims to have remained within it. Neither, however, is particularly predisposed to the allegedly rational, universalistic, and achievement ethics of the modern world. Yet both displayed remarkable entrepreneurial and organizational skills while sustained by mystical beliefs and primordial loyalties that are the antithesis of the Weberian model of the Protestant ethic.

Finally, several other instances of the dialectical relationship between tradition and modernity are being increasingly recognized lately. At least two such recent expressions can be noted here. One revolves around the role of informal groups, kinship networks, and other primordial ties in political development. James Bill and Carl Leiden (1984:74–131) provide persuasive evidence of the pervasiveness and profound influence such networks continue to have on political loyalties, power struggle, in relaying vital political information and arriving at consequential political decisions. The other focuses on the developmental potential of indigenous and other traditional grass-roots organizations in the formation of viable cooperatives, collectivities, and other peasant associations concerned with various rural development projects ranging from rotating credit and saving associations to the construction, maintenance, allocation and management of water schemes and irrigation projects.

To Nash, Dandler, and Hopkins (1976), cooperatives are conceived as communities which demonstrate how people direct themselves to form, out of the old human material, new institutions to cope with their changing world. They, too, speak of the "dialectic between structure and movement" and how "new forms of mobilization relate to existing traditional structures" (Nash, Dandler and Hopkins, 1976:19). They provide supportive evidence, from various cross-cultural settings, to demonstrate "the effectiveness of this kind of grafting of new organizations on the traditional kinship and communal organizations" (Nash, Dandler and Hopkins 1976:20).

Likewise, Cernea (1981), Siebel and Massing (1976) and Colletta (1975), among others, provide further substantive evidence along those lines. Cernea is quite explicit and maintains that policymakers or development practitioners in this area tend to develop one of two basic sets of attitudes:

The first consists of ignoring or underestimating the development function or potential of grass roots, production-oriented peasant organizations. This is the well-known attitude of certain national development agencies that perceive indigenous organizations and culture as a constraint on modernization, as a remnant of old times, and a nuisance to be eliminated, in order to really "modernize."

The second consists of idealizing the traditional organizations and culture and ignoring the historical necessity of changing them too; this is tantamount to not understanding the essence of organizational forms as a cultural adaptive mechanism to change and as a sociocultural form for absorbing and utilizing modernized technologies. (Cernea 1981:130)

To Cernea, clearly, neither of these two positions can guide, either in practical or in theoretical terms, an effective development policy. Instead of regarding traditional organizations as a constraint, could they not, Cernea asks, be utilized as a resource for development? "A sound modernization policy should make the best use of all available resources . . . when they are amenable to developmental activities. On the other hand, the need to strengthen, change, and develop these organizations themselves should not be overlooked" (Cernea 1981:130).

Colletta makes a similar plea for the use of indigenous culture. He concludes his Indonesian case study by writing, "All too often development has confronted culture as a bulwark of conservatism, infrequently looking towards its potential use for positive change. Anthropologists have been quick to document the confrontation between development and culture . . . [instead of] leading the creative discovery of how long-established cultural pathways of interaction, established roles, institutions and value incentive systems might be employed as levers for positive change" (Colletta 1975:62).

This charge does not apply to at least one anthropologist; Elizabeth Fernea who, after an absence of five years, revisited the Arab World and returned to speak of "new voices." In her recently published book (1985), an edited volume of evocative essays, stories, poems, life histories etc., she argues that despite the rich variety of expressions, there is a "great shift" in the aspirations of men and women: "No longer is the example of the West seen as the answer to the problems of the Middle East. . . . People are attempting to improve their lives through indigenous traditions and customs; through the dominant religion of the area, Islam; and through their own kinship and family patterns. They are improvising and combining the new and the old, adapting, changing, and building, trying to create their own form of independence" (Fernea 1985:2).

In Lebanon, as no doubt elsewhere in the Arab World, these "new voices" are far from new. They have always been there. Somehow, social scientists and historians failed to identify or recognize their true nature or the role they could play in generating and absorbing change. In fact, a generation of earlier scholars had either denigrated the presence of such traditional values and sentiments or prodded Arabs to disengage themselves from them, if they are to enjoy the fruits of modernity (see, among others, Lerner 1964).

Further such instances of the mutual reinforcement of tradition and modernity, from both developed and developing societies, can be easily furnished.[3] The foregoing examples are, hopefully, sufficient to establish the fact that such a dialectic is much more widespread and viable than has so far been admitted by interested observers. The oversight is understandable and may be accounted for in two ways. First, as has been suggested earlier, because of the predominance of certain perspectives and the emergence of radical revolutionary elites in the Third World, we have either overlooked or denigrated the modernizing potential of traditional values and institutions. Simply not enough social scientists have been trained to look for, recognize, and document such convergence. Second, forging a blend between seemingly discordant elements is admittedly difficult. At least it has not always been a simple and manageable task. These two historical forces—the desire for continuity and change, for coherence and dynamism, for institutional transformation and cultural reconstruction, to mention a few of the many labels by which this interplay may be expressed—are impelled after all by different sentiments and values and often derive their support from divergent and disparate social groups.

The experience of specific countries may be different, but the tensions and the broad patterns bespeak of essentially the same process or underlying concern: how to preserve cherished values while transforming the institutional and material basis of society. Expressed more pointedly: how is social cohesion to be maintained if change is accelerated?

The Lebanese experience is instructive in this regard because it had been, at least until the outbreak of civil hostilities in 1975, relatively successful in forging such a blend without the usual concomitant costs of either increasing alienation or increasing government centralization and repression. Rather than looking in either one of two directions—the rooted traditions of the past or the more secular and liberal components—Lebanon, perhaps more by necessity than design, has been inclined toward grafting or reconciling both dimensions. The result is often seen as an incoherent and precarious melange of disparate elements, but it has been at least at the micro and local level effective in generating and sustaining change while maintaining social cohesion and some measure of cultural continuity.

Three central features of adaptive modernization may be extracted from our discussion thus far. All three are essential for understanding the nature of modernization in Lebanon and justifying further the need for a dialectical perspective.

First, whether modernization is conceived in terms of "social mobilization," "structural differentiation," "role proliferation," "involution," "posttraditional order," or "convergence," it most certainly involves the will and capacity of a society to absorb and generate change or innovation. This capability for sustained growth, however, need not involve total and radical transformation. Nor should it necessitate incessant adoption and borrowing of new ideas and practices. Innovation can take place through the restructuring and rearrangement of existing institutions. Indeed, this is the distinctive feature of adaptive modernization: the capacity of existing institutions and agencies to rearrange themselves to confront new challenges and cope with continuing tensions and problems. In brief, a large measure of modernization can and does take place by mobilizing traditional networks.

Second, irrespective of how modernization is defined or brought about, it always generates discontinuities, imbalances, and tensions. Whether the process assumes a gradualist and spontaneous course or a more radical and revolutionary reconstruction; whether it originates from internal indigenous forces or from external social contact, modernization always produces disharmonies and strains that necessitate adjustments and continuous adaptation. No mode of social interaction is free of some of the occasional ramifications of internal tension. Accordingly, another attribute of modernity becomes the capacity of a society to cope with the discontinuities and discrepancies inherent in a changing social order.[4] Incidentally, proponents of dependency theory, perhaps more so than the developmentalists, share an overriding concern for recognizing the terrible human cost associated with rapid social change.

Finally, modernity, as Rousseau poignantly realized more than two hundred years ago, despite all its potential promises, remains a disruptive social process and a bitter and agonizing personal experience. If one is not to be mindless of some of its disquieting by-products—alienation, apathy, homelessness, over-urbanization, excessive materialism, pollution, senseless rebellion, pointless crime and deviance etc.—then there must be more cognizance of the need for stabilizing and integrative mechanisms that could provide some measure of social supports and psychic reinforcements. The "will to be modern," after all, and the desire to enjoy the material benefits of modernity are not the only overpowering urge among newly developing societies. Equally compelling is to survive with dignity and honor. Or what Mazzini called the "need to exist and have a name." In fact, the concern for national consciousness, cultural identity, and personal autonomy appears to be assuming more prominence than the heedless craving for unlimited growth and material progress.

If we accept these fundamental components, then modernization becomes ultimately a question of which are the appropriate agencies capable of generating change, absorbing and mediating tensions without threatening national identity. The viability and effectiveness of any agency of modernization should be assessed in terms of its propensity for providing such basic elements. In this sense modernization, contrary to what is often assumed (Huntington 1966:766), requires more than the expansion of production and communication, the broadening of loyalties from family, village, and community to nation, the secularization of public life, the rationalization of political authority, the promotion of functionally specific organizations, and the substitution of achievement criteria for ascriptive ones. These are no doubt essential for absorbing and generating change, but it is doubtful whether they are similarly effective in coping with imbalances while retaining a sense of national identity and social integration. Of equal importance is the capacity of a system to incorporate traditional social groupings that could act as palliatives in absorbing some of the imbalances and in maintaining some measure of political consciousness and national identity. In concluding his lucid and exhaustive survey of the economic history of the Middle East, Charles Issawi (1982:227) singles out this contradiction as a future source of social and political unrest in the region. Peoples of the Middle East, he maintains, much like those of the rest of the world, are seeking to achieve incompatible aims: economic growth, higher levels of living, national power and equality, a greater sense of community, cultural identity, and political liberty.

Modernization, then, should not be taken to mean necessarily the erosion of traditional loyalties and groupings, or a process of "disengagement from traditions" (Welch 1967). It is doubtful whether a pluralistic society like Lebanon could ever sustain substantial change and development if such transformations were to dislodge the rooted traditional interests and loyalties. Likewise, modernization need not involve the emergence of exclusively rational and secular agencies.

It is primarily because of such considerations that the central thesis of this volume argues in favor of an adaptive and reconciliatory form of modernization. Agencies and institutions such as family firms, kinship associations, confessional bureaucracy, parochial voluntary associations, company unions, and the political za'im have been fairly effective in reconciling some of the universal standards with particular interests, and in adapting certain rational elements to the traditional sentiments rooted in society.

At the expense of some oversimplification, it is argued that the basic problem of modernization, at least in Lebanon, has been and will continue to be one of convergence and assimilation: how to assimilate some of the rational instruments of a nation-state into the fabric of a pluralistic society that is still sustained by primordial allegiances and particularistic loyalties. The former are necessary for development; the latter for social and psychic reinforcement. Both, however, are necessary for sustaining modernization.

What is being suggested here is that insofar as modernization is, to some extent, a disruptive process, the effectiveness of a modernizing agency should not be measured solely in terms of its capacity to absorb and generate change. Of equal importance, as was suggested earlier, is its capacity to cope with tensions and discontinuities and promote a certain measure of cultural identity and national consciousness. The adaptive instruments of modernization that the Lebanese established at various stages of their history have proved to be effective on at least two of the three basic dimensions outlined above. While they have been effective in generating change and alleviating some of the tensions and disquieting effects of modernization, they have not been successful in generating the necessary conditions that sustain civic ties and national loyalties. The very factors that account for much of the viability, resourcefulness, and integration of the Lebanese are also the factors that are responsible for the erosion of civic ties and national loyalties.

Expressed differently, norms that enable in some respects, disable in other respects. This insight, attributed to Thorstein Veblen, John Dewey, Kenneth Burke, and which more recently has been judiciously used by Bruno Bettelheim (1960), W. F. Whyte (1943), and Bennett Berger (1966), can be appropriately applied to account for both the failure of specific instances of socioeconomic planning and development and to underscore the deeper and more encompassing predicament Lebanon is facing.

For example, the survival of primordial and other communal ties has been instrumental in containing the incidence of social disorganization and deviance in society to a relatively low level (Khalaf 1969). They have also insulated rapidly urbanizing districts from the temporal, segmental and impersonal types of social contacts often associated with urbanism (Khalaf and Kongstad 1973). But to a large extent, they also account for much of the deficiency in civility and the protracted violence and civil unrest Lebanon continues to suffer from. In short, the factors that enable at the micro and communal level, disable at the macro and national level. This is, indeed, Lebanon's predicament.

To a large extent, the political future of Lebanon, let alone the degree and pattern of socioeconomic development, will ultimately depend on how or when this dilemma or predicament will be resolved. The country clearly needs those types of sociopolitical institutions or structural arrangements that will permit the average Lebanese to preserve some of his primordial allegiances without threatening the already precarious and tenuous national sentiments and loyalties. This, among other things, will necessitate the development of a new political and national leadership; one that will encourage and sanction extensive political resocialization and restructuring of some of the existing values and loyalties. Without such restructuring or resocialization, Lebanon cannot possibly develop into a full-fledged nation-state. Compared to the purely "secular" or "traditional" institutions, the adaptive agencies we have in mind could still potentially be more effective, particularly if reinforced by such resocialization, in being the carriers of these transformations.

That these adaptive agencies have survived for so long is one indication that they continue to answer some durable and profound needs. That some of them degenerate or cannot as effectively mobilize and integrate human and other resources at higher levels of the social order is, in many respects, inevitable and expected given the pluralistic and multifarious nature of group affiliations in Lebanon. Such realities, as Durkheim often reminds us, are reasons to seek the reformation of these agencies, not to declare them forever useless, or to destroy them (Durkheim 1964:14).

Agencies of Adaptive Modernization

The preceding discussion should, it is hoped, have made it clear that in our conception of modernization it is not sufficient merely to consider the attributes or qualities of a modern man or modern society. If we are not to be mindless of some of the disquieting effects of rapid social change, we must be equally concerned about the instruments or agencies that produce such a man or society. Indeed, in Lebanon it may be more pertinent to undertake such an inquiry. If the three postulated features of modernization are accepted as central to the study of social change, then the focus of analysis is oriented toward those agencies that display the highest propensity for innovation, for coping with some of the imbalances and disruptive consequences of change, and finally for integrating the social order and retaining a measure of group identity and solidarity. This is being emphasized because there is a tendency in the literature to overrate the innovative aspects of modernization at the expense of the integrative and tension-reducing capacity of a particular agency or system. Once again, we reiterate that because of the persistence of certain perspectives of modernization, particularly those that place undue emphasis on rationality, growth and development, some of the integrative and sociocultural dimensions of modernization are often overlooked or treated only obliquely. Accordingly, the central problem of how social cohesion is to be maintained if change is accelerated, continues to be generally ignored.[5]

If this is the context—i.e., sustained changed and social cohesion—within which modernization is to be evaluated, then Lebanon can take one of three possible alternative courses of modernization.

One such course would be to adopt a coercive and disciplined model in line with many newly emerging nations where the state becomes the dominant agency of political socialization and modernization. In a Marxian sense, the state will presumably liberate man from his communal and primordial ties and establish collective allegiance on the basis of the "unmediated loyalties" and devotions of individuals.[6] All voluntary associations, special-purpose groups and social identities—traditional and rational alike—will be eroded or become virtually nonexistent. This unmediated approach to modernization, and for short of a better expression it can be labeled such, has not only been badly battered by academic critics, it has been faulted by events. Suffice it to note here that, given the pluralistic structure of Lebanese society along with the pervasive traditions of laissez-faire and individualism, it cannot possibly gain any widespread appeal. The totalitarian or authoritarian model is certainly effective in generating social cohesion and solidarity but only at the expense of sealing off most avenues of individuality and self-expression. Increasing centralization and state control may produce the desired goals of political stability and uniformity, but only by insulating the individual from modern life. Among other things, citizens in such a system are incapable of imagining any other values except those defined by the state. Also this model assumes that becoming modern is inherently revolutionary, in that it seeks to dislodge all the inherited basic institutions, a process that can only be carried out by, and under the guidance of, a radical elite.[7]

Durkheim, once again, can be appropriately invoked here. "When the state," he warns us, "is the only environment in which men can live communal lives, they inevitably lose contact, become detached, and thus society disintegrates. A nation can be maintained only if, between the state and the individual, there is intercolated a whole series of secondary groups near enough to the individuals to attract them strongly in their sphere of action and drag them, in this way, into the torrent of social life" (Durkheim 1964:28).

The critical question, then, is what sort of groups are more effective in "dragging," to use Durkheim's expression, individuals into the torrent of social life. Within this context, any authoritarian or centralized model which requires the elimination of such mediating groups, is not feasible for Lebanon. Indeed, of the three options, this is clearly the most perilous course Lebanon can take.

Lebanon could, however, opt for a more liberal and secular approach where change is mediated through predominantly rational agencies of modernization, and where political allegiance and loyalty is sustained by civic instruments of a nation state. Most proponents of developmentalism, particularly in their earlier writings, were more inclined to favor this approach. Daniel Lerner (1964), Edward Shils (1962), Manfred Halpern (1963), Karl Deutsch (1961), and S. N. Eisenstadt (1966), to mention a few, all identified the agencies of political development in terms of the instruments of the nation-state modeled after the experience of some Western countries. Modern man, whether through "empathy," "psychic mobility," or socioeconomic "mobilization," is defined in terms of psychological attitudes that predispose him toward secular, pragmatic, instrumental, and utilitarian ties and contacts. He is also a "participant" man in that he experiences modern citizenship by joining political associations or special-purpose groups. Accordingly, there is extensive consideration of the role of the mass media, the military elite, political parties, civil bureaucracy, and other so-called "institutional vectors of modernization" (Berger, et al. 1973:119–38), but hardly any recognition of the role of adaptive agencies in bringing about political development or promoting cultural identity and social integration. These secular institutions are seen as liberating agencies that free or disengage man from traditional loyalties and prepare him psychologically for modernity. Both these notions—the one of instrumentality and utilitarianism and the other of participation in secular political groups—do not correspond to realities or characteristics of modernization in Lebanon. At least at this juncture of Lebanon's socioeconomic and political development, this approach is not likely to be very compatible with the underlying features of the society. Even if they were to exist, the rational instruments of change are of doubtful value in coping with the imbalances and discontinuities inherent in a changing society. Neither can they be effective, as suggested earlier, as integrative mechanisms.

The third, and perhaps, most realistic and effective alternative, is the particularistic or adaptive path to modernity. This approach does not exclude the possibility of mobilizing traditional groupings in the process of modernization. It is an adaptive course in more than one sense. First, it attempts to mediate change through agencies that are not exclusively rational or secular. Second, it employs efforts to reconcile some of the universal and rational principles to the indigenous cultural traditions.

It is primarily for such reasons that it is being argued that the historical predisposition of the Lebanese to justify change within traditional contexts should not be dismissed as a conservative gesture to glorify the sacred traditions of the past. Recognizing the viability of some of the primordial ties and associations should not be taken to mean that the Lebanese seeks refuge in his past heritage and communal attachments to escape confrontation with the contemporary challenges of the modern age. The adaptive path to modernity is not a resigned and nostalgic flight. Rather, it emanates from a given socio-historical reality; a reality that cannot be ignored or simply willed away by prophetic visions of a secular social order free of all primordial attachments. Putting new wine in old bottles, to borrow a trite metaphor, can be quite salutary in absorbing conflict and in easing the acceptance of new ideas. Furthermore, the fact that an agency is traditional in form or structure does not imply that it must espouse traditional values, or that it must devote itself exclusively to passing on sacred values or preserving traditional lore and skills. Conversely, a seemingly modern institution, or exposure to modern values and practices, is no guarantee that man will undergo a drastic transformation in his spirit and that he will, after all, acquire modern life styles.

The case for adaptive modernization can still be justified on at least one further ground. There is a tendency in the literature to exaggerate the differences and discontinuities between so-called modern and traditional societies. The transition from one polarity to the other is seen as a "process in which major clusters of old social, economic, and psychological commitments are eroded and broken and people become available for new patterns of socialization and behavior" (Deutsch 1961:464). It is also asserted that one of the marks of the contemporary man is that "he will no longer live emmeshed in a network of primary kin ties . . . , but rather will be drawn into a much more impersonal and bureaucratic milieu" (Inkeles 1966:153).

The essays in this volume depart from this tradition of dichotomous schemes. Indeed, it is argued that we cannot begin to understand what is involved in the process of modernization in Lebanon unless we abandon this tendency of viewing change and development as an inevitable, directional, and unilinear movement from one polar end of the scheme to the other. Despite their rich insights, all such polarized dichotomies obscure some of the important adaptive mechanisms in Lebanese society.

For purposes of our analysis, then, we cannot think of modernization in terms of a quantitative decline in traditional features and the emergence of modern ones. We must consider instead what mixture, or rather blend, of traditional and modern patterns is most effective in meeting the three dimensions of modernization outlined earlier. In a sense we can think of modern patterns as providing the superstructure, and thus conclude that effective modernization depends upon whether the traditional patterns reinforce or undermine the superstructure of modernity. This is certainly a far more value-neutral approach than the ones that ipso facto declare the obstructive and unchanging character of all traditional values and institutions. The bulk of the evidence presented in the case studies to follow suggests that there are several instances where Lebanese traditions have had a reinforcing rather than a retarding effect on development and modernization.

Both historical and more recent empirical evidence appear to suggest that change mediated through exclusively nonrational or traditional agencies is not likely to be continuous or effective. Likewise, the socioeconomic and political structure of Lebanese society is not likely to sustain change of an entirely rational or secular character. The premature introduction of rational and secular ideas may be as much of an impediment to modernization as the excessively long retention of traditional practices. A shortcut, to repeat one of Charles Issawi's (1973:8) pungent aphorisms, is not only the longest distance between two points; it is quite often the most perilous route.

To insist at this stage on exclusively rational, formal, and professional criteria for assessing talent and allocating power and privilege in society not only runs the risk of disrupting the delicate but precarious sectarian balance; more important perhaps it carries within its wake a more disquieting consequence: that of depersonalizing the human content of the social structure. If the process of modernization in Lebanon were to truly assume an exclusively rational character, the more fundamental human need for intimacy, spontaneity, and extended personal contacts could quite possibly be sacrificed or restricted. At least these have been some of the concomitant consequences of modernization in the West, and a sizable portion of the intellectual concerns of the classic and contemporary social thinkers—from Rousseau to Marcuse—has been to either analyze or warn against such an irreversible historical force. In fact, modernity—in both its unbounded promises for generating fluid, open, mobile, and expanding social systems, and its negative potential for sacrificing individuality and restricting personal autonomy—has been the leitmotif of Western culture.[8]

The case is being made for the adaptive instruments of modernization in Lebanon precisely because agencies such as family firms, family association, confessional and communal voluntary associations, political patronage, urban quarters, etc. have been effective in meeting some of the secular and rational demands of modernization (i.e., openness, receptivity to change, the ability to cope with problems and imbalances) without diluting primordial loyalties or dehumanizing the social fabric of society. At the risk of some oversimplification, the alternatives to adaptive modernization at this stage are clear: increasing alienation (if Lebanon opts for the liberal-secular model), or increasing repression (if it opts for the authoritarian-disciplined model).

It is not being suggested here that the adaptive instruments of modernization have the potential of actually sealing off the "transitional" Lebanese from the abyss of modernization. Such an idyllic vision is hard to sustain. Alienation, after all, in one form or another, is an irrevocable historical condition that man is bound to experience. The adaptive instruments of modernization could, however, mitigate some of the corrosive effects of extreme alienation, particularly in periods of swift social change.

In short, the dialectical character of the relationship between tradition and modernity is basic to understanding the nature of modernization in Lebanon. The problem, to repeat, is not one of dislodging traditions or being disengaged from them; rather how to modernize without abandoning traditions. The patrimonial manager, the political *za'im,* the confessional bureaucrat, the company union, the parochial voluntary association, and the urban quarter are all, in fact, devices for achieving such a synthesis. Each, in its own way, has been effective in maintaining the appropriate blend necessary for sustaining change without a substantial measure of imbalances and discontinuities. They have done so, it is argued, because they have succeeded in adapting universal and rational principles essential for development and change to the indigenous traditions necessary for cohesion, continuity and cultural identity.

The "family firm," in this sense, becomes a sort of halfway arrangement between the corporate enterprise and the domestic putting-out system; and the patrimonial manager a cross-breed of the rational impersonal administrator and the paternalistic employer. The "political *za'im,*" in much the same way, becomes the mediating link between communal and local allegiances and the impersonal central bureaucracy. The "company union," too, is a halfway arrangement between craft guilds and national labor federations. "Family associations," are also a crossbreed of informal tribal groups and formal voluntary associations. The same is true of parochial and communal voluntary associations. They combine some of the rational and welfare features of formal organizations with the need for intimacy and identity inherent in communal and sectarian ties and loyalties. Finally, urban neighborhoods and residential quarters, as self-sufficient communities, serve all the conventional multiurban functions along with satisfying man's craving for a certain measure of intimacy and spontaneity in social networks.

In short, all these small units and seemingly nonrational and informal organizations have been quite effective so far in exposing the Lebanese to some of the requirements of modernization without eroding cultural identity or threatening the precarious sectarian or communal balance in society. Among other things, they demonstrate how traditional agencies can rearrange themselves to cope with particular problems and become open and receptive to socioeconomic, political, and cultural transformation. Conversely, they also provide vivid instances of how seemingly rational and modern agencies modify their structure and objectives to accommodate nonrational and particularistic considerations.

It is in this sense that the interplay between small and large units, local and national, communal and civic, informal and formal groups, etc. becomes essential for justifying the vital need for a dialectical approach to understand the nature of the relationship between tradition and modernity. As will become apparent, these small and adaptive agencies do not only mediate between the impersonal authority of the central government and the personal and communal interests of special groups (familial, ethnic, religious, or otherwise), they fill a void left by an inefficient and often suspected and mistrusted bureaucracy.

Since such adaptive mechanisms have been more effective at the communal rather than the national level, their future and continued viability will have to depend on the extent to which they can extend and broaden the scope of their concern to incorporate more civic and national attributes. It is only then that they will become equally effective in alleviating some of the consequences of deficient civility and in promoting the much-needed national sentiments and loyalties.

CHAPTER TWO

Abortive Class Conflict:
The Failure of Peasant Uprisings
in the Nineteenth Century

THE PROTRACTED CHAOS, unrest, and violence Lebanon has
been undergoing lately—much like its earlier repeated episodes of
civil strife—reveal, among other things, the fragility of its precarious democracy, its deficient civility, and perpetual grievances of dominant groups
within society.

That a fragmented and pluralistic society of this sort should display a
high propensity for civil unrest and political violence is not unusual. What
is remarkable is the frequency and pattern of such conflict. Its recurrence
suggests that previous resorts to violence have had little effect in redressing the gaps and imbalances in society, or in transforming its communal
and confessional loyalties into the more secular and civic attachments
typical of a nation-state. Indeed, the very persistence of civil strife means
that the basic problems are not being resolved.

The pattern or nature of civil unrest is even more remarkable. In recent, as in earlier, episodes of violence, what begins as predominantly
nonsectarian, factional rivalries and peasant seditions is almost always
transformed into confessional hostilities. On three specific instances in
the nineteenth century—1820, 1840, and 1857—peasants and commoners took the initiative and assumed leadership in organizing revolts against
some of the repressive abuses of the feudal or *iqta*ᶜ system of Mount
Lebanon. In each of these instances, the upheavals failed to bring about
the intended changes within society. More important, what seemed like

This essay is a revised version of one presented at the conference on "Hierarchy and Stratification in the Contemporary Near and Middle East," sponsored by the Joint Committee
on Near and Middle East, American Council of Learned Societies and Social Science Research Council. Seven Springs Conference Center, Mt. Kisco, N.Y., May 9–12, 1979.
Used by permission.

genuine class movements, sparked by collective consciousness and a concern for public welfare, were deflected into confessional conflict.

This persisting feature of Lebanon's pluralism reflects, among other things, the deficiency of secular loyalties, class ties and other civic attachments and the survival of sectarian, communal and primordial sentiments. One might perhaps argue that had the earlier class conflicts succeeded in eroding or containing these feudal and communal loyalties, Lebanon might have been spared much of its subsequent turmoil. It would at least have become more of a nation-state and less of a precarious mosaic of pluralistic and fragmented communities.

The persistence of nonclass loyalties in Lebanon is also conceptually significant since it provides evidence that departs from the general trend often attributed to other Middle Eastern countries, namely: the alleged obsolescence or erosion of the traditional "mosaic" system of allocating power, privilege, and status in society and its displacement by an emergent pattern of "social classes."

Within such a context, it becomes meaningful to reexamine the only instances of class struggle in Lebanon's recent history. What inspired and motivated the peasants, as commoners, to collective action? What, if anything, did the movements accomplish? Why did they ultimately fail in generating the necessary changes that could have transformed the rather amorphous strata and quasi-groups, which had characterized the social structure at the time, into cohesive social classes?

Since the uprisings were, to a large extent, a reaction to some of the institutions and loyalties of feudal society, it is instructive to begin our discussion by identifying those features of feudal society that are associated with both the grievances of peasants and the failure of their seditions as a collective class movement. The chapter will then treat, albeit briefly and eclectically, some of the antecedents and consequences associated with each of the three uprisings. The main focus is, of course, on accounting for the failure of the uprisings in bringing about the intended transformations. In conclusion the chapter will also make a few inferences regarding the persistence of primordial and nonclass loyalties within contemporary Lebanese society.

Feudal Society of Mount Lebanon

In its broad features, the socioeconomic and political organization of Mount Lebanon during the early part of the nineteenth century may be characterized as "feudal." In both its origin and evolution, the *iqtaᶜ* system had much in common with other feudal societies. For example, the system of vassalage and the institution of the fief, the idea of the personal bond, the hereditary and hierarchical nature of social relations, patron-client ties, and obligations, decentralization of the power of the state and the consequent autonomy of feudal chiefs in the appropriation of justice, collection of taxes and maintenance of law and order, these and other attributes were similar to the predominant form of European feudalism. Yet, the system of *iqtaᶜ* in Mount Lebanon had some peculiar features that differentiated it from both the European and Ottoman prototypes. We can only provide here a brief and sketchy overview of such features, particularly those pertaining to the political and socioeconomic institutions.

Political System

As the term itself suggests, *iqtaᶜ* denotes a system of socioeconomic and political organization composed of districts (*muqataᶜas*) in which political authority was distributed among autonomous feudal families (*muqataᶜjis*). The *muqataᶜji* was subservient to the amir or hakim who, as supreme ruler, occupied an office vested in a family—in this case the Shihabi Imarah or principality. Within the context of the Ottoman system of government, the sultan was formally the highest authority over the rulers of Mount Lebanon and their subjects. The amir received his yearly investiture through one of the sultan's representatives, the pashas of Saida, Tripoli, or Damascus, under whose administration Lebanon and its dependencies were divided. Through the pashas, the amir also forwarded his annual tribute *(miri)*, which he owed the Ottoman Treasury. In effect, however, neither the sultan nor the Pashas—with the noted exception of Jazzar's governorship of Saida (1776–1804)—meddled very much in the internal affairs of Mount Lebanon. The amirs enjoyed considerable autonomy in exercising their independent authority. They had the double task of dealing with the demands of the Ottoman pashas and acting as arbitrator among the *muqataᶜjis* in case of internal conflict. The specific duties of collecting taxes, maintaining peace and order, requiring a limited annual amount of unpaid labor from the peasantry *(corvée)*, and exercising judicial authority of first instance over all local, civil, and criminal cases involving penalties short of death were all part of the traditional authority of the *muqataᶜji*.

Four rather unusual political features of the *iqta*ᶜ system of Mount Lebanon, all of which have implications for understanding the peasant uprisings, can be emphasized:

First, and perhaps most striking, the *muqata*ᶜas in Lebanon were not organized as military fiefs. Nor were the fief holders expected to perform any military duties in return for the *muqata*ᶜas allotted to them, as was the case in Syria, Egypt, Palestine, and Iraq. The feudal sheikhs of Mount Lebanon lived in rural estates and not in garrison towns. The shihabi amirs did keep a small number of retainers mostly for administrative purposes, but they had no significant armies or police force.

Second, the nonmilitary character of Lebanese feudalism was an expression of the personal nature of political authority and allegiance. Legitimacy was more a function of personal loyalty between protector and protégé than an attribute of coercion or impersonal authority. In other words, the amir need not resort to coercion to generate and sustain conformity to his authority. Instead he relied on the good will of his *muqata*ᶜjis and the personal allegiance of their followers *(atba*ᶜ or ᶜ*uhdah).* The mutual moral obligations and feelings of interdependence inherent in such personal ties are aptly described and documented by Harik (1968:43). Typically, such relationships assumed the form of a patron-client network. They involved the exchange of support for protection. The client strengthens the patron by giving him support, and receives aid and protection in return. Primordial as it was this form of allegiance, however, was not sectarian. The *muqata*ᶜji usually presided over districts that were religiously mixed. In contrast to this nonconfessional system stood the government of *iltizam* where only Sunni Muslims had the right to hold authority (Harik 1965:420).

Third, the *muqata*ᶜji was a hereditary feudal chief whose authority over a particular district was vested within a patrilineal kinship group. He lived in his own village and maintained ties of patronage with his *atba*ᶜ. In contrast, the *multazim* was not indigenous to the tax farm he controlled. He was more akin to a government official than a feudal sheikh.

Finally, the *muqata*ᶜjis enjoyed more independence in exercising their control at the local level. Unlike the *multazim*s in other provinces of the Ottoman Empire, they were autonomous feudal chiefs and not officials in a decentralized Ottoman hierarchy.

The survival of such features account for the tenacity of patron-client ties in Lebanon and their predominance, particularly in times of conflict, over class or other collective interests.

Fiscal and Economic Organization

The system of taxation was flexible, obscure, and generally irregular in its exactions. A system, however, did exist. Whether the fiscal organization was technically an *iltizam*, or something peculiar to the *iqtaᶜ* system of Mount Lebanon is a moot point still debated by some historians, (Polk 1963:32; Chevallier 1971:82–89). What is undisputed, however, is that the Shihabi amirs were charged with the duty of forwarding taxes to the Ottoman Treasury by way of the governor of Saida, and that neither the amount of this yearly tribute *(miri)* nor their tenure in office were fixed.

Officially, the *miri* was supposed to be levied upon all sown land, and the amount of the tax depended upon the crop sown (Volney 1788:66). Yet neither in its assessment nor collection was the system consistent or regular. Indeed, the tribute was arbitrarily set and varied considerably with changing circumstances. Rather than being proportional to wealth (Burckhart 1822:188; de Lamartine 1835:294), the *miri* was often a reflection of the amir's power or special standing vis-à-vis the Ottoman pasha. In instances, when the Ottoman policy played rival amirs against one another, the governorship of Mount Lebanon normally went to the highest bidder.

The *miri* was not the only form of taxation demanded by the Imperial Treasury. In addition, a poll tax *(kharaj* or *jizya)* was imposed on non-Muslims who, for religious reasons, were not subject to military service. Another head tax *(fardah)* was also levied on occasion.

During the early nineteenth century, the system of *metayage* was beginning to transform the peasant-proprietor into a mere farm hand or *metayer*. As *metayers* or sharecroppers, the farmers were expected to pay their feudal landlord a specific share of the harvest, the size of which depended on conditions such as the type of crop cultivated, whether the *metayer* owned seeds and implements and the existing irrigation conditions. Typical of the *metayage* system common in Western Europe during the eighteenth century, the Lebanese sharecropper paid rent in kind and was bound by personal obligations of subservience to his feudal lord: he did not have the right to marry without the lord's permission, and he was also forbidden to leave his feudal lord at will, whereas the latter could forcibly transfer him to another estate. Furthermore the abusive practice of *corvée* often entitled the ruling amirs and feudal chiefs to demand free labor from peasants for the construction of palaces, forts, and other public works.

It is curious that despite the seemingly deplorable conditions of the peasants and the general impoverishment of the country, the economy of Mount Lebanon at the end of the eighteenth century was still considered by several observers as being relatively prosperous and viable. (See, for example, Polk 1963:75). Although the land is constantly referred to as *miri*, it was actually the private property of the person or group holding the *miri* rights. At the end of the eighteenth century, Volney estimated that about one-tenth of the Lebanese land was held directly by the *muqata'jis* as their estate *(arzaq or aqarat)*, often committed to managers. The remainder was held by their vassals *(atba')*—who became in effect the hereditary farmers of the village—and by Christian monasteries and churches (Volney 1788:64; Poliak 1939:58).

The economy of Mount Lebanon was also remarkably self-sufficient. The Biqa valley was a major source of grain and animal products. Caravans from Hawran and other parts of inland Syria and imported grain and rice from Egypt made up for the shortages not covered by what was grown locally. Cottage industry supplied much of the daily wants of the peasants.

The backbone of the Lebanese economy was silk production. For centuries, Lebanon's highly prized silk had been the most prominent item of its industrial and agricultural exports. The production of silk was compatible with the basic features of Lebanese agriculture and its labor-intensive household economy. For example, mulberry trees, suited to the climate and moisture pattern of the mountain, were relatively easy to grow and could be exploited for a variety of uses. Likewise, much of the process of cultivating and reeling silk did not require the peasant to interrupt his daily tasks; and virtually all age groups could be productively engaged in the activity (Guys 1850:170). European demand for Lebanese silk increased sharply during the eighteenth century and with the introduction of modern processing methods, by local and European entrepreneurs, entire village communities experienced considerable prosperity.

Social Structure

One of the striking features of Lebanon during the period was the successful integration of its pluralistic and differentiated social structure.

Vertically, the society was highly stratified with marked social distinctions on the basis of status and kinship affiliation. A recognized hierarchy of ranks among the feudal elites had evolved as a rather formalized system of social prestige sustained by elaborate forms of social protocol and rules of conduct. The distribution of prestige among the different families was not arbitrary, but reflected a continuity of traditional considerations. The following seem the most prominent: the actual power each of the families held (such as the hierarchy of noble titles differentiating that of an amir, *muqaddam* and sheikh), the vintage of their kinship genealogy, and the esteem the families enjoyed in the eyes of the ruling Shihabs. For example, only three houses held the title of amir (Shihab, Abillama, and Arslan), one *muqaddam* (Muzhir), and several (Junblat, Imad, Abu Nakad, Talhuq, Abd al-Malik among the Druze; and Khazin, Hubaysh and Dahdah among the Maronites) were entitled to the rank of sheikh. Together these eight sheikhly families formed a special stratum of "great sheikhs" *(al-mashayikh al-kibar)*, differentiated from other feudal families (such as Azar, Dahir, and Hamadeh) in terms of titular prestige and the extent of their feudal tenure and control over their respective *muqata'a*s (al-Shidyac 1970; Shihab 1933; Aouad 1933; Harik 1968; Salibi 1965).

Property in itself was not the principal factor in determining one's social position or, more precisely, the social honor and prestige the notables enjoyed in their respective communities did not vanish with diminished wealth.

Given this intimate association between kinship and social status, it is little wonder that the family survived as the fundamental socioeconomic and political unit in society. So strong was this consciousness of lineage that families were closely identified with the particular *jib* or *bait* ("branch" or "house") they descended from. The whole spatial configuration of a village or town and the physical arrangement of housing patterns into well-defined quarters and neighborhoods reflected kinship considerations.

Kinship solidarity was further reinforced by the prevalence of strong endogamous ties. Marriage outside one's family or village was rare. Doubtlessly, economic and moral considerations, such as the desire to concentrate wealth within the family, to avoid payments of dowries, and the concern for family honor and virtue all played some part in sustaining endogamy.

Typical of a highly stratified society, there was also little intermarriage between the various strata and no instance of social mobility. The possible exceptions were the movements of Abillama *muqaddam*s into the rank of amir and a few others—Talhuqs, Abd al-Maliks, Ids, Junblats—who were bestowed with their sheikhly titles by the Shihabi amirs after the battle of "Ayn Dara" in 1711. While the feudal aristocracy could be readily differentiated into well-defined strata of amirs, *muqaddams*, and sheikhs, no such hierarchies characterized the commoners. They were all lumped into one undifferentiated strata of *ʿammiyyah*.

Apart from the distinctions of status and kinship, the social structure of Mount Lebanon was differentiated horizontally into isolated and closely knit village communities. The mountainous terrain and the natural divisions of the country into distinct geographic regions, each with its own particular customs, dialect, folklore, and social mannerisms rendered the village community a fundamental unit in the society of Mount Lebanon. Strong endogamous ties, continuities in the patterns of residence and landownership, attachments to feudal families who also resided in the village, along with the geographic isolation from other communities all tended to reinforce village loyalties and make the villager more conscious of communal interests. So strong were these loyalties that village identity often superseded kinship, religious, or class attachments.

This is not to imply that feudal society in Mount Lebanon was factionless. There were certainly deep splits and rivalries between feudal families competing for power positions or seeking to win the favors of a governing amir or an Ottoman pasha. All such factional splits, however, were predominantly partisan or kinship in character. They rarely took the form of a class or confessional conflict.

Despite these divisions, the integrative institutions of feudal society managed to maintain a state of harmony and balance between the various sects and strata in society. If there were any tensions, they at least did not break up into open hostility until early in the nineteenth century. Indeed, the Druze and Christians, in the words of an impartial observer, had "lived together in the most perfect harmony and good-will" (Churchill 1862:25).

Peasant Uprisings

The state of harmony and security, however, did not survive for long. During the first half of the nineteenth century, Lebanon witnessed various forms of societal change that began to dislocate feudal relations and disrupt the balance of forces between the various groups.

Although the three uprisings were sparked off by different circumstances and expressed varying grievances, they had, nonetheless, much in common. In a general sense they were all manifestations of the same socioeconomic and political changes that began to weaken the feudal system and challenge the legitimacy of hereditary feudal authority. The more specific issues provoked by the uprisings—such as taxation, land tenancy, conscription, disarmament etc., were all reactions to essentially the same phenomena: attempts by successive Ottoman pashas to impose tight controls on Mount Lebanon, and an enfeebled feudal aristocracy trying to preserve its eroding power and privilege. The uprisings were also an expression of an emancipated peasantry and clergy who were articulating a new spirit of collective consciousness. All those features were making their presence felt at the turn of the century.

The Uprising of 1820

At the turn of the nineteenth century, Lebanon, without any official political identity, had just emerged from three prolonged and turbulent decades of the oppressive tyranny of Ahmad Pasha al-Jazzar. Appointed by the Ottomans to the Pashalik of Sidon in 1775, Jazzar managed to become the dominant figure in Syrian history until his death in 1804. Partly by intrigue and partly by inciting confessional rivalry and quarrels between Druze factions, he asserted his authority over bickering feudal chieftains, controlled lawlessness in the countryside, and was fairly successful in exacting and remitting the necessary dues to the Imperial Treasury. He detached Beirut from Mount Lebanon and proceeded, as he had intended, to bring the Shihabi Emirate under his complete control.

Jazzar's rapacious and tight control of the vilayet of Sidon offers the classic instance of monopolization of a province. He was in complete possession of the agricultural lands and had them cultivated for his own profit. He was virtually a partner of merchants and artisans, imposed himself as their money-lender and banker, fixed arbitrary prices for their goods and demanded excessive custom duties. He increased the revenues from direct taxation by farming out the towns and districts of his province at exorbitant sums. Growing insecurity in the countryside, usurious rates of interest, poor means of transportation, shortages of credit, and the primitive state of agriculture were beginning to deplete the modest economic prosperity the Mountain had enjoyed thus far.

The effects of all this were momentous. Jazzar had in effect converted the Druze amirs into "instruments of oppression on behalf of the Turkish authorities" (Gibb and Bowen, 1957:68). In doing so he contributed in no small part to the decline of feudal authority.

With Jazzar's exit, Amir Bashir proceeded to restore the diminished prestige of the Shihabi Emirate. To this end he sought to consolidate his position by curbing the power of the feudal families, particularly the Druze *muqata'jis.*

For a period of fifteen years (between 1804 and 1819), Bashir was the unrivaled master of Lebanon. He had eliminated all possible sources of local rivalry; he opened up the country to persecuted Christians, Druze, and other dissident Muslims and fugitives from the interior of Syria; launched upon an impressive array of public works; substituted his own stern but benevolent justice for the caprice and tyranny of feudal amirs and sheikhs; and could pose as the champion of the Ottomans in Syria (Salibi 1965:23–24). Circumstances, however took a sharp turn for the worse in 1819 and generated the set of events that were to plunge Lebanon into a series of protracted crises.

In 1819 Abdallah Pasha succeeded Suleiman as governor of Akka and like his notorious predecessor, Jazzar, he did not relish the prospect of a strong and autonomous amir in Mount Lebanon. Accordingly, shortly after his appointment, he started his incessant demands for an exorbitant tribute from Bashir. When the Amir showed reluctance, the pasha applied pressure by arresting Bashir's subjects who happened to be in Sidon and Beirut at the time. Eventually, Bashir was compelled to concede to the pasha's demands and had no recourse but to send his agents to collect the additional tribute. The tax agents had hardly started their work when the peasants of Kisrwan and Matn, incited by the clergy and two of Bashir's cousins coveting the emirate, rose in rebellion against Bashir. Unable to contain the uprising or to collect the needed revenue, Bashir went into voluntary exile to Hawran.

The central feature of the *'ammiyyah* uprising remains no doubt the changing perspective of the Maronite clergy and their emergence as a powerful group in challenging feudal authority and in generating new forms of Maronite consciousness and communal loyalties. A brief consideration of how these transformations came into being becomes vital for understanding the role of the clergy in the peasant uprising.

Typical of ties of patronage, the relationship between the *muqata'jis* and the clergy in the North until the end of the eighteenth century was one of mutual benefit and support. The *muqata'jis* provided the church with their protection and in return the clergy pledged their spiritual and material support. The Khazin sheikhs, throughout the period of their feudal authority in Kisrwan, which dates back to early eighteenth century, had almost total control over the wealth of the district. Together

with the Hubayshes and Dahdahs, they virtually owned all the land. They
also exercised considerable control over the administration of the affairs
of the church. Since it was part of their family prerogative to select prel-
ates, they influenced the election of patriarchs and had almost complete
control over the appointment of archbishops and bishops.

This convergence of interests between the *muqata'jis* and the Church
survived until the end of the eighteenth century. Under the impetus of
new ideas, reform-minded clerics began early in the nineteenth century
to advocate measures to rationalize church bureaucracy and to reorganize
its economic resources in a more enterprising manner. Achievement criteria and merit were introduced to replace nepotism in recruiting and
promoting clerics. Efforts were also made to render the Church free from
interference by notables and more economically independent.

To this end, monastic orders with considerable autonomy were established early in the eighteenth century. Typical of other monastic organizations, the orders led a disciplined, austere but productive life. Since
individually the monks were not entitled to possess any private property
or wealth, they worked hard as collective bodies to secure their economic
independence. Through their own labor, donations, gifts, and religious
services (such as education for which they were compensated in land),
they were able to extend cultivable land under their control and augment
their wealth. One estimate claims that by the middle of the nineteenth
century they occupied "nearly a fourth of the entire surface of the Mountain" (Churchill 1853:88–89). The orders were also very active in industrial crafts such as wine, spirits, bookbinding, and printing. To free
themselves from the domination of *a'yan,* they secured in 1812 a decree
that deprived the latter of the right to levy taxes on the order's monasteries. Instead, the monks themselves were now authorized to collect and
remit the *miri* directly (Harik 1968:116).

Such measures were incompatible with the traditional privileges of the
muqata'jis who were growing jealous of the burgeoning wealth and influence of the Church. Indeed, they resented seeing the Church free itself
from their domination. In short, Harik asserts, "By the end of the 18th
century, the Church had become the largest, the most organized, and the
wealthiest organization in the whole of Mount Lebanon" (1968:125).

More important for understanding the active involvement of the clergy
in the *'ammiyyah* uprising was their role as articulators and carriers of a
new Maronite ideology and communal consciousness that challenged the
sense of personal allegiance and kinship ties, which were the hallmarks

of feudal society. As we have seen, up until the last few decades of the eighteenth century, feudal society was held together by primordial ties of kinship and patron-client loyalties. With the recognition of Mount Lebanon as a sort of national home for the Maronite community, ethnicity and confessional allegiance were emerging as a new source of political legitimacy.

The Church, early in the nineteenth century and particularly in North Lebanon, was in a favorable position to assume the intellectual and political leadership necessary for changing the world view or political outlook of the peasants. The priest was doubtlessly the most ubiquitous and central figure in the village. He was not only entrusted with the task of attending to the spiritual needs of his community and administering sacraments at various stages of the life cycle, he was also authorized to resolve family disputes and marital problems and was often sought as mediator in factional conflict and village rivalry.

The enterprising priests were also a source of employment to the surplus manpower of the village. They were active in establishing voluntary associations and religious societies. But most important, they virtually monopolized the school system and the printing press—the only media available at the time.

In short, there was hardly an aspect of the secular life of the community that remained untouched or unaffected by the omnipresence of clerics or clerical education. Second to the family, no other group or institution figured as prominently in the daily lives of individuals. With a ratio of roughly one priest for every two hundred lay Maronites (Harik 1968:154), their presence was bound to be pervasive; let alone their growing prestige and influence.

The point being emphasized here is that even if the Church had chosen not to, it is doubtful whether it could have restrained itself from getting involved in the political life of Mount Lebanon. So when the occasion availed itself, as it did in 1820, they did their share in inciting and organizing the *'ammiyyah* uprising. The immediate issue at the time, as we have seen, was taxation. A newly appointed pasha at Saida had demanded an extra tribute from Bashir II. The Druze community in the South was solidly united under the leadership of Sheikh Bashir Junblat and would have certainly resisted such demands. Accordingly, the amir turned to what he thought were the leaderless *muqata'as* of the North.

Bishop Yusuf Istfan (1759–1823) emerged as the prime mover and architect of the rebellion. As Christian founder of the College of 'Ayn

Waraqah and judge for North Lebanon, he had already assumed a prominent role in the affairs of the mountain. His relationship with Bashir was strained. He was incensed by the Shihabs' ambivalent treatment of their true religious identity, and the proclivity of the amir in particular to disguise his Maronite faith in public. His innovative leadership proved instrumental in one significant respect: he organized the peasants into village communes and asked each village to choose a *wakil* ("representative") as a spokesman who could act on their behalf with other *wakils* and government authorities. (al-Shidyac 1970; Shihab 1933; Churchill 1862). Simple as it may seem, this innovative institution had revolutionary implications for transforming the political allegiance of peasants and challenging feudal authority. Insurgents from the Maronite districts of the North (Christians of the Druze-dominated districts of South Lebanon did not participate) drew up a covenant (composed by Bishop Istfan) in which they pledged their solidarity as *ʿammiyyah,* their unrelenting loyalty to their *wakils,* determination to oppose additional taxes and to struggle collectively in safeguarding their communal public interest. A similar covenant was drawn between the village of Bashʿalah and their *wakils* on August 15, 1821. (For a full text of this interesting document, see Harik 1968:213–14.)

Both the substance and tone of the covenant makes it clear that as an instance of social change the uprising should not be dismissed as a mere localized grievance against the heavy exactions imposed on the peasants. Underlying such concrete demands, lurked other more subtle issues and perspectives. First, and perhaps most important, the uprising reveals that *iqtaʿ* society was far from a closed system incapable of internal transformation. The very fact that the sedition was sparked off by the joint efforts of clerics and peasants is sociologically significant. It is one indication that the personal allegiance to the *muqataʿjis* did not restrain the *ʿammiyyah* from entertaining other forms of allegiance. Second, by choosing a *wakil* from among the *ʿammiyyah* and entrusting him with the task of being their spokesman on all matters of common interest, the covenants were, in effect, articulating a new concept of authority that necessitated a shift from the ascriptive ties of status and kinship to those based on communal and public interest. Third, this also involved a change in the peasant's political perspective: he no longer perceived himself as being bound by personal allegiances to his feudal lord. Instead, and perhaps for the first time, he was made conscious of his communal loyalties and the notion of public welfare *(al salih alʿumumi).* Finally, inspired by the

Maronite ideology of the clerical and secular writers of the day, the uprising embodied a nationalist fervor and a desire to seek independence
from Ottoman control.

Despite such new perspectives and the enthusiasm touched off by the
initial stages of the rebellion, the *ammiyyah* sedition failed in one significant respect. The initiative for political change remained essentially a
Maronite phenomenon and was predominantly confined to the Christian
muqata^cas of the North. Only one Druze feudal family—the Imads of
the Yazbaki faction—expressed willingness to support the *ammiyyah* cause.
Efforts to seek the assistance of others in the South proved futile. The
uprising failed to spark the same spirit of revolt among the *ammiyyah* of
the Druze. In this sense, one might argue, the ideological nationalism
generated and encouraged by the Maronite clergy was parochial not civic.
Even when perceived as a "class" rivalry, the commoners of the South
remained loyal to their feudal sheikhs and refused to heed the call of
"class" or "public" consciousness articulated in the North.

Altogether then, the *ammiyyah* uprising was the first instance in which
some of the established beliefs and institutions of *iqta^c* society were seriously challenged. Significant as it is, however, the challenge did not sig-
nal the obsolescence of the *a^cyan*, nor did it radically rearrange the forces
that held the society together. All it did was to initiate the transition
from the traditional ties of kinship, status, and personal allegiance to a
more communal form of social cohesion where the sources of political
legitimacy were defined in terms of ethnicity and confessional allegiance.
In short, it substituted one form of primordial loyalty for another.

The Uprising of 1840

The uprising of 1840 did not fare any better. It came in the wake of a
decade of Egyptian occupation when Mount Lebanon was subjected to
a thorough and intensive form of centralized control. Some of the reforms and changes introduced by Ibrahim Pasha, particularly in the economic sphere, were far reaching. The growth of public security, reforms
in the fiscal system, rationalization of land tenure, growth in foreign trade,
movement of capital, and the opening up of village society etc., produced
a pronounced shift in the relative socioeconomic and political positions
of the various groups and communities. The delicate balances that had
held the society together were disrupted.

Evidence of disenchantment with the Egyptian presence—particularly the despised measures of conscription, *corvée* and taxation—began to appear earlier in the decade. In fact, as early as 1834, there were uprisings in Palestine, Tripoli, and Lattakia against the imposition of such measures, and in each case Ibrahim Pasha was successful in subduing the insurrections with the assistance of Amir Bashir. He then turned to Mount Lebanon and requested from Bashir the conscription of sixteen hundred Druzes to serve for the regular fifteen-year term in the Egyptian army.

Of all the measures associated with the Egyptians, conscription was by far the most widely feared. Since it involved a prolonged absence from a village or town, it imposed a drain on the economic resources of Mount Lebanon. It meant isolation from kinship and other primordial ties that are the source of personal reinforcement and support in village society. Indeed, it was so despised that political conscripts would do their utmost to avoid its terrors. Beiruti Muslims—and their coreligionists in Saida and Tripoli—were known to seek refuge in European consulates and foreign residences, hide in caverns and excavations, or take to the sea in vain efforts to flee from the pursuit of Egyptian officers. Druze sought immunity in baptism or conversion, and there were cases of mutilation and emigration.

The initial success of the major Druze insurrection of Hawran in 1838 encouraged their coreligionists in Mount Lebanon to take up their arms in support of the same cause. Through French and European consular intervention, Christians had gained a temporary respite from conscription. They were, however, dragged into the confrontation in a more damaging manner. Ibrahim Pasha requested Bashir to recruit some four thousand Christian mountaineers to assist in subduing the Druze rebels. In appreciation of such assistance, the Maronites were allowed to keep possession of their arms and promised no additional tax increases (Hitti 1957:124).

This request was unprecedented in the history of Mount Lebanon. So far the "tradition of asylum" and the sort of peaceful confederacy that evolved between the various communities prevented any direct clash between them. As we have seen, for generations Lebanon was torn by internal strife, but it was the strife of factions and feuding families. Little of it took the form of religious rivalry. The Hawran episode, by pitting Christian against Druze, was bound to provoke bitter confessional hostility.

In 1840, however, Muhammad Ali reversed his decision and insisted on disarming all Christians of Mount Lebanon, which was correctly perceived by the population as a step toward general conscription. By then Bashir II had been reduced to a mere instrument of his Egyptian masters and despite his initial reluctance, had no recourse, but to obey their orders. Accordingly, in May 1840 he summoned the Druze and Christians of Dayr al-Qamar to surrender their arms. The outcry was total. First in Dayr al-Qamar and then in other towns and villages, armed resistance spread. Christians, Druze, Sunni Muslims, and Shi'ites temporarily ignored their differences and acted collectively to resist Bashir's orders.

Reminiscent of the *'ammiyyah* uprising of 1820, the insurgents held a conference at Intilias on June 8, 1840, drew up a covenant outlining their grievances, expressed firm determination to resist the oppressive injustices of Egyptian rule, and pledged "to fight to restore their independence or die." (For a full text, see Rustum 1934:102–3.) Though shaped by different circumstances, the parties involved, the organization, and the ideological overtones of the rebellion bore many similarities to the 1820 uprising. Initiative and leadership was, once again, assumed by Maronite peasants. After promises from Bashir to make them masters of the Maronite district of Kisrwan, the Druze withdrew their support. Some of the feudal sheikhs and *a'yan*, however, saw in the insurrection a chance to reclaim part of their lost privileges, and offered their support. So did the higher clergy. After some initial reluctance, the patriarch came out openly in support of the rebellion, and the clergy took an active part in encouraging the rebels.

Apart from specific grievances with regard to conscription, disarmament, *corvée*, and taxation, the expressed objectives of the revolt were similar to those of 1820. For example, the same confessional and class consciousness was manifested by the leaders in a letter to the patriarch: "We have come together in a real Christian unity free from (personal) purposes and from spite, made rather for the welfare of the common folk (*jumhur*) of the community" (Harik 1968:248).

Similarly, the rebels of 1840 were calling for the end of foreign rule and the restoration of Mount Lebanon's autonomy and independence. They were also demanding the reorganization of the administration by forming a new administrative council representing the various communities to assist the amir in governing the public affairs of Mount Lebanon.

The first phase of the revolt—roughly between mid-May and the end of July 1840—ended with failure. The rebels were dispersed and their leaders captured and exiled. By then, however, the "Eastern Question" was attracting the attention of European powers. Reinforced by the terms of the London Treaty of July 1840, in which they had agreed to expel the Egyptians from Syria, an Anglo-Austrian-Turkish fleet landed troops at the Bay of Junieh, reinforced the Lebanese insurgents, and bombarded Beirut. Within two weeks the allies occupied the main towns and cities and by early November, the Egyptians withdrew their demoralized forces from Syria. The defeat of Ibrahim Pasha carried with it the humiliating downfall of Bashir's illustrious reign of over half a century. He had steadfastly supported the Egyptians and had no recourse but to deliver himself up for exile.

The Uprising of 1857

The involvement of peasants in the political events of 1840 might have contributed to putting an end to both the Egyptian occupation and the eventful reign of Bashir II, but it did very little to transform the underlying loyalties of peasants or those aspects of the feudal system that were the source of their grievances and oppression.

Indeed, by the midfifties Mount Lebanon continued to display all the ingredients of a feuding and fractured social order: factional conflict between rival feudal chiefs, family rivalry between factions of the same extended kinship group, a bit of "class" conflict between a feudal aristocracy eager to preserve its eroding power and privilege and an emerging Maronite clergy and the mass of exploited peasantry determined to challenge the social and political supremacy of feudal authority. This intricate network of competing and shifting loyalties was reinforced, often deliberately incited, by Ottoman pashas playing one faction against another or the intervention of Western powers each eager to protect or promote the interest of its own protégé.

In short by the spring of 1858, the Christian districts in the North were in a state of total disorder bordering on anarchy. At both ends of the social hierarchy, there were growing signs of unrest. Feudal families, jealous of their feudal privileges and kinship consciousness, were challenging the authority of the *qa'immaqam* (sub-governor). Their rebellion succeeded in destroying his power over their districts. The peasant movement, as a protest against feudal abuses, was also beginning to gain considerable momentum.

It was, however, the peasant movement that proved instrumental in shaping the course of events in the years preceding the outbreak of confessional hostilities. Peasant agitation in the North can be better understood when viewed within the context of the economic transformations—particularly the expansion of European trade and the consequent emergence of a new urban bourgeoisie—which weakened the stability of the feudal economy. (For further details, see Dubar and Nasr 1976:51–59.) Feudal families tried to curtail their growing indebtedness and recoup their losses by intensifying the forced exactions and taxation on peasants. Others ceded or sold portions of their land to villagers and then tried to reclaim them forcibly through their armed retainers.

The protracted civil disturbances of the middle decades of the nineteenth century, which took the form of bitter political struggle over control of land, the power of taxation, and the rights and privileges of feudal families, were certainly provoked by arbitrary impositions and harsh exploitation to which the peasants were subjected. (for further details, see Saba 1976). These issues were apparent in the demands of the peasants in Kisrwan in their revolt against the Khazin sheikhs. Among other things they were demanding an equalized distribution of the land tax: an end to the exactions of gifts, dues, and the imposition of forced labor services; an abolition of contrived taxes on land already sold by the sheikhs to peasants; and the abolition of the right to authorize marriages and administer floggings and jail sentences (Porath 1966:101).

Peasant agitation began to assume violent forms. In one village after another, *sheikh shababs* organized village councils, usurped power, and demanded further concessions from their feudal lords. The reluctance of the notables to grant these concessions only provoked added bitterness among the peasants. Leadership also passed into more radical hands. For example, the relatively moderate Salih Sfeir (the *sheikh shabab* of Ajaltun) was replaced by the more intemperate, arrogant, and ambitious Tanyus Shahin of Rayfun.

The transfer of leadership to Shahin, the illiterate farrier who had "little to recommend him other than his tall and muscular frame and violent temper" (Salibi 1965:85), was a turning point. Almost overnight Tanyus Shahin became a legendary folk hero; the avowed and undisputed spokesman of peasants and their redeemer from feudal tutelage. (For further details, see Kerr 1959:49; Porath 1966:105–17.)

Shahin was clearly not acting alone. It is rare for uprisings of this sort to be inspired and sustained by local initiative alone. The peasant movement enjoyed, it seems, the moral encouragement of the Ottoman authorities and the French consulate in Beirut. As in earlier instances, the Maronite clergy also offered its blessings, although it remained suspicious of Shahin's character and personal ambitions.

By the spring of 1859, the peasant insurrection became a full-fledged social revolution; at least in the Christian districts of the North. The Khazins and other feudal families were evicted from their homes and stripped of their possessions. Feudal property, household provisions, and ammunition were parceled out among the peasants, and Tanyus Shahin was issuing his commands with the authority of a "republican government," or the self-appointed dictator of the so-called "peasant commonwealth" (Kerr 1959:53; Churchill 1862:111–12; Porath 1966:115).

Successful as the peasant revolt in Kisrwan had been in raising the hopes of other peasants throughout Lebanon, the movement remained predominantly a local upheaval. Druze peasants were apprehensive about taking similar action against their own feudal sheikhs. They were distrustful of their Christian neighbors and were counseled by their *ʿuqqal* (religious elite) to avoid sedition. As in earlier peasant uprisings, the enthusiasm for "class" struggle and public consciousness among Christian peasants in the North found little appeal among their counterparts in the Druze districts. The lapse of nearly forty years since the 1820 revolt, in other words, had done little in transforming the loyalties and attachments of the peasants, Confessional, local, and feudal allegiances continued to supersede other civic and class interests.

Indeed, the peasant movement in the Druze districts assumed a sectarian rather than a "class" conflict. Druze sheikhs were successful in muting and deflecting the discontent of their own peasants by provoking sectarian rivalry; particularly in the religiously mixed communities of the Shuf and Matn. From then on the conflict began to assume open confessional struggle until it culminated in the massacres of 1860.

Concluding Remarks

The three abortive peasant uprisings were the only instances in which peasants were collectively involved in organized political action. As organized acts of sedition against abusive features of the feudal system, they displayed some of the historic elements found in similar movements elsewhere: an enfeebled feudal system, a changing economy, and an emancipated peasantry aroused by a newly articulated spirit of collective consciousness, "class" struggle and common aspirations.

As we have seen, the uprisings were an expression of, or were provoked by, issues such as the legitimacy of hereditary feudal authority, taxation, land tenancy, conscription, disarmament, confessionalism, and the divisive strategies of Ottoman pashas and Western powers. More important, they signaled the emergence of the clergy as a powerful group in challenging the social and political supremacy of feudal aristocracy. All these issues continued to manifest themselves throughout the nineteenth century. Some, particularly the internationalization of Lebanese politics, ecclesiastical intervention in the political process, sectarian rivalry, and the persistence of primordial and semifeudal loyalties, have become inveterate features of Lebanese society.

That the insurrections should fail as a class movement is not surprising given some of the peculiar features of the *iqta* system and the other intervening circumstances that debilitated the burgeoning collective consciousness of the *'ammiyyah* and deflected the potential instances of class conflict into confessional rivalry.

As we have seen, despite some of its abusive features of the feudal economy, it was, on the whole, relatively prosperous and viable. There was sufficient evidence of an appreciable degree of security of life and property and continuity in land tenure. A fairly developed cottage industry and the surplus generated by its silk production rendered the economy largely self-sufficient. Its political system incorporated few of the conventional attributes of a nation-state. Personal loyalties to feudal chieftains and other forms of patronage, rather than public interest or ideological commitments, sustained political legitimacy. Likewise, a strong sense of kinship and village solidarity, reinforced by endogamous ties and localized residence, intensified the primordial attachments of peasants and diluted the nascent public or class interests that were emerging at the time.

The persisting nonclass loyalties of the peasants muted their grievances and eroded their solidarity, but the very nature and pattern of the uprisings themselves also account for much of the failure of the uprisings as forms of class struggle. Significant as they were in attempting to articulate a new concept of authority and in changing the peasants' loyalties and perspectives, the uprisings were not inspired or sustained by local initiative. The peasants were rarely acting alone. In all three instances, organizational and ideological leadership was assumed by the Maronite clergy. It was the clerical writers who first articulated the peasants' revolutionary attitude toward the *iqta'* system. They organized the peasants into village communes and appointed *wakils* as spokesmen for the *'ammiyyah*.

In addition to ecclesiastical intervention, the peasants almost always received either the direct or moral support of Ottoman authorities and foreign consuls who manipulated the uprisings for purposes unrelated to the grievances or interests of the *'ammiyyah* as a protest movement. The Ottomans, as we have seen, were eager to undermine the privileged status of Mount Lebanon and the local authority of feudal chiefs. Foreign powers, eager to gain inroads into the Middle East and win protégés, also sought to pit one religious community against another. Under such circumstances, it is easy to understand how the initiative for political change and the enthusiasm for class struggle and public consciousness could be readily deflected into confessional or factional rivalry.

Such considerations notwithstanding, the failure of peasant uprisings reflects, in essence, the deeply rooted and pervasive character of primordial loyalties and the consequent deficiency of class and civic consciousness. This has been one of the persisting features of Lebanese society throughout the nineteenth century, a feature that has also survived with remarkable tenacity in contemporary Lebanon.

The forces of socioeconomic mobilization Lebanon has witnessed during the past few decades—particularly widespread urbanization, literacy, commercialization, and the opening up of village society to secular and urban contacts—have generated further differentiation and disparities between the various groups in society. They broadened political recruitment and hastened the process of elite circulation. Political power and influence, which was once the exclusive preserve of the traditional feudal aristocracy and landed gentry, is being gradually transferred to a more literate, economically active, and occupationally mobile group. These changes were also accompanied by the inevitable decline in the economic status of feudal and notable families and the emergence of a new middle stratum composed mostly of businessmen, traders, money lenders, professionals, teachers, civil servants, and white-collar clerks and employees of the burgeoning service sector of the economy.

Significant as these changes have been, they should not be taken to mean that the old primordial loyalties have withered away and that the social structure is now being held together by class, secular or other civic

ties. Nor should they be taken to mean that class consciousness has become an effective source for determining group affiliations, collective
identities, and life-styles. Successive studies before the recent outbreak of
civil hostilities continued to reveal that religious and kinship attachments
superseded class, ideological, or national consciousness as forms of group
affiliation (Melikian and Diab 1959 and 1974). Similarly, parochial loyalties and religious affiliation were instrumental in shaping life-styles and
patterns of socialization (Smock and Smock 1975). Along the same lines,
kinship and communal ties and not ideological or class interests are the
forces that determine political recruitment and elite circulation. Despite
the broadening of the process of political participation, the political
dominance of notable families has not been seriously challenged. As will
be shown later, family ties and kinship networks continue to be viable
sources of political socialization and tutelage. They are also effective avenues for political power and perpetuation of leadership.

These and other specific studies on the changing patterns of social
stratification (Peters 1963; Khuri 1969; Khalaf and Kongstad 1973; Starr
1977), continue to reveal that the growing differentiation between groups
does not signify that each occupies a well-defined and clearly distinguish-
able position. Even in closely circumscribed and fairly homogeneous rural or urban communities, there is little evidence of any cohesive or self-
conscious social classes. If a class is to be defined as "the totality of individuals who share the same economic conditions, have common interests, way of life and culture, and whose identity of interests produce a
community consciousness stemming from their status, and leads them to
form national associations and engage in political action" (Karpat 1977:88),
then clearly there are no such classes in Lebanon. Groups with similar
economic conditions, common interests and life-styles have neither produced collective consciousness nor have they led to collective political
action or participation in national associations. A few concrete instances
will suffice here in way of demonstrating the absence or weakness of such
class consciousness.

The divisive and fragmented character of the labor movement and its
inherent weakness as a political force is, if anything, a reflection of the
persistence of traditional loyalties and the continued attachments of the
workers to nonindustrial ties. As has been demonstrated elsewhere, because of the survival of such parochial sentiments, workers transfer their
loyalties toward the workplace and the employer rather than to some
general industrywide or occupational form of association. Hence, "com-

pany" or "house" unions rather than industrial or craft unions have been the most proponderant form of union organization. The labor movement is further splintered on confessional and regional grounds. These, and other such features, have been a serious drain on workers' commitment to the labor movement as a rational and purposive group, and have not been conducive for the development of any occupational or class consciousness among the work force (see Khalaf 1967).

Voluntary and welfare associations suffer the same fate. The most typical voluntary associations are not organized along class or secular lines but along familial, confessional or communal grounds. For example, there are no purely national associations to attend to the welfare needs of the poor, orphaned, handicapped, infirm, or the elderly. These, like other health, educational and relief services, continue to be dispensed through kinship, confessional, or communal organizations (see chapters 8, 9).

The civil disturbances of the past eleven years have reinforced rather than diluted nonclass ties and loyalties. Virtually all the critical, and yet unresolved, issues provoked by the war—the presence of Palestinians, secularization, decentralization, the effective and equitable participation of religious communities in significant political decisions, foreign and Arab intervention, and the persisting debate over Lebanon's true national identity, etc.—have generated further religious cleavages but hardly any class or collective consciousness that cuts across confessional lines. The nature of political coalitions, the formation of "blocks," "fronts," and militia groups all continue to assume patent sectarian manifestations. Even the pattern and intensity of violence is largely a reflection of such confessional polarization.

It is considerations of this sort that prompt me to conclude that membership in a given "class" does not provide the average Lebanese with a sense of community or identity. This feeling is still, to a considerable extent, provided by nonclass loyalties, particularly familial, confessional, and other primordial affiliations. In this sense, it is more appropriate to speak about "status" differences, "strata," "hierarchies," "aggregates," "categories," even quasi-groups," but not "social classes."

CHAPTER THREE

Communal Conflict in the Nineteenth Century

THE SOCIAL AND POLITICAL history of Lebanon has experienced successive outbursts of civil strife and political violence. Dramatic episodes such as the peasant uprisings of 1820, 1840, and 1857; the repeated outbreaks of sectarian hostilities in 1841, 1845, 1860, 1958; and the protracted civil war of 1975–1986, reveal, as was suggested in the preceeding chapter, the fragility of Lebanon's precarious democracy, its deficient civility, and perpetual grievances of dominant groups within society.

Typical of small, communal, and highly factionalized societies, much of the earlier violence took the form of internal strife between factions and feuding families. Little of it assumed an open confessional conflict. At least until 1840, the bulk of violence was more in the nature of intermittent feuds, personal and factional rivalry between bickering feudal chieftains, and rival families vying for a greater share of power and privilege in society. Nineteenth-century travelers and local chroniclers all uniformly commented on the spirit of amity that had characterized confessional relations at the time.

During the two decades following the Egyptian occupation, from 1840–1860, civil unrest and communal conflict began to assume a more confessional form. Excluding, perhaps, the current civil war, they were also the most turbulent and violent decades Lebanon had experienced. One civil disturbance provoked another until the unrest culminated in the massacres of 1860. What brought about such conflict? More specifically, what transformed the earlier nonsectarian, factional rivalries and peasant seditions into confessional hostilities?

This is not an idle question. It reflects, among other things, the sur-

This essay is a revised version of a paper originally published in Benjamin Braude and Bernard Lewis, eds., *Christians and Jews in the Ottoman Empire* (New York: Holmes and Meier, 1982), 2:107–134. Used by permission.

vival of sectarian sentiments and the deficiency of civic and secular ties. In earlier, as in more recent, episodes of communal conflict, social and "class" issues have always been transformed or deflected into confessional hostility. Within such a context, it is meaningful to reexamine a few of these episodes to find out why they failed to bring about such a transformation.

It is no exaggeration to say that no episodes in the social and political history of Lebanon have been chronicled as much as the events surrounding the civil disturbances of 1860. Some of the chroniclers trace major events to trivial and inconsequential origins. Accordingly, an incidence of trespassing, a Maronite shooting a partridge on a Druze property, or a petty affray between a Druze and Maronite boy, etc. are often singled out as the immediate causes for the outbreak of confessional hostilities. (See, for example Hitti 1957:434; Salibi 1965:44.)

There were, of course, deeper and more profound causes for the conflict. Despite the confessional character of the tension, it was neither motivated nor sustained by purely religious sentiments. There were socioeconomic disparities underlying the confessional enmity. Furthermore, these disparities did not just unfold shortly before the outbreak of hostilities. Christians in general had had a head start over other groups in cultural and material advancements. Throughout the seventeenth and eighteenth centuries, they were able to maintain close cultural, commercial, and political contacts with Europe and had, as a result, grown disproportionately richer and more influential. Political and socioeconomic developments early in the nineteenth century reinforced these imbalances.

More specifically, I will argue in this chapter that Christians, on the whole, were the main beneficiaries of the socioeconomic changes generated by the Egyptian presence. Two more decades of Ottoman reforms, with the concomitant improvements in civil and social liberties, limited as they were, accentuated the disparities further. To understand, then, the nature and pattern of communal conflict we must consider some of the changes during the Egyptian occupation and the period of Ottoman reforms.

The Egyptian Occupation of Mount Lebanon (1831–1841)

The circumstances that culminated in the Egyptian occupation of Syria are multiple and diverse. They include Muhammad Ali's ambitious expansionist designs and development projects, which necessitated an intensive exploitation of Syrian resources (particularly timber, tobacco, and Lebanese silk as an exportable cash crop) and easier access to Egyptian-Syrian trade routes, the growing hostility of Europe, a weakened Ottoman Empire, and Muhammad Ali's eagerness to pose as the protector of Christian minorities in Syria. These and other contributing factors have been documented by several historians (Shidyaq 1970; Rustum 1937; Polk 1963). What concerns us here is not so much the motives and events surrounding Muhammad Ali's expedition as the impact and consequences of a decade of Egyptian rule for accentuating socioeconomic disparities and communal conflict.

To several historians Ibrahim Pasha's ten-year interlude in Lebanon continues to be perceived as the beginning of the "modern" period; a dawn of a new era of change marked by the disintegration of feudal society and the so-called "opening" up of the country to foreign influence (see, for example, Polk 1963; Maʿoz 1968; Issawi 1967). The reforms introduced by Ibrahim Pasha are seen as "bold" and "profound" changes that transformed "almost every aspect of the old life" (Maʿoz 1968:12). Others speak of a "brief golden age which set in motion certain trends and movements which were to influence profoundly the future course of Middle Eastern history" (Polk 1963:226).

Can one not advance a more realistic appraisal of the modernizing impact of the Egyptian occupation? A view that recognizes the transformations generated by the Egyptian presence, but one that also recognizes the disruptive impact of such changes on communal conflict.

The kind of political regime Muhammad Ali envisaged for Mount Lebanon, which would permit a more efficient exploitation of the country's resources and maintain law and order, required a greater degree of government control. This was apparent in the measures undertaken by the Egyptians to promote public security and safeguard the freedom of movement of both goods and people. In some respects, the significant developments associated with the Egyptian presence in Mount Lebanon—economic development, religious equality, conscription, disarmament and tax innovations—were a by-product of Ibrahim Pasha's concern with public security.

The Egyptians had every reason to be concerned. The people of Mount Lebanon, with their tradition of feudal autonomy and spirit of independence, have not been very hospitable to any system of centralized control. The rugged mountainous terrain and the isolation of villages rendered certain areas beyond the effective reach of any government authority. Bedouin tribes, encamped in the Biqa valley, derived much of their income from pillaging trade caravans and imposing "protection money" and "brotherhood" tributes upon villages (Polk 1963:109). Many villages and towns levied their own tolls and duties while cities prevented the entry and restricted the mobility of certain religious minorities. Even Beirut, "by all odds the most open of the cities of the Levant, was under restraints. On the eve of the Egyptian invasion, none of the numerous family of Shihab was allowed to enter without special permission" (Polk 1963:112).

These and other forms of public insecurity restricted the flow of goods and people, handicapped commercial transactions, and prevented easier access to the country's natural resources. Accordingly, early in the occupation, the Egyptian government determined to take the necessary steps to assuage the adverse effects of such conditions. Hence, it resorted to measures as conscription, disarmament, and the imposition of a more regular system of exactions. Such involuntary enforcements were not only extremely unpopular; they proved to be damaging in inciting confessional jealousy and discord. This was particularly so since the measures were not uniformly applied. Eager to win European good will, the Egyptians allowed Christians differential treatment by exempting them from many of the impositions levied on Muslims and Druze. It is instructive to note that the first major act of Ibrahim Pasha's government was the declaration he made before the fall of Akka in November 1831, in which he ordered the notables of Jerusalem to cease levying extra taxes on native Christians, places of worship, and pilgrims (Shihab 1933:825–26). Likewise, in the imposition of personal or head taxes (fardah), there is evidence that Muslims were paying higher rates than Christians (Polk 1963:135; Ma'oz 1968:16–18). They were also exempted from conscription and disarmament, permitted to hold responsible positions in government, appear in public on horseback, and wear a white turban—all exclusively Muslim privileges (Hitti 1957:423).

Indeed, so privileged had the Christian community become as a result of these and other socioeconomic benefits, that the conversion to Christianity witnessed at the time may be attributed to the disproportionate rights and advantages they enjoyed under the Egyptians. Writing from Beirut in December of 1835, Eli Smith, the American missionary, observed: "The Christian community apparently escaped all of the fears of sudden arrest and conscription experienced by Muslims and Druzes. Indeed, there was a certain amount of conversion by the latter to escape conscription" (Polk 1963:131).

It is the central argument of this chapter that this growing disparity between the religious groups, a feature that has had a lasting impact on Lebanese society, was one of the by-products of the Egyptian occupation. To understand how this disparity emerged, we must consider some of the transformations that occurred during that eventful decade.

The most visible changes were in the economic sphere. This was to be expected. Economic motives, after all, loomed high in Muhammad Ali's justification for occupying Mount Lebanon. The Egyptians were eager to reform the fiscal and economic organization to permit a more efficient utilization of the country's resources.

One of the initial changes in the tax structure was the lifting of taxes levied upon pilgrimage groups and religious establishments. This did not mean, however, that Christians had become entirely free of exemptions. A portion of the poll tax (*jizya*) was earmarked as a "toleration tax," which the Christians of Mount Lebanon were compelled to pay. The *fardah* was retained. The same was true of the *miri*. So were the other impositions and fines levied on public baths, animals, customs and monopolies. (For further details, see Polk 1963:153–57.) The system of *corvée*, which took the form of a direct tax on the community, continued to drain the resources of the peasants. Henri Guys cites an instance in 1837 when Bashir drafted some two hundred peasants to work in the government-controlled coal mines of Qurnayil in the Matn and were paid only three piastres daily. Since this was hardly adequate to support their families, the villages from which the laborers were drawn were compelled to contribute five piastres further to each person (Guys 1850: 131–32).

Conscious of the apprehensive and restive mood of Mount Lebanon and eager to woo the populace, Ibrahim Pasha exercised initial moderation in his tax collection and other exactions. The moderation, however, did not survive for too long. By 1835, acting on stern instructions from his father, Ibrahim Pasha raised taxes to about three times their size, extended state monopolies over silk, soap, and other necessities, and insisted on disarmament and conscription. The last two were the source of much outrage and bitter resentment.

Altogether, then, the tax structure during the Egyptian period may not have had sufficient time to develop into a coherent system. The same inconsistencies, local variations, and deficiencies that characterized the fiscal system at the turn of the century continued to exist. Without these changes, the administration was still able to "regularize, to an extent before unknown, the system of exactions and to squeeze out of the population money, men, and goods on a scale quite out of line with previous experience" (Polk 1963:159). The point to be underscored here is that, on the whole, Christians were favorably treated. Despite the stringent exactions and tighter controls, they somehow found more circumstances to escape them than Muslims and Druze.

Of the extensive economic changes introduced during the Egyptian period, no factor had as significant an impact on the local economy as the change in the scale and pattern of foreign trade. This, too, had its effect on widening disparities between the religious communities.

Prior to the Egyptian invasion, the little international trade that did exist was predominantly an Asian trade. Beirut, still confined to its medieval walls, was just emerging as a major entrepôt for the hinterland. Until then, and because of the traditional "caravan navigation," the main cities of Syria, such as Damascus and Aleppo, were inland cities oriented toward the desert. Ports on the Syrian and Lebanese coast were, by comparison, relatively small towns. Beirut's population before the Egyptian occupation barely reached 10,000. The rise of Beirut, as Dominique Chevallier (1968:205–22) among others has argued, is linked with the shift of trade from the interior to the Mediterranean. This shift would not have occurred without the revolution in shipping and the introduction of steam navigation lines into the Eastern Mediterranean. Vessels with deeper drafts for mass cargos were established first by the British in 1835 and then shortly after, competition from French and Austrian lines increased the number of vessels operating in the Mediterranean. Beirut's harbor was naturally more endowed to accommodate deeper vessels and began to attract the bulk of growing traffic. Other coastal cities, without such natural advantages, like Sidon, Tripoli, and Tyre, began to witness a decline. (For further details, see Bowring 1840:167; Neale 1852:247; Chevallier 1968:214.)

Beirut's prominence as a trade center was more than an accident of geography and natural harbor facilities. Muhammad Ali took a keen interest in encouraging and stimulating trade. Commercial treaties, intended as a compromise between the provisions of the old capitulatory privileges and modern requirements, were introduced to regularize custom duties and facilitate the circulation of goods (Chevallier 1968:208). The opening of Damascus to Europeans, the transshipment of Western goods to the interior, growing public security and safety in the transport of goods and travels, growth of foreign community and freedom granted to missionaries to expand their activities all assisted in Beirut's development as a major Mediterranean seaport. During the decade of Egyptian occupation, Beirut's population rose rapidly from 10,000 to nearly 15,000, and tax returns for the same period increased fourfold (Bowring 1840:167).

The growth of Beirut did not mean draining the hinterland of people and resources. The noticeable growth in public safety and revival of security in villages encouraged the movement of capital from urban to rural areas. Direct measures were taken to encourage agriculture by urging people to settle and invest in land and by introducing new crops and extending areas under cultivation. Government monopolies over items such as timber, which Egypt needed for growing fleet, animal hides, coal, iron, wool for army uniforms, and olives were introduced (Polk 1963:167–68). Other commodities, such as wines and liquor, though not made into state monopolies, received much encouragement as exportable items to Egypt. And of course Egypt was in urgent need of Lebanon's silk as an exportable cash crop. In fact, Muhammad Ali had hoped to impose a state monopoly over the entire silk crop of Mount Lebanon. European opposition, however, and the difficulty of controlling such a widely diffused crop prompted him to abandon his plans (Polk 1963:271). Planting of mulberry trees, nonetheless, continued to receive encouragement and government support. So widespread was silk cultivation that it almost became a national pastime, like apple growing had become more than a century later. Lured by the growing demand for silk, villagers started converting their farmlands to mulberry trees, and "city dwellers began to buy or rent lands and to make arrangements to share the crops with peasant laborers. Land devoted to mulberries increased from 25 to 50 percent; in addition to 37,000 trees planted along the coast under government auspices, others were privately planted in every part where its growth presents a probability of success" (Polk 1963:171).

These new forces of regeneration—introduction of order and security, revival of foreign trade, easing of restrictions from which Christians had previously suffered, opening up the hinterland by extending agriculture and stimulating economic activity—had compelling social implications. Some of the most visible consequences were the changes in tastes and life-styles. Travelers in the late 1830s and early 1840s were already describing Beirut as the "Paris of the East." As the seat of diplomacy, residence for consul-generals, headquarters for French, American and British missions and a growing center of trade and industry, Beirut was "rapidly increasing in wealth, population and dimensions. . . . Stupendous new mansions, the property of opulent merchants, were daily being built; beautiful country houses, summer residences of the wealthy; hotels and billiard rooms and cafes, elegantly fitted. . . . Everywhere utility was blended with magnificence" (Neale 1852:209). Travelers, particularly those coming to Beirut after visiting other towns and cities in Syria and Palestine, were all struck by how "European" the character and amenities of the city had become. The British traveler Frederick Neale, like several others, was almost rhapsodic when describing the stylish lounging bars and Italian locandas "with the latest European journals and French papers" (Neale 1852:235). Others were more impressed by the freedom of movement and the new liberties people were beginning to enjoy in their dress and appearance in public places (Stanhope 1846:216–67).

The economic and technological changes, particularly the upsurge in foreign trade and the consequential growth of Beirut, had other less favorable implications. To begin with, the stimulation and growth of commercial exchange with the more advanced industrial countries of Europe—France and England in particular—began to generate a chronic deficit in the balance of trade. In 1833, for example, Beirut's imports were nearly twice the value of its exports. The deficit declined in subsequent years but continued to provoke a "grave monetary hemorrhage" throughout the 1830s and 1840s (Chevallier 1968:210). In fact, it was not until 1854 that Beirut had a surplus on its balance of trade (Chevallier 1968:214). Both French and British consuls of the period repeatedly noted the gravity of the trade deficit and its consequences for draining the country of its currency and precious metal. One of consul Bouree's dispatches of 1842, quoted by Chevallier (1968:211–12), is a poignant summary of this situation:

> This state of affairs [the deficit in the balance of trade with Europe and the decline of Syrian production] has already exhausted the country to the point that all silver and gold coins whose intrinsic value approximates their face value have flowed out. Those that are still found do not have the intrinsic worth of their quoted value and, for this reason, are not exported. Anyway, these coins have the indelible sign of their origin for they are all pierced, that is, they come from necklaces or from other women's ornaments which had to be parted with. They are jewels which misery transformed into coins and thus returned to their intended purpose.

Along with this loss of precious metals, the country was gripped by a general inflation characterized by a rapid rise in the cost of living, value of urban property, rent, and food prices (Polk 1963:173).

More important than the trade deficit and inflation were the growing disparities in the relative position of the various religious groups. The first symptoms of the uneven distribution of wealth and privilege—a feature that became endemic to Lebanese society ever since—were becoming more visible. This was particularly noticeable in Beirut where a small segment of the population enjoyed a disproportionate share of prosperity. A new mercantile middle class—mostly Christian merchants and agents for European traders and firms—emerged as the most prosperous group. Foreign travelers who were so impressed by the conspicuous consumption, lavish display of wealth, and Parisian life-styles in Beirut at the time must have been observing the changes within the rather exclusive community. Other groups were largely excluded from these manifestations of prosperity. The most prominent Druze feudal families, such as the Junblats, Abu Nakads and Imads, were dispossessed and exiled by Amir Bashir, and the bulk of the middle and lower classes did not fully participate in the new economic opportunities.

By virtue of their European predispositions and contacts and the security and privileges they were enjoying, Christian capitalists ventured in commercial speculations and dominated the burgeoning free enterprise activities. Colonel Charles Churchill (1862:29–30) had this to say about the growing disparity between Christian and Druze during the Egyptian occupation:

> Christians were admitted into the local councils. Their evidence, before mixed tribunals of Christian and Mussulman, was valid. All distinction of dress was abolished. As secretaries, as local governors, even as military officers, in all departments of the State their services were accepted and rewarded. Numbers, who had for years been hiding themselves up in the mountains amongst the Druze, to escape the tyrannous exactions of Djezzar and of Abdallah Pasha, returned to the sea-coast towns, and recommenced their commercial business. A brisk trade with European merchants was quickly opened, and the harbour of Beyrout, in particular, soon became thronged with the shipping of London and Marseilles.

This disproportionate prosperity of Christians was in part achieved at the expense of other groups, particularly the Druze feudal lords. Indeed, we are told that it is possible to observe Christians "in the 1820's as serfs of such Druze shaikhs as the Abu Nakad and at the end of the Egyptian period as the chief moneylenders to the same shaikhs" (Polk 1963:137). Furthermore, Christians in general appear to have benefited considerably from the improvements of public health as evidenced by their growing numbers relative to other religious groups (Guys 1850:275–77).

Manifestations of the economic prosperity of Christians during the Egyptian period were not confined to Beirut. The town of Dayr al-Qamar, which at the beginning of the eighteenth century was no more than a "small straggling village inhabited by Druzes" (Churchill 1862:104), under the patronage of Amir Bashir and impetus from its reputable silk trade, rose to a major town of nearly eight thousand, composed mostly of Maronites and Greek Catholics. Once again, Colonel Churchill (1862:104–5) has this to say:

Its merchants built spacious houses with marble courts and foun-
tains, and furnished in a style of costly luxury. All the Druze landed
property in the neighborhood passed into their hands. Thus they
finally attained a position of wealth and affluence which excited the
jealousy and cupidity of their feudal superiors, the Druze sheiks of
the family of Abou Nakad. . . . Released from the restraints which
had hitherto weighed upon them from being placed under a Turkish governor, the Christians of Deir-el-Kamar enjoyed the full and
unimpeded development of commercial activity. Their leading men
amassed riches; they kept studs; their wives and daughters were
apparelled in silks and satins, and blazed with jewelry, gold, and
pearls, and diamonds. The few Druze who still inhabited the town
were reduced to absolute insignificance, were always obliged to be
on their good behavior, and, to use their own expression, often
repeated in the bitterness of their hearts, had become to the Christians as "hewers of wood and drawers of water."

The same is true of other towns like Zahle and Hasbaya. Zahle, which formed a kind of federal alliance with the Christians of Dayr al-Qamar for the general protection of Christian interests, had also risen "with as-tounding rapidity to a state of affluence and consideration" (Churchill 1862:107). Its predominantly Greek Catholic population of about twelve thousand carried on a large trade with inland Syria and farmed the fertile land of the Biqa (for other pertinent details, see Churchill 1862:95–131).

By disrupting the delicate balance between the various communities, these growing disparities deepened confessional antagonisms between Christian and Druze and renewed hostilities between peasants and feudal lords. The economic transformations had also helped generate a group of commercial capitalists potentially able to threaten the wealth, power, and prestige of the traditional elite.

The change in the pattern of trade produced further dislocations within the rural economy. The village was no longer a self-contained economic community. The peasant and village craftsman became increasingly dependent on urban creditors and entrepreneurs, and their economic well-being was now linked to fluctuations in the world market. The primitive methods of local production could not face competition from European products. Even silk, Lebanon's major cash crop, suffered from native reeling methods. It was not until the end of the Egyptian period that steam-powered silk reeling was introduced and the output was more suitable for European factories. Furthermore, some of the new legislations were not to the advantage of the villagers or the products of their labor. The commercial treaties of 1838 were designed to favor foreign trade. Accordingly, these treaties stipulated that local products be taxed when circulating within the Ottoman Empire, while foreign trade merchandize required duty only upon entrance or exit from Ottoman territory (Chevallier 1968:218).

During the last few years of the Egyptian occupation, conditions were getting progressively worse. Some of the favorable aspects of the Egyptian presence were wearing off, and the population—both Christian and Druze—was growing increasingly restless. Disenchantment with the despised measures of conscription, *corvée,* and stringent taxation was more widespread. As early as 1834, there were uprisings in Palestine, Tripoli, and Lattakia against the imposition of such measures, and in each case, Ibrahim Pasha was successful in subduing the insurrections with the assistance of Amir Bashir. He then turned to Mount Lebanon and requested from Bashir the conscription of sixteen hundred Druzes to serve for the regular fifteen-year term in the Egyptian army.

The horrors of conscription, as we have seen before, have always provoked armed rebellion. There is no need here to recount the circumstances, events, and outcome of the peasant uprising of 1840. This has already been done in the preceeding chapter. It is sufficient to note that like earlier uprisings, particularly that of 1820, the civic and public consciousness articulated by Maronite peasants in the North did not find much support among the Druze in the South. Once again, in other words, a genuine civic revolt was muted and deflected into a parochial and confessional struggle.

By the end of the so-called "brief golden age," Mount Lebanon was in a less enviable position. The growth of public security, reforms in the fiscal system, rationalization of land tenure, growth in foreign trade, movement of capital, and the opening up of village society, etc., produced a shift in the relative socioeconomic and political positions of the various religious groups. The delicate balance that held the society together was disrupted. Civil crisis and confessional rivalry, so far kept in abeyance, had become imminent.

The Ottoman Reforms of 1839 and 1856

The end of the Egyptian affair and the consequent collapse of the Shihabi Emirate mark a significant turning point in the political history of Lebanon: the traditional Lebanese privilege of autonomy under hereditary rule was seriously challenged. The Egyptian threat, and the growing recognition of Western superiority prompted the Ottomans to advance a new ideology of reform. The traditional system of Ottoman reforms, it must be recalled, had recognized the autonomy and importance of various millet communities. Accordingly, the scope of the reforms was limited to military and administrative changes. Matters such as health, education, social security, communications, and the promotion of industry, trade, and agriculture remained within the scope of local religious authorities (Shaw 1968:32–33). Care was taken, in other words, to preserve the old institutions even when they were being superseded by new ones.

The edicts of 1839 and 1856 mark a fundamental departure from the traditional system: rather than sustaining the autonomy of the millets, they sought to introduce new institutions and to extend the scope of the central government. This also necessitated increasing measures of autocracy and centralization. More important, the secular tones of the edicts—particularly in their promises of religious equality—generated as we shall see considerable tension and hostility. A brief review of the events and circumstances that led to the outbreak of conflict is in order.

Foremost among these was the residue of ill-feeling and resentment the Druze continued to bear against Bashir for undermining their feudal authority and privileges. Not only were they dispossessed and forced into exile, but Bashir had assisted Ibrahim Pasha in suppressing the Druze uprising in Hawran. During the Egyptian interlude, the Druze enjoyed none of the preferential treatment accorded to Christians. At least they could not escape as readily from some of the hardships of conscription and disarmament. Returning from exile, they were embittered further by the heightened prestige and prosperity of Christians and the comparative destitution of their own communities. Much of their property was now held by Christians, and all their traditional rights and prerogatives—collection of taxes, maintenance of law and order, and judicial authority—had been absorbed by the Shihabi Emirate.

The political vacuum generated by Bashir's exile doubtless played a part in encouraging such hostility. Until the end of his reign, Bashir remained master of the internal politics of Lebanon and managed to keep the sectarian and partisan divisions under control. Furthermore, during the 1840 insurrection, common hostility toward his tenacious allegiance to Egyptian presence brought the contending groups—Maronites and Druze, peasants and feudal lords—together. With Bashir out of the way, there was no common force or cause to keep the various factions united (Salibi 1965:44).

The downfall of Bashir II and the appointment of his incompetent cousin, Bashir III, as his successor, gave the Ottomans a welcome opportunity to undermine the local autonomy of Lebanon's feudal chiefs. Upon the insistence of the Ottoman authorities, Bashir III organized a council or *diwan* of twelve men (two from each of the dominant sects; Maronites, Druze, Greek Orthodox, Greek Catholics, Sunni Muslims, and Shi'ites) to assist him in the administration of justice. Both Druze and Christian feudal sheikhs saw in this an encroachment on their traditional authority and refused to cooperate in this arrangement. Druze sheikhs in particular, especially the Junblats, Arslans, and Talhuqs, who were eager to restore the rights and privileges they had lost during Bashir II's reign, were not prepared to suffer further usurpations. More provocative was the circular issued by Patriarch Yusuf Hubaysh, and signed by leading Maronite families, calling on their coreligionists in the Druze districts to assume the judicial authority traditionally held by the feudal chiefs. "This was tantamount to an assertion by the Patriarch of the power to withdraw authority from the Druze shaikhs" (Kerr 1959:4).

Following a dispute in October 1841 over the distribution of taxes, a party of Druze led by the Abu Naked sheikhs attached Dayr al-Qamar, set the town on fire, pillaged Christian homes and besieged Bashir III. The incident touched off other sectarian clashes throughout the Shuf, Biqa, and Zahle. This was the first sectarian outburst, and it left a staggering toll: a loss of about three hundred people, the destruction of half a million dollars of property (Churchill 1862:63–64), the dismissal of Bashir III under humiliating conditions, the end of the Shihabi Emirate, and a large residue of ill-feeling and mutual suspicion. (For further details, see Churchill 1862:46–62; Hitti 1957:434–5.) The animosity was further aggravated by the complicity of the Ottoman authorities. Eager to undermine the autonomy of Mount Lebanon, the Ottomans supported the Druze in an effort to disrupt or discredit the Shihabi Emirate. Not only were they suspected of having been involved in the initial Druze plot against the Christians (Salibi 1965:50; Hitti 1957:434–35); there were instances which Ottoman troops participated in the acts of plundering. Such instances gave rise to the saying common then among Christians: "We would sooner be plundered by Druzes than protected by Turks" (Churchill 1862:52).

By 1842 it was becoming apparent that an irreparable breach was drawing the religious communities further apart. The Maronite-Druze confederacy, which had sustained Lebanon's autonomy for so long, suffered its first serious setback. The Ottomans were eager to step in and impose direct rule over Mount Lebanon. They declared the end of the Shihabi Emirate and appointed Umar Pasha "al-Namsawi" ("the Austrian") as governor. The Druze, already jealous of Christian ascendancy in power and prosperity, greeted the downfall of the Shihabs with enthusiasm, without realizing that the introduction of Ottoman centralized rule would ultimately have adverse effects on their own community. The Christians, naturally, refused to recognize the new arrangement and insisted on a restoration of the Emirate, which could only be achieved with Druze cooperation (Salibi 1965:53).

Umar Pasha's main concern was to gain support for his efforts to establish direct Ottoman rule. He turned first to the Druze and Maronite feudal sheikhs who had been dispossessed by the Shihabs. By restoring their estates and traditional prerogatives and appointing several of them as his advisors and agents, he won their support for the new regime. Second, he was eager to demonstrate to European powers that direct Ottoman rule enjoyed wide support in Lebanon. To this end, agents were hired to circulate petitions and secure signatures—a sort of plebiscite by coercion—in favor of direct Ottoman rule. He resorted to bribery, entreaties, false premises, threats, intimidation, blackmail, and "every species of personal indignity" (Churchill 1862:66–75) to procure the necessary signatures. So flagrant were the extortionist pressures that European consuls in Beirut collectively protested against the use of such measures, and declared the petitions to be "completely unrepresentative of true Lebanese opinion" (Salibi 1965:55).

In the meantime, internal alignments with Lebanon were being swiftly redefined. The petitions had hardly been circulated, when the Druze had serious afterthoughts about direct Ottoman administration and their place within it. They had considered themselves responsible for the collapse of the Shihabi Emirate and the establishment of Ottoman rule, and were therefore reluctant to assume a subservient position and accept the arbitrary dictates of Ottoman officials. Confronted with such Druze pretentions, and in desperation, Umar Pasha turned to the Maronites for support and started his policy of ingratiation to win their favors; which only aroused the suspicion of the Maronites and the bitter resentment of the Druze. So intense was Druze opposition that Umar Pasha was forced to arrest seven of their prominent sheikhs. The outrage was instantaneous. An open Druze rebellion was declared demanding the immediate dismissal of Umar Pasha, immunity from conscription and disarmament, and exception from taxes for a three-year period (Salibi 1965:62). Despite strong resistance, a joint Turkish-Albanian troop forced the surrender of Druze leaders.

The rebellion, nonetheless, was a clear indication that direct Ottoman control was disagreeable to both Druze and Maronites. Efforts for a new Druze-Maronite coalition had failed, but the insurgents enjoyed the moral support of Maronite leaders (Kerr 1959:5–6; Churchill 1862:64–79). Druze feudal sheikhs were resentful of the loss of the traditional prerogatives and the arbitrary arrests and imprisonment they were subjected to under the autocratic control of Umar Pasha. The Maronites were equally appalled by the demise of the Shihabi dynasty and, with it, the frustration of their hopes for establishing an autonomous Christian Imarah (Harik 1968:268). In the face of such opposition, the Ottomans were forced to dismiss Umar Pasha before he completed his first year in office. So ended this brief interlude with direct Ottoman rule. But more important, this interlude had intensified the enmity between the religious communities. The desperate efforts of the Ottomans to assert their direct authority over Lebanon prompted them to resort to their time-worn ploys of inciting sectarian suspicions and hostility.

Such is the way in which the Turks ever maintained their power. Not by vindicating their authority, as a legitimate government ought to do, but exciting and playing upon the worst passions of human nature; by setting sect against sect; subdividing again, by corruption and intrigue, these sects amongst themselves; by bribing the worthless to betray their relations, their religion, and their country; and by dissolving all the ties which create confidence and happiness amongst mankind. (Churchill 1862:76–77)

European intervention—particularly on behalf of France and Britain—prevented the Ottoman government from imposing direct control over Lebanon, but failed to reconcile the Druze and Maronites. Consequently, the five powers and the Porte agreed in 1843 to a scheme of partitioning under a Christian *qa'immaqam* ("sub-governor"), and a southern under a Druze *qa'immaqam,* each to rule over his coreligionists and both responsible to the local Ottoman governor residing in Beirut. The Beirut-Damascus road was used as an arbitrary line of demarcation. The partition scheme was a compromise plan—advanced by Prince Metternich—between the French and Ottoman proposals. The French—supported by the Austrians—continued to hope for a restoration of the Shihabi Emirate; while the Ottomans—backed by the Russians—insisted on the complete integration of Lebanon in the Ottoman Empire and opposed any reinstatement of Lebanese autonomy.

The double *qa'immaqamiyyah* was an ill-fated plan from the day of its inception. The partition was an artificial political division that aggravated rather than assuaged religious cleavages. In the words of a contemporary observer, "it was the formal organization of civil war in the country" (as quoted by Salibi 1965:64). According to the scheme, each *qa'immaqam* was to exercise authority over his own coreligionists. The religious composition, however, of the two districts was far from homogenous. This created the problem of how to treat those who belonged to one religious community but happened to be living under the political authority of another, especially in areas like the Shuf, Gharb, and Matn.

To overcome the jurisdictional problems created by the mixed districts, the Porte decided to limit the authority of each *qa'immaqam* to his own territory, thus denying Christians in the Druze districts the right of appealing to a Christian authority in judicial and tax matters (Kerr 1959:6–7). As usual, European powers intervened on behalf of their protégés. France, as the protector of Maronite and Catholic interests, opposed the Ottoman plan and encouraged the church to remove Maronites from the jurisdiction of the Druze *qa'immaqam* and to place them directly under the Christian one. Britain, eager to safeguard the prerogatives of the Druze feudal sheikhs, approved of the revised scheme. In the meantime, Russia maintained that the Greek Orthodox community of 20,500 was populous enough to justify the creation of a special *qa'immaqamiyyah* (for further details, see Salibi 1965:63–66). In the face of such conflicting expectations, an arrangement was arrived at whereby in each of the mixed districts, a Christian and Druze *wakil* would be chosen, each with judicial authority over his coreligionists and responsible to the *qa'immaqam* of his sect. Mixed cases, involving Christians and Druze, would be heard jointly by the two *wakils*. The *wakils* were also empowered to collect taxes, each from his own sect, on behalf of the feudal chief (Kerr 1959:8–9; Salibi 1965:66–67).

A fresh outbreak of hostilities in the spring of 1845 finally convinced the Ottomans of the inadequacies inherent in the double *qa'immaqamiyyah*. Nevertheless, the Ottomans opted not to resort to a thorough reorganization of Mount Lebanon. Instead, they modified the existing arrangement by settling the jurisdictional problems of Christians living in Druze districts. A review of the articles and provisions of the Règlement Shakib Efendi, as the plan is identified by historians, reveals that altogether it reinforced rather than undermined the prevailing social and political power of the feudal families. (For further details, see Jouplain 1908:297–353; Chevallier 1971:174–79; Poujade 1867:34–35.) In the words of Shakib Efendi—the Ottoman foreign minister who was dispatched to Beirut in September 1845 to implement the revised plan—"The goal of my mission is to apply fully and completely the arrangements and the more recent enactments on local administration while preserving the particular privileges granted by the sultan." (for an English translation of the full text of the Règlement, see Hurewitz 1956: 132–35). Accordingly, the *qa'immaqam* was to be appointed from the princely families (Arslans in the case of the Druze and Abillama in the case of the Maronites) after consultations with the *a'yan* and clergy. An elected council of twelve members (two from each of the major six religious communities) was to be selected at large from the people without restriction to birth and status, yet the Christian clergy had the strongest voice in determining the election, while the Muslim members were appointed by the *wali* of Saida (Harik 1968:273). Furthermore, in the event that any vacancies were to arise in the council, the heads of the religious sects were to appoint the new members.

Feudal families throughout Lebanon had recognized Shakib Efendi's Règlement as a direct threat to their status and traditional privileges and did their utmost to resist its application. Shortly after the departure of Shakib Efendi, both Christian and Druze feudal sheikhs began "to resort to the old ways and to revive old fiscal abuses, much to the distress of the peasants" (Salibi 1965:73). For example, the enforcement of many of the provisions envisaged by the Reglement required carrying out ca- dastral surveys and a census to ascertain land ownership and population estimates. Both these measures were perceived by the feudal sheikhs as an encroachment on their feudal privileges, and the projects were aban- doned in 1847 because of feudal opposition (Salibi 1965:73).

It is within this context that the Ottoman reforms should be viewed and interpreted: growing social and political unrest generated by the pe- rennial problems of taxation, feudal authority, disarmament, and con- scription; the rather fluid state of affairs existing after the expulsion of the Egyptians and the demise of the Shihabs; growing disparities be- tween religious communities; increasing foreign intervention in the in- ternal affairs of Lebanon and the eagerness of the Ottomans to impose direct rule on Mount Lebanon and to undermine all vestiges of its local autonomy.

In their general and overall conception, the Tanzimat essentially in- volved a series of Western-inspired reforms directed towards a radical transformation of all aspects of Ottoman society (Ma'oz 1968:333). The basic drive behind the movement was to "revitalize the Empire through measures of domestic reorganization which should include the adoption or adaptation of some western ideas and institutions" (Davison 1963:7), involving practically every dimension of the social structure: military, economic, social, intellectual, legal, and political. The earlier phase of such reforms—roughly covering the era of Mahmud II (1809–1839)— was very limited in scope and involved predominantly military and ad- ministrative changes. Historians are in agreement that most of the earlier efforts, generally sporadic attempts to eliminate certain administrative abuses, were largely unsuccessful. They were almost always foiled by powerful local resistance to change. (For a critical treatment of these and earlier military reforms, see Davison 1963:21–31; Lewis 1968:74; Mar- din 1962:133–55.) At least in Mount Lebanon, the early reforms had little effect on controlling the powerful feudal chiefs. Autonomous life and communal loyalties continued unabated in a population that had little faith in the power of a central government.

It is not within our scope here to elucidate the underlying objectives, ideology, and specific circumstances that led to the promulgation of the two edicts. It is sufficient to note that they were both inspired by the belief in the need to treat with equality people of all creeds within the Empire. They were also motivated by the desire to introduce order into government, to enhance the role of ministers and to safeguard the bureaucracy against the arbitrary whims of the sultans (Davison 1963:37).

The edict of 1839, the Hatti-i Sharif of Gulhane (Noble Rescript), was explicit in its promises. Its espoused three major guarantees to ensure: "1) perfect security for life, honor, and fortune. 2) A regular system of assessing and levying taxes. 3) An equally regular system for levying of troops and the duration of their service." In addition, other provisions were made regarding the compilation of a penal code that would apply to all irrespective of "rank, position or influence"; payment of suitable salaries to public servants; and legislations against the "traffic of favoritism and bribery." (For a full English translation of the edict, see Hurewitz 1956:113–16.) There was nothing novel or outstanding about the edict. To a considerable extent, it was echoing the eighteenth-century principles of "life, liberty, and property" of the American and French revolutions as a charter of civil liberties (Davison 1963:41).

The general reaction in the Empire was mixed: the promises of security, life, and property, of tax and conscription reforms drew favorable reactions; but the promise of "equality without distinction as to religion and sect," which was to become a sort of leitmotif of the entire Tanzimat period, was met with strong opposition, particularly among Muslims (Ma'oz 1968:25).

The large measure of toleration and autonomy the non-Muslim communities were granted within the Ottoman Empire was predicated on the assumption that the tolerated communities or millets were separate and inferior. "The Muslim could claim that he assigned to his inferiors a position of reasonable comfort and security; he could moreover claim that his discrimination related not to an accident of birth but to a conscious choice on the most fundamental question of human existence. Infidel and true believer were separate; to equalize them and to mix them was an offence against both religion and common sense" (Lewis 1968:107). In this sense, the call for religious equality represented the most radical breach with traditional Islamic practice. Little wonder that it was met with strong resistance.

The principle of equality of all Ottomans, Christians, and Muslims was implicit in the adoption of mixed tribunals, secular education, and Western law. But these efforts were for foreign consumption—to win the good will of Western powers or to stave off European intervention—and did not reflect a genuine desire for reform. Indeed, the implementation of many such schemes was never put into effect. The fundamental changes, for example, promised in the conduct of courts, provincial administration, the assessment and collection of taxes, and the terms of military service, were never wholly executed (Hurewitz 1956:113; Maʿoz 1968:25–26). Muslims, likewise, could not bring themselves to accept Christians as officers, and Christians were reluctant to serve in the army, preferring to pay the traditional exemption tax (Davison 1963:45).

Altogether, the outcome of the reforms generated by the edict of 1839 were disappointingly few. The edict of 1856 did not fare any better. Like the edict of 1839, the Hatti-i Humayun had something for everybody. It confirmed the promises of 1839 but went further in identifying the specific changes to be made. Since the edict was designed to weaken Russian claims to the right of protecting Greek Orthodox Christians in the Empire (a claim that, incidentally had been one of the major causes of the Crimean War), it once again promised to take "energetic measures to insure to each sect, whatever the number of its adherents, entire freedom in the exercise of its religion. Every distinction or designation pending to make any class whatever of the subjects of my empire inferior to another class, on account of their religion, language, or race, shall be forever effaced from administrative protocol" (Hurewitz 1956:151).

The edict made further guarantees that all subjects, without distinction to sect or nationality, should have access to military and civil schools, should be admissible to public employment, and be qualified to fill them according to their capacity and merit. Mixed tribunals were called for to hear commercial, correctional, and criminal suits involving Christians and Muslims. It reiterated the same concern for introducing administrative reforms in the system of taxation (a system of direct collection was to replace the abuses of tax farming), recruitment and exemption from military duty and constitutional reforms in provincial and communal councils. More than the edict of 1839, the Hatti-i Humayun expressed concern for works of public utility, monetary and financial reforms, and encouragement of commerce and agriculture. (For an English translation of the edict, see Hurewitz 1956:149–53.)

Like its predecessor, the edict of 1856 "left nothing to be desired but its execution" (Hitti 1957:430). At least in Lebanon, the effect of the reforms on the social order was negligible. None of the three general objectives professed by the two edicts—the imposition of direct centralization rule, improving social and economic conditions, and the promotion of equality between religious communities—was adequately realized. Effective provisions for implementing the reforms were deficient, and the secularizing and sweeping tone of the edicts, particularly the second Hattii, seemed too threatening to some of the vested traditional interests. A word about each of these objectives is in order.

To undermine the local autonomy inherent in *iqta*ʿ society and impose direct rule on Mount Lebanon, the Ottomans had to resort to the detested measures of conscription and disarmament. They also attempted to introduce a system of direct taxation to replace the quasi-feudal system responsible for perpetuating the power of the feudal sheikhs. The earlier experience of the Lebanese with such instances of direct rule and tight controls under Ibrahim Pasha did not leave much room to expect that the Ottomans would succeed where the Egyptians had failed. The same outcome occompanied Ottoman efforts to organize local councils (*majlis* or *diwan*). Both Christian and Druze feudal sheikhs perceived such arrangements as an attempt to undermine their local autonomy and refused to participate. (For further details, see Davison 1954:848; Maʿoz 1968:81–84; al-Shidyaq 1970:345.)

The impact of the Tanzimat on social and economic conditions was even more negligible. The reforms, by the admission of several historians, had failed to bring about any significant change in rural areas. Reports and accounts of consuls, missionaries, and travelers repeat the same theme: "Life and property in the country were becoming daily more insecure" (Maʿoz 1968:151–52). Peasants continued to be subjected to the high interest rates demanded by urban creditors and other exploitations. The high incidence of mass migration during the 1840s and 1850s was a by-product of the peasants' state of impoverishment and dispossession (Smilianskaya 1966:234–35).

Works on public utilities such as roads, bridges, canals, post and telegraph services, port facilities, and the like—which had a direct impact on the state of agriculture and commerce—were also generally neglected. This neglect was all the more flagrant because the Ottomans during the same period displayed little reluctance in lavishing disproportionate sums of public expenditure on military barracks, forts and guard houses, government buildings, and ostentatious palaces for their resident pashas, which had no bearing on enhancing general welfare.

The prosperity and private initiative the local economy was able to generate were further depleted by the instability of the Ottoman monetary system. Inflationary practices and the debasement of the currency, measures frequently resorted to by the Ottomans, inflicted drastic hardships on the population. The first bank in Syria, a branch of the "Ottoman Bank," was established in 1856 in Beirut but was unable to regulate the monetary system, guarantee securities, and advance the needed credit (Farley 1959:36). Nearly all the monetary affairs were in the hands of bankers who monopolized the currency and charged exorbitant rates of interest.

The socioeconomic changes observed during this period did not act evenly upon the various elements of the population. Once again, the burgeoning urban middle class—mostly Christian merchants and agents for European traders—continued to prosper. The rest of the society, particularly craftsmen, artisans, peasants, and small traders, were adversely affected by the growing dependence of the Lebanese economy on European production and trade. The new trading patterns deprived a large portion of the rural society of its traditional sources of livelihood and rendered the economy sensitive to external circumstances. Any disturbance in the European economy had its reverberations within Lebanon. The French consul general in Beirut noted that the French financial crisis of 1857–58 had had "disastrous consequences for Syrian business. Numerous and important bankruptcies, an extraordinary financial uneasiness felt until the end of 1859, loss of credit everywhere, and all this added to by two years of poor harvest (Chevallier 1968:219). Furthermore, in violation of the Anglo-Turkish commercial Treaty of 1838, which established the principle of free trade and laissez-faire, the Ottomans imposed a tax on silk cocoons at the place where they were raised, an act which contributed to the consequent ruin of many of the local reeling factories (Issawi 1967:115; Chevallier 1968:218).

More damaging than the socioeconomic disparities were the widening religious cleavages and confessional hostility. The two edicts, which espoused the principle of equality between Christians and Muslims, did in fact achieve just the opposite: a complete rift between the two dominant groups which ultimately provoked the massacres of 1861. It is instructive that the two decades of widespread turmoil and bitter civil and confessional unrest in Lebanon's history should have also coincided with the epoch of Ottoman reforms. The coincidence could not be dismissed as accidental. The liberal policy of Ibrahim Pasha, the egalitarian provisions of the edict of 1856, and the efforts of the Ottomans to subject Lebanon to more intensive centralized rule, generated a large residue of confessional hostility. Muslims, on the whole, found the secularism inherent in the reforms too repugnant. This was apparent in the educational and judicial reforms introduced by the Ottomans which undermined rather than reinforced existing traditional systems (Tibawi 1969:132–34). They were also jealous of the religious liberties and economic prosperity the Christians were generally enjoying. Christians were the main beneficiaries of the socioeconomic changes generated by the Egyptian presence. The Tanzimat accentuated the religious disparities. Initially, Christians in Lebanon, as elsewhere in the Ottoman Empire, welcomed the egalitarian provisions of 1856 with much exuberance. Church bells were sounded in the countryside; and in some instances the French flag was hoisted above churches and monastaries and religious processions were held in public, often in open defiance of Muslims and Druzes (Ma'oz 1968:203). Gradually, however, Christians began to doubt the motives behind the reforms and continued to perceive Ottoman presence as an instrument to reinforce the predominance of Islam.

Factional, Class, and Confessional Conflict

Around the middle of the nineteenth century, Mount Lebanon had all the ingredients of a feudal and fractured social order: factional and family rivalry, a bit of "class" conflict between the feudal aristocracy and an emerging Maronite clergy, and the mass of exploited peasantry determined to challenge the social and political supremacy of feudal authority. This, as we have seen, was reinforced, often deliberately incited, by Ottoman pashas playing one faction against another or the intervention of Western powers eager to protect or promote the interest of its own protégé.

The interplay of all these forces was apparent in the early phases of conflict. The Khazins, as feudal masters of Kisrwan, were outraged by the appointment of an Abillama (Bashir Ahmad) as Christian *qa'immaqam* of the North. They were reluctant to recognize the Abillamas as social superiors and were incensed by the encroachment on the aristocratic rights and feudal privileges that they enjoyed for ages. To cope with the growing challenge and displeasure of the feudal families, the *qa'immaqam* turned to the Maronite clergy and peasants for support. Encouraged by the French and Austrians, he posed as the champion of Roman Catholics. He also incited a number of intersectarian conflicts between Maronites and Greek Orthodox Christians. The British, aware of the support of the French and Austrian consulates, threw their weight on the side of another Abillama, Bashir Assaf, who was making a bid for the *qaʾimmaqamiyyah*. This persuaded other feudal families, particularly Khazin and Hubaysh, to support Bashir Assaf. With this in mind, the townsmen of Zahle were encouraged to form a village council and elect a *sheikh shabab* (a village strongman) to manage the public affairs of the town. Such a move was an open defiance of the authority of the *qaʾimmaqam*. It set the pattern for townsmen elsewhere to establish similar defiant and rebellious movements. In some of the towns of Kisrwan and Matn the uprisings, which first took the form of mass agitations and public rallies, openly challenged the supremacy of feudal families. Petitions were drafted and public assemblies were organized to articulate the grievances of commoners against feudal injustices and oppression.

In short, by the spring of 1858, the Christian districts in the North were in a state of total disorder bordering on anarchy. At both ends of the social hierarchy, there were growing signs of unrest. Feudal families, jealous of their feudal privileges and kinship consciousness, were challenging the authority of the *qaʾimmaqam*. Their rebellion succeeded in destroying his power over their districts. The peasant movement, as a protest against feudal abuses, was also beginning to gain considerable momentum.

We have already, in the preceeding chapter, provided an account of the peasant uprising of 1857: the circumstances that provoked it, the form it assumed, its leadership and some of its consequences. It is sufficient to note here that successful as the peasant revolt in Kisrwan had been in raising the hopes of other peasants throughout Lebanon, the movement remained predominantly a local upheaval. Druze peasants were apprehensive about taking similar action against their own feudal sheikhs. Indeed, the peasant movement in the Druze districts assumed a sectarian rather than a "class" conflict. Druze sheikhs were successful in muting and deflecting the grievances and discontent of their own peasants by provoking sectarian rivalry; particularly in the religiously mixed communities of the Shuf and Matn. The communities were already seething with confessional enmity and required little provocation. After the first clash of 1841, both Druze and Maronite continued to rearm themselves. The supply of arms and amunition that cleared Beirut customs in the years preceding the war was quite voluminous (Tibawi 1969:123). The two communities had also been preparing for the confrontation, although Christians went about it much more openly, and with greater deliberation and boasting, often taunting their adversaries. Several of the Christian villages, for example, were in a state close to actual mobilization. Units of armed men, with special uniforms, led by a *sheikh shabab,* were organized in each of the villages. In turn, these small units were placed under the command of higher officers. In Beirut the Maronite Bishop himself organized and headed such an armed group, while wealthy Maronites competed with one another in raising subscriptions for the purchase of arms and amunition (Jessup 1910:165–66).

In short, the affray between the two boys, the shooting of a partridge, or the collision of two pack-animals—often cited as sources of provocation—were no more than a spark that set ablaze an already explosive situation. Once ignited, agitation and violence became widespread. With every renewed confrontation, the ferocity of the fighting was intensified. So was the magnitude of damage to life and property. Although the Maronites, with an estimate of fifty thousand men, were expecting to overwhelm the twelve thousand Druze forces (indeed, they often boasted of exterminating their adversaries) early in the struggle, the Druze manifested superiority in fighting effectiveness. In one battle after another, they defeated and humbled the Maronites.

So sweeping was the Druze victory that historians talk with amazement about the "flagrant temerity of the Druzes . . . and the seemingly inexplicable Christian cowardice" (Salibi 1965:93). The Druze forces were better organized, disciplined, and fought more fiercely and menacingly; while Christians suffered from inept and bickering leadership (Churchill 1862:142–43). The magnitude and intensity of violence was more astonishing.

Sometimes within hours entire villages and towns would fall, often with little resistance. Townsmen, seized with panic would abandon their villages and homes to be burned down, plundered, and pillaged and seek refuge in Christian strongholds. Other fugitives on their way to Beirut or Sidon were often overtaken, robbed and killed indiscriminately by their assailants. Even the Christian strongholds were not spared. In fact, it was in these towns that the worst atrocities were perpetrated. First in 'Ayn Dara, then in Babda, Jazzine, Hasbayya, Rashayya, Zahle, and Dayr al-Qamar the same atrocious pattern of violence repeated itself with added intensity. The Ottoman garrison commander would offer the Christians asylum in the local serai, request the surrender of their arms, and then stand idly by watching the carnage.

In the short span of four weeks—from mid-May until June 20—an estimated twelve thousand Christians lost their lives, four thousand had perished in destitution and a hundred thousand became homeless and about 4,000,000 pounds worth of damage to property had been done (Churchill 1862:132; Hitti 1957:438; Salibi 1965:106). Added to this devastation of life and property was the legacy of confessional bitterness and suspicion the civil war had generated. Lebanon was clearly in urgent need of swift and sweeping measures to pacify, rehabilitate, and reconstruct the fabric of a dismembered society. It was also clear that more than a mere restoration of order and tranquility was needed. The political reorganization of Mount Lebanon became imminent. Once again the future of Lebanon was at the mercy of foreign powers.

Concluding Remarks

During the short span of twenty years, Lebanon witnessed at least five major episodes of civil strife and communal conflict. Not only did the scale and intensity of political violence increase during this period, it also assumed a new form. Until the end of the Egyptian occupation, civil strife was largely nonsectarian. Feuding families and bickering feudal chiefs fought one another and, on two occasions, peasants revolted against their overlords. All such alignments were sustained by partisan, feudal, or class rivalry but rarely took the form of outright confessional hostility. Travelers and observers continued to be impressed by the spirit of amity and harmony that characterized relations between the various religious communities. As late as 1840, Maronites and Druze were still signing joint declarations in opposition to Ibrahim Pasha's repressive measures.

An attempt was made in this chapter to identify some of the internal and external sources of change that disrupted the balance of forces between the various religious communities. Factors such as the demise of the Shihabi dynasty, efforts to undermine local autonomy and traditional authority of feudal sheikhs, Maronite involvement in crushing the Druze uprising in Hawran, and the divisive consequences of the partition scheme all contributed to the intensification of confessional hostility.

The great power rivalry and the consequent internationalization of Lebanese politics also left their toll. Foreign powers, eager to gain inroads into the Middle East and win protégés, sought to pit one religious community against another. Added to this was the new centralized policy of the Ottomans directed at undermining the privileged status of Mount Lebanon and the local authority of feudal chiefs.

More important in this regard were the consequences of the liberal policies of Ibrahim Pasha and the egalitarian provisions of the two Ottoman edicts. A decade of Egyptian rule opened up the village society of Mount Lebanon to all sorts of societal changes and secular reforms but also generated a pronounced shift in the relative socioeconomic and political positions of the religious communities. The precarious balance that held society together and sustained confessional harmony was disrupted. The Ottoman Tanzimat did little to assuage these dislocations. On the contrary, the secular and innovative tones of the reforms were a threat to the vested interests of traditional Muslims, and the egalitarian provisions of the second edict provoked further hostility between the sects.

What general inferences, if any, can be made about the nature and consequences of communal conflict in pluralistic societies like Lebanon?

In some obvious respects, Lebanon then and now had all the features of a fragmented political culture. Sharp divisions, sustained by striking differences in religious beliefs and communal and regional allegiances continue to split the society and reinforce segmental and parochial loyalties. Superimposed on these traditional divisive forces were new forms of socioeconomic differentiation generated by the asymmetrical growth Lebanon witnessed during the nineteenth century. In short, there were both vertical and horizontal divisions that pulled the society apart and threatened the delicate balance of power. Accordingly, much of the communal conflict—factional, class, and confessional—Lebanon has repeatedly experienced might very well be an expression of its fragmented political culture and deficient civity.

That a fragmented and pluralistic society of this sort should display a high propensity for conflict is not unusual. What is unusual is the frequency, intensity, and form of conflict or violence. The recurrence of violence suggests that the resort to violence has had little effect so far on redressing the gaps and imbalances in society, or in transforming its communal and confessional loyalties and institutions into more secular and civic entities typical of a nation-state. Indeed, the very persistence of conflict means that something is not changing.

The persistence and changing form of conflict also reveals another curious feature of Lebanon's pluralism. The exposure of a growing portion of the population to secular forms of social control, the extension of state services, and the spread of market economy did little to weaken the intensity of communal loyalties. Confessional, kinship, and regional attachments continued to serve as viable sources of communal solidarity. They inspired local and personal initiative and accounted for much of the proverbial resourcefulness of the Lebanese at the time. But they also undermined civic consciousness and commitment to Lebanon as a political entity. Expressed more poignantly: the forces that motivated and sustained prosperity, harmony, and balance were also the very forces that on occasion pulled the society apart and contributed to conflict, tension, and civil disorder.

CHAPTER FOUR

Changing Forms of Political Patronage

All human societies and their institutions are, at the root, a barrier against naked terror.
—Peter Berger, *The Sacred Canopy.*

A NY CURSORY REVIEW of the local section of a daily Lebanese newspaper is bound to reveal a preoccupation with one or more of the following items of news that attracted public attention during the past few months:

Sabri Hamadeh, the traditional political *za'im* of the Shi'ite community of Baalbeck, declared his intention to seek his 25th nomination as Speaker of the Chamber of Deputies—the second ranking position in the formal hierarchy of power in Lebanon. Like most other veteran politicans (*aqtab* as they are popularly labelled by the press), Hamadeh is an absentee landlord, a descendant of a feudal family that can trace its genealogical descent to the 15th century and the undisputed head of an extensive clan. Typical of the traditional *zu'ama,* he has been a prominent figure in the political life of Lebanon close to half a century, and has succeeded in representing his constituency in every parliamentary election held thus far. He served as minister a score of times and has had a virtual monopoly over of the speakership of the Chamber of Deputies. Of all forty-two regular parliamentary sessions since independence, Hamadeh was elected twenty-four times. The remaining rotated among two other prominent Shi'ite feudal families of the South: Assad (nine times) and Usayran (eight times). In declaring his intention to seek the speakership yet another round, Hamadeh identified no program or platform other than his purely personal whim to cap his political career by celebrating a golden jubilee.

This essay is a revised and updated version of a paper originally published in Ernest Gellner and John Waterbury, eds., *Patrons and Clients* (London Duckworth, 1977), pp. 185–205. Used by permission.

Camille Chamoun, though not a scion of a feudal family, has also been one of the most ubiquitous and entrenched political figures of contemporary Lebanon. He was first elected to the National Assembly of 1934–37, and like the spirited politicians of the day, he participated in the national struggle for independence, served as minister in successive cabinets, and became eventually President of the Republic (1952–58). Rather than retiring after his eventful term as President, he established his own "National Liberals" political party, regained his parliamentary seat, and has since been instrumental in the formation of several coalitions—often with some of his earlier and most bitter adversaries—to assert his continued influence on the political life of the country. Like other *aqtab,* he has formed his own militia group—a paramilitary organization of trained and disciplined retainers—for the professed purpose of assisting in maintaining law and order and safeguarding Lebanon's sovereignty. In recent months, the whole question of the presence of private militias within a nation state, because of their growing visibility in public places and the concomitant display of arms and explosives, has become a hotly contested issue with charges and counter charges of arms smuggling, espionage and the demise or erosion of state power.

Practically everyday, the papers carry sensational headlines of a new "scandal" involving deals, kickbacks, *quid-pro-quos* and other such flagrant evidences of corruption, nepotism, graft and squandering of public funds. Some of the most recent are the "Regie Scandal" (the state tobacco monopoly) involving the sale of defective tobacco, mismanagement and bribery; the sale and resale of municipal real estate property; technical incompetence of government officials; ministers, taking advantages of their short-term in office, to appoint some of their own clients in excess of positions available; the disproportionate allocation of public funds for projects in politically "desirable" regions to the exclusion of others currently out of favor; the personal and often arbitrary intervention of the President of the Republic in expediting certain public projects while obstructing or suspending others.

Papers also carry repeated stories of long-standing family and tribal feuds being liquidated without retributive justice; of mutinous *qab-adayate* (henchmen) of known political leaders taking the law in their own hands in defiance of government authority; of offenders wanted for honor crimes seeking the protection of their local *za'im;* of marginal and interest groups (Shi'ites, Palestinian Resistance, banana growers etc . . .) demonstrating their grievances against government abuse and indifference by imposing road blocks and cordoning off urban districts and neighborhoods; of dismissed university students seeking the patronage of politicians and religious leaders.

Monday morning papers, at least during the three months of summer, almost always carry engaging accounts of a day in the life of President Frangieh while on his family homestead in Ihden. Every Sunday, and often on other days, the President literally holds an open house. All protocol is lifted and any person, regardless of station or background, can seek his audience without previous appointment. He personally enquires about each of his visitors' relatives, recalling nostalgically past moments they might have shared together, listens to their grievances and promises prompt attention. Much like the fief holder of old, presiding over the private concerns of his estate, he is more the affable, benign and personable "bey" displaying genuine empathy and compassion in the lives of his subjects than a stately President carrying on with the affairs of state. He is no longer President Frangieh but "Abou Toni" or Suleiman Bey," the tribal za'im of a tightly knit community.

Though seemingly unconnected, all these instances—the resilience of traditional leaders, veteran politicians seeking to extend their political clientage, corruption, tribal feuds, the grievances of dispossessed groups and marginal communities, and the personal and affective style of political leadership—are all manifestations of essentially the same phenomena: the ubiquity and survival of patronage in Lebanon. This is far from unusual in a pluralistic society marked by persistent disparities in status and opportunity and sustained by highly personalized networks of reciprocal obligations and primordial loyalties. In fact, in all known societies, with or without such diffuse and ascriptive loyalties, individuals and groups normally seek to advance their private ends particularistically. As Carl Lande (1973:117) has argued, "The powerful, the rich, and the well-connected, can obtain favored treatment through personal office holding, through the use or threat of force, or by offering material rewards to bureaucratic decision makers. The weak and the poor often can hope to obtain leniency either by becoming the clients of persons in positions of power or, in the case of those who lack such connections, through appeals for pity." Unlike other societies, however, very few underprivileged groups in Lebanon resort to appeals for pity and mercy. The concern for family honor and preserving one's face and integrity leaves little room for such appeals. It is certainly far more honorable and dignifying to seek the patronage of the powerful, the rich, and the well-connected. To a large measure, much of the sociopolitical history of Lebanon may be viewed as the history of various groups and communities seeking to secure such patronage: client groups in search of protection, security and vital benefits, and patrons seeking to extend the scope of their clientage.

Within such a context, the middleman, the *wasit,* and the broker—one who provides "crucial linkages between the center and the periphery" (Lemarchand and Legg 1972:198), and promises greater access to opportunity, needed services, and protection—emerges as the most prized and viable political actor. Likewise, patron-client ties become one of the most fundamental of all social bonds to hold the society together. In their most rudimentary form, all such ties involve the "reciprocal exchange of extrinsic benefits" (Blau 1964:314; Lemarchand 1972:75–76). Both parties, in other words, the patron and the client, have a vested interest in maintaining this kind of mutually beneficial transaction. Despite their asymmetrical nature—and all patron-client ties bring together people with marked disparities in wealth, status, and power (Scott 1972:93; Lemarchand and Legg 1972:151)—they remain essentially an exchange partnership. As will be shown, clients in Lebanon have no equally accessible avenue to secure some of their personal services, favored treatment, and protection other than through their allegiance to a patron (particularly in the form of gratitude and compliance which in some instances boarders on filial loyalty), and patrons can only maintain their power by extending the size of their clientage support. In this lies the ubiquity and survival of patronage in Lebanon.

We cannot, in this essay, explore all dimensions of patronage. Both in its structural and dynamic features, the phenomena has varied manifestations and consequences. The most we can do is to identify a few of its political forms, trace its emergence and transformation within the context of Lebanon's feudal society and account for its persistence and viability. More specifically, our basic concern is to identify some of the conditions associated with the survival of patronage and to explore some of its functional features in terms of inducing and absorbing change while integrating the social order.

Feudalism and Patronage

The broad socioeconomic and political features that characterized the feudal society *(iqta')* of Mount Lebanon have already been identified in chapter 2. It was noted then that both in its origin and evolution, the *iqta'* system had much in common with other feudal societies. Yet, as several writers have suggested, it also had unique features of its own that distinguished it clearly from the *iltizam* system of tax-farming prevalent in other provinces of the Ottoman Empire. (For further details, see Chevallier 1971; Harik 1965; Harlik 1968; Poliak 1939; Polk 1963.)

What needs to be underscored here are those features of Lebanese feudalism that have implications for the survival of patronage. It is not that difficult, after all, to trace the origin of some of the persisting peculiarities of patronage to that special variety of Lebanese feudalism.

One of the striking political features of the *iqta'* system of Mount Lebanon, one that had implications for patron-client networks, was its non-military character. It was clearly not organized as a military fief. Unlike the fief holders in Syria, Egypt, and Palestine, those of Mount Lebanon had no fixed military duties and were not required to maintain a specific contingent of troops. At one point under the Ayyubids and Mamluk sultans, we are told, they were occasionally involved in the communication of intelligence regarding activities of the Crusades (Poliak 1939:26). That was the closest they got to a military function. The Shihabi amirs did keep a small number of retainers mostly for administrative purposes, but they had no army or police force to speak of. Indeed, their attitude toward military or security officers was one of low regard and outright disdain.

This nonmilitary feature reveals a subtle but basic characteristic of the nature of political legitimacy and allegiance in the *iqta'* system. Legitimacy was based more on personal loyalty than on coercive obedience to an impersonal authority. The amir as we have seen, need not resort to coercion to generate and sustain conformity to his authority. Instead he relied on the good will of his *muqata'jis* and the personal allegiance of their followers *(atba'* or *'uhdah)*. Furthermore, this form of political allegiance was not sectarian or confessional. It was predominantly personal. Regardless of a person's religious affiliation, he was identified as a *'uhdah* of a *muqata'ji*. The mutual moral obligations and feelings of interdependence inherent in such personal ties are aptly described and documented by Harik (1965:411).

To be of the *'uhdah* of a *muqati'ji* placed moral obligations not only on the followers but also on the *muqati'ji,* who would come to the aid of his men and protect them. This duty was usually expressed as *haq al-riayah wa al-himayah* (to tend and protect). To maintain his integrity and position in the political life of the Imarah, a *muqati'ji* was well aware that he had to have a strong following and a loyal one. Sometimes *muqati'jis* went so far in protecting their followers as to place political considerations above accepted rules of good conduct.

This is clearly a typical form of a patron-client tie. Characteristically, it involved the exchange of support for protection. The client strengthens the patron by giving his support, and receives aid and protection in return. This form of patronage, with all its moral under-tones of mutual benefit and avowed loyalty between protector and protégé, could be easily sustained under the special variety of Lebanese feudalism. Unlike the system of *iltizam* prevalent in other Ottoman provinces, where the *multazim* was essentially a government official official with no special ties to the village or tax farm under his control, the *muqata'ji* usually lived in his own village among his own *atba'*. Much like the bureaucrat of a centralized administration, the *multazim*'s sole concern was to remit the yearly tribute and maintain law and order in his district. Since his tenure in office was usually at the mercy of a pasha's capricious whim, he developed little interest in the welfare of his subjects and tried instead to enrich himself at their expense. These and other oppressive side effects of the system of *iltizam* have been noted by several observers (Polk 1962; Bowring 1840).

In contrast, the *muqata'jis* power and economic well-being depended on the continuous support and loyalty of his *atba'*. Accordingly, he was less likely to be oppressive and rapacious toward them. The beneficial effects of such a system of patronage, particularly since it involves a propinquity between feudal lord and peasant, should not be overlooked. More important, the *iqta'* system permitted more responsibility to be exercised at the local level than was the case under iltizam. The multazim was essentially a representative of the government in the village. Quite often, he was a city notable with whose assistance the Ottoman pashas sought to exercise their control over the various districts. As such, he had no independent jurisdiction over his subjects. On the other hand, as an autonomous feudal chief, the *muqata'ji* enjoyed a much larger measure of independence in his jurisdiction. Indeed, both the amir and the *muqata'ji* did all they could to ward off Ottoman encroachment on their own traditional rights.

Despite the rigid gradations of authority and the well-defined sanctions at all levels of the political hierarchy, the *muqata'ji* had virtually complete supremacy over the affairs of his own *muqata'*. Ottoman authority, as we have seen, was too far removed and limited to the payment of the *miri* by the hakim. The hakim himself had no direct relations with the subjects; and if he had any particular wish or grievance with regard to any particular subject, it had to be mediated through the *muqata'ji*. In most such instances, the *muqata'ji* invariably came to the rescue of his own *atba'*, in much the same way that the hakim would have protected his *muqata'ji* from the punitive demands of an Ottoman pasha or sultan. In such a differentiated hierarchy of authority, the *muqata'ji* emerged with almost undisputed sovereignty over his own district. This sovereignty was further reinforced and perpetuated by the hereditary character of the *iqta'* system. "Power and transference was subject to blood relationship . . . Both title of nobility and government rights were passed from father to son and thus authority was kept within the patrilineal kinship group" (Harik 1965:420). In this sense Iliya Harik is of course correct in arguing that the *iqta'* system was neither an aristocratic form of government nor a tribal one, although it had some elements in common with both. Since the *muqata'ji* lived on his fief and attended personally to the affairs of his subjects, he was clearly not part of a court aristocracy. Nor was he a tribal leader, although political authority and succession were kept within the same family. The feudal districts he presided over were composed of heterogeneous kinship and religious groups (Harik 1968:64–73).

This brief characterization of some of the salient political features of the *iqta'* system of Mount Lebanon should have made it clear that it departs in some significant respects from the system of *iltizam* common in other provinces of the Ottoman Empire. In surveying such features, several historians have noted that the *iqta'* form of government in Mount Lebanon had perhaps more in common with European feudalism than with the *iltizam* system of neighboring Ottoman provinces (Harik 1965:420). In a comparative study of feudalism in the Buwayhid dynasty of Baghdad (946–1055), Southern France, and Japan of the same period, Archibald Lewis (1969) underscores nearly the same distinctions. On all four counts—the nonmilitary character of the Midi and Japanese form of feudalism, the nature of personal allegiance and reciprocal loyalties, their noncentralized form of government, and the subsequent autonomy feudal lords enjoyed in their local districts—the *iqta'* system of Mount

Lebanon is clearly closer to the French and Japanese variety than that of the Buwayhids.

Though in a different context, Charles Issawi (1968) was essentially referring to the same tendency when he maintained that in contrast to the centralized bureaucratric system found in Egypt and other countries, Lebanon and Japan "were the only two countries in Asia where one could find a semblance of feudalism." He goes on to say, "It may be, as I believe, that the critical point is that, under the systems of these two states, Lebanon and Japan, a certain spirit of independence was developed. And it was the spirit which laid the groundwork of later development. This is, of course, a tenuous hypothesis; but I do not think it is completely irrelevant" (as quoted by Polk and Chambers 1968:16).

Varieties of Political Patronage

Throughout the nineteenth century, most of the conditions associated with the survival and vitality of patron-client networks—marked disparities in the distribution of wealth, status and power; isolated and closely knit communities; factional and partisan rivalries; and highly personalized and diffuse social obligations and loyalties—continued to display themselves under varied forms. They also generated different forms of patronage. A brief word about each of the conditions associated with the patron-client network is in order.

The vertical differentiation of the social structure generated marked class distinctions on the basis of status and kinship affiliation. A recognized hierarchy of ranks among the feudal elites had evolved as a rather formalized system of social prestige sustained by elaborate forms of social potocol and rules of conduct. As we have seen earlier, the distribution of prestige among the different families was far from arbitrary. It reflected considerations such as the actual power each of the families held, the vintage of their kinship genealogy, and the esteem the families happened to enjoy in the eyes of the ruling Shihabs. The Arslans, for example, could trace their lineage back to the pre-Islamic Arab kings of the al-Hira; while the Shihabs, to a Quraysh companion of Muhammad. The Talhuqs and Nakads traced their lineage to the twelfth century; the Dahdahs to the fourteenth; the Hamadeh to the fifteenth; the Junblats, Hubayshes, and Khazins to the sixteenth, and so on until one may arrive at a ranking that corresponds fairly consistently with the vintage of a family's genealogy (Poliak 1939:57–58). While the feudal aristocracy could be readily differentiated into well-defined strata of amirs, muqaddams, and sheikhs, no such hierarchies characterized the commoners. They were all lumped together into one undifferentiated class of *ammiyyah*.

The social structure of Mount Lebanon was also differentiated horizontally into isolated and closely knit village communities. As we have seen earlier, the mountainous terrain and the natural divisions of the country into distinct geographic regions, each with its own particular sociocultural traditions rendered the village community a fundamental unit in the society. Strong endogamous ties, continuities in the patterns of residence and landownership, attachments to feudal families who also resided in the village, along with the geographic isolation from other communities all tended to reinforce village loyalties and make the villager more conscious of communal interests. So strong were these loyalties that village identity often superseded kinship, religious, or class attachments. William Polk (1963:70), cites the interesting case of how the village of Ammatur in South Lebanon made a collective effort in 1777 to halt the encroachment of the Junblati overlords on the water resources of the village. The villagers, regardless of their kinship, confessional, or class allegiances acted in concert to ward off such encroachment.

This is all the more remarkable since the village communities, like the feudal districts, were generally of mixed confessional composition. Neither the predominantly Christian communities of the North nor the predominantly Druze communities of the South were exclusively homogeneous in their sectarian structure. In fact, of all the feudal districts, only three in the North (Bcharri, Zawiya, and Futuh) were Maronite, and one in the South (Jabal al-Rihan) was Shi'ite (Chevallier 1971:61–63).

The implications of such communal and regional isolation, with its concomitant village attachments, for patron-client networks are self-evident. Villagers, among other things, required protection from the oppressive tyranny and rapacious controls of distant pashas and amirs. They also needed protection from the excessive demands of central administration, particularly the ruinous impositions of *corvée,* taxation and arbitrary conscription. Warding off the encroachment of competing factions or other village communities was also a persistent fear. Any person or group that could offer the needed security and protection and who was in a position to alleviate the heavy exactions levied on the peasants was bound to inspire allegiance among his clients. Initially, the *muqata'jis,* by virtue of the authority and autonomy they enjoyed, were the most likely group to offer such patronage. No other group, at least until 1820, could have challenged their supremacy or offered alternative avenues for protection and security.

Feudal society of Mount Lebanon, all other integrative evidences of harmony and balance notwithstanding, was far from factionless. There were deep splits and rivalries between feudal families competing for power positions or seeking to win the favors of a governing amir or an Ottoman pasha. In fact, the Ottoman pashas encouraged such rivalry so much that it had become virtually a policy of theirs to play off one amir against another as a means of containing the growing influence of a powerful vassal. All such factional splits, at least initially, were predominantly partisan or kinship in character. They rarely took the form of a class or confessional conflict. They were also fairly fluid and loose in that the factions could easily reorganize themselves into new alignments. No sooner, for example, had the classic Qaysi-Yemeni rivalry vindicated itself in the battle of 'Ayn Dara of 1711 than feudal families and their followers began to align themselves into new dual factions along Yazbaki-Junblati lines.

The factional and kinship rivalries soon developed into broader "class" and confessional conflict. The peasant uprisings of 1820, 1840, and 1857 and the outbreak of confessional hostility in 1841 and 1860 generated new forms of patron-client relationships. The peasant seditions, even if temporarily, ushered in the Church as an alternate source of patronage and political leadership. As has already been demonstrated, for the first time in the history of modern Lebanon, commoners and clerics took the initiative in organizing a revolt against some of the repressive abuses of the *iqta'* system. Though the sedition was initially limited in scope to a protest against the imposition of additional taxes by the Ottoman Pasha of Saida, it generated some unanticipated consequences that had significant implications for changing the nature of political legitimacy. Clerics helped organize the peasants into village communes and asked each village to choose a *wakil* as a spokesman who could act on their behalf with other *wakils* and government authorities. As was shown earlier, this innovative institution had revolutionary implications for transforming the political perspectives of peasants and challenging feudal authority and the nature of political allegiance to it. Among other things, it expressed a new concept of authority; one which generated a shift from the ascriptive ties of status and kinship to those based on communal and public interest. It also involved a change in the peasant's political perspectives: he no longer perceived himself as being bound by personal allegiances to his feudal lord. The significance of this new awareness is aptly underscored by Harik (1968:221): "No universal ideas like private versus public welfare had been entertained in the past. The individual viewed himself as an integral part of *uhdah* with no sense of political individuality of his own. To start to think in terms of public interest implies an awareness of new relations and an outlook in which the traditional idea of subject and master are no longer acceptable."

One must not, however, overrate the impact of this episode. The ʿammiyyah revolt remained, despite the new enthusiasm it generated in its initial phases, essentially a Maronite phenomenon and was predominantly confined to the Christian *muqataʿas* of the North. Efforts to mobilize the support of Druze peasants in the South was met with failure. They remained loyal to their feudal lords and clearly refused to be drawn into any rivalry which would undermine such ties of fealty and personal allegiance.

All other subsequent efforts in the nineteenth century to undermine the authority and local autonomy of the feudal sheikhs proved equally futile. For example, the decade of centralized and direct Egyptian rule (1831–1841), in which sweeping reforms were introduced by Ibrahim Pasha from above, had little visible effect on controlling the powerful feudal chiefs. True, the power of some of the prominent Druze feudal families of the South was temporarily destroyed by Amir Bashir in 1825. Much of their property was confiscated, and they were forced into exile. Most of these families, however, had little difficulty in restoring their usurped rights and privileges. After 1840, they began to reclaim their former estates and regain their feudal prerogatives.

The same is true of the efforts of the Ottomans, following the outbreak of sectarian hostilities of 1841 and 1845, in reorganizing the administrative divisions of Mount Lebanon. Both the double *qaʿimmaqamiyyah* (the partition scheme advanced by the European powers in 1843 to divide Lebanon into separate Christian and Druze districts each with its own subgovernor) and the so-called Règlement Shakib Efendi of 1845 (which attempted to rectify some of the jurisdictional inadequacies inherent in the scheme) did not undermine the power of the feudal chiefs (for further details see Jouplain 1908:297–353; Chevallier 1971:174–79; Poujade 1867:34–35). Indeed, as some observers have argued, the traditional authority and privileges of the feudal families remained virtually untouched (Churchill 1862:109–10). For example, the enforcement of many of the provisions envisaged by the Règlement required carrying out cadastral surveys and a census to ascertain land ownership and population estimates. Both these measures were perceived by the feudal sheikhs as an encroachment on their feudal privileges, and the projects were abandoned in 1847 because of unresilient feudal opposition (Salibi 1965:73).

The same outcome accompanied other Ottoman efforts to organize local councils *(majlis* or *diwan)*. Both Christian and Druze feudal sheikhs again perceived such arrangements as an attempt to undermine their local autonomy and refused to participate. In the coastal cities, the system of local councils reinforced rather than undermined the power of notables and *ʿayan*. The general population was barely represented on the councils, and consequently local notables and Muslim religious leaders were able to consolidate and extend their patronage by playing their traditional role as intermediary between the general population and general government. In fact, throughout the Tanzimat period (1839–1856), some form of cooperation between the urban elite and Turkish officials was gradually evolving into a rather consistent feature. The power of urban notables also extended to rural areas, and they were able to form alliances with feudal families. In Lebanon this was particularly true after the demise of the Shihabi dynasty, when the sphere of power and influence was gradually shifting toward Beirut. Different families or factions in the mountain began to seek new contacts among the bourgeoning urban elite. It was in this period, for example, that the alliances between Druze feudal sheikhs of the Shuf and Muslim notables of Beirut began to be established (Hourani 1968:62–63).

The *mutesarrifate* (governorate) of Mount Lebanon (1860–1920) generated new forces that reinforced rather than undermined the power of the traditional feudal families. The Règlement Organique of 1861 called for another geographic rearrangement of the country. Lebanon was now stripped of its three major coastal cities (Beirut, Tripoli, and Sidon) and its fertile regions of the Biqa valley and Wadi al-Taym and divided into seven districts *(qadaʾ)* each under a *qaʾimmaqam* with further divisions into smaller counties *(mudiriyahs)*. The Règlement also called for a central Administrative Council composed of twelve members presided over a Christian governor designated by the signatory powers. The distribution of seats within the council was on a purely confessional basis, with each of the major six sects (Maronite, Greek Orthodox, Catholic, Druze, Shiʿite, and Sunni Muslim) claiming two seats.

These and other provisions of the Règlement no doubt undermined the security and social standing of the feudal families and threatened to make a disgruntled class out of them. So did the burgeoning agricultural and commercial class, mostly urban money lenders, who were already vying for a greater share of the influence and exclusive privileges the feudal families have been enjoying. Accordingly, the mutesarrif "undertook to keep them content by arranging for their gradual absorption into the new administration. During the seven years of (Dawud Pasha's) *Mutesarrifate* no less than sixteen feudal emirs or sheikhs were appointed to the leading government positions, the later mutesarrifs followed Dawud Pasha's policy in this respect" (Salibi 1965:111–12).

This gradual absorption of prominent families into the new government bureaucracy generated some of the conditions conducive to the emergence of a new breed of political leadership or patronage; a patronage more bureaucratic than feudal in nature, and one that came to play a prominent role in the political life of Lebanon in subsequent decades. Individuals with legal and bureaucratic skills began to develop their political careers under the tutelage of the Ottomans and the French. The political power and social prestige that this new "administrative aristocracy" came to enjoy was a reflection of their participation in the movements of reform, independence, and Arabism that had consumed the intellectual resources of the emerging elite at the time. Consequently, and unlike the earlier "feudal" patrons, their status was relatively more achieved than ascribed. Furthermore, by virtue of their administrative positions, they offered more of the desired linkages between "center" and "periphery" that clients almost always seek in their patrons.

The leadership that emerged during this period, along with their second- and third-generation descendents, constitutes today the bulk of the political elite of Lebanon. If the country can boast of any political heroes, ideologists, reactionaries, or popular urban activists, they all received their political socialization, in one form or another, during this eventful period of Lebanon's political development. The Khuris of the Shuf, the Solhs of Saida, the Khalils of Sour, the Salams, Beyhums, Daouks, Taqlas, and Chihas of Beirut, the Karamis of Tripoli, the Eddes of Batroun . . . these and a score of other prominent names were drawn—partly by accident and partly by design—into the political and national struggle of their communities. Little wonder that they began to offer new sources of patronage.

The composition of the Parliament, as will be shown in chapter 6, continues to reflect this intimate association between this form of legal and administrative patronage and political leadership. There is more than just historical accident in this association. With the declining influence of feudal families, lawyers, magistrates and government officials became the closest groups to the loci of power and consequently were in a better position to offer the needed benefits to their clients. This may partly account for the continuing popularity of the legal profession in Lebanon. It is still largely considered, by many political aspirants, as the natural and most effective means for extending their political clientage. The Chamber continues to draw 35 to 40 percent of its Deputies from legal and auxiliary professions.

The socioeconomic and political transformations after World II, particularly in the form of rural exodus, burgeoning economic opportunities, rapid urbanization, and the growth of political parties and pseudo-ideological groups, led to the emergence of a new form of political patronage. Self-made entrepreneurs and popular political activists, more receptive to the secular and ideological interests of urban masses, began to offer some novel and alternate sources of patronage. Since this form of patronage derives much of its support from the relatively amorphous and heterogeneous urban masses, it is more politically oriented and often resorts to catchy and popular slogans to incite mass appeal. Leaders like Saeb Salam of Beirut, Rashid Karami of Tripoli, the late Ma'ruf Saad of Saida, the late Emile Bustani of Shuf, and more recently younger upstarts like Abdel Majid al-Rafi'i of Tripoli, and Ali Khalil of Sour and Najah Wakim of Beirut, to mention a few, have all invoked ideological and pseudo-ideological slogans to capture a transient political mood or capitalize on a concern over some overriding public issue. When not courting Ba'thist, Pan-Arabist, Nasserist, Nationalist and, more recently, Palestinian resistance rhetoric, some of the leaders within this group have formed their own parties and parliamentary blocs. Others sponsored or patronized labor organizations and established benevolent voluntary associations to extend the scope of their clientage.

More than the other forms of patronage, this pseudo-ideological variety, no doubt, subsumes within it a rather mixed and heterogeneous group of political leaders. They all display, however, one underlying feature in common. The basis of their patronage remains largely personal and tightly circumscribed. In supporting a Salam or a Karami, the followers pledge their support more for the person than his programme. In this sense, this form of patronage shares some of the attributes of the other more traditional types.

This sketchy overview of the three forms of patronage, and to a large measure they represent three different stages in the political history of Lebanon, should have made it clear that what sustain the *za'im* as a political figure—whether feudal, administrative or pseudo-ideological—are the personal and communal ties of fealty. His political assets are those typical of most patron-client ties—namely, reciprocal loyalties and obligations. It is in this sense that the seemingly more liberal and emancipated political leaders have much in common with the *aqtab* they frequently admonish and deride. These younger aspirants for public leadership, with rare exceptions, all seek to establish their political base not by articulating a program or identifying critical issues or specific problems requiring reform but by building up a personal entourage of clients and followers. Much like the *aqtab,* the bulk of their time and efforts is devoted to interceding with public officials on behalf of their clients. Both the private interests of clients and the political careers of patrons are served by such a system of patronage. Clients, who normally lack the power, wealth, and connections to obtain favored treatment would be more than willing to pledge their allegiance in return for the benefits and private goals the patron can secure on their behalf. To the patron, such devoted following is a priceless political capital and, in most instances, the only capital that can guarantee his tenure in office.

This, more than any other feature, accounts for the relatively small part played by Lebanese politicans in formulating broad policy issues of national and civic significance. To launch and sustain one's political career on the basis of a clearly defined ideological program or platform of reform requires, among other things, continuous critical study and devotion to public issues and nagging societal problems. Such civic-minded concerns, if they are to be more than ad hoc and arbitrary pronouncements, necessitate some disregard for the personal demands and favors of clients. But politicians in Lebanon rise or fall more on the size of their clientage and competence at dispensing personal favors than on their merit in articulating and coping with public issues and problems. To refuse favors is to risk losing votes, and ultimately dimish one's base of client support. Instances of this kind of failure are legion in Lebanon. Resourceful and spirited young intellectuals, sparked by a genuine concern for public service and civic reform, have consistently failed in national elections. The few that have succeeded are invariably ones who have been adopted or sponsored by a traditional *za'im*.

Survival and Consequences of Patronage

What perpetuates political patronage in Lebanon and how do patrons, whether "feudal," "administrative," or "pseudo-ideological," retain and extend the scope of their clientage? The discussion thus far has under-scored some of the socio-historical circumstances associated with the sur-vival of patronage. We turn now to a consideration of two further, and perhaps more vivid, conditions that account for the ubiquity of patron-age in the contemporary political life of Lebanon; namely kinship loyalty and the pecularities of the electoral system.

Familism

I will, in the following chapters, explore the impact of pervasive fam-ilism and other primordial loyalties on the nature of political leadership and political succession in Lebanon. Evidence will be cited to demon-strate how the family continues to be a viable agency of political sociali-zation and tutelage and an effective avenue for political power and per-petuation of leadership. The monopoly that a handful of leading families continue to exert over the political process in the country, by almost any comparative measure, is truly staggering.

This is particularly true of the so-called *aqtab* of today. With rare ex-ceptions, they are all heirs of a long political tradition and continue to exercise much of their political influence by virtue of their kinship ties. Like their fathers and grandfathers before them, they too are initiating their own sons—at least those who have politically inclined offspring—into the political life of the country. A few obvious and current examples can be readily made.

Of course the political career of Pierre Gemayel and his two sons (Amin and Bashir), in light of the recent momentous and tragic events, stands out as one of the most striking and dramatic instances. It clearly deserves fuller and more detailed treatment that we can afford at the moment. A few passing observations will, however, suffice. As founder of the Phal-ange (Kataeb) party, Pierre Gemayel has been actively involved in the political life of Lebanon since 1936. Despite the repeated bids he made, neither he nor any member of his party could win a seat in the Parliament until 1960. The civil war of 1958 enlarged the political constituency of the party and transformed it from a paramilitary youth movement into a disciplined and highly organized mass party. The political events of the past two decades, particularly the threatening presence of Palestinians and other borrowed ideologies and left-wing groups, enhanced further the mass appeal of the party among its predominantly Christian-Maronite adherents. Today, it claims a membership of approximately forty thousand, occupies nine seats in the Parliament, runs its own newspaper and private broadcasting station, and more significantly perhaps, has a highly trained militia of more than 25,000 men who fought fiercely during the civil war.

Typically, Amin's ascendancy to power was largely an act of family inheritance. He won his first parliamentary seat in 1970 (he was only twenty-seven at the time) in a contested by-election to replace his deceased uncle, Maurice Gemayel. He was reelected again in 1972 and has been a resourceful member of the Party and Parliament since.

The civil disturbances of the past eleven years also propelled his younger son, Bashir, into political prominence. Tougher and more defiant than his mild-mannered brother, he played a more militant and hawkish role throughout the civil war. He was leader of the Lebanese Forces of the Lebanese Front and substantially broadened the popular base of his appeal among the Christian constituency. So much so, in fact, that he emerged, at thirty-four, as the sole and uncontested candidate to the Presidency of the Republic. In a political culture that pays deference to age, this was unprecedented, even more so since Bashir, because of alleged ties with Israel and the ruthlessness with which he eliminated his political foes, was feared and suspected by many political factions and groups. Indeed, he barely received (by a margin of one) the necessary quorum required by the constitution but was nonetheless elected President in a tense and dramatic session on August 23, 1982. But in the brief interlude of twenty days, between his election and assassination on September 14, he left an indelible mark on Lebanese society. He had all the ingredients of an inspiring charismatic leader: youthful, engaging, highly energetic and spirited, firm in his convictions, and clear-sighted in his visions about Lebanon's future. Even his demeanor was refreshingly different: casual in appearance, personable and modest, he articulated his views in candid, simple, and colloquial Arabic. He managed, in this short span, to transfer his image as a factional, ruthless warlord into a visionary and reconciliatory leader determined to liberate Lebanon from all foreign armies, reinforce the enfeebled state agencies, uprooting corruption, and unite the dismembered social fabric. By the time of his death, even those who had opposed or boycotted his election began to genuinely mourn his passing.

The almost total outcry and outrage with which his assassination was received promptly made his brother Amin the heir apparent to succeed him. The Parliament convened a week later and elected him almost unanimously to the six-year term as President. He received 77 votes of the 80 Deputies who attended the session.

The inferences that can be made from the involvement of the Gemayels in politics are many and need not concern us here. What needs to be underscored, however, is the impact of family tutelage in preparing and propelling the two sons for the highest political office in the country. It is after all unusual that one family, in a society where political competition is both democratic and intense, should produce two Presidents who are strikingly different in character, temperament, and political style. In pledging their support to the Gemayels, several of the traditional politicians rationalized and justified their choice of the basis of family heritage and the political and national legacy of Sheikh Pierre, their father. Indeed, the two sons themselves have on more than one occasion publicly acknowledged such heritage. Both Bashir and Amin, often in highly evocative and touching tones, expressed the debt they owe to their father's "political school."

When Suleiman Frangieh's parliamentary seat was vacated upon his election as President of the Republic in 1970, he encouraged his own son, Antoine, to make a bid to perpetuate the presence of a Frangieh in the Parliament—a succession which dates back to 1934 when Hamid Frangieh was first elected to the Assembly under the French Mandate. The young Frangieh, a virtual unknown and with clearly none of his father's stature or abilities, was able during his brief political career to establish his own parliamentary bloc and secure two cabinet appointments, incidents that touched off outcries of criticism with charges of flagrant nepotism at the time. Since his assassination in June 1978, his younger brother, Robert, is being groomed to step into his role. He is always seen with his father when receiving and visiting other political figures and dignitaries, and on occasion makes public statements on his father's behalf.

Other *aqtab*, with an eye on their imminent retirement, are making every effort to bequeath their political capital and influence to their children. Camille Chamoun continues to encourage his two sons (both in their early fifties) to assume more visible public roles. His eldest, Dory, particularly during his father's absence, finds it necessary to take on some of his father's unofficial responsibilities. His youngest, Dany, was made head of his father's militia group and took an active part in the fighting until the group was disbanded in 1980. Both lack their father's charisma and do not particularly relish the demands of a political career but may find the temptations of inheriting their father's distinguished political record too irresistible to bypass.

Saeb Salam, too conscious of the rich political heritage of his own family, will certainly not deprive his own sons of the political resources he himself drew from. Indeed, he has taken tangible measures to safeguard and insure such succession. Of his two sons, Tammam and Faysal, the former has clearly emerged as the heir apparent. In 1974–75 he inherited the leadership of his father's private militia group and, more important perhaps, he was "elected" in 1982 to succeed his father as president of the Maqassed Society; one of the most viable Sunni-Muslim voluntary associations in Lebanon.

Kamal Junblat, with all his ideological pretensions of party-base support, cannot disclaim the relevance of his kinship descent for his eminence as a za'im. It is doubtful, for example, whether he could have wielded as much influence had he derived his political legitimacy exclusively from the ideological base of his progressive socialism. Indeed, his own entry into politics was more a by-product of fortuitous family circumstances than firm and well-articulated ideological commitments on his part. The unexpected death of Junblat's uncle, Hikmat, in 1942, who was the heir apparent to inherit the leadership of the Junblati clan from the inveterate Sit Nazira, propelled the young intellectual recluse of the family into public life. Of course, since Junblat's assassination in March 1977, his own son, Walid, with clearly none of his father's charisma, political stature, or determination, has assumed the leadership of both the Progressive Socialist Party and the National Movement.

The point of all this—and similar instances may be easily cited of other families with a long tradition of political succession—is that when patronage is supplemented by ties of kinship it is bound to acquire added intensity and survival. The son, himself his father's client, attains more credibility as a patron if the source of his patronage is reinforced by family loyalty. Even if he were to disavow such primordial heritage, as

Junblat himself has attempted to do, it is questionable whether his traditional clientele will accept such disavowal. To them he is a Junblati, a member of a Druze community before he is a progressive socialist.

Electoral System

The electoral system, which was promulgated by the Constitution of 1926 and has since undergone no fundamental modifications, is based on a combination of a single electoral college and proportional representation of the various communities or confessions. Conceptually, the system was conceived to enable each community to be represented in the Parliament in proportion to its size,[1] but without becoming a sort of state within the state.

To accomplish this, the electoral system, to a certain degree, compels each candidate to depend on votes outside his own religious community. For example, in the district of Aley, two Druzes, two Maronites, and one Greek Orthodox are to be elected. Two or three contesting lists or ballots are formed bearing the same confessional composition. Electors are free to vote for any candidate from among the lists as long as they observe the confessional proportion established for that district. In this case, the second Greek Orthodox who might have received more popular votes than the other successful Maronite and Druze candidates will not be elected. What this single-college system has meant is that each elected candidate, though competing with a confessional rival, is, to a large measure, a representative of communities other than his own. In fact, in mixed electoral districts (and of all twenty-six districts only nine are homogeneous confessional communities) a candidate cannot be elected unless he is reasonably well-accepted by other confessional groups of his constituency. Indeed, in some instances it is the religious communities other than that of the candidate's that guarantee his success or failure. In the last national elections of 1972, Najah Wakim, a virtually unknown candidate—supported by the so-called Progressive Nasserist coalition popular among the urban Sunni Muslims—won one of the Greek Orthodox seats in Beirut while in fact receiving few of the votes of his own religious sect.

These safeguards or constitutional peculiarities of the Lebanese electoral system, reinforced by the National pact of 1943, may have done much to promote harmony, justice, and balance among the various communities, but they accomplished little in curtailing the power of the zu'ama. If anything, the division of the country into small electoral units gives the *zuʿama* a freer hand to assert their influence and perpetuate their power over local communities.[2] Each of the *aqtab* reigns supreme in his own district and runs virtually unchallenged electoral contests. They exercise complete authority in selecting the candidates on their lists, set the going or market price for each candidate (i.e., the sum they owe the *zaʿim*) and dictate whatever strategy or policy the list as a collectivity is to follow. The candidates are usually more than happy to oblige. In addition to paying the set tribute, they defray the full financial burdens of the campaign, act on behalf of their *zaʿim* in dispensing favors and services and, in some instances, declare their total and unrelenting obedience to him. In short, they are no longer partners in a joint venture but "clients" in a reciprocal though asymmetrical exchange. A poignant manifestation of this rather extreme form of patronage appears in a pledge signed by those on the list headed by Suleiman al-Ali in the elections of 1953.[3] The text reads as follows:

> We swear by God Almighty, by our honour, and by all that is dear to us, that—having agreed to participate in the battle of legislative elections on the same list—we pledge ourselves, in the case of victory by the grace of God, to follow in the Lebanese Parliament the directives and the policy that will be dictated to us by His Excellency our companion in the struggle, Sulaiman Bey el Ali el Ma-ra'aby, and to act in a manner to carry out all that he wills. We pledge ourselves to back him in all that he desires, in the Ministry or outside of it, and not to swerve one bit from the attitude he intends to adopt with regard to the authorities as a partisan or as an opponent. If we do not keep our promise and fail to fulfill this oath we recognize ourselves to be unworthy of the human species, and deprived of honour and gratitude.

All other such instances notwithstanding, the relationship between the *zaʿim* and his clients remains fundamentally one of reciprocity. The *zaʿim* throws in his political weight, influence and social prestige, and his clients reciprocate by providing other resources he (the *zaʿim*) may be deficient on: money, youthfulness, advanced education, a progressive outlook, and most significantly a kinship, regional, or communal affiliation that might weaken the strength of an opposing list. The late Kamal Junblat, for example, had persistently and skillfully relied on the latter—i.e., incorporating some of the Maronite notable families in the Shuf—to erode the electoral strength of his archrival in the area, Camille Chamoun. In other instances, two or three of the *aqtab* may resort to coalitions, mostly in the form of temporary ad hoc alliances to extend the scope of their patronage and to ward off possible defeat at the polls. The Triple Alliance *(al-Hilf al-Thulathi)* between Chamoun, Edde, and Gemayel in the wake of the 1967 Arab-Israeli war was one such effective though short-lived coalition.[4]

Certainly not all the coalitions between the *aqtab* are prompted by ideological or national interests. In more cases than not, purely Hobbesian motives of self-interest and political survival underlie such coalitions. During the last national elections of 1972, the late Kamal Junblat and Majid Arslan, representatives of a feudal rivalry for Druze supremacy for over two centuries, found it politically expedient in the face of emergent political threats to ignore their traditional enmity and assist each other in their respective districts. The alliance guaranteed the return of both traditional leaders along with their clients and safeguarded Druze hegemony against possible sources of new challenges.

The survival of primordial allegiances (particularly in the form of kinship, fealty, and confessional sentiments), the peculiarities of the electoral law along with the adaptability of the traditional politician have enabled some of the *aqtab* and lesser *zu'ama* to enjoy a measure of substantial power that is sometimes not commensurate with their own personal electoral strength. The consequences of such survival for political change are many and grievous.

First, it has doubtlessly meant the persistent failure of any truly secular and ideological parties or candidates in making any significant dent in undermining the power of the *aqtab*. The only notable exceptions are the election of Ba'thists Ali al-Khalil in Sour and Abdul Majid al-Rafi'i in Tripoli and the Nasserite Najah Wakim in Beirut during the last elections.

Second, and more important, the survival and extension of this form of political clientelism, as several writers have observed (see Yamak 1966; Kerr 1966) has crippled the role of the Legislature as a forum for national debate and eroded the powers of the state. Theoretically, the cabinet has been fairly independent of the collective will of the Deputies. Indeed, no government since Lebanon's independence in 1943 has had to resign because of a vote of no confidence. The so-called "parliamentary game"—often invoked during the frequent cabinet crises in Lebanon—is no more than a game of musical chairs among its *aqtab* jockeying to extend their share of clients in the government. In this sense, "Politics exists only in

Laswell's limited sense of 'who gets what, when, and how,' as a competition for the honors and spoils of office" (Kerr 1966:190). And the abiding concern of politicians, once in power—particularly since their tenure in office rarely exceeds a year—is to enlarge the scope of their patronage. Accordingly, politics, like practically everything else in a society sustained by the reciprocal exchange of favors, becomes a delicate art of distributing and managing patronage. Squabbles over civil service appointments, jurisdictional competition, allocation of public funds—all essentially patronage squabbles—assume more prominence (if judged by the time and attention devoted to them) over controversies involving substantive issues of national and public policy. (For empirical documentation of this feature, see Kerr 1966:193–96.)

Finally, the erosion of legislative and executive powers and the reduction of the entire political process to one of squabbles over patronage rights and boundaries relegates to the Chief Executive exceptional presidential powers. The constitutional prerogatives of the President are immense. Since ultimate executive authority is invested in his office, it is with his consent that the government submits all legislative and budgetary proposals to Parliament and conducts foreign policy. He reserves, in some instances, the powers of veto over the passage of such legislative acts and constitutional amendments. He may, with cabinet approval, dissolve Parliament before the termination of its regular term; or he may summon it to a special session. Unlike the cabinet, the President is not accountable to Parliament except, of course, in instances of constitutional or criminal violations.

More formidable is the amount of unofficial powers and prerogatives he can easily muster and mobilize. With, or without his consent, an unofficial retinue of opportunists, troubleshooters, middlemen, self-appointed experts, political entrepreneurs, brokers, and retainers emerge to claim their fair share of privilege. Once again, the distribution of material benefits and opportunity begin to be the prominent concern of the highest office in the land. In this sense the President as patron and his unofficial entourage of clients fulfill one of the distinguishing features of all patron-client ties. He comes to hold, as James Scott would argue, a position of monopolist or obligopolist over vital services (protection, security, employment, and access to other critical needs etc.), the demand for which is highly inelastic. "Being a monopolist or oligopolist, for critical needs, the patron is in an ideal position to demand compliance from those who wish to share in these scarce commodities (Scott 1972: 93).

In short, he becomes the supreme patron manipulating or coordinating the unscrupulous and skillful machinations of lesser patrons and their own clients who, ad infinitum, are the patrons of yet other clients . . . all seeking a greater share of the spoils and privileges of office. It is then that a regime acquires the injurious label of becoming (in Lebanese parlance) a "bazaar," an open marketplace for middlemen and political brokers. And very few regimes have, thus far, been spared this label.

Both President Khuri (1943–1952) and Chamoun (1952–1958), adroit politicians that they were, thrived on political manipulation and used these unofficial powers to the fullest. Both conducted, if not blatantly fraudulent and rigged, then certainly subtle but scarcely impartial national elections in which many of their prominent rivals were excluded from office. Accusations of corruption, nepotism, and excessive personal influence were rife; though slightly more favorable in the case of Chamoun (at least in the eyes of the public) because they were associated with visible economic prosperity and development in the country. President Shihab (1958–1964) carried a clear distaste for political manipulation and waged an almost self-righteous crusade against professional politicians whom he derisively dubbed as "fromagists." His Deuxieme Bureau, however, assumed exceptional powers and developed its own tightly controlled and subtle system of patron-client networks. The Bureau became notorious for employing state machinery in dispensing favors for its clients and undercutting its critics and opponents. President Helou (1964–1970), despite his initial efforts at civil service reform, never really managed to disassociate or free himself from the Shihabist mold. Nearly the same network of forces continued to operate almost unabetted throughout his regime. While President Frangieh (1970–1976) initially succeeded in eradicating virtually all signs of "dualism," from which the Helou regime suffered (i.e., the coexistence of military and civil powers), he clearly resorted to the more traditional pattern of patronage without even the subtleties of some of his predecessors. Even President Sarkis (1976–1982), noted for his administrative prudence, impartiality, and fair-mindedness could not restrain some of his enterprising associates from taking advantage of the political chaos in the country to indulge in favorable quid pro quos.

Prime Ministers, often victims of such unofficial powers, have persistently complained of their excessive use by Presidents. Sami al-Solh, who served as Premier under Khuri and Chamoun, wrote bitterly in 1960 about how Presidents relied more on the advice of their unofficial "sultans" than their own Prime Ministers. Little has happened to change the substance of Solh's poignant admission. "Every sultan" he wrote then in his *Memoirs*, "had an entourage and a group of followers, relatives, in-laws, in-laws of in-laws, associates, middle-men, and hangers-on from every faction and class and every village and street. Whichever of us should come to power, to the crematorium of Cabinet office, found himself obliged to pay homage to those sultans and their followers and the followers of their followers. It is they who govern and direct, plan, and execute policies, while we are only the instruments which they set up before the eyes of the public to bear responsibility for their errors and misdeeds" (al-Solh 1960:320).

Concluding Remarks

At the expense of some oversimplication, I have suggested that the political history of Lebanon may be seen as the history of three forms of political patronage. Though not mutually exclusive, each of the three forms made its appearance at different epochs and was generated by particular sociopolitical and economic circumstances. They have, nonetheless, much in common. Whether "feudal," "administrative," or "pseudo-ideological," they continue to be sustained by highly personalized, tightly circumscribed, and reciprocal obligations typical of all patron-client networks.

The survival of such patronage, it was suggested, is not too unusual in a society that continues to be characterized by a large residue of primordial allegiances. The ascriptive ties of family solidarity and communal loyalties have for a long time provided the only trustable and meaningful basis for integrating the social order. Any other form of collaboration, particularly if it is sustained by the rational instruments of a nation-state—i.e., anonymous large-scale organizations such as political parties, civil bureaucracies or class loyalties—have not had an enthusiastic reception in Lebanon. Indeed, in some instances, they have proved disastrous and too disruptive.

As we have seen, all efforts to bring about any significant transformations in the basic structure of society throughout the nineteenth century were neither lasting nor substantive. The peasant uprising, a decade of centralized Egyptian rule, the Ottoman reforms, and the mutesarrifate generated no doubt some far-reaching institutional and infrastructural changes. Other dimensions of the social structure, however, especially those that have traditionally held the society together, remained almost untouched. Kinship loyalty, village solidarity, ties of patronage, and to a considerable extent the power and autonomy of feudal chiefs survived, with a large measure of fixity and tenacity.

More recent efforts have scarcely been more successful. The two attempts of the Syrian National Party (Parti Populaire Syrien, or PPS) in 1949 and 1962—the only organized revolutionary attempts to bring about political change in Lebanon—have both been abortive. The impact of other progressive parties has certainly not been more decisive. In fact, the distinction between a political party and a client group is not always very clear in Lebanon. The fact that a party has an internal structure, formal by-laws, elected officers, and specific aims does not mean, as Arnold Hottinger (1966:85–105) has suggested, that it no longer serves as a locus for patron-client networks. A sizeable number of the *aqtab* and lesser *zuʿama* have formed their own blocs and parties. The basis of support in most such collectivities, remains essentially confessional or personal, and to a much lesser degree ideological.

Even the more gradualist efforts directed at undermining the political power and economic base of the traditional *zuʿama* has accomplished very little in eroding the extensive patronage such leaders continue to enjoy among their clients. The so-called "Shihabist" doctrine associated with President Shihab and his followers was, if anything, an effort to discredit or bypass the traditional *zuʿama* as the exclusive intermediaries or spokesmen of underprivileged groups and communities. Measures were taken to modernize state bureaucracy to gain more effective and direct access of individuals in remote communities. State planning was encouraged to curtail or moderate the adverse effects of free enterprise. Specific administrative reforms—geared mainly toward rescuing bureaucracy from the direct and personal pressure of *zuʿama*—were also undertaken. Finally, national social security and other state agencies emerged to provide citizens with much of their needed welfare and services. None of these measures, however, as Shihab himself painfully admitted after his retirement from politics, accomplished their intended objectives. Like confessionalism, patronage has become almost institutionalized into Lebanon's body politic.

Until new parliamentary elections take place, one cannot realistically assess the impact of the civil disturbances on traditional patron-client networks. During the past decade, a variety of paramilitary and ideological groups emerged that drew their support from the radicalized masses at both ends of the political spectrum; right and left. The Israeli invasion of 1982 and the consequent withdrawal of the PLO from Lebanon has undermined significantly the power and appeal of leftist groups and their alliances; groups that could have potentially challenged the political leadership of the old patrons. The survival and tenacity of their power was strikingly visible during the eventful months of August and September of 1982 when the Parliament convened in two successive sessions to elect Bashir and then his brother Amin Gemayel as Presidents of the Republic. The same old veteran politicians—Majid Arslan, Camille Chamoun, Saeb Salam, Suleiman Frangieh, Pierre Gemayel—to mention a few, either through their absence or presence continued to demonstrate their indispensability in shaping the course of events.

Continuities of this kind prompt us to argue that patronage is not, as some writers have suggested, a transient phenomenon, one that is bound to disappear as other more secular agencies and institutions emerge to offer alternate avenues for gaining access to privilege and opportunity. In assessing the nature of political change in Lebanon, Leonard Binder (1966:302) has, to cite one such instance, suggested that the extension of roads, health, electrification, and other amenities to more remote parts of Lebanon; the emergence of a modern middle class capable of exerting its influence among rural communities; and the recruitment of younger political aspirants are bound to "open a gulf between traditional political leaders and the increasingly educated and politically alert population." It is doubtful, in the light of evidence supplied earlier, whether this "gulf" has taken place. Even if it has occurred, it certainly has not weakened the traditional patron-client ties; nor has it eroded much of the political legitimacy of patrons.

More important perhaps, patrons have been able, by skillful maneuvering and adaptability, to forestall and circumvent their possible obsolescence. All the *aqtab*, at one point or another in their political careers, sought to extend the scope of their patronage by incorporating secular and ideological elements. By forming political coalitions, parties, and blocs; sponsoring labor organizations and other voluntary and benevolent associations; and by invoking liberal and progressive rhetoric, they have been able to retain and extend their clientage support which could have, under other circumstances, sought alternate sources of patronage. Expressed differently, the persisting influence of patrons stems from their ability to provide services, goods, and values that no other group has so far been able to provide as effectively. These services and benefits are so desired by others as to induce them to reciprocate these gratifications in the form of gratitude and compliance which often boarders on filial loyalty. In this lies, I have repeatedly suggested, the ubiquity and survival of patronage.

Indeed, the power veteran politicians continue to enjoy in Lebanon is partly due to their monopoly over such vital benefits. Two simple but effective strategies are often pursued to retain this form of monopoly. First, access to alternative suppliers of these or substitute services is blocked. Much like the patrimonial manager, who employs every paternalistic ploy to discourage his workers from joining labor unions, quite often the *zu'ama* resort to similar measures to retain the allegiance of their clients. In instances where more than one *za'im* happens to be vying for supporters within one electoral district or region, direct efforts are sought to prevent or block a service to an individual unless he turns to a particular patron for support. (For further details, see Gubser 1973:181–82.) Second, the traditional scope of patronage is extended to meet or incorporate a variety of new demands and services. By establishing benevolent or welfare societies, political parties, militia groups, or by sponsoring labor unions and other voluntary associations, many political leaders have been able to extend or secularize the scope of their patronage without eroding their traditional basis of political support. Two such fairly successful instances are the Maqassed and 'Amiliyya welfare associations. The former, as we shall see, evolved from a traditional benevolent society to one of the most effective Sunni Muslim associations with extensive cultural, educational, and welfare activities. Saeb Salam was skillfully patronized the Maqassed to extend the popular base of his political clientage. The same is true of the *'Amiliyya*. The late Rashid Beydoun exploited this Shi'ite benevolent association for good political advantage. He too was able, through the association's activities and membership, to cope with some of the welfare and secular requirements of his Shi'ite constituency (mostly recent migrants and marginal urban groups from the South) while retaining his traditional clientage.[5]

The shortcomings and abuses of patronage are many and grievous and have been variously underscored by several observers: endemic corruption, nepotism, favoritism, the erosion of legislative and executive powers, the reduction of the entire political process to one of squabbles over patronage rights and boundaries, the absence of any serious concern for formulating broad policy issues of national and civic significance, and the consequent "sacrifice of long-range planning for short-run expediency" (Lemarchand 1972:71).

We should not, however, overlook some of the inherent advantages of patronage. Beginning with its feudal variety, patronage has been able to generate and absorb new forms of reciprocal and universalistic loyalties, provide some measure of political integration and the means for maintaining a modicum of stability and harmony in an otherwise differentiated and pluralistic social structure. More important it has offered a relatively viable form of political action—among others which have thus far been less effective—that allows individuals and groups a greater measure of leverage in securing benefits, services, and a more equitable distribution of resources. In this sense, patronage in Lebanon is one of the most accessible and effective strategies for coping with vulnerability and relative deprivation. That it has survived when access to resources was made possible through other means—such as the spread of market economy, centralized bureaucracy, class-consciousness, party-based and ideological loyalties—attests to its tenacity and continued viability.

In this sense too, political patronage shares much with other adaptive instruments of modernization. Much like the family firm, kinship association, and confessional and communal voluntary associations, patronage has been equally effective in meeting some of the secular and rational demands of modernization (i.e., openness, receptivity to change, the ability to cope with tensions and imbalances) without diluting primordial loyalties or dehumanizing the social fabric of society. Indeed, it has survived because it has been a device for achieving such a synthesis. But it has also obstructed, in often grievous ways, the emergence of civic consciousness or allegiance to state-sponsored agencies of reform or development.

CHAPTER FIVE

Primordial Ties and Politics

B Y THE ADMISSION OF many dispassionate observers—indige- nous and foreign alike—the political system in Lebanon stands as a curious phenomenon. A pluralistic confessional society, it enjoys a par- liamentary system of government with a freely elected Chamber of Dep- uties. Outwardly, the country appears to be bolstered by liberal and dem- ocratic traditions, yet Lebanon hardly possesses any of the political instruments of a civil polity. A National Pact, a sort of Christian-Moslem entente, sustains its so-called national entity, *Al-Kayan,* yet this sense of identity is neither national nor civic. Its politicians, masterminds at the art of flexibility and compromise, are local *zuaʿma* not national heroes. The few parties that do exist are so closely identified with sectarian groups and so unconcerned with a larger national identity that they can easily engender political disintegration. Likewise, its political blocs and fronts are so absorbed with parochial and personal rivalries that they fail to serve the larger national purpose of mobilizing the population for the broader aims of society. Politicians and pressure groups alike have not been able to transcend their petty personal feuds to grapple effectively with the public issues of the country.

Precarious as this may seem, the political system has maintained a bal- ance of power among its heterogeneous, confessional, ethnic, kinship, and communal groups. Despite recurring crises, this mosaic-like structure with its multiple allegiances and loyalties has been relatively stable. Even eleven years of civil unrest, with its consequent terror, breakdown in law and order, and traumatization of a large portion of the population, has not as yet generated any fundamental change in the political system. In both substance and form, the political actors and various coalitions, old and new, have evinced little change in their political perspectives or in their willingness to transform the political structure.

This essay is a revised and updated version of a paper originally published in *Middle Eastern Studies* (April 1968), 4(3):243–69. Used by permission.

The resilience of the political system will not appear so curious if one understands the nature of social and political change in Lebanon. Preceding discussions should have made it clear by now that change in Lebanon is not entirely a process of conversion and swift transformation. It has rarely involved a complete break with the past. It is much more a process of selective adaptation and assimilation. Likewise, political modernization has at no point involved a clear transfer of sovereignty from primordial allegiance to secular and ideological commitments. The metamorphosis of political life, given the persistence of primordial sentiments, may never involve such a sharp transformation.

Ultimately, it is a question of what kind of society or political system would be most compatible with the value patterns and historical traditions rooted in the culture. It is not, as often implied, a choice between traditional culture and "Mass Society." Nor could it be an instance of transformation of a traditional society into a secular nation-state or civil polity. It is doubtful whether Lebanese society can ever be a duplicate of a rational, secular, and egalitarian society based exclusively on achievement-oriented and universalistic criteria. Rather the problem boils down to a question of fusion and assimilation: how to assimilate traditional culture into the culture of a rational and secular society without destroying both.

This is indeed a delicate task. As we have seen, the political history of Lebanon provides ample proof of the persistence of primordial ties in local and national politics. Throughout its continued contacts with other civilizations, Lebanon has successfully managed to assimilate ideas and styles of life of other cultures without drastically changing its basic character. Judging by the unfolding of recent events, history is bent once again on repeating itself.

The persistence of traditions, it should be emphasized, need not mean the absence of innovation. Modernization involves, after all, the ability to absorb and generate change, not the repudiation of traditional values (Halpern 1964). Innovation as such is not generally resisted by the Lebanese. They have been receptive to change matched by a remarkable predisposition for empathy. Rather, what is resisted is the abandonment of traditions or the erosion of primordial sentiments.

This can be readily seen in the type of political and economic institutions that have been emerging in society. The most typical of these institutions are neither "traditional" nor "rational" in character; rather they are a hybrid of both. To exercise effective political leadership, as will be remarked later, requires above all skills of flexibility in fusing the compatible elements of a traditional society and a secular state. This, in concrete terms, means expressing "traditional sentiments in modern idioms, to assimilate and transform attitudes and to mould them into modern genres" (Shils 1961:64). As such, the successful political leader in Lebanon is not the party boss or ideologist of the variety of Antoun Saadeh or Mustafa al-'Aris;[1] he is a Salam, Junblat, Edde, Gemayel, and Karami—disguising his traditionalism behind the garb of political slogans and pseudo-ideological platforms.

It is the intention of this paper to document some of the above propositions. More specifically, an attempt is made to account for the persistence of primordial ties in the political life of Lebanon. The term primordial is employed here in the conventional sense to encompass ties of kinship, fealty, religion, and all such congruities of blood, personal, and sacred affinities. (For further details, see Shils 1957; Geertz 1963:105–57.) The central thesis of this chapter converges on the recurrent theme running throughout this volume: that the survival of primordialism is not entirely an unmixed blessing. While kinship, fealty, and religious ties and loyalties have been functionally instrumental in providing the much-needed social, psychic, and spiritual supports, they have also served as divisive forces by reinforcing the traditional cleavages in society. For example, in the absence of effective voluntary associations, publics and other rational instruments of political change, primordial loyalties have provided alternative avenues for preserving individual sovereignty, democratic institutions, and a modicum of political stability. But it is, nonetheless, these same ties that continue to undermine and inhibit the growth of civil and national loyalties.

Primordial Loyalties

Kinship

Kinship has been, and is likely to remain, Lebanon's most solid and enduring tie. The extended and patriarchal family, all other evidence to the contrary, has demonstrated remarkable resiliency as a unit of social organization. In fact, there is still much truth to the often repeated observation that in Lebanon the family, not the individual, is the basic social unit. To a large extent a person's status in society, his occupation, and social and political prestige are defined largely by it. One's status, class, and power, in other words, are still partly ascribed by the accident of birth. To say that a person is a "son of a family" *(ibn ʿayleh)* prompts one to bypass other attributes that he may possess. The concept of *ahl* ("kin") extends beyond and differs from the lineal concept typical of Western culture.

All this is by way of saying that Lebanese society is predominantly a kinship culture. Society starts with the family and is fashioned after it. Even the behavior of the individual in various life situations is mainly an expression of his family pattern. Since blood ties are intimate and binding, the sovereignty of the family transcends all other loyalties, and the individual is compelled at times to suppress his individuality if it happens to clash with the whims and rigid dictates of the family. As part of an intimate primary group, the individual no doubt derives a good deal of emotional support and security from his family, but it also exacts a price. In return he pledges his loyalty and subordination. Filial piety is almost a sacred norm; a debt one owes his kin, and a prerequisite for gaining approval and support.

It must be emphasized that the intense attachment to one's *ahl* and the solidarity of kinship as a primary group cannot be simply a reflection of intimate association or social interaction as some sociologists would have it. As expressed proverbially, blood runs thick and deep in Lebanon, and this intense affinity to kinship is to a large extent attributed to the tie of blood. Even where intimate interaction is absent, deference to one's elders and loyalty to one's kin remain almost a scared value in society.

It is not the intention here to trace the cultural roots of this pervasive value pattern. Suffice it to note that it has far-reaching implications for the political life in the country. Since the family dominates the life experience of an individual, it becomes almost an exclusive agency of political socialization and tutelage. "Ever since my eyes saw the light of day, I found myself immersed in an atmosphere of civil servants and political life." So begins the political memoirs of Bishara al-Khuri (1960:20), the first President of independent Lebanon. His political background is certainly not unique. It is typical of a whole generation of Lebanese politicians whose careers and even specific political ideas are inextricably associated with certain kinship traditions.

Not only is the family an agency of political socialization and tutelage; it is also an avenue for political power and a means for perpetuating leadership. Almost a quarter of the 1960 Chamber, for example, was composed of Deputies who have "inherited" their parliamentary seats;

people who are heirs of a long political tradition. To be exact, twenty-three members are the descendants of men who were appointed in the Legislative Assemblies under the French Mandate (as-Safa 1964:2). The 1960 Chamber, which was in no way peculiar, also included members of the same family who held office simultaneously. Joseph and Michel Skaff are brothers, the latter having changed his religious domination to become eligible for the Greek Orthodox seat in Zahle; Nicolas and Yousef Salem are twins; Pierre and Maurice Gemayel are first cousins; Samih and Adel Osseiran are cousins; Souleiman and Ali Abdel Karim el-Ali are close relatives. There are also other types of kinship association: Sabri Hamadeh is the brother-in-law of Kamel al-Asᶜad, though the two remain politically at odds; likewise, the marriage of Majid Arslan to a Jumblati has not brought the two arch-Druze factions closer together. Succession to office is also linked with kinship. During the four-year term of the 1960 Chamber, four Deputies died in office, three of whom were succeeded by their own children at the partial elections held in their respective districts. Ahmad al-Asᶜad was succeeded by his son Kamel; Yousef al-Zein, by his son Abdel Latif; and Emile Bustani, by his only child, a daughter, Myrna el-Khazin, the first Lebanese woman to ever become a Deputy.[2]

Not only the Legislature but the Executive also bears the traces of kinship. The Premiership, for example, has usually been the preserve of four traditional Sunni Muslim families, namely: Solh, Karameh, Yafi, and Salam. Excluding the Shafik Wazzan cabinet of October 1982, the first in Amin Gemayel's tenure as President, a total of fifty-three cabinets have been formed since Lebanon's independence in 1943. Of this total, forty cabinets have rotated among these four families. The four Solhs—Riyad, Sami, Takkiyyedin, and Rashid—alone held the Premiership fifteen times. Abdel Hamid Karami and his son Rashid held it ten times; Abdallah Yafi, nine; and Saeb Salam, six.

Because of recurring cabinet crises, the life span of a government in Lebanon does not, on the average, exceed nine months. The shortest, formed by Abdallah Yafi in November 1968 survived for only one month and twenty-five days. The longest, formed by Salim Hoss in December 1976, lasted for two years, seven months, and six days.

The four traditional families have not only monopolized 76 percent of all cabinets formed since independence, they have also had the lion's share in terms of their tenure in office. Together they served a total of approximately twenty-nine years; again close to 75 percent of the forty years since independence. The Solhs alone served for twelve years (30 percent; the two Karamis, seven; Yafi, five and a half years; and Salam four and a half years.

Other ministerial positions are also associated with certain families and/or individuals. The Ministry of Foreign Affairs, for example, was for a long time held mainly by the Taqlas; first by Salim and later his brother Philip. Likewise, until recently, the Ministry of Defense had almost become the preserve of Majid Arslan. (For further such details, see Salem 1966.)

In more than one respect, the whole political history of Lebanon, without undue exaggeration, can be described in terms of not more than a handful of leading families—families competing to reaffirm their name, power, and privilege in their respective regions: the Arslans and the Junblats in the Shuf, the Karamis and the Ahdabs in Tripoli, the As'ads and the Khalils in the South, the Duwaihis and the Frangiehs in the North, the Hamadehs and the Haidars in the Biqa, and so on.

This kinship rivalry, intense and persistent, has not been confined to two feuding families. The rivalry very often takes the form of a dual organization—a loose, informal two-fold faction that extends beyond the immediate kin groups of the prominent families. As such one may be neither an Arslani nor a Junblati, yet he is invariably drawn into one faction in times of political struggle. The slightest provocation—anything from the bitter contest for electoral office to the appointment of a village night watchman—may easily incite the deep-seated hostility. Elections, though, remain the broadest arena where the factional rivalry vents itself. As in other personalistic and kinship societies, local and national elections in Lebanon are not merely a process of electing representatives or a device through which the ruling elite seeks to perpetuate itself. It is not an ideological contest between political systems or figures. Rarely, if ever, have elections been sought and fought on a programmatic and impersonal basis. In more cases than not it is a bitter and long-standing conflict between extended families and communal factions. It is a chance to vindicate some of the old feuds that have traditionally mobilized and divided electoral districts. Irrespective of the positions of the contestants, the contest is almost always a source of friction and hostility. Since elections are fought in a personal and vindictive manner, the results bring glory to the victors and shame to the losers. The former take their victory with indulgence; the latter accept their defeat with bitterness and humiliation. Needless to say, a personal and familial rivalry needs few ideological platforms. It leaves no room for organized debates where contestants

can challenge the ideas of their rivals. Gaining access to voters is still
largely accomplished through traditional contacts, such as visits and social calls and through the services of "election keys" who act as self-appointed intermediaries between candidates and voters. They organize
meetings, arrange for contacts, and sometimes go as far as to guarantee
a certain number of votes or returns. (For further details, see Salem 1965.)

Nor has the kinship rivalry been confined to contests for electoral offices. The political energies of the leading families have also been consumed in a ceaseless competition for government positions. In some respects this is where the political rivalry might have all begun. During the
mutesarrifate, for example, the leading feudal families insisted on, and
duly received, the lion's share of the highest government positions. In
fact, the abolition of feudalism by the Règlement Organique of 1861
undermined the security and social standing of these families and threatened to make a disgruntled class out of them. Accordingly, the mutesarrif, as we have seen, arranged for their gradual absorption into the new
administration.

The late President Bishara al-Khuri (1960:30) expresses this intimate
association between the feudal aristocracy and civil bureaucracy in even
more pointed terms:

> High government positions virtually became the exclusive preserve,
> a *waqf,* for the leading families of the country. This came as a con-
> sequence of the continuing influence of feudalism though officially
> abolished by the "Règlement Organique." Office in those days was
> everything. It was the object of ambition and the source of all in-
> fluence and prestige. Members of the same house and close friends
> would fight for it; they could risk peril to secure a coveted govern-
> ment job. It became a cause for hostility and heavy expenditure.
> Many an aristocratic house has been shaken, even ruined by it. This
> competition for office helped the Mutesarrif perpetuate his influ-
> ence over the Lebanese families and dispense with Lebanese affairs
> according to his own whims and without any restraints.

True as this may be, the gradual absorption of prominent families into
the new government bureaucracy was inevitable and, to some extent,
functional. To begin with, "through this administrative aristocracy, a political continuity was maintained in Lebanon's government, linking the
period of the mutesarrifate with the earlier periods . . . and preparing

the way for later developments" (Salibi 1965:117). It generated, as shown earlier, some of the conditions conducive to the emergence of a new breed of political leadership; a leadership more bureaucratic than feudal in nature, and one that came to play a prominent role in the struggle for independence.

The persistence of kinship rivalry and the political dominance of prominent families has, on the whole, however, been more dysfunctional. Among other things, it has given the political process a rather personalistic and opportunistic character. Political alliances, parliamentary blocs, and opposition fronts are still predominantly initiated and sustained by personal and not ideological considerations. Passing references to a few such instances will suffice here. The "Socialist Front," which was formed around the beginning of President Khuri's second term, was no more than a temporary alliance combining diverse and incompatible factions and blocs. Though the "Front" bore an ideological name, all that its members had in common was a personal opposition to President Khuri. Apart from Junblat, who had organized his Progressive Socialist Party in 1949, the so-called "Socialist Front" included factions and figures like Chamoun, the Kata'ib, the Najjedeh, the National Bloc of the Eddes, and the Syrian Nationalists—all ideologically opposed to the "socialism" the Front was professing. Having grown disillusioned with the apparent administrative corruption and the alleged widespread influence of Khuri's closest kin (particularly his brother Salim), the Front by September 1952 demanded the resignation of Khuri and the complete reorganization of the state.

Political history very often repeats itself in Lebanon. No sooner had Chamoun come to power in 1952 than the political alliance disbanded only to appear again in a different guise. By 1957, Chamoun's political opponents (and he had managed to antagonize quite a few) had organized a new opposition group now under the name of the "National Front." Among others, the Front this time included Kamal Junblat, Rashid Karami, the Constitutional Bloc of the Khuris, and other prominent leaders like Salam, Yafi, and As'ad, most of whom were embittered by their loss in the elections of the summer of 1957. Having had no effective access to constitutional opposition from within the Parliament, the National Front resorted to terrorist activity which ultimately led to the crisis of 1958.

This pattern of personal and opportunistic alliances is certainly not of recent vintage. As far back as 1928 Bisharah al-Khuri—then Prime Minister of a short-lived three-man cabinet—was already bitten by it. In a resounding address to the Legislature he had remarked: "As for us, we differ from others in that we are negative blocs. Opinions meet today to destroy what is present but part tomorrow and we know not why. The party with us is the child of opportunism and the victim of aimlessness, at a time when the country awaits a plan or a program to uproot some of our evils" (al-Khuri 1960:159).

Made current under the French Mandate and carried over into the era of independence, this pattern of alliance making still permeates all levels of the political process. Electoral slates and lists often produce some un-natural combinations. Personal and opportunistic considerations pit can-didates sharing the same views against one another, while others with incompatible ideological stands pledge a common front. Even the rela-tionship between the President and the Premier often follows a similar pattern. All presidents, beginning with Charles Dabbas, sought to estab-lish some kind of a political alliance with a leading Sunni Muslim figure. During the two terms of his Presidency (1926–32), Charles Dabbas could rely for consistent Muslim support on Sheikh Muhammad al-Jisr, a Sun-nite jurist from Tripoli. President Edde found in Khayr al-Din al-Ahdab, another Sunnite from Tripoli, such a man. During the nine years of Khuri's presidency, Riyad al-Solh was Premier for a total period of five years and two months. Out of the sixteen regular cabinets formed then (1943–1952), Riyad chaired eight. Had he survived Khuri's term, he would have undoubtedly served more, and Khuri's own tenure in office might have possibly been marked by a different ending. The relationship be-tween the two men is certainly unique in the political history of Lebanon and warrants closer scrutiny than has been accorded to it by historians and political scientists so far. The two leaders were not only the archi-tects of the National Pact, but they articulated and blended together the political formulae that have sustained the national entity of Lebanon since Independence.[3]

Camille Chamoun (1952–58) found a similar relationship with Sami al-Solh. Though Chamoun, like Khuri, did rotate the Premiership in an effort to broaden his political support, he called on Solh frequently. In fact, during Chamoun's six-year term, Solh was premier almost three years. Even the sectarian strife of 1958 did not attenuate the personal and po-litical alliance between the two. President Shihab (1958–64) leaned toward Rashid Karami in continuing this pattern. Except for two provisional temporary cabinets to supervise elections, and two short-lived ones formed by Saeb Salam, Karami monopolized the Premiership for nearly four years.

Charles Helou (1964–70) relied almost equally on Rashid Karami and Abdallah al-Yafi. Except for two brief cabinets formed by Hussein Oueini during the initial period of his term, each lasting a few months, Karami and Yafi were called upon four times each, each serving for about two years and ten months. Suleiman Frangieh (1970–76) maintained nearly the same pattern of reliance on typical traditional Sunni Muslim families. Except for two short-lived cabinets formed by Amin Hafiz (April 25–July 8, 1973) and Nureddine Rifa'i (May 23–July 1, 1975), he called upon familiar figures like Saeb Salam, Takkiyyedin and Rashid al-Solh, and Rashid Karami. The personal alliance he had with Saeb Salam, however, dominated nearly the first half of his six-year term.

Elias Sarkis (1976–82) was the first President to depart from this pattern in two significant and obvious respects: He formed fewer cabinets (only 3 compared to the usual 13, 10 or 7 formed by his predecessors), and cooperated with only two Prime Ministers (Salim Hoss and Shafik Wazzan), both of whom do not belong to the traditional Sunni Muslim families.

Opportunistic and unprogrammatic as most personal relationships are, the political process in Lebanon has certainly not lost all ideological undertones. It would be an error to assume that the whole structure of the body politic is sustained by personal and kinship alliances. Rather, what is being suggested here is that the continuing dominance of personal and kinship loyalties does not preclude the presence of ideological rifts, and that the persistence of such loyalties has at times made for political stability and continuity. The political history of Lebanon abounds with instances where purely personal and kinship rivalries are transformed into doctrinal conflicts, and where ideological commitments have been supported by kinship loyalty. In other words, it is a dialectical rather than a dichotomous relationship. The two spheres—the personal and the ideological—are constantly infiltrating and influencing each other. The personal rivalry, for example, between Emile Edde and Bishara al-Khuri which dominated the political scene during the early years of the Republic (1926–41), did not remain a purely personal struggle. Not only were the two different in character and background, but their political careers were marked by ideological differences and orientations. Likewise, there was much more to the political alliance between Khuri and Solh than personal admiration and mutual respect for one another and for the kinship traditions they represented. Their relationship, above all, was cemented by an ideological rapport and a common political struggle. The same is true of the relationship between President Shihab and Rashid Karami. There was clearly a personal dimension to the relationship between the two men. This alone, however, could not have accounted for the unusual political rapprochement between them had it not been sustained by the political commitment Karami displayed towards the Shihabist Nahj (political program and orientation) as it was called at the time.

A more recent example is the mutual political support and admiration President Sarkis and Prime Minister Wazzan exhibited toward each other during the turbulent days of the civil war and the Israeli invasion. In retrospect, it is the amicable relationship between them reinforced by their common perception of the imminent threats to national unity and legitimacy that kept the two major communities—Christian and Muslim—from drifting further apart.

Fealty

Another pervasive primordial tie—one that is closely associated with kinship—is fealty, which still survives in the personalized relationship between follower and leader. Among other things, fealty involves the recognized obligation of a leader in return for the loyalty and unquestioned allegiance of a follower. Far from being a contractual or rational relationship, fealty is sustained by personal commitments and a system of political obligations in which a powerful local leader or *za'im* is owed the personal loyalty of followers and servile dependents.

In feudal Lebanon, as we have seen, the whole fabric of the social structure was based on the fidelity of a man to his overlord. The bond of fealty, typical perhaps of the epochs of feudalism elsewhere, served a dual function. First, it helped create a small but decisive group of followers. Second, it was instrumental in sustaining the cohesion and solidarity of local communities and possibly the whole society.

As a social bond, fealty is not merely a relic of the exotic past of Lebanon. Though predominantly a feudal institution, it is still very much alive, in both form and content, in contemporary political life. Its manifestations are deep and extensive. There is hardly a phase of the political process that remains untouched by it. The discussion below will be mainly concerned with one of its predominant features, namely the persistence of the *za'im* as the most typical political actor.

Much like its feudal antecedents, the system of *zu'ama* is cemented by ties of fealty. The *za'im,* like the feudal overlord or fief holder, is the unquestioned leader of a tightly knit local community. By virtue of his lineage and ascribed prestige, he sustains and perpetuates his political power by dispensing favors for, and protecting the interests of his clients or *zilm.*[4] The *za'im-zilm* relationship—like that between fief holder and peasant, warlord and warrior—is personal, not ideological or programmatic. Likewise, the authority of the *za'im,* in the Weberian sense, is partly traditional and partly charismatic, but rarely rational.

Both as a concept and as a concrete phenomenon, the term *za'im* implies shades of meaning and subsumes within its rubric a multitude of political types. We have already identified three evolving forms of political patronage—feudal, administrative and pseudo-ideological—and explored reasons for their persistence. Since nearly the same set of circumstances is associated with the survival of the *za'im,* there is consequently little need for further discussion. One underlying feature, however, needs to be emphasized. What sustains the *za'im* as a political figure in Lebanon are the communal and personal ties of fealty. His political assets are those typical of most personal relationships—namely, reciprocal loyalties and obligations. In fact, the present-day *za'im* appears to capitalize on the needs and misfortunes of his political clients and followers. Not only does he dispense favors and secure jobs for the unemployed, but he very often intervenes in the bureaucratic and judicial process on behalf of his clients. In return, clients pledge their loyalty in gratitude for past favors and in anticipation of future ones. In several respects the entrenched evils of favoratism and graft are part and parcel of the syndrome of *zu'ama.*

The *za'im* also capitalizes on the apathy and political indifference of the masses. In this sense he becomes the prototype of Michel's "Oligarch"—someone who takes advantage of the dependence and willing submission of his followers to perpetuate his leadership within his closely circumscribed community. It is little wonder that the leadership of some of the traditional *zu'ama* stands virtually uncontested in certain regions. Barring a few exceptions, almost all the "feudal" *zu'ama* cited earlier have been continuously elected to the Legislature since independence. Record holders in the cabinet (i.e., people who have served in ministerial positions the largest number of times) are also from this group. With the exception of veteran politicians like Philippe Taqla, Gabriel Murr, and Habib Abu-Shahla, the rest all fall within our definition of *zu'ama,* namely, Majid Arslan, Sami al-Solh, Rashid Karami, Hamid Frangieh, Ahmad al-

Asa'd, Philippe Bulos, and Sa'ib Salam (For further details, see Kerr 1966:211–12).

Most of these leaders, it must be recalled, are local notables, not national heroes. They are guardians and trustees of whatever privileges and benefits their communities are entitled to, not the articulators of new platforms or political principles. Any attempt to challenge or tamper with the sovereignty of such leadership spells political suicide. The civil crisis of 1958, and lesser but chronic cabinet crises Lebanon continues to experience, are partly a consequence of such attempts.

It is considerations like these that prompt us to suggest that the system of *zu'ama* is likely to persist in Lebanon as long as the primordial sentiments of kinship and fealty remain rooted in the culture. It will survive not because it has done so in the past, or that the Lebanese have an innate predisposition to venerate traditions for their own sake. Rather, because the *za'im*, in the absence of other rational agencies or ideological pressure groups and parties, still serves some vital political functions. First, as has been suggested throughout, insofar as the system of *zu'ama* has served as an agency of political socialization and tutelage, it has been instrumental in maintaining political continuity and stability. Second, the *za'im* acts as a "tension manager" in the informal process of adjudication and reconciling tribal and communal conflict. Finally, and perhaps most important, he serves as a mediating function, a link between his community and the central bureaucracy. Since an impersonal and rational system of bureaucracy is still relatively alien to the primordial sentiments rooted in rural regions, the *za'im*, by reinterpreting some of the formal requirements in a more personal and particularistic manner, tends to soften their impact and ultimately facilitate adjustment to them.

Religion

That religion and politics are intimately associated in Lebanon has been almost self-evident and has been ably and extensively surveyed. Any such further discussion runs the risk of becoming a painful elaboration of the obvious. Much like the persistence of primordial ties of kinship and fealty, religion permeates every aspect of the political process or administrative structure, especially since sectarian and confessional representation has long been a legitimate and formally recognized feature of the political system.

In appraising the nature of such association, most observers have been predisposed to document its disruptive and dysfunctional consequences. As a result, the literature abounds with references to the evils of confessionalism, such as the bankruptcy of ideological parties and pressure groups, the paralysis of Parliament, excessive meddling of religious leaders in the political life of the community, and the sacrifice of competence and efficiency on the altar of sectarian balance. Eager to highlight the abuses of such tendencies, and they certainly cannot be overlooked, observers nevertheless have been less concerned with some of the functional consequences of religious and confessional loyalties. The brief remarks to follow are a preliminary attempt in this direction.

The institutionalization of confessionalism, which can be traced back to the mutesarrifate, did at least provide Lebanon relatively early in its political history with the opportunity of experimenting with a representative form of government. Though it limited electoral competition, it was nevertheless an inevitable and natural framework given the pluralistic and sectarian foundation of the society. Religious sentiments, particularly after the decline of feudalism, came to assume a more intense role in sustaining identity and communal solidarity. Consequently no realistic political arrangement could have ignored or bypassed such sentiments without endangering the delicate sectarian balance.

The National Pact of 1943 (Al-Mithaq al-Watani), it must be recalled, did not obliterate confessional differences. Rather, it consecrated them. In essence, it is no more than a pragmatic modus operandi, an entente between religious groups whose political orientations and frames of references are basically different. What the architects of the Mithaq sought to do was to immobilize those differences and thus hopefully avoid the emotional and confessional upsurges associated with them.

Whether by default or conviction, the Mithaq not only promoted political balance, it also guaranteed a semblance of democracy and freedom of expression. Among other things, it has regulated the interplay of the various confessional groups that underlie the body politic of a pluralistic society. Precarious and immobile as it seems, the Mithaq has proved to be an effective palliative. It is true it may have, along with other socio-cultural variables, inhibited the emergence of organized political parties and other ideological pressure groups, but it has also been a "bulwark against the disruptive potential of irrational confessionalism" (Maksoud 1966:241).

Furthermore, and like perhaps most other Lebanese institutions, the Mithaq is a cross breed of rational and traditional elements, contractual and communal considerations. Recognizing the legitimacy and political relevance of confessional loyalties, it also sought a national identity and consequently "came to fill the national vacuum in which the state was super-imposed after World War I" (Saab 1966:276).

It is of interest to note that the Mithaq has accomplished all this, although it remains at heart no more than an oral mutual pledge between Bishara al-Khuri and Riyad al-Solh. Though unwritten, it is also a contractual pledge in the sense that it is based on reciprocal interests, mutual consent, and reason. The Mithaq is after all a practical, political pact, not a sentimental and emotional settlement, as is often implied. Prompted by rational and national considerations, the architects of the Mithaq and the core of political leaders behind them were certainly not oblivious of their confessional and communal loyalties. Bishara al-Khuri and Riyad al-Solh, as much as Abdul Hamid Karami, Majid Arslan, Salim Taqla, Ahmad al-Asʿad, Adel Osseiran, Sabri Hamadeh, Camille Chamoun and a handful of others were all consumed by the passions of religious, communal, and kinship ties. Yet in transcending or incorporating these loyalties into the National Pact, the "fathers of independence"—as they have come to be called, succeeded in reconciling the rational and traditional ingredients of the political system.

By and large then, the consecration of confessional loyalties through the National Pact is a realistic and effective formula. It is more than just an "expedient deal among a few politicians" (Binder 1966:319). It is something akin to a "social contract"; a solemn and almost sacred covenant. Like all other contracts, it exacts a price: the renunciation of some of the politically charged claims or sentiments of each of the major religious groups for the sake of national concord and amity. That this should be confused with immobilism or the paralysis of initiative and political innovation is hardly justified.

Confessionalism has also been associated with the inveterate evils of nepotism, graft, and bureaucratic inefficiency. In fact, almost any of the failures and shortcomings of civil bureaucracy has been attributed to the persistence of confessional and sectarian loyalties. So much has been written about bureaucratic inefficiency and its inextricable association with confessionalism, that one is led to believe there exists a special "cult" in Lebanon that condones inefficiency and sustains its growth. The charge of inefficiency is certainly justifiable and can be amply substantiated. But to hold this as prima facie evidence of confessionalism is an entirely different matter.

To begin with, the persistence of confessional loyalties has in no way precluded administrative innovation and reform. Neither has it inhibited the development of new personnel laws (such as those promulgated in 1959), which set forth the general obligations of civil servants with regard to organizational efficiency. (For a brief summary of these laws, see Crow 1966:170–71.)

Second, there is no inherent contradiction between the principle of guaranteeing "equity and amity" by a proportional representation of the different confessional groups, and administrative efficiency. There is no inherent reason why both goals cannot be maintained without subverting either. The current system of confessional distribution as such cannot be singularly blamed if this dual objective has not been achieved thus far. Rather, what should be decried and ameliorated is the unequal distribution of talent and qualified candidates among the various religious communities. Once such discrepancies are bridged, confessional distribution need no longer be sustained at the expense of organizational efficiency.

Finally, confessionalism has become a convenient scapegoat for abuses whose roots lie elsewhere. Deviations from ideal bureaucratic norms and practices are universal and no particular sect or group in Lebanon—as elsewhere—can claim complete monopoly over them. Consequently it is doubtful whether many of the more serious problems associated with Lebanese bureaucracy would disappear if confessionalism were to be completely eradicated. For instance, petty and personal rivalries, the absence of civic responsibility, low motivation and financial rewards, individual incompetence and lack of training, and a score of other problems are above and beyond confessionalism. They are rooted in the sociocultural traditions of society, and they are likely to persist with or without confessionalism. The *wasta* mentality has virtually become institutionalized. The familiar pressures that are brought to bear by *zuʿama* or their spokesmen in favor of some of their clients are likely to continue no matter what fate befalls sectarianism. Furthermore, religion is rarely, if ever, an isolated variable. It is intimately bound with kinship, fealty, and communal considerations. Consequently, the elimination of one in no way involves the exclusion of the other.

Rather than making unrealistic attempts to abolish confessionalism and in so doing run the risk of fomenting the vulnerable sectarian factionalism, a less drastic and more effective remedy would be to upgrade the present bureaucratic structure within the framework of confessionalism. There is certainly ample room for extensive administrative reform without amending Article 95 of the Constitution.[5]

In brief, a "confessional bureaucracy" need not be a contradiction in terms. The universalistic and rational criteria of allocating and utilizing manpower can still be retained without diluting the sectarian loyalties that underlie a confessional society. In fact, it is doubtful, given the resurgence of confessional sentiments and loyalties, whether any other bureaucracy can function effectively at present in Lebanon.

Future Prospects

Some of the recent studies on political development appear to carry an unjustifiable implication, namely, that political change should involve a transfer of loyalties from primordial allegiances to secular and ideological commitments. Ultimately, the underlying problem of any political system, it is argued, is one "of asserting and legitimizing the priority of the nation-state over tribal and traditional loyalties" (LaPalombara and Weiner 1966:1–7).

It was the intention of this paper, at least with respect to the political history of Lebanon, to cast some doubt on such assertions.

As has been implied all through, and contrary to what is often suggested, these traditional links are not "shattered beyond repair" (Halpern 1963:28). They have a way of reappearing again and again; overtly if possible, in disguise when necessary. Not only are the traditional loyalties still rooted in the culture, some have long been legitimized by the political system. Hence the success of a party system or any other attribute of the nation-state depends not on diluting or overriding these traditional elements but on the extent to which they can be incorporated into the emerging body politic.

The whole question of the so-called "crisis of identity" can be viewed within this context. As long as the social structure remains predominantly ascriptive and particularistic in character, the Lebanese citizen will derive greater satisfaction and security from his kinship and communal ties than from his involvement or participation in purely rational or ideological associations. It is still largely within these traditional networks that he derives and sustains his sense of identity.

The average Lebanese politician is naturally not above all this. Not only is he himself a product of such primordial attachments, he frequently resorts to them as a means to court the masses by appealing to their traditional sentiments during elections. In this he differs little from the urban secular politician who invokes catchy slogans before elections and ignores them afterwards. There is one subtle difference however: primordial affinities, like all other personal and primary group attachments, cannot be lightly dismissed or bypassed. Consequently, the Lebanese politician is likely to stand or fall not on the merit of his political platform; rather on how intense or attenuated primordial attachments are.

Needless to say, this crisis of identity cannot be resolved by fiat. Legislation cannot turn a confessional, kinship and personalistic society into a nation-state. Nor can a sense of legitimacy of government be created by constitutional arrangements and a representative electoral system alone. These constitutional prerequisites have long been guaranteed in Lebanon, but the traditional loyalties of people have not undergone substantial change. Kinship, fealty, and confessional loyalties still supersede those of the nation, state, or party. Accordingly, a Christian is first a Christian, a member of a given family, and from a specific region before he is a Lebanese. Likewise a Junblati is a Junblati first and a progressive socialist second.

All this is by way of saying that if the modern nation-state presupposes that the "link between governmental authority and inherited privilege in the hands of families of notables is broken" (Bendix 1964:106), then in this sense the idea of a nation-state is not firmly rooted in the Lebanese political system. Political prerogatives and access to political power and privileges, as shown above, are still largely a reflection of kinship, fealty, and sectarian loyalties. The so-called "antiquity of blood," to use Machiavelli's phrase, is not only a relic of Lebanon's medieval past, it is still alive today.

It is not being suggested that the present particularistic and ascriptive system is a paragon of political virtues. Rather—and notwithstanding its personalistic and unprogrammatic character—the system has nevertheless been politically viable in integrating the pluralistic factions of the society and in solving some of the pending political issues. Somehow, and until the outbreak of the current civil hostilities, successive Lebanese governments had succeeded in maintaining a relatively generous amount of freedom of expression, evolved a foreign policy, protected and encouraged a free economy, and most of all remained a free, independent, prosperous country. Such a system is clearly not faultless. It no doubt entails many pitfalls and shortcomings.

The persistence of civil unrest is one dramatic indication that at least at the macro level the system has not been effective in warding off society from the trials and tribulations of recurrent violence and disorder. But then, as has become clear recently, the sources of such unrest are only in part due to the internal contradictions and imbalances within society. The external loads on the system—particularly the presence of Palestinians, inter-Arab and superpower rivalries—are to a larger extent more responsible in generating and sustaining civil unrest.

At another level, it is also equally clear that leadership and access to power are still partly a function of ascribed attributes and primordial affinities. But then where is that idyllic society where equal access to power and privilege is guaranteed? Not even the most "open society" has been able to eliminate all barriers of class, caste, and kinship.

One conclusive observation is in order. In more than one respect, the major argument of this essay and the evidence provided is far from novel or peculiar. It is in the good company of some of the great classical traditions of sociology. The pioneering work of Charles Cooley on the substantial harmony between primary and secondary group orientations, Mayo's research on the supportive function of small groups in large-scale industrial organizations, Shils' and Janowitz's studies of primary groups in military organizations, these along with the theoretical formulations of Weber, Simmel, Tonnies, and Durkheim provide ample evidence in support of the major orientation of this essay. They all, among others, confirm the proposition that primordial ties, like perhaps most primary group relations, are both inevitable and functional. As such the persistence of such ties in political institutions should not be deplored as pathological and intrinsically subversive. Rather, they can be incorporated into the rational instruments of political change and ultimately make for the viability of political institutions.

The classic and more contemporary theoretical tradition in sociology posits another proposition that also finds ample support in the encounters of Lebanon with primordialism. Robert Merton (1957), among others, has maintained that because of the uncertain and latent relations within systems, particular elements may be functional for part of the system and dysfunctional for the overall system. In this sense it could be argued that the survival of primordial ties might very easily serve better the interests of certain groups and individuals than it does the maintenance of civility and national loyalties. Once again, in other words, what enables in one respect could disable in another.

CHAPTER SIX

The Parliamentary Elite

S UCCESSIVE STUDIES OF the Lebanese parliamentary elite continue to reveal some inconsistent and paradoxical tendencies. One such striking feature is the wide discrepancy between the relatively flexible and changing background of the Deputies and the continuities in their political behavior and orientations. The rapid socioeconomic transformations Lebanon has witnessed, particularly during the past few decades, have broadened processes of elite recruitment and circulation. They have drawn a more literate, professional, and skilled elite into the body politic and politicized a growing segment of the population. Such changes, however, have not been accompanied by any perceptible change in political attitudes and behavior of the elite. Nor have they rendered the Parliament more effective as a legislative body.

From one perspective, the changing social composition of the Parliament attests to the decline of descendants of feudal aristocracy and notable families and the gradual ascendancy of Deputies with more plebian and bourgeois social origins (Harik 1972:15–27; Harik 1975:201–2). Occupational background also reveals a sharp shift from landed proprietors to lawyers, professionals, and businessmen. This trend, among others, bespeaks of a shift away "from the traditional and parochial and toward the achievement oriented and sophisticated" (Hudson 1968:241). The high educational level of the Deputies is equally impressive. The proportion of Deputies with university degrees has been persistently increasing. While 51 percent of the 1943 Chamber held university degrees, the proportion rose to 73 percent for the current Chamber (Harik 1975:28; Messarra 1974:257–64).[1]

The electoral process, particularly on indices such as voter participa-

This essay is a revised and updated version of a chapter originally published in Jacob Landau, Ergun Ozbudun, and Frank Tachau, eds., *Electoral Politics in the Middle East* (London: Croom Helm and Hoover Institution Press, 1980), pp. 243–71. Used by permission.

tion, competitiveness in parliamentary elections and turnover rates, also reveals some encouraging manifestations. The persistent increase in the number of people voting since 1943 suggests a broadened suffrage, increasing popular involvement and greater civic consciousness among a growing segment of the adult population (Hudson 1968:219–25; Harik 1972:79–82; Messarra 1974:30).

Electoral contests have also become steadily more competitive. The number of candidates competing for a given seat has been increasing; consequently they have been winning by smaller margins. This, among other things, suggests that Deputies do not have a substantial popular backing and hence cannot afford to be indifferent to their political constituencies. More important, a competitive electoral process is seen by Hudson (1968:225) as a sign of "a healthy pluralistic system because it indicates flexibility and responsiveness . . . and that a process of institutionalized change is developing."

Successive studies of elite circulation clearly indicate a comparatively high rate of turnover of Lebanese Deputies (Messarra 1974:39; Harik 1972:47–52; Hudson 1968:239). With an average turnover rate of 40 percent for the nine Parliaments since independence, it is evident that political recruitment has been significantly broadened. This incessant change in the parliamentary elite is, once again, seen as a symptom of the system's fluidity (Hudson 1968:239). It has at least prompted one observer to deny the often-made charge regarding the oligarchic character of Lebanon's political elite (Harik 1972:49–52).

Finally, other observers point out to the growing role of political parties and organized caucuses in both parliamentary representation and election campaigns. The proportion of Deputies representing various organized political parties, as opposed to loosely organized cliques and coalitions, has been persistently increasing. This, too, is seen as a reflection of greater organizational development and politicization as prerequisites for political modernization (Zuwiyya 1972:92; Hudson 1968:231–27).

Altogether, changes in the socioeconomic composition of the Parliamentary elite along with other trends in the direction of increasing voter participation, competitiveness in elections, and the broadening of the recruitment process, are taken to mean that the "system is capable of limited, self-induced, structural modernization" (Hudson 1966:174).

From another perspective, particularly if one were to make inferences regarding the political behavior and attitudes of the elite, one emerges with an entirely different impression. The image of the Deputies as political actors and the general impact of the legislature on the political system are far from favorable. In fact, both invite considerable derision and scorn from the popular and more serious literature on the subject.

Regardless of their background and professional skills, Deputies emerge more as political brokers concerned with the parochial and often petty interests of their local constituencies than with formulating and articulating broad policy issues of national and civic significance (Harik 1975:214–15). Although the proportion of Deputies with what Hudson (1968:246; see also Suleiman 1967:265) terms "sophisticated and modern" political orientations has been increasing, "the great majority of Lebanon's parliamentary deputies have no political orientation beyond the list or clique that got them elected."

The fragmentation, ineffectiveness, hesitation, and impotence of the Parliament has been repeatedly decried by several observers. Much like its individual members, the Parliament is notorious for its subservience to the Executive and is often reduced to a "puppet" to be manipulated and managed by a skillful President (Kerr 1966:202; Binder 1966:287). It avoids critical and controversial issues (Rondot 1966:133), and makes only a minimal contribution to the policy-formation and rule-making functions. Nor is it effective as a check on the Executive and bureaucracy (Crow 1970:296–97).

The foregoing evidence should be sufficient to caution us against drawing too many inferences about the elite's attitudes and political behavior from its social background. An analysis of the background and changing composition of the Deputies, in of itself, is clearly not a meaningful gauge of their political behavior. Fruitful as such analysis is in identifying changing trends in political representation, it does not tell us much about the power structure of society. Nor does it explain why there is such a discrepancy between the seemingly progressive and changing elite and the rigidities in their behavior and political orientations.

In his study of the Turkish political elite, Frederick Frey (1965:157) is similarly reluctant to admit the existence of a causal link between background characteristics of a political elite and its behavior. "To leap from the knowledge of social background of national politicians to inferences about the power structure of society is quite dangerous. Even to proceed from such knowledge to judgments about the political behavior . . . can be treacherous." It is instructive to heed Frey's caution, particularly since the bulk of the studies of Lebanon's political elite have been excessively concerned with its background characteristics and in identifying patterns of elite circulation and recruitment.

No such "leaps" will be made in this study. If we are to understand the discrepancy between background and political behavior of the parliamentary elite, we need, instead, to look elsewhere beyond a mere documentation of the changing patterns of elite composition. An exploration into the nature of patronage and political clientelism would, I think, offer a more meaningful context for such an analysis. Accordingly, the paper has a three-fold objective. First, it reexamines some of the changing trends in elite composition and circulation. Second, it identifies a few of the continuities in patterns of political behavior, particularly with regard to political orientations and the ineffectiveness of the Parliament as an innovative legislative body. Third, an attempt will be made, through a brief analysis of the nature of patronage, to account for the persisting disjunction between changing composition of the elite and the continuities in its behavior.

Except for occasional reference to the so-called "Representative Councils" of the pre-Independence era, the bulk of the data and analysis in this paper is based on the nine Chambers since Independence. Constitutionally, Deputies are normally elected for a four-year period. Accordingly, the term of the current Chamber should have ended in 1976. The protracted civil disturbances, however, have made it impossible to hold any national elections and the Parliament has had to pass special legislative decrees to renew its own mandate on three successive occasions: in 1976, 1978, and 1980.

Composition and Circulation of the Elite

Age

The average age of the Lebanese Deputy has been gradually increasing since 1943. On the whole the Deputy in the current Chamber is almost six years older than his earlier colleague in 1943. As shown in table 6.1, the average age has risen from 45.6 in 1943 to 51.1 in 1972. Some observers see this as a sign that electoral and political processes are producing a more mature and stable elite (Hudson 1968:240; Messarra 1974:247), a feature that compares favorably with the age profile of U.S. Senators and British members of Parliament, though it is considerably

Table 6.1
Age Distribution of Deputies in Nine Lebanese Parliaments
(As percentage of all deputies)

					Parliament				
Age Group	1943	1947	1951	1953	1957	1960	1964	1968	1972
25–30	7	7	5	5	1	1	—	1	3
31–35	11	6	10	6	6	6	8	6	5
36–40	13	16	13	18	14	14	12	11	9
41–50	31	38	48	43	52	49	30	30	32
51–60	33	27	17	14	15	26	39	38	33
Over 60	5	6	7	14	12	4	11	14	18
Total	100	100	100	100	100	100	100	100	100
Average Age	45.6	46	45.1	46	47	48.4	49.3	50.5	51.1

older than elites in revolutionary and unstable political regimes such as those of Syria and Libya (Winder 1962).

In the light of such evidence, it is rather surprising to find occasional reference being made to the "youthful character" of the Lebanese Chamber (Landau 1961: 131; Zuwiyya 1972:95). One writer, in particular, after comparing the age composition of the 1964 and 1968 Chambers, concludes: "Clearly, the elections of 1968 marked a turning point in what appears to be a quickening shift of power, from the traditional older elites to a more youthful leadership by modern politicians" (Zuwiyya 1972:95). No such quickening shift of power has taken place. In fact the trend is unmistakably in the opposite direction.

The progressive maturity or aging of Lebanon's parliamentarians becomes more apparent when one examines changing trends in three major age groups. While 31 percent of the 1943 Deputies belonged to a younger generation (i.e., between 25–40), the proportion declined to 17 percent in 1972. Conversely, the proportion of older Deputies increased from 38 to 51 percent over the same thirty-year period. It is instructive to observe that the most appreciable increase occurred among those over sixty years old. Their share of seats in the Parliament increased from 5 to 18 percent (see table 6.2).

What might have given this misleading impression regarding the alleged youthfulness of the parliamentarians is the tendency of the average Deputy to begin his parliamentary career at the relatively early age of forty. As shown in table 6.3, nearly one-third of the Deputies in the

Table 6.2
Trend in Age Groups of Lebanese Deputies
(As percentage of all deputies)

	1943	1947	1951	1953	1957	1960	1964	1968	1972
Young (25–40)	31	29	28	29	21	21	20	18	17
Middle (41–50)	31	38	48	43	52	49	30	30	32
Old (51 and above)	38	33	24	28	27	30	50	52	51
Total	100	100	100	100	100	100	100	100	100

current Chamber first entered the Parliament when they were less than thirty-five years old. In a political culture that venerates old age and pays deference to elders, this may seem, at first glance, surprising. A closer look, however, at the manner in which younger Deputies seek entry into the Parliament prompts us not to attach too much significance to this phenomenon.

Virtually all fourteen Deputies who had an early initiation into politics—Sabri Hamadeh (23), Kamel al-Asʿad (24), Magid Arslan (25), Joseph Skaff (25), Kamal Junblat (26), Talal Mirʾabi (27), Zahir al-Khatib (28), Salim Dawoud (28), Suleiman al-Ali (28), Rashid Karami (30), Antoine Frangieh (30), Amin Gemayel (30)—are descendants of feudal or notable families or those who "inherited" their Parliamentary seat from a close relative. They also all represent traditional political communities where primordial ties and personal allegiances sustain the political loyalties and motivations of the electorate. The only notable exception is Najah Wakim (26), who, as we shall see, won one of the Greek Orthodox seats in Beirut by receiving the votes of a religious community other than the one he represents. Given such evidence, we certainly cannot interpret this "youthfulness" as one writer has inferred (Zuwiyya 1972:95), as a "clear sign of systematic evolution away from traditionalism and towards

Table 6.3
Age at Which 1972 Deputies Began Their Parliamentary Careers
Age Groups

	25–30	31–35	36–40	41–50	51–60	Over 60	Total
Number of Deputies	14	17	20	31	14	3	99

modernity." Likewise, the fact that 84 percent of the Deputies were born in post-Ottoman times,[2] in of itself, is not very significant given the traditional loyalties that continue to underlie much of their behavior and political orientations. Even the few who are products of post-Mandate times seem intensely bound by such traditional commitments.

Finally, the advanced age or maturity of the Deputies becomes more pronounced given the relative youthfulness of the Lebanese population in general. Since 53.7 percent of the population are under nineteen years of age (Courbage and Fargue 1973:52), the generational gap between the elite and the masses they are supposed to represent is quite striking and should have considerable implications for the political alienation of youth.

Level of Education

The exclusive character of the parliamentary elite is quite visible in its relatively high educational accomplishments. In comparative terms, particularly if one considers the trend in the direction of increasing university and professional education, then the general educational profile of the Lebanese Deputy is quite impressive. With 73 percent of the current Deputies (Messarra 1974:261; Harik 1972:28) holding university degrees, their educational level is considerably higher than the average adult Lebanese citizen. This is expected since the political elites of newly developing countries are normally better educated than the people they represent. But the Lebanese Deputy is also better educated than other modernizing elites in Lebanese society, such as entrepreneurs, industrialists, and labor union leaders (See Sayigh 1962; Khalaf 1963; Khalaf 1967). Even a highly educated university community like Ras Beirut, perhaps one of the most literate communities in Lebanon and the Arab world, where 47.5 percent of household heads are university graduates, is still below the educational level of the Deputies (Khalaf and Kongstad 1973:74–76).

The high literacy of the Deputies, as an earned and achieved attribute, becomes more pronounced when it is considered that many of them are "heirs" of political families and could have, instead, relied on some other ascribed traditional quality to reinforce their political career. Only 25 percent of the 1960 Deputies, for example, reported that their fathers had attained the equivalence of a university education (Gebara 1964:76). The proportion of university graduates in the parliament has been persis-

Table 6.4
Type and Place of Education

Type of Education[a]		University attended[b]	
Law	41	Saint Joseph University	33
Medicine	10	American University of	
		Beirut	11
Engineering	4	Other foreign universities	18
Pharmacy	1	European 9	
Social sciences	5	Arab 4	
Liberal arts	3	United States 1	
Secondary	35	Other 4	
Total	99	Secondary	37
		Total	99

SOURCE: Messarra 1974:260–64.
[a] Based on averages of past three chambers.
[b] For 1972 Chamber only.

tently increasing. While only 17 percent of the Deputies in the first Representative Council of 1922 had higher education, the number increased to 50 percent for the Parliaments of the 1940s, 55 percent for those of the 1950s, and 60 percent for the 1960s. Estimates for the current Chamber range from 68 to 73 percent (Messarra 1974:261; Harik 1972:28).

The type of education, both in terms of professional training and the universities or schools the Deputies attended, continues to reflect the well-entrenched bias in favor of legal and French education. More than 40 percent of the Deputies are graduates of law schools, and a significantly larger proportion, if one considers those who received their education in Europe or French-oriented secondary schools, are French educated. One-third of the Deputies alone are alumni of Saint Joseph University. This is perhaps the one homogeneous and persisting feature in the Deputies' background. Possibly in the future, graduates of less elitist universities—such as the Lebanese National or Arab universities—might begin to have more access to Lebanon's exclusive political club. For the time being, no trend in that direction is very visible.

Occupational Background

The occupational composition of the Parliament continues to reflect this intimate association between legal training and the political career of

the Deputies. There is more than just historical accident in this association. As we have seen, the social and political disturbances between 1840
and 1861 had eroded the political supremacy of feudal chieftains and
began gradually to introduce a new administrative aristocracy into the
political life of the country. With the declining influence of feudal families, lawyers, magistrates and government officials emerged as the closest
groups to the loci of power in society, and consequently many of them
were drawn into the movements of reform, independence and Arabism
that had consumed the intellectual resources of the emerging elite at the
time.

The abolition of feudalism by the Règlement Organique of 1861 undermined the security and social standing of feudal families and threatened to make a disgruntled class out of them. The Ottomans, accordingly, pursued the policy of absorbing such families into the new
administration. A civil-service appointment became the surest and most
prestigeous source of livelihood. And legal education, with its concomitant bureaucratic and administrative skills, was naturally the most relevant for such career mobility.

Considerations of this kind, plus, of course, the relative accessibility of
legal education, must no doubt account for the continuing popularity of
the legal profession. It is still largely considered by many political aspirants as a natural stepping stone for grooming a political career. It is the
one traditional source of political recruitment that continues to attract a
disproportionate number of Deputies.

It is quite apparent from table 6.5 that occupationally the parliamentary elite is far from stable and is characterized by significant shifts in its

Table 6.5
Occupational Composition, 1943–1972
(As percentage of all deputies)

					Parliament				
Occupation	1943	1947	1951	1953	1957	1960	1964	1968	1972[a]
Landlords	46.5	48.2	42.5	40.9	33.3	23.0	23.2	10	10
Lawyers	33.9	27.3	25.0	34.1	36.3	29.0	27.3	44	45
Businessmen	10.2	10.9	12.5	6.8	11.1	14.0	17.2	17	21
Professional	10.2	12.7	20.0	18.2	19.0	34.0	32.3	28	24
Total	100.0	100.0	100.0	100.0	99.7	100.0	100.0	99	100

SOURCE: Harik 1975:203.
[a] Updated by the author of this chapter.

Table 6.6
Distribution of Basic and Secondary Occupation, 1968 Parliament

	As a Basic Occupation	As a Secondary Occupation	Total	Percentage of Total
Landowning	10	18	28	17
Legal professions	44	—	44	27
Business	17	28	45	27
Other professions	28	20	48	29
Total	99	66	165	100

SOURCE: Harik 1975:205.

occupational composition. Consistent with the broader socioeconomic changes in Lebanon, the proportion of landlords has sharply declined from 46 percent in 1943 to 10 percent of the current Chamber. Conversely, the number of professionals has increased from 10 to 24 percent over the same period. Professionals—particularly doctors, engineers, and to a lesser extent intellectuals, journalists, and teachers—account for almost 30 percent of the four successive Chambers since 1960. The number of businessmen and entrepreneurs has also exhibited a moderate increase, particularly during the past three Chambers.

Since many of the Deputies hold multiple occupations, it is instructive, as Harik has done (1975:203–6), to distinguish between basic and secondary occupation on the basis of a Deputy's primary economic pursuit. For example, several of the Deputies are the heirs of large estates but are also practicing lawyers. Others are entrepreneurs and urban professionals who have acquired small or extensive areas of agricultural land.[3] Such a compounded computation of occupations is certainly a more realistic measure of the diversity and trend in occupational composition. It also reveals a slightly different profile than the simple occupational distribution. For example, if multiple occupations are considered, lawyers, businessmen and professionals become almost equally represented in the Parliament. In fact, the professional character of the Deputies becomes a bit more pronounced. Altogether, law, business, and professions are the chief occupational bases from which Deputies are recruited in Lebanon.

Michael Hudson (1968:244) noted some regional and religious differentiation in the occupational composition of the Parliament. Interestingly, Beirut and Mount Lebanon appear to exhibit a greater degree of consistency in the occupational affiliation, while the other predominantly rural regions have been characterized by more striking occupational changes. For example, the increase in the number of professionals has been greater in the hinterland. The same is true of the decline in landlords. There are also notable occupational differences between Christian and the non-Christian Deputies. While the rate of increase of professional Deputies is roughly the same, the proportion of non-Christian landlords has been declining faster. Conversely, the percentage of non-Christian Deputies recruited from legal professions has been increasing faster (Hudson 1968:244–45).

Significantly, the crisis of 1958 makes a sort of watershed in changing the occupational composition of the Parliament. The shift in the direction of greater professionalization of the political elite was most apparent then. The incidence of professionals leaped from 19 percent in 1957 to 34 percent in 1960. It is interesting to speculate whether the protracted crisis of 1975–1986 could not produce, slight as it might be, yet another shift in the direction of the "proletarianization" of the elite. It is doubtful, however, whether this gradual process of broadening the occupational base from which Deputies have been recruited will become more accessible to laborers, peasants, small businessmen, school teachers, and other such groups that have thus far been excluded from political representation.

Elite Circulation

How exclusive or stable is Lebanon's parliamentary elite? If we perceive the "circulation of elites" statistically—i.e., in terms of the growing incidence of new entrants and the changing socioeconomic composition of the Deputies, then the parliamentary elite gives a clear impression that it is neither stable nor exclusive. Pareto's concept, after all, draws attention to the fact that this process of replacement—by virtue of the natural process of human attrition and replenishment—is bound to occur. Furthermore, Lebanon, particularly after World War II, has experienced sufficient socioeconomic mobility to allow individuals with relatively modest social origins to join the ranks of the powerful and influencial. In this sense the process of elite recruitment is fairly open and has been significantly broadened. But if one probes into the nature of this process—who are the new entrants, and how are they recruited—and explores further certain dimensions of their political behavior, than the extent of this circulation and its impact on the orientations, commitments and political styles of the new recruits must be qualified.

The turnover of Deputies in the nine successive Parliaments since Independence, by almost any comparative standard, is very high. If one adopts a specific measure of elite circulation—i.e., in terms of the incidence of new entrants appearing in the Parliament for the first time—the Parliament is certainly characterized by an impressive degree of incessant change and fluctuation in its personnel. Such a new-entry rate of 40.6 percent[4] for all nine Parliaments is considerably higher than comparable rates observed in some Western democracies. (See Froman 1967:170; Ross 1949:107; Matthews 1960:240.)

Such deceptively high rates of elite circulation could, it may be argued, reflect changes in electoral laws that have on several occasions increased the number of seats in the Parliament. For example, the highest turnover rates in newcomers occurred in the Chambers of 1951 and 1960, each of which was considerably enlarged over preceding Chambers. The 1951 Chamber was increased by twenty-two seats, and the 1960 by thirty-three. A more realistic measure would be the past four Chambers (1960–1972), when the number of Deputies was stabilized at ninety-nine. The new-entry rate over this period is 37 percent compared to 43 percent for the preceding five Chambers (1943–1957). Thus, the high turnover tendency is confirmed regardless of the fluctuating size of the Parliament.

Elite circulation is still considerably higher if one broadens the definition of turnover to include newly reelected Deputies or those with previous but interrupted parliamentary experience. In such instances the general turnover rate adds up to 57.8 percent for the first five Chambers and is slightly lower—54.7 percent—for those between 1960 and 1972.

Such numerical measures of elite circulation, impressive as they may be, become meaningful only if one probes into the background of the new entrants, particularly their kinship ties, and the process by which

Table 6.7
Elite Circulation in Nine Lebanese Parliaments

	1943	1947	1951	1953	1957	1960	1964	1968	1972
General turnover	65.4	52.7	62.3	54.5	54.5	71.7	44.4	49.4	53.5
Newcomers	54.5	45.4	54.5	27.3	36.4	51.5	28.3	28.3	39.4
Total Deputies	55	55	77	44	66	99	99	99	99

Table 6.8
New Entrants with Family History of Parliamentary Representation

	1943	1947	1951	1953	1957	1960	1964	1968	1972
Number	14	10	22	9	7	10	18	14	22
Percentage	46.6	40	52.4	75	29.6	19.6	64.3	50	56.4

they are normally coopted or recruited by other political veterans. As shown in table 6.8, 48 percent of all new entrants are, in fact, descendants of families with a history of parliamentary representation.

The incidence of such family succession is even higher—56 percent— for the last three Chambers. It is only the Chambers of 1957 and 1960 that experienced a relatively lower degree of family succession. It is instructive to find out what happens to such Deputies, particularly the newcomers to the 1960 Chamber which, as we have seen, is also marked by the highest incidence of turnover rates. Thirteen Deputies (i.e., 56 percent) of the new entrants to the 1957 Chamber and 15 (30 percent) of those to the 1960 served only one term. This is a relatively high casualty figure and does demonstrate, as we shall see, the continuing relevance of kinship ties in political succession. A closer examination of the type of new Deputy who demonstrates staying power beyond one or two terms confirms this tendency. A considerable number of such new entrants are either heirs of notable political families or candidates with little personal political support but who secure a seat on the coattails, so to speak, of a traditional political *za⁽im* or one of the *aqtab*. The patrons, in short, both the *aqtab* and lesser *zu⁽ama* rarely change. It is the clients that experience the turnover.

Kinship Ties and Political Succession

The socioeconomic transformations Lebanon has been undergoing have broadened, as we have seen, political recruitment and hastened the process of elite circulation. Political power and influence, which was once the exclusive preserve of the traditional feudal aristocracy and landed gentry, is being gradually transferred to a more literate, economically active, and occupationally mobile group. Wider political participation, party slogans, and popular ideological movements have also politicized a growing segment of the population and have, on occasion, introduced individuals with more plebian social origins into the political system. The political dominance of notable and privileged families, however, has not been seriously challenged. Family ties and kinship networks continue to be viable sources of political socialization and tutelage. More important, they continue to be—all other evidence to the contrary—effective avenues for political power and perpetuation of leadership.[5]

At more than one instance in the preceding chapters, I have suggested, and perhaps in an exaggerated manner, that the whole political history of Lebanon may be viewed as the history of a handful of leading families competing to reaffirm their name, power, and prestige in their respective communities. An analysis of the extent of kinship ties among parliamentarians and the persisting impact of the family in political succession and recruitment clearly reconfirms such an inference. One, in fact, is prompted to argue that a comparatively small number of prominent families continues to exert almost monopolistic control over the political process in the country.

Over the entire span of fifty years of parliamentary life (1920–72), 425 Deputies belonging to 245 families have occupied a total of 965 seats in 16 Assemblies.[6] Deputies are considered to belong to the same family if they are characterized by close kinship ties and carry the same name. For example, Deputies with a surname of al-Khuri—one of the most numerous families in the Parliament—are not all descendants of the same lineage. Khalil of Aley, Ilyas of Babda, Shahid of Jbeil, and Rashid of Zahrani are all unrelated Khuris who occupied seats in the 1964 Chamber. The same is true of the Beydoun, al-Husayni, and Shihab families, to mention a few. Care was taken to keep such distinctions in mind in identifying family units. If distant relatives and those related through intermarriage were to be included then the estimate would certainly not exceed two hundred families.[7]

It is revealing that only 129 Deputies (28 percent) of all parliamentary representatives are unrelated to other parliamentarians. The remainder, with the exception of approximately 10 percent of the earlier pre-Independence cases whose family ties could not be ascertained, bear some close or distant relation to other Deputies. As shown in Table 6.9, 45 percent of all parliamentarians can be considered closely related, through direct kinship descent or marriage, to other colleagues in the Chamber. Another 17 percent might be considered distant relatives. Altogether, in other words, 62 percent of the entire universe of Deputies have some kinship attachments to other parliamentary families.

That there are oligarchic or "dynastic" tendencies is also apparent in

Table 6.9
Kinship Ties among 425 Parliamentarians

Kinship Ties	Number	Percentage
Fathers[a]	36	9
Sons[b]	41	10
Brothers	33	7
Cousins	37	8
Nephews	12	3
Uncles	19	4
Brothers-in-law	16	4
Distant relatives	76	17
Unrelated	129	28
Not determined	44	10
Total	443	100

SOURCE: Messarra 1974:201.
[a] Includes two grandparents; Qabalan Frangieh and Ahmad al-Khatib.
[b] Includes two grandchildren; Antoine Frangieh and Zahir al-Khatib.

the disproportionate share of parliamentary seats a few of the prominent families have enjoyed. Table 6.10 identifies the year each of those families were initiated into politics, the number of assemblies they served in and the parliamentary seats they occupied. Altogether, not more than twenty-six families have monopolized 35 percent of all parliamentary seats since 1920. What this means in more concrete terms is that 10 percent of the parliamentary families have produced nearly one-fourth of the Deputies and occupied more than one-third of all available seats.

A few other striking features of family succession are worth noting. Once initiated into political life, almost all the families have virtually had uninterrupted tenure in all successive Chambers. With the exception of one family (Gemayel), which entered the Parliament in 1960, the majority had initiated their political career in the 1920s. This is quite telling, considering the prominent and decisive role the Gemayels, Pierre and his two sons Amin and Bashir, came to play in the political life of the country during the past two decades.

In some instances, it is one man (Sabri Hamadeh), or fathers and sons (Arslan, Edde, Karameh, Ghusn, Khazin, Asᶜad, Skaff, Khuri, Zayn, Zu-wayn, Gemayel), brothers (Zayn, Edde, Shahin, Skaff), cousins (the five Solhs, four Khazins, two Gemayels, two Sihnawis, and two Kayruzes), or brothers-in-law (Hamadeh-As'ad, Salam-Karami, Arslan-Junblat, Saf-iuddin-Arab) who perpetuate family succession. In two particular instances—Frangieh and Khatib—three successive generations of grand-

Table 6.10
Prominent Parliamentary Families (1920–1972)

Family	Year of Initiation	No. of Deputies	No. of Seats	No. of Chambers
Arslan	1922	4	19	15
Zayn	1920	5	18	13
Fadl	1922	4	17	10
Husayni	1922	4	17	14
Khazin	1920	6	16	15
As'ad	1925	4	16	12
'Usayran	1922	3	15	13
Haydar	1920	3	15	13
Edde	1922	3	15	13
Hamadeh	1925	1	14	14
Junblat	1920	3	14	13
al-Solh	1943	5	14	7
al-Khuri	1925	5	13	12
Skaff	1925	4	13	11
Frangieh	1929	4	13	12
Ghusn	1920	2	12	12
Salem	1925	3	11	10
Qaz'oun	1922	3	11	11
Lahhoud	1943	5	11	8
al-Khatib	1937	5	10	8
Beydoun	1937	7	10	7
Zuwayn	1925	2	9	9
Karami	1937	3	9	9
Gemayel	1960	3	9	4
Harawi	1943	5	9	8
Chamoun	1934	2	9	8
Totals		98	339	

fathers, fathers, and sons have already ensured the continuity of their family mandate in Parliament. This is rather remarkable given the comparative recency of Lebanon's experience with parliamentary life.

The staying power of the family is particularly demonstrated during by-elections. In several instances when a parliamentary seat is vacated in mid term, the Deputy is succeeded by a son, if he has an apparent successor, or a relative. Magid Arslan, Kamel al-As'ad, Antoine Frangieh, Zahir al-Khatib, Bahij al-Fadl, Maurice Zuwayn, Myrna Bustani, Abdal-latif al-Zayn, Amin Gemayel, Philip Taqla—to mention a few—have all inherited their seats from a father, brother, or uncle.

Because no general parliamentary elections have been held since 1972, such familial succession often takes place outside the official or constitutional political process. In typical patrimonial and feudal fashion, sons—their qualifications notwithstanding—are bequeathed their fathers' political "estates." Given the resigned and unchallenged attitudes that sustain the survival of this tradition, the succession often assumes all the attributes of an endowed estate in the very strict meaning of the term. At least three recent occasions attests to such survival.

When Sabri Hamadeh, the veteran politician and feudal chieftain who had been reelected to all fourteen successive Chambers since 1925, passed away in January 1976, his constituency in Hermel-Ba'alback, in a traditional but dramatic gesture, vowed its allegiance to his 30-year-old son, Majed.

Walid Junblat was also the heir apparent to his father's momentous political heritage. Soon after his father's assassination in March 1977, he stepped into his role, first reluctantly and then much more assertively and convincingly. Like his father, he is now not only the leader of the Junblati faction of the Druze community and the head of the Progressive Socialist Party and the Nationalist Front, he is also emerging as the undisputed spokesman of the entire Druze community. Because of the role he played in the mountain war during the summer of 1983 and the political coalition (the Liberation Front) he formed with Suleiman Frangieh and Rashid Karameh in opposition to some of the policies of Amin Gemayel's regime, he is bound—unless his political fortunes are eclipsed by some unforeseen event—to assume a decisive role in the political future of the country.

Feysal Arslan, in many respects less promising than Hamadeh and Junblat, likewise stood uncontested in inheriting the political fiefdom of his phenomenal father—Amir Majid—upon his death in September 1983. In a ritualized but muted ceremony, and as the war raged on in other parts of the mountain, his investiture as the amir of the Yazbaki faction of the Druze community was observed.

Nearly all the other *aqtab,* with an eye on their imminent retirement, are making every effort to bequeath their political capital and influence to their children. Camille Chamoun, Saeb Salam, Suleiman Frangieh, and Pierre Gemayel have all, as was documented earlier, encouraged their sons to assume more visible public roles and relegated to them some of their official and unofficial responsibilities.

The above evidence is hopefully sufficient to confirm the continuity of kinship ties in political succession. In terms of both the number of seats

Table 6.11
Family Succession in Nine Lebanese Parliaments: Sons of Deputies

	1943	1947	1951	1953	1957	1960	1964	1968	1972
Sons of Deputies	6	4	13	11	12	12	23	21	13
Percentage of membership	10.9	7.3	16.9	25.0	18.2	12.1	23.2	21.2	13.1
Number of seats	55	55	77	44	66	99	99	99	99

they occupied and the successive assemblies they served in, it is clear that a disproportionately small number of families have been able to retain and extend their power positions. Expressed differently, at least a significantly larger number of families have demonstrated staying power in comparison to those whose political fortunes have suffered sudden setbacks. The political casualty rate among prominent families, in other words, is remarkably low. Only nine such families—Daouk, Beyhum, Sa'd, Thabet, Trad, Munthir, Nammur, Istfan, Abdel-Razzaq—who were prominent politically in the pre-Independence era have since lost or disinherited their positions.

What is even more striking is that this trend in kinship succession does not at all, contrary to what Harik (1975:210–11) suggests, evince any decline. If the nine successive Parliaments since Independence are any measure, both the incidence of sons of Deputies and descendants of parliamentary families have definitely persisted. In fact, over the past three Parliaments, the proportion of sons who have "inherited" their seats from their fathers is 19.2 percent compared to 10.9 percent in 1943. Nearly the same magnitude of change occurred among the Deputies who are descendants of families with a history of parliamentary representation.

Table 6.12
Family Succession in Nine Lebanese Parliaments:
Descendants of Parliamentary Families

	1943	1947	1951	1953	1957	1960	1964	1968	1972
Deputies from parliamentary families	23	27	40	26	33	35	50	48	44
Percentage of membership	41.8	49.1	51.9	59.1	50.0	35.3	50.5	48.5	44.4
Number of seats	55	55	77	44	66	99	99	99	99

The incidence of such family succession increased from 41.8 percent in 1943 to 47.8 percent over the past three Parliaments. The magnitude of such change, it may be argued, is not too significant. It is at least one indication of the survival of kinship ties and their continuing relevance for political recruitment.

Patterns of Political Behavior

Given the survival of kinship and communal loyalties, the persisting disjunction between the seemingly progressive background of the Deputies and their traditional political behavior becomes an inevitable phenomena. This is not meant as a categorical denial of the impact factors such as education, occupation, and age might have on the ideas and outlook of the parliamentary elite. Such background characteristics, under normal circumstances, certainly help determine what skills and experience a Deputy is likely to bring to the decision making process. They also might determine the interests he represents and is prone to promote once in office. The impact of such factors, however, are circumvented by other considerations that quite often override and dilute the presumably secular and rational interests of one's professional or occupational background. Primordial loyalties and personal allegiances are clearly more significant in determining a Deputy's stand or outlook with regard to a particular issue or event.[8]

Deputies in general, irrespective of their political affiliations or ideological commitments, continue to show greater concern for their constituencies than for national issues. In an opinion survey of seventy Deputies, more than half of the respondents showed strong local orientations and only one-third were nationally oriented (Harik 1975:214–15). Such localism is inevitable given the strong communal ties that attach the Deputy to his client groups in his political constituency. Except for rare instances, almost all the Deputies are born in the constituencies they represent and are consequently compelled to devote much of their time and attention to the petty and private interests of their clients.

Manifestations of this form of political localism are legion: the nonprogrammatic nature of electoral campaigns, the almost total absence of ideological platforms in national elections, the political styles, public fronts, and demeanors Deputies have to assume. It is also visible in the ritualistic concern politicians display for the ceremonial and social obligations of their communities. Even the veterans among them cannot afford not to be seen in funeral processions, weddings, receptions, or other such religious and social functions.

The electoral system sustains such localism and accounts, in part, for the survival and unchanging character of the *aqtab* and political patrons. It also accounts for the political subservience of the newer deputies to such *aqtab*. Much of the clientelistic character of the political process in general is, to a large extent, a reflection of the peculiarities of such a system. The distinct features and implications of the electoral system for the survival of clientelism have already been fully elaborated in chapter 4. It is sufficient to note here that the survival and extension of this form of political clientelism has, among other things, crippled the role of the legislature as a forum for national debate and eroded the powers of the state. Like other highly personalized political cultures, political processes in Lebanon take place largely in informal cliques and through the pervasive networks of kinship and personal ties. Formal institutions are not the settings for political decision making and bargaining. The Chamber is certainly no exception. As the legislative body, it is a forum for public debate and the airing of views. It acts as a buffer for balancing power and mitigating tension. In this sense, it is more of a "deliberative" than a legislative assembly (Landau 1961:147). The most cardinal decisions, however, are taken elsewhere. For example, while constitutionally the Parliament is designated as having sole legislative powers, on repeated major occasions it has granted such powers to the executive. And cabinets, once empowered, do in fact promulgate decrees of a fundamental nature (reorganization of bureaucracy, new tax laws, a purge of civil service etc.) which are too controversial to be handled by an open forum such as the Parliament (Crow 1970:296–97).

Much of the behavior of the Deputies within the Parliament—particularly voting on bills, casting of ballots during sessions devoted to the election of the President of the Republic, Speaker of the House, or parliamentary committees—is conducted in such a manner as to confirm promises and concessions made outside the Parliament. In casting their votes, for example, Deputies resort to the ingenious but devious practice known as "election keys" by which they enter the name of their candidate in a specific prearranged manner to confirm their predetermined commitments. The implications of such a practice for limiting the Deputies' freedom and deepening their political subservience are self-evident. The Parliament, however, passed a special decree in 1982 forbidding such a practice. It was effectively observed for the first time during the presidential elections of Bashir and Amin Gemayel in August and September of 1982. All deputies cast their ballots without any prefixes, titles, or clues that might reveal the identity of the balloter.

The regular sessions of the Parliament, though frequent, are drained by much formalistic and ritualized behavior, a high degree of absenteeism, and exchange of personal invective, so that the time during which the Chamber is truly active in the course of a year is rather limited (Crow 1970:288).

The most serious indictment against the Parliament is its impotence in times of crisis. During every major crisis the country has faced so far, the Parliament has been virtually crippled.[9] Political initiative reverts back to the real actors in the political system: clerics; communal leaders, a handful of *aqtab*, prominent bankers and businessmen, and as of late, the various spokesmen of Palestinian resistance groups, private militias, and some of the newly politicized "counter-elite" who are excluded from pratication in the formal political system. Even the Deputies among them cease to act as parliamentarians and assume their roles as defenders of the particular interests and privileges of their client groups or local communities.

The behavior of the Parliament during Lebanon's protracted civil war of 1975–86 was no exception. While the country was being besieged and beleaguered by endless rounds of violence, civil disorders, bitter sectarian rivalry, sedition, and total anarchy, the Parliament—particularly in the early stages of the conflict—could not even muster enough collective will, let alone a quorum, to convene and take appropriate measures to contain the crisis.[10] On the few occasions during the initial phases of the crisis that the Parliament was able to meet, two sessions stand out. The first session occurred after the dramatic putsch staged by Brigadier General al-Ahdab in which he proclaimed the "Corrective Movement" of March 11, 1976, and, among other things, demanded the resignation of the government and the President of the Republic and called on the Parliament to elect a new President within seven days. Frantically, the Parliament did produce a petition with seventy signatures requesting the resignation of the President. The second session occurred on April 11, 1976, when a majority of ninety Deputies made it to the makeshift Parliament premises[11] and voted a constitutional amendment permitting the President to resign six months prior to the expiration of his term.

Antoine Messarra (1983) provides further evidence to substantiate the diminished and inept role of the Parliament particularly in periods of crisis and national conflict. He surveys the performance of the Parliament in 1952, 1969, 1975–76, 1977, 1979, and 1980 to arrive at the self-evident conclusion that most of the decisive and crucial decisions were debated and resolved outside the Parliament. The sessions of the Parliament were, in most these instances, devoted to the study of nonconflictual problems and issues.

Concluding Remarks

It should have become clear by now that the survival of primordial allegiances and the nature of patronage account for much of the persisting discrepancy between the progressive background of the parliamentary elite and their clientelistic behavior. On nearly all the attributes underlying the socioeconomic characteristics of the Deputies, they are clearly distinguished from the rest of the society, and they do stand out as an elite. They are highly educated and enjoy elevated social origins and the acquired professional skills that go with high-status positions. While they might not be true descendants of Lebanon's feudal aristocracy, they certainly belong to notable and prominent families. More important, they are economically very active and occupationally mobile. In terms of their loyalties, however, and their supporting orientations and patterns of behavior, the Deputies do not depart much from the prevailing norms and expectations of the rest of the society.

Because of the survival of primordial loyalties, kinship, communal, and sectarian commitments supersede secular and ideological groups as agencies of political socialization or as avenues for political power and leadership. This is far from unusual in a pluralistic society marked by persistent disparities in status and opportunity and sustained by highly personalized networks of reciprocal obligations. Within such a context, the "middleman" (*wasit*) or the broker—one who provides crucial linkages between the center and the periphery and promises greater access to opportunity, needed services, and protection—emerges as the most prized and viable political actor. It is precisely for such reasons, it was argued in the preceding chapter, that patronage and clientelism have survived as the most distinctive features of the Lebanese political system.

The ubiquity of patronage reveals another attribute of the political elite that cannot be understood solely in terms of the qualitative superiority of its socioeconomic composition. More important, in other words, than elevated social origins are the patronage and manipulative skills to which the politicians have access for securing protection and privilege on behalf of their clients. In this sense the parliamentary elite, despite their varying backgrounds or political orientations, are all fundamentally alike. Their power and influence, as we have seen, rarely extends beyond their closely circumscribed communities. Likewise, their political assets are those typical of most patron-client ties—namely, reciprocal loyalties and obligations.

From this perspective the seemingly more liberal and emancipated political leaders have much in common with the *aqtab* they frequently admonish and deride. These younger aspirants for public leadership, with rare exceptions, all seek to establish their political base not by articulating a program or identifying critical issues or specific problems requiring reform but by building up a personal entourage of clients and followers. Much like the *aqtab,* the bulk of their time and efforts is devoted to interceding with public officials on behalf of their clients. Both the private interests of clients and the political careers of patrons are served by such a system of patronage. Clients, who normally lack the power, wealth, and connections to obtain favored treatment would be more than willing to pledge their allegiance in return for the benefits and private goals the patron can secure on their behalf. To the patron such devoted following is a priceless political capital and, in most instances, the only capital that can guarantee his tenure in office.

This, more than any other feature, accounts for the relatively small part played by Lebanese Deputies in formulating broad policy issues of national and civic significance. To launch and sustain one's political career on the basis of a clearly defined ideological program or platform of reform requires, among other things, continuous critical study and devotion to public issues and nagging societal problems. Such civic-minded concerns, if they are to be more than ad hoc and arbitrary pronouncements, necessitate some disregard of the personal demands and favors of clients. But politicians in Lebanon, as we have seen, rise or fall more on the size of their clientage and competence at dispensing personal favors rather than on their merit in articulating and coping with public issues and problems. To refuse favors is to risk losing votes, and ultimately diminish one's base of client support. Instances of this kind of failure are legion.

All earlier and more recent efforts directed at undermining the political power and economic base of the traditional *zuʿama,* as shown earlier, has so far accomplished very little in eroding the extensive patronage such leaders continue to enjoy among their clients. The protracted civil war of 1975–1986, by far the most violent and devastating Lebanon has ever experienced, has done little so far in way of preparing for any fundamental changes in the social and political structure of society. It remains yet to be seen, for example, whether the urgent appeals made during the early phases of the war for secularization, deconfessionalization, changes in the electoral law, democratic reforms of political institutions, and more equitable redistribution of power and privilege will in fact be realized in the near future. In the meantime, eleven years of bitter hostility, diffuse hatred and violence, fear, widespread distruction, chaos, and anarchy have only polarized the various factions, deepened the fragmentation of society, and retrenched the position of traditional leadership. Moreover, threats of partition, escalation of confessional violence, concern over Lebanon's sovereignty, and withdrawal of all foreign troops have only reawakened, as they have done at similar instances in the past, the same old soothing rhetoric and elusive appeals for confessional unity and harmony and an almost exclusive concern with the immediate problems and dislocations generated by the war.

Such concerns are no doubt vital and urgent, particularly since they involve interest in some of the fundamental issues of state sovereignty, legitimacy, reconstruction, and the more humanitarian day-to-day problems of the homeless and uprooted and the imminent needs of devastated and besieged communities. Legitimate as these concerns are, they have nonetheless deflected interest from some of the more basic and existential issues. Once again, the deeper social and historical sources of the crisis are either ignored or mystified, and politicians seem more concerned with squabbles over the honor and spoils of office. The established elite, in short, is reluctant to entertain or consider any change that might undermine the very system that sustains and reinforces its patronage.

The reawakening of primordial and communal loyalties has then contributed to the diminished role of the Parliament as a forum for national debate. Parliamentarians have become more conscious of their communal and confessional identities and consequently become more receptive to the local and particular interests of their parochial constituencies. This is unfortunate. At the very time when Deputies are called upon to transcend their local attachments and safeguard the threatened national sovereignty and public welfare, they become instead obsessively preoccupied with their communal interests. While paraparliamentary groupings assume more prominent and visible roles, coalitions and fronts within the Parliament are initiated and organized on purely confessional or regional grounds.

One inference that might be drawn from our discussion so far is that this anomalous disjunction between the rather impressive socioeconomic profile of the Deputies and their clientelistic behavior is, to a large extent, a reflection of the survival of patronage and other primordial allegiances. Patronage, then, is clearly not an unmixed blessing. While it continues to provide greater leverage and vital services and some measure of personal security and communal integration, it has done so, however, at the expense of diluting civic consciousness and national loyalties.

CHAPTER SEVEN

Family Firms and Industrial Development

THE RELATIONSHIP BETWEEN traditions and industrial development or economic growth has always been subject to some moot and controversial considerations. Ever since Max Weber made the distinction between rationality and tradition as the prime variable in differentiating technologically advanced economies from underdeveloped societies, this debate does not appear to be losing any of its polemical fervor. The prevailing view is that advanced societies are characterized by rational and universalistic forms of organization, whereas underdeveloped societies are more traditional and particularistic in nature.

Reflecting this underlying trend of thought, most of the relevant literature falls in one of two categories. First, and perhaps in a sizable portion of the literature, tradition is generally seen as a factor inimical to industrial growth. Second, particularly when traditions are distinguished from traditionalism as an ideology,[1] traditional norms or practices are treated more functionally as palliatives or stabilizing agents that may prove useful in the solution of current economic and industrial problems. In other words, although it can be argued that traditionalism may be incompatible with industrial growth, the same is not true of traditions.

Of the two positions, proponents of the former appear to state their case in more emphatic terms. Some, particularly economists, go to the extent of arguing that traditions in general are always adverse to industrial employment, and that a society must do away with such traditional practices and beliefs if any progress and development is to be attained.

Of all these traditional factors or agencies, the extended kinship system

This essay is a revised version of a paper published jointly with Emilie Shwayri in *Economic Development and Cultural Change* (October 1966), 15(1):59–69. Used by permission of the University of Chicago.

and its associated attitudes seem to be most widely decried by students of economic development. In fact, many failures and shortcomings of the industrial system are frequently attributed to the continuing dominance of the family firm or family-dominated enterprises. The so-called "patrimonial manager"[2] is often depicted as a person with an inevitable and almost built-in disposition for nepotistic and paternalistic inclinations. By virtue of his position and loyalty, he is also portrayed in the image of a security-minded conservative who resists change while insisting on retaining a vast amount of authority within his own hands. In short, it is argued that these and other derivative consequences of the extended kinship system render family firms incompatible with the logic of industrialization as a rational process.

It is the intention of this essay to support the contrary point of view: that which maintains that traditional norms in general and family firms in particular may exert a supportive rather than a subversive influence on industrial growth. This is particularly true in a society like Lebanon, which is in the throes of rapid industrialization and social change. Desirable as it may seem as a goal, industrial development remains a painful process because it entails a considerable degree of disruption and change in the socioeconomic institutions.

In such times of flux and uncertainty, one can find some refuge and security in certain traditional forms of social organization. Such refuge, as argued earlier, need not be interpreted as a fatalistic flight from the disquieting demands of a complex and competitive world, nor should it be taken as a fatuous gesture to glorify the sacred traditions of the past for their own sake. Rather, they are effective in coping with some urgent industrial problems. In the absence of other agencies, such as a powerful and organized labor movement and a more consistent policy of government control, family firms have performed some vital functions. Indeed, as they have been functioning in Lebanon, they do not appear to be incompatible with the demands of industrialization. Instead, they combine the virtues of the two worlds: some of the secure and tested traditions of the past along with the rational and secular requirements of a contemporary society. Insofar as they have been able to reconcile these two tendencies, they have remained adaptable and viable organizations. The history of Lebanon's industrial development, together with the results of the preliminary study summarized here, provide ample proof of this contention.

The central thesis, then, of this essay is plain and simple: given the scope and stage of industrialization in Lebanon, and some of its socio-cultural and institutional patterns, one could easily think of instances where family firms may have reinforcing rather than retarding effects on industrial development.

The Evidence

The bulk of the evidence for this paper is derived from an extensive case study of ten family firms. Apart from being the largest, both in terms of size and capital invested, the family firms selected are among the most important industries in Lebanon. They represent the following industrial establishments: food processing, textiles, tanning, leather articles, wooden and metal furniture, soap, paints and polishes, metal working, and water pumps. In order to assess the practices and attitudes of patrimonial managers with respect to the operation of their organizations, the survey explored the following areas: history of the firms, ideologies of top management, organizational structure, delegation of authority, personnel policies, and the performance of managerial functions such as planning, organization, staffing, directing, and controlling (for further details, see Shwayri 1964).

Our observations in this essay will be more limited in scope. They will be confined to some of the main charges made against family firms, particularly those reiterated by students of economic development who hold that patrimonial enterprises act as deterrents to industrialization. Four such charges will be discussed below.

Nepotism

Among the most frequent charges made against family firms is that of nepotism. The extended family's control of an enterprise, it is argued, enables less competent members of the family to hold managerial positions for which their training and ability would not otherwise qualify them. Family loyalty and obligations take precedence over other loyalties and obligations, with the result that kinship ties rather than competence and training constitute the principal avenue to key managerial positions. In short, it is maintained that family firms in general fail to conform to two vital requirements of industrialization as a rational process, namely, functional specificity and universalistic criteria (Levy 1952:431).

While it should be recognized that no management is completely free of nepotism, and that even the most professionally oriented organization builders may sometimes favor the persons they know over the ones who have the best education and experience, the fact remains that the charge of nepotism is made much more frequently against patrimonial than professional management. A number of studies about French, Italian, and Indian family enterprises lend support to such accusations. In India, for example, "the proprietorial element is a fundamental determinant of top executive management. It sponsors heredity in management at the highest level, and circumscribes the field recruitment to a small, essentially non-competitive group" (Myers 1959:141).

At first glance it would appear that Lebanese family firms constitute a particularly conducive area for nepotism to flourish. In fact, so much has been written about industrial and organizational inefficiency and its inextricable association with family nepotism, that one is led to believe that there is a special "cult" in Lebanon that condones inefficiency and sustains its growth. The argument usually runs as follows: since family loyalty is deeply rooted in Eastern behavior, and since the subordination of the individual to his family and his participation in larger social groupings on a family basis are still predominant characteristics of the culture, this naturally has had a great effect upon economic life. Economically speaking, the extended family is often regarded as the basic social unit. And since the average business unit is relatively small, industry is often regarded as a purely family affair.

The argument goes on to point out that this narrow conception of business as a family affair has led many employers to "view their firms in much the same way as they view their private house and estate. . . . The firm is the source of the family income and prestige, to be managed, inherited, or sold in the interests of the family alone" (Mills 1956:40). Moreover, the focal position that the family occupies in Lebanese culture and its unshaken internal loyalty is also seen to be reflected in the lack of any broader sense of social responsibility among many industrialists.

Plausible as these charges may appear, we found no evidence to warrant their support. True, the administration of the enterprises under study is entirely in the hands of the patrimonial group, and no employee possesses decision making power in the strict meaning of the term. But to hold this as prima facie evidence of nepotism and to associate this nepotism with inefficiency is an entirely different matter. A few considerations may be advanced here to support this contention.

First, there is a critical shortage in Lebanon of professional and managerial skills that qualify a person for positions of authority without ownership. In fact, the organizational elite and the supervisory talent required for industrialization are virtually absent. Such a shortage, particularly at the levels of middle management, has had far-reaching consequences on the country's capacity for disciplined and rational growth. Under such conditions, and in view of their training and experience, patrimonial managers should not perhaps be blamed for drawing upon their own resources for the needed talent and skills. Furthermore, they still harbor the conviction that "ownership creates a sense of responsibility." To them, such assertions are not trite platitudes employed to disguise their nepotistic inclinations. Rather, they reflect a genuine belief sustained by long experience that their competent employees who are also sparked by a sense of kinship loyalty seem to have a higher degree of involvement in the affairs of the enterprise.

Second, among the basic value-orientations of Lebanese society is the presupposition that the environment is hostile; that people outside one's family or group are generally antagonistic and may take advantage of one another at any time. The cultural persistence of this peculiar orientation has helped the perpetuation of in-group—out-group relationships. This, more than anything else, makes the outsider a suspect and has intensified rivalries and factions at all levels of the social structure. Under such circumstances, it is little wonder that patrimonial managers should be predisposed to avoid placing "outsiders" in key positions. In itself this preference for kin, then, should not be feared and decried. Indeed, it would be foolhardy to do so, particularly when the relatives happen to possess the needed skills and experience. The situation in Lebanon, incidentally, is not peculiar. In Brazil, key positions are also reserved for relatives "not only out of sentiment of family solidarity but . . . above all they can count on the loyalty of their own kin" (Siegel 1955:407).

Finally, Lebanese family firms have not as yet reached such a size as to render the employment of outsiders in managerial positions a question of real meaning. Typically, the members of the patrimonial group are in adequate number and can effectively share among themselves the responsibilities of managing the firm. Furthermore, they do recognize that the process of dividing responsibilities between themselves cannot continue indefinitely, and that as the firm grows beyond a certain point, the hiring of outsiders to fill managerial positions becomes a vital and inevitable requirement.

The foregoing remarks should, hopefully, restrain us from indulging in the tendency of overrating the dysfunctional consequences of nepotism all too often. No one denies that ascriptive and particularistic considerations may impose serious limitations on the effective functioning of industrial organizations, but nepotism as such need not always betray the rational and universalistic principles of utilizing productive resources. Indeed, in societies "where trained skills are scarce and the sons of the wealthy have much of the training, nepotism may be relatively costless" (Harbison and Myers 1959:70). Furthermore, particularly at this stage of Lebanon's industrialization, the family has not only proven to be a source of talent and faithful service, but also a rather handy source of initial capital for investment. Hagen might have as well been talking about Lebanon when he said: "Where one can neither trust a stranger or an acquaintance as a business associate, nor persuade him to lend one money, then the extended family may be a necessary source of capital and a necessary bond between business associates. Its abolition would not modernize the society; in the circumstances it would merely paralyze large-scale business relationships" (Hagen 1957:198).

Centralization of Authority

There are those who have been more alarmed by the extent to which family loyalty tends to limit the process of delegation of authority in industrial organizations, a concern that is closely associated with nepotism. Since the patrimonial manager is engrossed in the effort of remaining the master of his own house, he is often depicted as an autocratic despot who monopolizes and jealously guards a sizable amount of authority and decision making prerogatives. Furthermore, it is argued, he tends to think of this authority in terms of personal power rather than as functions inherent in an office. Given this conception of an enterprise as some sort of a private kingdom, any division of responsibility may not only undermine the sovereign authority of the patrimonial group but may also dilute the family's prestige.

Literature on the subject is replete with such overtones. The profile of the German *Unternehmer,* (Hartmann 1959:60) or his counterpart in Italy, France, and Belgium is cast almost in the same image (Harbison and Burgen 1954:18). In general, the patrimonial manager is seen as an uncompromising "pasha" who is nevertheless suspicious of his subordinates and who persistently complains that people in his organization lack initiative, imagination, or just plain common sense. He delegates too little, does too much, and thus has scarcely any time left for effective and creative management. As a consequence "this type of management is likely to be defensive, enervated, and static. It breathes only at the top, and when the top disappears, the organization either collapses or must be completely rebuilt" (Kerr et al., 1960:147).

Much has also been written about the consequences of such overcentralization of authority: the marked absence of precise job definitions and classifications; the organizational gaps between the few in command on top and the ranks of the lower echelons, particularly middle-management and first-line supervisors; and the almost extinction of the foreman as a managerial resource. The cumulative effect of all these, among others, is to discourage the growth and expansion of the enterprise. Opportunities for younger executives are limited, incentives are stifled, and initiative is drained.

That Lebanese industrialists in general should subscribe to many of these practices is no surprise to anyone. As long as authoritarianism and the presupposition of hostility remain persistent cultural themes, it is natural to expect all managers—patrimonial, salaried, or otherwise—to be inimical to delegation of authority in both theory and practice.[3] If this is so, family firms need not be singularly blamed for generating attitudes or condoning practices that are deeply rooted in the culture. That such attitudes and practices are not something inherent in, or peculiar to, family firms is also suggested by a preliminary comparison of the ten firms under study with a broader sample of Lebanese industrialists. It is true that both groups are not much predisposed to delegation of authority, but the patrimonial group did at least delegate and/or share part of their managerial responsibility with other members of the family.

Our argument thus far does not entirely absolve family firms from some of the charges frequently leveled against them. It can now be stretched a bit further. Accordingly, several reasons may be advanced that prompt us to maintain that centralization of authority in Lebanon is not as serious a hindrance to industrialization as some writers are inclined to argue.

As has been suggested earlier, authority in Lebanese family firms does not appear to be exclusively concentrated in the hands of one single individual but is shared by the members of the patrimonial group, which may involve at times anywhere between five to ten persons. Far from resembling the German *Unternehmer*, who is uncompromising in his insistence on undivided authority, the Lebanese patrimonial manager at least favors the "horizontal" sharing of authority at the top. Joint decisions are made when the issue is of a certain magnitude, and each department head is usually left on his own to handle the matters pertaining to the regular, day-to-day operations of his division.

Such a state of affairs is akin to that prevailing in Japan—another instance where centralization of authority has not apparently been dysfunctional. The Japanese enterprise, as Harbison (1959:255) has indicated, illustrates a rather unique mixture of highly centralized authoritarianism along with democratic-participative management. To a considerable extent, so does the Lebanese family firm. In one sense, major authority is concentrated at the top, and even the most routine decisions are often pushed up from below because of reluctance of subordinates to assume responsibility. In another, there is apt to be rather wide participation in decision making. Top executives (members of the patrimonial group) seldom take individual responsibility. They act only after thorough discussion and examination of alternatives by the group. Under such conditions, then, centralization of authority cannot be said to be of the "suffocating" variety.

It could also be noted that even though there is no vertical delegation of authority, subordinates are generally allowed to "speak out their minds" and encouraged to express their opinions on matters where their knowledge and experience may be appropriately put to use. Moreover, and contrary to what is frequently charged, Lebanese patrimonial managers appear to utilize the services of the foreman as a link between managers and workers. Instead of being demoted into the ranks of labor, he is correctly perceived as the "man in the middle."

Unlike the German *Unternehmer,* then, the Lebanese patrimonial manager does not believe that he is born to rule his enterprise and that his authority is based upon a kind of natural law or "calling" in the Weberian sense of the term. Rather, he justifies the legitimacy of his authority primarily on the basis of his functions in the organization, and to a lesser extent by virtue of his ownership or property rights. Firmly believing that property creates a sense of responsibility, he may still sustain some skepticism about the earnestness and motivation of salaried employees. But such attitudes have not been uncommon in the early stages of industrialization of even the most developed economies, and there is no reason to believe why they should act as serious deterrents to industrial growth in Lebanon. With time, and as the inevitable process of secularism takes more root in the society, patrimonial managers are likely to acquire more rational theories of motivation and consequently modify their present attitudes toward delegation of authority.

Finally, the charge that centralization of authority hinders the growth of an enterprise must also be qualified. The Lebanese patrimonial manager is more than eager to expand his business, provided market conditions are favorable. In fact, he has fared quite well. In all ten firms, the number of employees has increased considerably since their establishment. More important, perhaps, he has also displayed some adaptive and innovating qualities that have rendered his enterprise dynamic and viable.

Paternalism

Another traditional feature often commented upon when discussing industrial growth in Lebanon has been the persistence of relatively small, tightly controlled enterprises and the survival of a good deal of paternalism in employer-employee relationships. It is not within our scope here to trace the historical or cultural foundation of such a phenomenon. Suffice it to note that paternalism in industry has its roots in the feudalistic tradition where the employer expresses his responsibility toward the worker by providing him with the desired welfare services and social benefits. In return, the worker expresses his obligation by being loyal and productive. In short, the image of the "industrial pater" takes the place of the head of the family, tribe, or communal primary group in preindustrial society.

Of all forms of managerial organization, patrimonial management is more inclined to exhibit many of the paternalistic features. To some extent, "the employer's attitude to his workers is one of superiority, a legacy of the feudal system which still persists, in spirit if not in form, in most Arab countries, including parts of Lebanon" (Mills 1956:10). The predominance of paternalistic management, it is argued, is simply an extension of this master-serf mentality.

Such relics of the feudal tradition are certainly not peculiar to Lebanon. The early stages of most industrializing societies are usually marked by socioeconomic conditions that are congenial for the survival of paternalistic attitudes. In Italy, for example, where "the individual firm, owned and operated by a single family group, is still the prevailing pattern," paternalism is the dominant managerial philosophy. It also survives in India, where "the top management of private enterprises is essentially patrimonial" (Ferrarotti 1959:235). There are many examples of "benevolent paternalism" based on an apparent willingness of the employee to accept a subordinate status and of the employer to play the role of the wise father. In Germany paternalism has almost become institutionalized. The so-called "Social Department"—which is a subunit of the personnel office or a separate department by itself, and which is concerned with providing a multitude of employee services, including housing projects, preventive health programs, etc. is a traditional device of patriarchal companies (Hartmann 1959:97).

In Lebanon paternalism has taken a slightly different form. Outwardly, it is not manifested by a profusion of social services. Neither has it become institutionalized in the creation of special "Social Departments." Nevertheless, a good deal of employer-employee relationships are still characterized by a quasi-familial paternalism patterned after the master-serf mentality. The patrimonial groups usually maintain personal relationships with their employees, know their names and their families, and rely upon such relationships to ensure the discipline and work performance required in the factory.

The survival of such paternalism, it is often charged, has posed many obstacles in the face of industrial development. Among other things, it has restricted mobility and incentives and furthered the growth of apathy by promoting timidity and a lack of venturesomeness among subordinates. It is further argued that, by obligating workers to reciprocate management's paternal responsibility, industrialists can easily manipulate the docile and faithful workers for their own ends. Finally, this reciprocal obligation has been also held responsible for retarding the growth of an effective and aggressive labor movement.

That these features have been, in some form or other, a liability to the industrial system in Lebanon is not to be questioned. What is to be questioned is the charge that family firms should bear the guilt for generating such impediments. It is evident, for example, that the timidity of the work force and the weakness of the labor movement reflect some underlying socioeconomic conditions that have little or no bearing on the nature of patrimonial management. The persistent surplus in the labor supply with which Lebanese industry has been faced accounts for a good deal of the prevailing apathy and the weak bargaining position of labor. The paternalism of the employer may in fact be a reaction to, and not a cause of, such conditions.

Indeed, an industrialist sparked by a spirit of paternalism may, for whatever motive, offer his workers certain welfare benefits and social services that other agencies in society have so far failed to provide. With a minimum of government intervention in the industrial system, and with a weak and ineffective labor movement, and in the absence of collective bargaining and other means of labor negotiation, the paternalistic employer may be one of the few remaining agents who can still provide some of the benefits that the worker fails to derive elsewhere. In addition to such material benefits, paternalism "often serves to smooth the major dislocations which an industrial way of life forces on the newly recruited worker" (Kerr et al., 1960:150).

Such considerations are often overlooked by those who persist in decrying the evils of paternalism. Lebanon, at the turn of the century, had all the essential features of a feudal society. Its underlying social structure and economic and political systems were sustained by primordial ties and patron-client obligations. These traits, as we have seen, have evinced a large degree of continuity. Little wonder, then, that there is still a legacy of feudal attitudes that find expression around the workplace. As Amitai Etzioni (1958:35) observes, "The worker from the traditional society tends to accept paternalistic-authoritarian supervision as a natural extension of the father, teacher, patriarchal community and religious authority he experienced before." Brought up under strict paternal authority, Lebanese workers may not after all bitterly resent the paternalistic approach to which they are culturally attuned.

Naturally, this state of affairs cannot go on indefinitely. "As industrialization proceeds, and as the expectations of industrial workers rise, employers and managers are often forced to become less authoritarian and less paternalistic in dealing with their employees and tend to function as constitutional managers."[4] Management then, faced with an increasing pace of industrialization, cannot possibly sustain its paternalism. Various pressures, in the form of more militant labor organization or government labor legislation, may be brought to bear upon it. In highly industrialized societies, pressures such as these have been exerted upon employers and forced them to relinquish some of their authoritarian and paternalistic practices for a more constitutional approach. None of these pressures, however, have taken any substantial root in Lebanon. The country is still at too early a stage of industrialization for such forces to have gathered momentum.

In the absence of such pressures, the paternalistic employer in Lebanon does not appear to have become a ruthless despot. If nowhere else, this is at least evidenced in the relatively low incidence of industrial unrest and labor protest in these firms. It is pertinent to note that none of the ten family firms under study fell in the category of "conflict-prone industries" surveyed elsewhere. Judged by their record of labor disputes and grievances brought before the Conciliation Board, family firms are relatively more "conflict free" than the average industrial establishment in Lebanon (for further details see, Khalaf 1963). Rather than being resented as an intruder who meddles with the private lives of his employees, as has been perhaps the experience in some advanced societies, the paternalistic employer in Lebanon still plays the role of the benevolent provider.

Finally, it should also be recalled that this benevolent paternalistic employer is not of the feudal variety, the type who owns, controls, and operates an organization by virtue of the absolute authority of his family ties. Neither is he of the manipulative type, the one who affects a genuine paternal concern for his employees "to buy off loyalty or prevent disloyalty." Rather, he appears to be more akin to that brand of paternalism that Ferrarotti (1959) labels "democratic and participative." In other words, the enterprises are still predominantly family owned and family members may still hold the key positions, but they are subject, by and large, to rational and meritorious principles of control. Performance is slowly becoming the prevailing criterion for reward and promotion. Authority is no longer exclusively associated with property rights or ownership.

These considerations prompt us once again to suggest that paternalism, at least the way it has manifested itself in Lebanon, is not entirely dysfunctional. It has not violated the workers' sense of justice and equality in competitive opportunity. Neither has it betrayed some of the rational and universalistic principles of evaluating talent. Instead, it has offered some of the needed social and welfare benefits and served to soften the impact of some of the major dislocations associated with industrialization.

Conservatism

That conservatism should be considered a characteristic of patrimonial management is not surprising in the light of what has been said thus far. Family firms have been often charged with being guilty of predisposition toward preserving the familiar and resisting the new. The patrimonial manager is seen as a person motivated by the desire of assuring a regular income and protecting the family's status and prestige. He is the proto-type of the ritualist, the type who has an almost compulsive aversion to innovation and change. In short, he is depicted in the image of a "care-taker rather than a risk-taker" (Harbison and Burgess, 1954:19). Driven by an excessive prudence and an over-whelming concern with security, the patrimonial manager is constantly "playing it safe" and is haunted by the risk of "stretching his own neck out." The cumulative effect of such attitudes, among other things, is to create rigid and timid enterprises drained of any dynamic and venturesome attributes.

As in charges of nepotism, centralization of authority, and paternalism, students of economic development have had ample evidence, from both developing and advanced economies, to document such arguments. Charles Myers (1959a:148) for example, makes the following observation in his study of Indian management:

A prominent Bombay millowner explained the presence of a young man sitting at a nearby desk in his office in these terms: "This is my nephew, and he is learning the business just the way I did from his grandfather years ago. I sat at the desk he is at now, and I listened to everything the old man did, the people he met, and the problems he discussed with them. This is the way I learned the business, and that's the way he is learning it from me now."

To demonstrate the family firm's innate preference for security rather than expansion, David Landes (1957:336) describes the typical French family firm as that which places "inordinate stress on safety and security. It fears change and is unwilling to borrow for fear that the lender, whether individual or bank, will gain a foothold in the enterprise." Similarly, in the Chilean family firm, "traditional patterns have strengthened and le-gitimized tendencies to the habitual, to continuing with old methods, products, and customers, to remaining within the circular flow" (Myers 1959a:171).

From the evidence supplied by our case studies, an entirely different impression emerges. The Lebanese patrimonial manager does not appear to fit the mold of the security-ridden caretaker who resists innovation and conforms to the habitual and familiar. When asked, for example, what they conceive their major function to be, the respondents rated things like "following up the developments taking place in the West" and "studying market conditions" as the most important. "We must not only keep ourselves informed about the machines already existing in Europe and the techniques being used," said one of the respondents, "but we must also be aware of the new technical advances."

These are hardly timid responses. They indicate, rather, an inclination to search for improvements by keeping track of advances made abroad and examining local conditions to see whether they could be profitably applied by their firms. Furthermore, far from learning the business by sitting at the desk and listening to what his father says, the Lebanese patrimonial manager gets his training by traveling abroad. In fact, all ten respondents have traveled extensively within and outside the Arab world.

All in all, the patrimonial group displays a remarkable facility and readiness to adopt new ideas and practices. Indeed, in all fields but marketing, Lebanese family enterprises seem to be animated by the same propensity for adaptive innovation that played an important part in Japan's economic transformation from an agrarian to an industrial society. True, they display a striking timidity in facing the market, but such an attitude is far from being peculiar to patrimonial managers. Writing about Lebanese entrepreneurs, Yusif Sayigh (1962:87) observes: "It is indeed puzzling that a group of men that seem so active in trying to innovate in their production and organization should declare themselves largely unaggressive in their sales policies and practices."

Under the circumstances, such a nonaggressive approach to marketing should not be regarded as symptoms of conservatism and resigned attitudes. Rather, it stems from a realistic appraisal of the limited size of the internal market.

Concluding Remarks

The central aim of this essay has been to shed more light on the nature and direction of the relationship between traditions and industrial development. Largely, this effort has been in the form of demonstrating that some of the traditional norms and practices need not, as is often charged, be inimical to industrial growth. Indeed, the essay advanced the proposition that given some of the salient features of the industrial and sociocultural environment, family firms have exerted a positive effect on industrialization.

Compared to other developing societies, industrialization in Lebanon has been a relatively slow and gradual process. To a considerable extent, the sociocultural environment has been quite receptive to the changes or requirements of industrialization. As a consequence the traditional norms of the Lebanese culture have not been swept aside by industrialization. Instead, the culture has assimilated and reinforced a good part of the demands of industrialization as a rational process. It is for this reason perhaps that many of the managerial norms and practices that are rapidly becoming obsolete in advanced societies are still effective and functional in Lebanon.

That patrimonial managers should display some paradoxical combinations of attitudes and practices is to be expected given the nature and stage of industrialization in the country. To cite one instance, the group under study tended to exhibit, on the one hand, an apparent receptivity for adaptive innovation that denotes progressive and dynamic predispositions. On the other, their conception of managerial functions of control is inclined to be more conservative and authoritarian in character.

It is true that the limited nature of the case studies do not allow us to generalize. Further and more extensive research is needed before we can arrive at more emphatic assertions. The evidence presented thus far, however, tempts us to suggest that under certain socioeconomic conditions or at certain stages of industrial growth, the relationship between traditional norms and industrial growth may lead to mutually reinforcing tendencies.

CHAPTER EIGHT

Family Associations

F AMILY ASSOCIATIONS ARE perhaps unique to Lebanon. No other comparable institutional arrangement, as far as we could ascertain, exists elsewhere. As early as 1860, families in Lebanon started to employ kinship affiliations as the basis for the formation of formal organizations to attend to some of their unmet welfare and benevolent needs.

Initially, the Lebanese had little access to other forms of association. Primordial ties of fealty, kinship, and religion were the conventional avenues for reinforcing their threatened sense of security and solidarity and for securing some of their humanitarian and benevolent interests. Even when other more secular and rational forms of association became more accessible, the Lebanese continued, however, to use their family networks to establish voluntary organizations.

That such associations should be a predominant and persisting form of voluntary organization is not surprising given the survival of kinship sentiments and the continuing dominance of the family in virtually all dimensions of society and everyday life in Lebanon. What is rather unusual is the preponderance of such groupings despite the proliferation of other welfare and public voluntary associations.

Until the late sixties and early seventies, there were about five hundred such registered associations. According to officials in the Ministry of Interior, where all such licensed organized groups have to apply for legal recognition, their number continued to increase until the beginning of civil hostilities in 1975. By then, however, security conditions made it impossible to organize or establish such associations, let alone secure official certification to sanction their formal status and operation. Unfortunately, all records and registers have been either destroyed or ransacked during the war. Hence, it has not been possible to extend, in any con-

This essay is a revised version of a paper originally published in *Journal of Comparative Family Studies* (Autumn 1971), pp. 235–50. Used by permission.

crete manner, our exploration to cover the five-year interlude before the outbreak of civil hostilities in the country. The span of over a century, however, is sufficient for documenting the nature, magnitude, and role of family associations within the context of some of the distinctive features of Lebanese society.

It is essential, before the structural and functional dimensions of family associations are elucidated, to underline first a few conceptual considerations and some of the salient features of the kinship system in Lebanon that account for the emergence and survival of such unusual institutional arrangements.

Virtually all family systems, regardless of their diversity, undergo some decline under the impact of urbanization and industrialization. With or without a high degree of technological change and impersonal forms of association, urbanization is almost always accompanied by the dissociative processes of secularization, individuation, and sociocultural differentiation. The consequences and implications of such processes for the structural-functional aspects of the family and its psychic climate have been extensively surveyed.

That "urbanization exercises an incontestable influence upon nuclear family individualization" (Kooy 1963/164:22) is not disputed. There is little theoretical or empirical obscurity regarding either the factors leading to, or the consequences of, such a decline in kinship. What is still disputed, and remains relatively obscure, are some of the specific reactions to these underlying changes—particularly in a so-called kinship culture that begins to experience a certain loosening of family ties.

The central concern then of this essay is not so much with the correlates and consequences associated with the decline in kinship as with the particular responses to such a decline. The Lebanese case offers a rather unique example of how a kinship culture reacts to some of the disruptive forces that inevitably bring about a decline in the sense of kinship. Given the pervasiveness of familism, it is safe to assume that with urbanization and increasing secularism there has been a corresponding increasing need to reorganize the family by establishing formal associations or corporate kin groups. Such associations, then, not only reflect the decline in kinship, they are also significant manifestations of an attempt to mitigate this decline. They are a kind of "pseudo-gemeinschaft," as Robert Merton aptly suggests, attempting—perhaps vainly—to revive the traditional sense of kinship and communal bonds that insured group solidarity in traditional societies (Pappenheim 1959:68).

From one general aspect, the main problem of this essay is in part related to Tonnies' central concern with the nature and implications of the shift from gemeinschaft to gesellschaft forms of social organization. It should be recalled that although Tonnies recognized the dissociative consequences of such a trend, he did not lament the alleged virtues of gemeinschaft. To him, the process is inevitable and irreversible and consequently any attempt to restore the sense of gemeinschaft would be fraught with too many hazards. Such efforts could, at best, produce artificial and empty forms of only nostalgic significance. So instead of restoring gemeinschaft in its purer forms, Tonnies urged that we accept the transition to gesellschaft and try to achieve a higher form that could integrate the virtues of both (Pappenheim 1959:69). This is, in effect, what family associations in Lebanon attempt to accomplish. The very urge, after all, to form and join associations may be indicative of the isolation felt by individuals living in a world that is becoming increasingly impersonal and atomized. The fact, however, that the Lebanese continue to seek refuge in family associations is in itself significant in terms of the survival of kinship sentiments and their viability in providing the needed social, psychological, and economic reinforcements and supports. This is at least one indication that urbanization in Lebanon has not as yet created a depersonalized and atomized society. It may also be taken to mean that the directional trend from gemeinschaft to gesellschaft is not as irreversible a process as depicted by Tonnies and other subsequent writers.

From another, and perhaps more indirect respect, the main argument of this essay supplements the hypothesis that extended family relations need not be inconsistent with urban and industrial societies.[1] In this sense, it similarly questions Parson's (1949) assertion that the extended family is dysfunctional for contemporary society and that the isolated nuclear family is the only type that is functional for such a society. Instead it will be suggested that efforts to coalesce the family by creating formal kinship associations should not be treated as an irrational and nostalgic gesture. Rather, they may be a response to some unmet needs, and they continue to serve some meaningful, albeit symbolic, functions in Lebanon.

Finally, it will be argued that family associations have survived as viable agencies of social organization and social control because they combine some of the rational features of formal organizations with the needs for intimacy and identity inherent in primary relations. The former are essential for coping with uniform and universal situations; the latter for handling particular and idiosyncratic cases.

Pervasive Familism

If there ever has been a culture with an exclusive kinship orientation, Lebanon comes close to being such. Kinship has been, and is likely to remain, Lebanon's most solid and enduring social bond. The extended family, as we have seen, has a social and psychological reality that pervades virtually all aspects of society. There is hardly a dimension of one's life that is untouched by it. To a considerable extent, a person's status, his occupation, political behavior, personal values, and various events in his life cycle are largely defined by his kinship affiliation.

So intense and encompassing are kinship attachments that the average Lebanese has small appreciation for the solitary ego. The lone creature—derelictlike and unattached—is a rare phenomenon. He seeks and finds refuge and identity within close family circles. One's society begins and ends with his family; so much so that anyone outside the family tends to be regarded as though he is outside society. In Lebanon to be private quite often carries the connotation of being deprived.

Since familism as a value orientation permeates society and stamps all institutions with its mark, it is little wonder that ties of blood in themselves should become the basis for the formation of family associations. Inasmuch as the average Lebanese is inclined to recognize no society or community outside the family, he is naturally not predisposed to seek social support on a communitywide basis. Outside the relatively closed kinship networks, his ties are on the whole tenuous and amorphous.

To say that familism is pervasive is not to assert that there are no evidences of a decline in the sense of kinship. Urbanism in Lebanon, as no doubt elsewhere, has already left its dissociative impact on the family. Kinship has been growing less important in the total social organization of the society, and the family is beginning to lose some of its conventional functions. It is clearly no longer the exclusive agency of socialization it once was. Where it used to monopolize the life experience of an individual, many agencies and groups are now competing with the family in carrying the main burden of social control. Even where this competition of gaining access is not as intense as in other less kinship-oriented societies, the mass media has begun to expose the individual to alternative sources of satisfaction and new values. As a result, and particularly in the more urban and secular parts of Lebanon, adolescents are not as much under the direct surveillance of their families.

This is certainly not something peculiar to Lebanon. Other societies, at different stages of their development, must have gone through similar transformations. What is rather peculiar are some of the consequences and reactions to this inevitable transition and the survival of kinship units as relatively insular groups. Kinship relations, despite the emergence of other secular and specialized functional groupings, remain the most meaningful, and familistic norms the most important mechanisms of social control. The family is still the major security device in society. It is a most sobering palliative. It serves as a tranquilizer pill, a confessional stand, a safety valve, and a "security blanket" all put together.

Given the survival of a large measure of families, a fundamental question poses itself: What happens to a kinship culture when its basic unit of social organization (i.e., the family) begins to decline in social significance? To say the least, people begin to lose the emotional supports and restraints that an intimate group like the family provide. One may easily advance the hypothesis that the incidence of suicide, alcoholism, drug addition, and other mental and psychological disturbances is still relatively low in Lebanon because of the persistence of primordial attachments associated with family solidarity. All preliminary evidence thus far points out that family disorganization or the breakdown of primary group ties seems a crucial variable in accounting for prostitution, juvenile delinquency, vagrancy, and other symptoms of personal and social disorganization. In short, family disintegration is a predisposing, and not merely an incidental, factor in social disorganization (see Khalaf 1965:45–50).

Faced with such inevitable consequences, it is not too surprising that the Lebanese should respond in a protective and defensive manner. Typical perhaps of most kinship cultures, the Lebanese does not wish to be disarmed of his basic security device. In this sense he is bent, to borrow a trite metaphor, on eating his cake and having it too. He is eager to enjoy some of the liberal and material rewards of urbanization, but he is equally eager to ward off some of its unsettling consequences, particularly if they threaten to dilute the primordial bonds of kinship. He is understandably touchy about his kinship ties, because he is moved by little else. It is true that other nonkinship loyalties are beginning to attract the allegiance of the more secular segments of the society. Most such ties, however, particularly those of party, class, or profession, as we have seen, are still relatively weak and tenuous. They have not found deep roots in the social structure to displace the sentiments crystallized around kinship loyalties. The so-called crisis of identity in Lebanon is to a large measure the crisis of the family. Stripped of his kinship supports, the individual is sustained by little else. He is bare and helpless.

The point I am trying to make is that because of this pervasive familism, the scope and range of family activities often extend those functions universal to kinship systems. Family associations are not simply an expression of kinship sentiments. As will be shown, they discharge certain social and integrative functions that in other societies are handled by special nonkinship organizations.

Structural and Organization Features

Like any other formal organization in Lebanon, a family association cannot be legitimately recognized unless it has been licensed by the government. To become licensed, each family association prior to its establishment must submit a statement of its by-laws or constitution, along with its aims, functions, and objectives. For all such licensed associations, the year and place of their establishment, the names of elected officers, and a brief statement of their objectives are recorded in a special government register in the ministries of Interior and Social Affairs. The first such recorded association dates back to 1860, and since then their incidence has shown a persistent and steady increase. The records for November 1968 show a total of 477 such associations.[2]

It is of interest to note that this constitutes the largest number of any organized groups or voluntary associations of any kind in Lebanon. By comparison, there were, until the late sixties, 405 nongovernmental welfare agencies, 127 labor unions, and 85 employer associations.

By the sheer force of size, some of these associations bring together a compelling number of members. The president of the Atallah association, in their general assembly meeting in Zahle, August 1968, claimed a membership of fifteen thousand. Very few single associations in Lebanon, political, industrial, or otherwise, can boast of similar numbers. It should also be remarked that these family associations in no sense exhaust the scope and activities of kinship groups. A large measure of benevolent, welfare, and cooperative activities are no doubt discharged by family members outside the formal boundaries of organized associations.

What structural patterns mark the organizational features of family associations? Have the kinship and presumably nonrational sentiments they espouse obstructed the development of formal and impersonal expectations? Judged by their official by-laws and the specific prescriptions for the conduct of their operations, family associations appear not to depart significantly from any other formal association.

Except for some minor modifications, there is little variation in the organizational features and operational procedures of most of these family associations. Qualification for membership and holding office, duties of officers, frequency of general meetings, solicitation of funds, and the nature of sanctions stipulated all comply to a uniform and standardized pattern.

Since the underlying rationale of family associations is kinship solidarity, membership is naturally restricted to descendants of the same lineage. Carrying the same family name, however, is necessary but not sufficient to qualify one for membership. The individual must be related to the family through ancestral kin, particularly since many unrelated families in Lebanon may still bear the same family name. Tracing family geneology to a specific locale, town, or village of origin becomes imperative in several instances to establish or confirm the identity of a particular family. This is why the official title of some family associations carries the name of a particular village, town, or district. In other instances, families related through intermarriage may form a joint or collective association bearing all or some generic name. For example, the Shaheens, Madis, and Yassins have formed a joint association carrying the name of the three separate families. Another association—"The League of United Families"—is in fact, a union of six families related through intermarriage, namely: Shadeed, Salameh, Asmar, Hjeili, Hajj, and Zeidan of Zouk Musbih in Mount Lebanon. In such instances, membership is often restricted to the immediate kin and cannot extend beyond members of the same nuclear family. In the case of such associations, the constitution frequently specifies that patriarchal heads have the right of recommending relatives to membership if they fall within one of three categories: parents, sons and daughters, or brothers and sisters.

Age and sex also impose certain limitations on membership. Minimum age is eighteen, though in most cases a person cannot become an active member before twenty-one. Women, particularly among Muslim associations, are denied equal and effective rights of participation. They can only become dues-paying members. Christian associations allow more flexibility in this regard, and unmarried women are not denied the privilege of active membership. In both cases, however, when a woman changes her maiden name through an exogamous marriage, she forfeits her rights to membership.

Family loyalty is often implied as a prerequisite for membership. In some specific cases, an explicit family oath is required to ensure fidelity and kinship solidarity. With or without the rituals of an oath, all members are expected to manifest their kinship loyalty through deeds of benevolence or goodwill, otherwise the executive committee may reserve the right of denying them membership.

Finally, like any other formal association, payment of dues—no matter how nominal—is a prerequisite for membership. Fees vary from L£3 to L£25 ($1–$8) annually. In cases of proven financial need, this requirement is often waived. All associations, however, stipulate the payment of a fee before one attains eligibility for membership. Income from membership fees is the main source of revenue. Other sources are solicited through charitable donations and recreational activities during which lotteries and other such inducements are employed to encourage contributions. In some instances, the government regards family associations like any other welfare or voluntary agency and accordingly contributes to the financial support of the active among them. Among some Muslim associations, contributions in the form of *zakat*, particularly during the holy month of Ramadan, also forms a significant source of financial support. It is of interest to note that in the event an association is disbanded, its capital or financial assets are frequently bequeathed to religious and charitable institutions.

In their administrative structure, too, family associations do not diverge much from the features characterizing other formal and rational associations. The by-laws call for a general assembly comprised of all members, which meets at least once a year for purposes of electing an Executive Committee. The size of the Committee and its duration in office varies from one association to another. The number of executive officers ranges from four to twenty-five, while tenure in office varies from a minimum of six months to a maximum of five years. On the whole, the Executive Committee meets rather regularly, on an average of once a month. Special ad hoc committees may be appointed from time to time to resolve some pending familial problems. Expert advice from outside the ranks of the kinship group is often sought, but under no circumstances are such advisors admitted to membership. The Executive Committee may also appoint an honorary president who in many instances is an elderly or a religious figure. As in most other appointments, special consideration is given to age and religiosity, both of which add weight and prestige to the position. A member, for example, regardless of his special skills and competence, cannot be eligible for election before the age of thirty. In cases of a tie between two contestants, priority is given to the elder.

Since these kinship associations are a kind of pseudo-gemeinschaft group existing primarily to promote the welfare and solidarity of particular families, it is little wonder that their formal structure should also prescribe sanctions to protect the interests and integrity of the family. Penalties for unacceptable behavior, which range from warning to ostracism, are often enforced by special disciplinary committees. Minor offenses, such as the failure to pay dues or recurrent absenteeism from family meetings, may result in withdrawal of membership. Criminal acts or serious offenses that may stigmatize or taint a family's reputation result in complete ostracism and censure of the offender. Very often, if a member of a certain family has been implicated in a scandalous or public offense, the family association issues a prompt condemnation of the act in the form of a public statement absolving the family name and urging the authorities to inflict the severest penalty upon the offender.

Other measures of social control are also stipulated with respect to any type of deviant behavior inclined to damage or impair the image of the family. An individual, for example, who has been prosecuted or imprisoned for any offense loses membership in the association and is denied whatever assistance or pressure the family may exert on his behalf. Deviant activities like gambling, alcoholism, and theft are condemned, and members who are involved in them are first admonished and, if they do not reform, are ultimately ostracized from the family.

It is apparent from the preceding remarks that the structural features of family associations are a blend of rational and traditional elements. It could also be argued that the survival and viability of such associations are in fact a reflection of their ability to assimilate particular and universal expectations without much damage to both.

Another feature should also be noted: though family associations bear some resemblance to "corporate kin groups" observed in some nonliterate societies, they are nonetheless more elaborate and formally organized. As described by Radcliffe-Brown (1968:250) a kinship group may be spoken of as "corporate" when it possesses any one of the following characteristics: "if its members, or its adult male members, or a considerable portion of them, come together occasionally to carry out some collective action; if it has a chief or council who are regarded as acting as the representative of the group as a whole; if it possesses or controls property which is collective, as when a clan or lineage is a land-owning group."

As has been made clear, family associations fulfill all the above features. In one form or another, they serve as instruments of collective action. They also possess a representative council that acts on behalf of the whole group. Finally, though they may not have any claims over collective land-ownership, they still possess collective capital and financial assets amenable for investment. But they are also much more. In both their organizational features and professed functions, they go beyond the relatively amorphous and unstructured character of the corporate kin groups described by Radcliffe-Brown. As they have come to survive in Lebanon, family associations are more specific and formally organized. They are also multidimensional and more diffuse in their scope and activities.

Trends and Patterns of Family Associations

The incidence of family associations and the trends they display, along with their professed objectives, provide further evidence that they could be appropriately conceived as symptoms of, and reactions to, some of the dissociative forces inherent in urbanization and secularism. The ecological and religious variations in the functions they serve also bear some witness that family associations reflect and cope with some of the unmet needs of various groups and communities in Lebanon. This is all the more apparent particularly since the incidence of family associations continues to increase despite the proliferation of welfare agencies and other voluntary associations.

The first striking feature, as shown in table 8.1, is the steady and continuous increase in the incidence of family associations. From an average of less than one family association per year being formed between 1860–1919, the incidence has risen gradually to 18.5 in the sixties. In and of itself, the fact of persistent increase is meaningful. Contrary to what is often remarked, it does suggest that kinship associations are not undermined and finally swept away by industrialization (Nash 1960).

It is no sheer coincidence that the genesis of these associations dates back to the 1860s. To be exact, the first such recorded association was established in 1857.[3] No doubt, the widespread turmoil and civil strife

Table 8.1
Trends in Family Associations: Ecological Variations

	1860–1919	1920–1929	1930–1939	1940–1949	1950–1959	1960–1968	Date unknown	Total
Urban	23 (43.4)	25 (53.2)	21 (53.8)	38 (52.8)	53 (56.4)	82 (49.4)	4 (66.7)	246 (51.6)
Rural	24 (45.3)	14 (29.8)	14 (35.9)	27 (37.5)	41 (43.6)	79 (47.6)	2 (33.3)	201 (42.1)
Urban-Rural	6 (11.3)	8 (17.0)	4 (10.2)	7 (9.7)	—	5 (3.0)	—	30 (6.3)
Total	53 (100.0)	47 (100.0)	39 (99.9)	72 (100.0)	94 (100.0)	166 (100.0)	6 (100.0)	477 (100.0)
Average/year	0.9	4.7	3.9	7.2	9.4	18.5		

of 1860 must have been a major source of threat to family security and status. That responses to such a threat should take the form of either efforts to coalesce the family or to seek refuge in religious organizations should not be surprising given the pervasiveness of kinship and religious values and sentiments in Lebanese society. In the absence of other voluntary agencies, the bulk of welfare and benevolent activities at the time were in fact assumed by kinship and religious organizations. All the eighteen welfare agencies in existence during the second half of the nineteenth century were, without a single exception, sponsored by or affiliated with religious organizations (Lebanese Republic, Ministry of Planning 1965). An equal number of family associations was also in existence during the same period.

The rural-urban distribution is also worth noting. As shown in table 8.1, there is a slight preponderance of urban over rural family associations.[4] More interesting and pertinent evidence is provided by the variations in the rates of growth. While urban family associations have maintained an almost stable and uniform rate of growth with signs of decreasing incidence during the sixties, rural associations have demonstrated a consistent and gradual increase with a sharper rise occurring during the sixties. This may perhaps be taken as evidence of the encroachment of secular and urban features into rural communities and the decline in the sense of kinship that normally accompanies such tendencies.

It is of interest to note that the incidence and trend in welfare associations display almost an identical pattern. As shown in table 8.2, the ecological distribution and rate of annual increase of all nongovernmental welfare agencies do not depart significantly from those manifested by family associations. The fact that both have been increasing at the same rate could be taken to mean that family associations continue to satisfy certain needs that cannot be adequately fulfilled by other associations. This is also further evidence, particularly since opportunities to participate in other voluntary associations have been growing, that secular and rational associations have not as yet undermined the functional significance of kinship groupings.

The religious distribution is equally instructive. It is apparent from table 8.3 that the major religious groups have displayed varying intensity to organize family associations at strikingly different time intervals. In intensity of organization, the Christian community reached its peak during the thirties. More than 71 percent of all family associations formed during that period belonged to Christians; compared to 15.4 percent for

Table 8.2
Trends in Welfare Associations: Ecological Variations

	1860–1919	1920–1929	1930–1939	1940–1949	1950–1959	1960–1964	Date unknown	Total
Urban	28 (59.6)	18 (51.4)	25 (50.0)	36 (56.2)	50 (42.0)	35 (42.6)	5 (62.5)	197 (48.7)
Rural	16 (34.1)	12 (34.3)	20 (40.0)	23 (35.9)	62 (52.1)	44 (53.6)	3 (37.5)	180 (44.4)
Urban/ Rural[a]	3 (6.3)	5 (14.2)	5 (10.0)	5 (7.8)	7 (5.8)	3 (03.6)	—	28 (6.9)
Total	47 (100.0)	35 (99.9)	50 (100.0)	64 (99.9)	119 (99.9)	82 (99.8)	8 (100.0)	405 (100.0)
Average/ year	0.8	3.5	5.0	6.4	11.9	16.4		

SOURCE: Data is based on the *Directory of Social Welfare Agencies* prepared by the Ministry of Planning, Lebanese Republic (Beirut 1965).
[a]Established in Beirut with branches in rural regions.

Table 8.3
Trends in Family Associations: Religious Variations

Religious groups	1930–1939	1940–1949	1950–1959	1960–1969	Total
Christians	28 (71.8)	32 (44.4)	35 (40.2)	51 (31.3)	146 (40.4)
Sunni	6 (15.4)	29 (40.3)	22 (25.3)	17 (10.4)	74 (20.5)
Shi'a	5 (12.8)	3 (4.2)	23 (26.4)	77 (47.2)	108 (29.9)
Druze	— —	8 (11.1)	7 (8.0)	18 (11.0)	33 (9.1)
Total	39 (100.0)	72 (100.0)	87 (100.0)	163 (100.0)	361 (100.0)

Sunnis and 12.8 percent for Shi'ites. Since then, however, Christian family associations have gradually and consistently declined. During the sixties they constituted less than one-third of all family associations formed then.

Sunni Muslim associations were relatively very low during the thirties, witnessed a sharp increase during the forties (from 15.4 to 40.3 percent), and have been sharply declining since. Shi'ites, on the other hand, were just beginning to reach the highest level of organization during the sixties. While Shi'ite family associations made up only 4 percent of those organized during the forties, they constituted close to 50 percent of all associations established during the sixties.

It is generally in this order that these major religious communities began to undergo some of the unsettling and disruptive experiences associated with urbanization. It is in this sense, too, that family associations are treated as both symptoms of and reactions to social change. Having experienced modernization relatively earlier than other groups, it was by and large the urban Christian groups that had to face the brunt of social change first. With urbanization, particularly if it involves some loosening in kinship and other supportive networks, comes the dissociative forces of secularization, and consequently a greater need to seek an integrative outlet through family associations.

During and after World War II, Sunni Muslims began to undergo similar experiences; hence a greater proportion of such families established their associations during that period. It was not until the middle and late sixties that Shi'ites began to witness similar tendencies. This period also corresponds with the heavy outflow of Shi'ite rural migrants into urban areas. Consequently, the larger proportion of family associations among them may be taken as a reflection of the same dissociative forces experienced by other religious groups earlier.

It is of interest to note that the incidence of Druze family associations is relatively low. This should not be taken to mean that the Druze are still untouched by the demands of secularization. Rather, as a community they are comparatively more cohesive and clannish, and their communal structure is sustained by stronger primordial affinities.

Professed Objectives

That the need to coalesce the family seems to correspond with secularization and rural exodus should not be too surprising. As has been repeatedly suggested so far, family associations are quite effective in providing some measure of economic, social, and psychological support to those in the throes of transition. Even where voluntary associations are available, recent migrants may find it comparatively difficult to establish new personal contacts with institutional and nonkinship agencies. Accordingly, family associations need not only function as integrative mechanisms; they also serve an equally important protective function for recent migrants—a form of social insurance and an effective palliative for smoother adaptation to urban life.

Empirical evidence provides adequate support for some of the above assertions. At least in terms of the professed objectives as stated in their formal by-laws, family associations seem quite extensive and multifunctional in the services they expect to dispense.[5] Tables 8.4 and 8.5 provide

Table 8.4
Objectives of Family Associations: Ecological Variations

Objectives	Rural	Urban	Rural/Urban	Total
Solidarity	65 (48.9)	117 (65.4)	3 (50.0)	185 (58.0)
Benevolent	88 (66.2)	94 (52.5)	1 (16.7)	183 (57.4)
Educational	62 (46.6)	84 (46.9)	5 (83.3)	151 (47.3)
Social	42 (31.6)	63 (35.2)	4 (66.7)	109 (34.2)
Economic	25 (18.8)	38 (21.2)	5 (83.3)	68 (21.3)
Cooperative	14 (10.5)	15 (8.4)	— —	29 (9.1)
Health	9 (6.8)	17 (9.5)	— —	26 (8.2)
Moral-Religious	8 (6.0)	7 (3.9)	— —	15 (4.7)
Mediation	2 (1.5)	7 (3.9)	— —	9 (2.8)
Recreational	2 (1.5)	2 (1.1)	— —	4 (1.2)
Total	133	179	6	319

NOTE: Totals add up to more than 100 percent because of multiple response. An association may state an interest in more than one objective.

Table 8.5
Objectives of Family Associations: Religious Variations

Objectives	Christian	Sunni	Shiʻa	Druze	Total
Solidarity	70 (58.8)	36 (60.0)	56 (50.9)	18 (60.0)	185 (58.0)
Benevolent	65 (54.6)	29 (48.3)	69 (62.7)	20 (66.7)	183 (57.4)
Educational	35 (29.4)	36 (60.0)	65 (59.1)	15 (50.0)	151 (47.3)
Social	26 (21.8)	24 (40.0)	50 (45.4)	9 (30.0)	109 (34.2)
Economic	24 (20.2)	17 (28.3)	20 (18.2)	7 (23.3)	88 (21.3)
Cooperative	11 (9.2)	8 (13.3)	5 (4.5)	2 (6.7)	29 (9.1)
Health	2 (1.7)	9 (15.0)	13 (11.8)	2 (6.7)	26 (8.1)
Moral-Religious	6 (5.0)	4 (6.7)	3 (2.7)	2 (6.7)	15 (4.7)
Mediation	5 (4.2)	2 (3.3)	1 (0.9)	1 (3.3)	9 (2.8)
Recreational	1 (0.8)	2 (3.3)	1 (0.9)	1 (3.3)	9 (2.8)
Total	119	60	110	30	319

NOTE: Totals add up to more than 100 percent because of multiple response. An association may state an interest in more than one objective.

a general summary of these objectives and explore whether variations are likely to occur among various religious groups and ecological communities.

Since some decline in the sense of kinship and loosening of family ties is to be expected with increasing urbanization, it is little wonder that family associations in Lebanon should express an overriding concern for family solidarity. Fifty-eight percent of all associations mentioned this concern as one of their prime objectives. In some respects all the other collective activities of family associations—ceremonial, ritualistic, or otherwise—are in fact occasions to demonstrate and reinforce family solidarity. Apart from the conventional welfare and benevolent activities, there are countless occasions where such kinship sentiments are expressed: weddings; funerals; feasts; extended bereavement over deceased members of the family; the show of concern and sympathy during hard times, sickness, and other such crises; and the continued allegiance some families pledge to traditional political leaders—all serve to strengthen family solidarity and reinforce family values. There are also other manifestations that perhaps are of a more symbolic nature, such as the preservation of family property, the restoration of old houses, the concern for ancestral homes or family homesteads, the drawing up of family trees and genealogies, and the manner with which family folklore is remembered—all are cherished symbols of family unity.

Some have published special books to record, often in a highly evocative and glorifying manner, their family history, its trials and tribulations, and the exceptional accomplishments of family members. The volumes vary in form and content, but they are almost always motivated by a desire to reconstruct a success story, to publicize outstanding attributes of the family, and to inspire a sense of pride and esteem in one's kinship attachment. Three such recently published books demonstrate the varied scope and content of such endeavors.

The first (Abu Jawdeh 1973), chronicles the history and geneology of the family, its genesis, migratory movement, branches, and settlement in various parts of the world. Typically, the volume provides detailed family trees of each lineage and valuable demographic data and vital statistics on marriage and career patterns. The second, written by an amateur historian (Tarabey 1983), is a predominantly historical account of how the family evolved and adapted to diverse sociopolitical and cultural circumstances with particular emphasis on the contributions the Tarabeys have made to the cultural and political life of Lebanon. Both volumes are modestly produced and printed and distributed by commercial publishing houses. The third (Sinnu 1983) is a glossy and pretentious *Who's Who* of the family that is privately printed and distributed. It contains little historical documentation and focuses more on the current accomplishments and activities of the Sinnu family. The volume, like many of its kind, includes portraits of outstanding members of the family along with their curriculum vitae. It also includes pictures and accounts of family reunions and other collective activities sponsored by the family association.

In these and other such publications (see, for example, Attallah 1965; Imad 1973; Hubeiysh 1978), one encounters recurrent concern for family solidarity and the need to cement or reintegrate the dismembered parts of the family. Such concern often assumes the form of generalized sentiments or efforts to "strengthen and revive family ties," "spread the spirit of amity and unity among family members," "deepen the ties of brotherhood," "unite the voice of the family," "revive kinship acquaintance," or "awaken interest and familiarity with the outstanding historic and present figures of the family."

Platitudinous as these avowed and lofty objectives seem, they are not merely trite and meaningless expressions. They do reflect a legitimate concern for protecting family ties from further erosion and disintegration. That this is not an empty claim is also seen in the varying concern expressed by rural and urban associations. While 48.9 percent of rural family associations mentioned family solidarity as one of their objectives, 65.4 percent of the urban did so. This difference could not be fortuitous. It is a realistic expression of the greater need the urbanite normally feels for reintegrative mechanisms.

Closely associated with kinship solidarity is the concern for benevolence, which manifests itself in a wide range of activities and interests designed to assist the needy and the poor. Solidarity, after all, does not only give members the motivation, as Durkheim observed, to abide by the norms and expectations of the group, but it is equally important in dealing with individual and group problems.

The concern for benevolence, or at least the way it has been formally expressed, takes one of two forms: an expression of general concern for charity and adoption of welfare projects, or more specific efforts such as the support of orphans, assisting in the costs of funerals, and extending assistance to poor brides by providing bridal trousseaux.

As shown in table 8.4, rural associations, and perhaps realistically so, express more concern for welfare and charitable activities than those in urban areas. Religious communities, however, do not seem to display any significant differences here.

The desire to raise the educational and cultural status of the family also looms high in their multivariant interests. Forty-seven percent expressed this as one of their objectives. The interest in education has also been expressed in two ways: a general concern ranging from "reviving the spirit of learning," "preparation of an enlightened and responsible youth," to organizing illiteracy campaigns and rendering elementary education mandatory; or more specific efforts such as establishing libraries, reading rooms, cultural clubs, and scholarships for the needy and gifted students.

Though there are no significant rural-urban variations, Christian family associations seem to profess a markedly lower interest in education compared to the other three religious groups. This, too, it may be argued, could be taken as a realistic reflection of the varying needs of these communities.

The social and economic objectives follow the same pattern. There is first a general interest in uplifting the social and economic standards of the family through the adoption of "development projects." This concern for the well-being and comfort of the family is seen in such activities as campaigns for fighting unemployment. Quite often though, this interest assumes more specific efforts, such as job hunting and extending credit in times of need.

Two of the other remaining objectives are worth noting: mediation and the concern for moral and spiritual values, areas where the actual activities and accomplishments of the family may well exceed their professed objectives. Even without the reinforcement of kinship associations, a large measure of family bickering and private problems are still resolved outside the impersonal and rational proceedings of a legal court. Family mediation does not only avoid the costly and complicated court system, but it also serves as an effective mechanism for resolving conflict without public embarrassment.

The concern for "piety and righteousness" and efforts to "enhance the spiritual and moral awareness of the family" and to protect "family virtue and morality" are set as precepts for moral conduct. Family honor and the care that is often taken not to blemish or taint the family's name or integrity are after all expressions of this pervasive value orientation.

Several inferences may be easily drawn from this brief consideration of the functions or professed objectives of family associations. That the family should continue to serve as a source for social, economic and psychological support should not be surprising in a society where kinship is still a deeply rooted and trusted sentiment. A decade of civil unrest, with its protracted and diffuse violence, widespread demoralization, terror, intimidation, homelessness, and reckless and senseless destruction of life and property has, in fact, reinforced rather than undermined such loyalties. As the public world grew more menacing, threatening, and insecure, the Lebanese sought shelter in one of their most accessible and reassuring institutions. Since state and other civic voluntary agencies had either become defunct or inaccessible, it was understandable why the family should become even more appealing as a source of refuge. A significantly larger proportion of Lebanese have been interacting with and feel closer to members of their immediate and extended family than they did before the war. They have also been expending more effort, resources, and sentiments on family obligations and interests. As a result, the traditional boundaries of the family have expanded even further to assume added economic, social, and recreational functions.

Along the same lines, the extended family need not be, as is often assumed, inimical to social and occupational mobility. Kinship networks, with or without the formal support of family associations, continue to have a marked influence on the career and occupational choices of individuals. In a recent empirical survey, it was found that a relatively large proportion of university students are either influenced by their parental attitudes or preferences as to the careers they ought to pursue, or they actually follow identical occupations and family business (Shuayb 1984). In addition, family associations appear to provide sufficient aid to members who are either downwardly mobile or in the initial stages of mobility to influence their status positions.

Finally, family associations in Lebanon bear some resemblance—at least in some of their functions if not in their structural organizations—to Le Play's classic model of the stem-family or *"famille-souche."* Le Play considered the stem-family to be the form most suited to cope with the changing conditions of an urban society. Insofar as it incorporates the characteristics of both the "patriarchal" and "unstable" types, the stem-family reconciles the need for change with the need for continuity within the same structural framework. Zimmerman and Frampton (1935) describe this type in the following manner:

> This stem-family consisted of a parent household (the stem) which preserved the organic basis of society, and of a number of individuals (the branches) who leave the parent household in order to fit into industrial organizations and urban environments where high but fluctuating money incomes were produced. The stem of the family helps to preserve the society and to insure that the branches which fail in their adaptations to contractual relations have havens of safety to which they may return. Thus, the stem part of the family reduces to a minimum the needs for public charity for the unemployed. At the same time, the successful branches contribute to the embellishment of society by their rapid adjustment to new opportunities, by the development of industrial areas, and by the increase in new types of production.

In much the same way, the relationship of the family association to member families bears a remarkable resemblance to that of the "stem" and "branch" families. They similarly act, among other things, as "haven of safety" to which members can return in times of need or stress. Apart from the conventional welfare and benevolent functions, they do assist individuals in the quest for opportunity and employment. They are also a vehicle for family solidarity and the advancement of the social, economic, and political interests of the family as a social group.

Concluding Observations

The central concern of this chapter has been an effort to supplement the hypothesis that extended family relations need not be inconsistent with urban requirements. The need to coalesce the family by creating kinship associations, it was suggested, should not be dismissed as a nostalgic and irrational gesture. Rather, they are a response to some unmet needs, and they continue to serve some vital functions at least at the local and micro level. In their functional and organizational development, family associations have displayed a configuration of elements that blend together features of social insurance, welfare, benevolence, and charity together with all the attributes of gemeinschaft community. Tentative as the nature of the data is, several concluding observations may still be advanced.

First, the persistence of family associations and the multiple functions they serve questions a misleading assumption often implied in the literature: that extended families, tribal clans, and other such communal groups come to assume certain functions by default. In other words, it is often suggested that it is the absence of welfare agencies and other voluntary specialized associations that accounts for the survival of such corporate kin groups (Bell and Vogel 1968). In fact, the very survival of such groups is often interpreted as a relic of primitive societies and tribal communities.

In much the same vein, it is also asserted that the inevitable emergence of special-purpose groups and voluntary agencies—insofar as they now assume some of the functions that were once performed within traditional family networks—will ultimately undermine the significance of family associations as agencies of social organization and social control in society (Goode 1963).

Both these observations have not been borne out by our preliminary findings. It is true that the process of modernization in Lebanon has been marked, as elsewhere, by the emergence of a variety of voluntary associations and welfare agencies to cope with the unmet needs of various groups. The proliferation of such agencies, however, has not spelled the obsolescence of family associations. Likewise, the increasing efforts of both governmental and nongovernmental agencies in the fields of social welfare and community development have not been accompanied by a decline in the incidence of such associations. In both absolute numbers and their rate of annual increase, family associations exceed those of all other active voluntary associations in the country.

It is considerations like these that prompt us to maintain that the survival of family associations should not be dismissed as a transient feature, or at best a futile effort to recreate the sense of gemeinschaft. Rather, they appear to be a functional and modestly viable attempt to cope with certain local and parochial needs that have not been met by other agencies in society.

Second, the fact that family associations are ascriptive and particularistic in their orientation does not imply that they are based exclusively on traditional and nonrational criteria. In most of their organizational features and operational procedures, they subscribe to formal and impersonal expectations. Qualifications for membership and for holding office, duties of officers, frequency of general meetings, solicitation of funds, and the nature of sanctions are all clearly stipulated in written by-laws. True, insofar as membership is restricted to descendants of the same lineage, the association cannot be thought to possess an "open" structure and as such fail to satisfy one of the basic requirements of a modern agency. Yet admission to membership is no guarantee that one will retain his membership. There are uniform norms and expectations to which one has to subscribe to if one is to maintain his position within the corporate group. Strict sanctions are imposed to ensure conformity. Penalties for disapproved conduct, ranging all the way from warnings to discharge and public censure, are frequently meted out to ward off deviant behavior that might otherwise taint or defame the family's reputation and honor.

Duties and prerogatives of officers are also clearly prescribed. Tenure in office rarely exceeds five years, and in the majority of instances it rotates yearly through competitive elections. Though deference is occasionally expressed to elders and religious figures, most such expressions are honorific gestures and in no sense have they involved arbitrary judgment and unlimited powers on the part of those vested with such deference.

Kinship-consciousness, regardless of its intensity, has not bridled the efforts of these associations to seek the assistance of outside experts. If the appropriate talent is lacking within the ranks of the kinship group, outside assistance is sought in coping with some impending problems.

In short, in their organizational structure and operational procedures, family associations appear to be a crossbreed of informal tribal groups and formal bureaucracies. In so doing, they combine the wisdom of kinship elders and rational administration.

Third, this combination of tribal and bureaucratic aspects accounts for the survival and functional significance of these associations. Though family associations are outwardly an expression of kinship sentiment and profess an overriding concern for family loyalty and solidarity, they should not be dismissed as a sheer nostalgic gesture to glorify traditional values for their own sake. Neither should they be interpreted as a fatalistic flight from the disquieting and unsettling demands of a competitive and impersonal urban world. Rather, they have been effective in performing some vital social and welfare functions without destroying the sense of gemeinschaft.

As demonstrated earlier, they provide certain services and functions that are akin, if not identical, to the three major tasks of any welfare institution: namely, income maintenance, deviance prevention, and social participation. In addition to such conventional benevolent and welfare activities, they have also provided a measure of primary group reinforcements and mediation services, both of which are vital for coping with some of the private troubles and tensions of a society in throes of civil unrest.

Fourth, on a more general and conceptual level, the survival of such associations sheds some light on the nature and character of urban social groupings that are likely to persist within developing societies.

The city, as has been repeatedly observed, represents socially a relatively novel form of human association; a large, densely concentrated aggregation of heterogeneous individuals living for the most part under conditions of anonymity and indirect social control. Social contact is temporary, segmental, and generally impersonal. By virtue of such segmental relationships and participation in impersonal and contractual groups, urbanites, it is often asserted, "hang together by the slenderest threads" (Ericksen 1954:304). The Lebanese evidence tends to question such assertions. At least they cannot be accepted without some reservation.

While there is undoubtedly a large measure of truth in the portrayals of Wirth, Tonnies, Maine, Durkheim, and Simmel, they have nevertheless described the rural and urban worlds as extreme poles of life, a description that hardly fits the outstanding features of urban development in Lebanon. Such polar typologies and ideal-type constructs and dichotomies, as we have been suggesting all along, must be modified if they are to correspond with realities of urbanization and the nature of social groupings in Lebanon.

Formal professional associations and political parties are still sustained by nonrational and personal considerations. Conversely, traditional associations are not devoid of rational and impersonal elements. Despite their outwardly traditional character, family associations do rest upon certain elements that they share with any formal large-scale organization, namely, a certain degree of division of labor and delegation of authority, formal and impersonal relations, and structural rationalization.

Furthermore, it should also be noted that the survival and viability of these associations as functional agents in society rest to a large extent on their ability to reconcile the essential properties of secondary and primary groups: the attributes of formality, impersonality, and rationality of the former with the needs for intimacy and identity inherent in the latter.

Finally, important as these attributes are, one should not overlook a fundamental shortcoming inherent in these and other such adaptive agencies of social change. The more effective they are in providing such vital functions and services, the more likely that the already enfeebled civic and national sentiments will be undermined. In this sense, family associations have much in common with the political za'im, patrimonial manager, confessional bureaucrat, urban neighborhood, and parochial voluntary association. By being accessible vehicles for securing needed benefits, services, and opportunities, they are prone to reinforce kinship and other primordial loyalties at the expense of the more secular, civic and state allegiances. Once again, in other words, what enables at the family, local, and communal level disables at the civic and national level.

CHAPTER NINE

Cultural Values and Family Planning

TO ANYONE CONCERNED WITH the interplay between cultural values and population policy, Lebanon offers a rather interesting and curious case study. At least five general considerations render such an exploration instructive and meaningful.

First, in no other country, perhaps, are demographic considerations as intimately bound up with the fundamental issue of distributing and maintaining political power in society. Generally, in all pluralistic societies operating within a confessional system of government based on proportionate representation, demographic variables are bound to have profound consequences for the balance of power and sociopolitical stability. This has been especially true in Lebanon.

As we have seen, throughout the nineteenth century, Lebanon witnessed various forms of societal change that produced pronounced shifts in the relative socioeconomic and political positions of the various religious communities. As early as the 1840s, in the wake of the first episode of sectarian conflict, the numerical distribution of the various religious communities began to assume serious implications for the political management of the country. Since then successive efforts were made, often in the form of geographic reorganization of the administrative divisions of the country, or the numerical rearrangement of the basis of representation, so as to avoid the political subordination of one sect to another. All the partition schemes Lebanon has been subjected to, particularly those of 1843, 1845, and 1861, were, among other things, efforts to institutionalize confessional representation (e.g., Salibi 1965; Khalaf 1979; Gordon 1983). As confessional representation became rooted into the political system, demographic variables assumed more prominence.

With the creation of the State of Greater Lebanon by the French in 1920, the numerical distribution of the various sects became a more sensitive political issue. On the basis of the census of 1932 and the National Pact of 1943, a political formula was arrived at that distributed parliamentary seats, cabinet positions, and other civil service appointments according to the ratio of six Christians for every five Muslims. It is on this basis also that Maronites, who were reportedly the largest single sect in 1932, were assigned the presidency of the republic. The Sunnis, the second largest sect, received the premiership; and the Shi'ites, the third largest, the speakership of the Chamber of Deputies.

Pluralism in and of itself, it should be remarked, would not have been problematic had not the various religious communities been also marked by striking imbalances in socioeconomic conditions. Differential rates of fertility and corresponding religious differences in growth rates are also associated with other disparities in sociocultural and economic attributes (Chamie 1977a). It is then that demographic variables will translate into changes in the religious composition, which in turn generate tension on the precarious balance of forces. These dislocations almost always touched off renewed outbreaks of civil unrest and political violence.

The protracted civil war of 1975–1986 once again demonstrates the volatile demographic nature of the crisis. In some significant respects, all the critical, and yet unresolved, issues provoked by the war are fundamentally demographic issues: the naturalization of alien residents, the Palestinian presence, electoral law, secularization, decentralization, confessional balance, the effective and equitable participation of religious communities in significant political decisions, and the persisting debate over Lebanon's true national identity, etc—these and other associated issues are either generated by or have consequences for the salient demographic features of the society. Even as benign and neutral a problem as a taking a national census becomes highly politicized. No such census, for fear of upsetting the delicate sectarian balance, has been taken since 1932.

The results of the 1970 national survey on the composition of the economically active population, conducted by the Lebanese Ministry of National Planning,[1] clearly indicate, however, that the proportional distribution of sects among the population has no doubt been drastically altered since 1932. For example, it is generally conceded that given the considerable fertility differentials among the religious communities, the Shi'ites are now decidedly the most populous group. If they are not already, then they will certainly be in the very near future if existing rates of fertility are maintained without substantial changes in mortality or migration. Similarly, the second largest sect is, or will soon be, the Sunni (Chamie 1977a:118).

Since these and other such estimates, are only unofficial approxima-
tions, they cannot be used by any confessional group to demand a change
in the political structure or a redistribution of parliamentary seats. But
such demands have been repeatedly made. In fact, the issue of a more
proportionate political representation consistent with the assumed new
demographic realities is bound to be one of the most hotly contested
issues in the impending controversy over the political reorganization of
Lebanon.

Within such a highly charged political context, it is meaningful to consider how a family planning association can emerge to address population issues and problems.

A second consideration is Lebanon's lack of an explicit and direct governmental population policy, an understandable absence given the politicization of population variables. The clear formulation and articulation
of such a policy is certainly not possible or feasible under the circumstances. Yet Lebanon has an officially registered Lebanese Family Planning Association (LFPA), which receives the support of the ministries of
Health, Social Affairs, and Planning.

Politicians, religious leaders, government officials, and other public figures have publically endorsed the activities and goals of the LFPA. Successive Prime Ministers have on repeated occasions inaugurated conferences on population policy sponsored by the Association. Since its
inception in 1969, the Association has been very active and visible in
extending and publicizing the scope of its family-planning services. The
Secretary General of the LFPA is also a full-time head of the government's Social Development office in Southern Lebanon. This double role
has given the Association access to government-sponsored agencies and
services. Indeed, centers of the Office of Social Development are frequently used by the LFPA as bases or clinics for offering medical advice
on side effects of contraceptives, fitting IUD's, giving injections, and
providing referrals for sterilization at the American University Hospital
(AUH) in Beirut.

It is instructive to find out how has this anomalous situation has been
maintained and justified, particularly when the state prohibits even the
collection of demographic data, let alone the articulation of a population
policy or program.

Third, the status of contraceptives in Lebanon is another paradox that
reveals the wide discrepancy between prevailing laws, public sentiment,
and actual behavior. While articles 537 and 538 of the Penal Code pro-

hibit the use, sale, or distribution of any contraceptive devices for the purpose of birth control, there is almost an open and totally uncontrolled contraceptive business, including importation, distribution, selling, and advertising. The same is true of abortion. Eight articles of the Penal Code (539–546) spell out prohibitions of and punishments for the specific criminal offenses involving abortions, yet abortion is widely practiced despite prohibitive laws and public sentiment, which disapproves of abortion on religious and other grounds (Dib 1975:5–8).

It is of interest again to explore how this seemingly paradoxical situation came into being: a situation where political authorities find it more expedient and judicious to ignore the widespread illegal traffic in importation and distribution of contraceptives and where family planning services are sanctioned and often dispensed in conjunction with government supported agencies and voluntary associations, yet these same political authorities feel hesitant or impotent to accept a change in the law which legalizes contraceptives or sanctions the taking of a national census.

Finally, given our basic concern with the dialectical interplay between traditions and modernity, it is equally meaningful to consider how a relatively "modern" notion of family planning has been introduced and incorporated into a sociocultural context in which seemingly "traditional" values and sentiments are expected to militate against such an introduction. No matter how one perceives family planning, it introduces the idea of rationality and control into an area previously left to God, fate, or to the chance combination of other societal changes. Furthermore, despite all manifestations to the contrary, Lebanon continues to be sustained by predispositions and preferential interests that encourage pronatalism. It is of particular interest, in such an instance, to find out how a kinship culture in which norms of the extended family and other pronatalist values regarding the place of children, early marriage, and the status of women can become receptive to family planning.

These and other related considerations render an exploration of the role of the LFPA in introducing and mediating change into such a sensitive area of social life meaningful and interesting. Since the LFPA has emerged as an almost semiofficial organization, and since it is the only such voluntary association with professed family planning aims and activities, it is instructive to review its emergence and development. How did the LFPA perceive and formulate its goals and objectives? How did it secure permission and authorization to initiate and extend its family planning services? How did it advocate and present its views to the public?

What sort of rationalization has it employed to justify and legitimate such introduction? More specifically, what are its distinctive views regarding both the guiding ends and permissible means for such activities? How did it implement or translate such views into specific programs in areas and communities known for their resistance to such programs?

Finally, in view of the ethical controversy involved in such forms of social intervention (for further details, see Warwick 1982; Lapham 1978), it is also significant to find out whether the LFPA reveals any sensitivity to some of the moral issues underlying family planning programs and activities. More specifically, how has it coped with or adjusted to the cultural and institutional barriers and other sources of resistance to family planning?

In addressing these questions, the chapter will focus on three related issues. Since our primary concern is for the interplay between cultural values and population programs, we begin first by considering some of the normative and institutional barriers to family planning in Lebanon. Second, we trace the emergence and development of the LFPA and assess its efforts to overcome such barriers. Finally, we focus on the role of the *wasita* ("mediator"), the fieldworker of the community-based program, to find out how she was effective in mobilizing indigenous local traditions to generate favorable attitudes and practices towards family planning.

Obstacles to Family Planning

Pronounced differentials in fertility and some of the socioeconomic disparities between the various religious communities are associated, as one would expect, with considerable variations in knowledge, attitudes, and practices of family planning. Because of the varying incidence and pattern of social change, various groups have shown greater receptivity and eagerness to adopt the norms and practices associated with fertility control.

Despite the general favorable predisposition toward family planning, results of the national and other subsample surveys continue to reveal some marked differentials, particularly on measures such as attitude toward contraception and desire for additional information on the subject. There are also gaps between such favorable predispositions and actual usage. For example, while 56 and 58 percent of the Shi'ites—the least predisposed group—approve and desire additional information about family planning, only 35 percent are currently using contraceptives. Similarly, and as in other societies, there is some lag between desired and achieved family size.

These and other such results point to an inescapable conclusion: there are still factors that militate against a more widespread diffusion and acceptance of family planning in Lebanon. Two general sources of such resistance will be briefly considered: persisting cultural values that continue to encourage and reinforce pronatalist norms and conceptions and structural disinsentives and institutional blockages, particularly the manner in which family planning has been introduced and implemented, which might arouse suspicions toward the ends and means of family planning as a movement.

Pronatalist Values

We cannot possibly exhaust here all the normative elements and belief systems that are associated with fertility or encourage pronatalism. The discussion will simply identify a few—such as the survival of extended kinship norms and preference for large families, the economic, moral, and recreational value of children, the subordinate status of women, pervasive religiosity, and the role of sexuality in Islam—which are of particular relevance to the Lebanese situation.

The survival of kinship norms and sentiments, we have argued repeatedly in the preceding essays, has had a pervasive effect on virtually all aspects of public and private life. If, as we have seen, kinship networks and loyalties continue to influence the nature of political leadership, industrial development, and social welfare and benevolent organizations, then they are more likely to leave their imprint on features more closely identified with the family. Consequently, it is little wonder that pronatalist norms and expectations should become predominant in so pervasive a kinship culture. It is doubtless for this reason that widows, orphans, fatherless children, and childless marriages—despite the support they are expected to receive from the extended family—continue to evoke feelings of pity tinged with social stigma.

Most of the conventional economic justifications associated with pronatalist values and preferences for children are also present in Lebanon. In rural areas wives and children are perceived as valuable economic assets, as extra hands in domestic chores or as sources of extra cash in harvest time or other forms of seasonal employment. Boys assist their fathers in the field, and girls help their mothers around the house and attend to younger siblings. As in other developing and rural communities, children assume such domestic responsibilities and other activities pertaining to livelihood at a relatively early age (al-Hamamsy 1972:335–57).

Children working in the fields, particularly since the nature of agriculture employment (tobacco, fruit and vegetable harvesting, and packing, grazing etc.) is conducive for child labor, continues to be a familiar sight in rural areas. The proportion of children of school age who are not attending school is correspondingly higher in such areas (Lebanon, Ministry of Planning, 1974).

A large family in Lebanon, particularly in rural and less developed communities, is more than a source of welfare and a hedge against social isolation and economic insecurity. In a fundamentally gregarious and leisure-oriented culture and in the absence of institutionalized outlets of recreation, a large family is also an important source of amusement and entertainment. "The more, the merrier," is more than just a terse aphorism. It is rooted in the very fabric of a social order where much of the social interaction and everyday life occurs within small and closely knit family circles. Expecting an additional child, pregnancy, childbirth, child rearing, socialization, and all the rituals and ceremonies associated with the early stages of a life cycle become infused with added meaning and significance in an otherwise drab and uneventful existence. It is then that children live up to the Koranic saying and truly become "the adornment of life." An added child is not only an added source of entertainment, but members of an extended family often share the responsibility of looking after younger children and reduce the burdens of child rearing.

As in other patrilineal, patrilocal, and patriarchal societies, there is strong preference for male children. The birth of a boy is greeted with joy; it is an occasion for lavish festivities. The birth of a girl, on the other hand, is generally hushed and muted. Despite evidence to the contrary, such preference is understandable. A male child perpetuates the family name, reinforces the continuity of the family and, perhaps more important, preserves inherited land and wealth within the family. Inheritance laws among Sunni Muslims—since a boy inherits twice as much as a girl—continue to place a higher premium on male descendants.

On moral and ethical grounds, a son is also perceived more favorably. He is a source of security for his sisters and parents in old age, a provider in times of need, and a protector and defender of his sisters' virtue and family honor. This is increasingly so since the relaxation of sexual standards is already threatening conventional morality and weakening the family as a source of moral and social restraint. The preference for early marriage, as a means for protecting a girl's chastity, is no doubt an expression of this ethical concern. Despite the relaxation of sexual standards, a high premium continues to be placed on a girl's virginity. Early marriage frees parents from such anxiety and protects the girl's honor.

Pronatalist values are also a reflection of the relatively poor public health and hygienic conditions prevalent in underdeveloped regions of Lebanon. The high infant mortality observed in such regions must no doubt encourage procreation, if only to ensure the survival of an optimal number of children into adulthood. Accordingly, it is very common for such families to wait until a large number of children have survived beyond the precarious years of infancy before they are predisposed to entertain notions of family planning.

In a male-oriented society, the subordinate status of women and the consequent limitations of their activities to narrow social circles might well also militate against any notion of family planning. There is a definite relationship between the participation of women in the labor force and fertility. It is in areas or communities where such participation is low that fertility is the highest. Since women in such communities have little access to employment opportunities outside the house, the wife derives much of her self-esteem and recognition from her traditional role as wife and mother. Procreation, like other associated domestic chores and activities, becomes highly coveted and infused with social significance. These become virtually her only avenues for status and self-esteem. Through them she asserts her identity and secures privileges and attention that are normally denied a sterile and childless woman. Within such a context, pregnancy, procreation, and child rearing may be easily perceived as advantageous and beneficial circumstances. Indeed, there is evidence that married women are quite instrumental in this regard and deliberately manipulate these circumstances to secure some of these benefits. For example, during pregnancy women are culturally expected to pass through periods of "craving," during which they duly receive unusual items of food or other gifts they desire and crave for. Expectant women are known to exaggerate and dramatize the discomforts of pregnancy to invite attention and sympathy. Several of the fieldworkers involved in the community-based family planning services program of the LFPA reported that a considerable number of women resort to pregnancy as a means of committing and sustaining the attention and interest of their husbands.[2] It is also a hedge, it seems, against divorce since they believe that they are less likely to be divorced as long as they are pregnant.

The impact of religiosity, Islam in particular, on family planning has been the subject of continuous discussion. Both theoretical interpretations of the position of Islam and recent empirical evidence is inconsistent. For example, while Muslim women are often characterized as suppressed and subordinate to men and are normatively expected to display modesty and preserve their sexual purity, Islam in general is frequently described as being favorably predisposed towards sexuality, with strong preference for children and little interest in family planning (Kirk 1967; Clarke 1972). Such viewpoints have been challenged recently on grounds that Islamic ideology holds a potentially more positive approach to sexuality and fertility than does Christianity. Basim Musallam, in a comprehensive and thoughtful study of birth control in Islam before the nineteenth century, provides well-documented evidence in support of such a perspective. By reviewing medieval Arabic discussions of contraception and abortion in areas like Islamic jurisprudence, medicine, erotica, and popular literature, he shows that birth control was sanctioned by both Islamic law and popular opinion. Likewise, knowledge of effective methods of birth control was also available throughout premodern times (Musallam 1983).

Though in a different context, Fatima Mernissi (1975a) also argues that since Islam treats sex as a mere instinct that does not necessarily connote good or evil, sexual energy may be harnessed as a source of inspiration in society and need not be procreative (Mernissi 1975a:3–11). In other words, with such a positive view of sexuality, the use of contraception is not likely to create excessive guilt or anxiety among Muslim couples. Mary Chamie (1977) provides empirical evidence from a sample of 450 Lebanese women who visited the sterilization clinic at AUH in Beirut to support this argument.

Earlier and more recent empirical evidence on the effects of religion upon fertility and fertility control in Lebanon suggests repeatedly that there are some social and structural dimensions other than religious affiliation—such as the educational level of women, urbanization, participation of women in the labor force, sexual compatibility and responsiveness—that are more significantly correlated with birth control (Yaukey 1961: Chamie 1977b).

Religious motives and associated ethical and spiritual considerations continue, nonetheless, to act as a barrier to fertility control. Results of the KAP (Knowledge, Attitude, and Practices) survey of the town of Tyre in southern Lebanon (Tanas 1974), indicate that 24 percent of the men interviewed object to the practice of contraception on religious grounds. They expressed one of the following refrains in justifying their refusal to adopt means of birth control: "Children are the gift of God"; "It is *haram* ("forbidden") to prevent the birth of a soul", "It is against religion"; "God does not permit it" (Tanas 1974:84).

Results of a more recent community-based survey involving a sample of 310 fertile women from 44 villages in the Zahrani district of Southern Lebanon reveal similar tendencies. When the respondents were asked about their preferred family size or how many children they expect to have, 6 percent of the sample refused to answer on grounds that such matters are entirely in God's will (LFPA 1974:10).

Most of the fieldworkers interviewed who were involved in the LFPA community-based project reported that religiosity, particularly where it is accompanied by vague and often ill-defined beliefs in ritual, superstition, and resignation to overwhelming whims of fate and destiny, continues to pervade the attitudes of many women toward pregnancy and birth control. According to the fieldworkers, a significant number of village women continue to perceive any form of birth control as *haram* because it is a violation of God's wish and an intervention with a divine and natural process.

It should not be inferred from the preceding remarks that pronatalism and its associated values are absolute and intransigent. The very existence of wide differentials in fertility—generated and sustained by variations in religious affiliation, socioeconomic disparities, specifically rural-urban considerations, and literacy—reveals changing patterns in fertility behavior. The general trend, in fact, is toward declining rates (see Chamie 1977b).

There are, nonetheless, strong normative preferences for procreation which continue to encourage high fertility. The persistence of traditional sociocultural values and behavioral patterns associated with a kinship culture and extended family networks are interrelated with a host of other considerations that encourage natality and place a high premium on the value of children and larger families. The importance of the family as a source of social and economic security and psychic reinforcements; the preference for early marriage on both economic and ethical grounds; the value of children as economic assets as well as a future security for parents in old age; and the subordinate status of women and the large measure of self-esteem they derive from their child-bearing potential—all these factors, along with pervasive religiosity, seem outwardly incompatible with some of the values underlying family planning.

If one accepts this portrait of traditional culture—and recent evidence from at least Southern Lebanon suggests that it bears a large measure of truth—then some degree of normative conflict between the demands of population planning and control and the residue of pronatalist expectations becomes inevitable. Expressed more concretely, the perceived benefits and values derived from children continue to outweigh the perceived costs and disadvantages.

Institutional Blockages

The conflict, however, is not exclusively normative in character. Other than the pronatalist values and cultural beliefs that continue to militate against family planning, there are some structural and institutional constraints that act as disincentives by discouraging potential recipients from accepting contraception as a mode of behavior.

Foremost among these is the legal restrictions imposed on any form of birth control. As mentioned earlier, Lebanon is in that peculiar and anomalous situation where the Criminal Code of 1943 continues to prohibit the use, sale, distribution, and advertisement of any contraceptive device, yet the government sanctions the creation of a family planning association and supports its activities and services. Articles 537 and 538 of the Penal Code are quite explicit:

Article 537—Whoever uses one of the methods mentioned in paragraphs 2 and 3 of Article 209 to prescribe, or spread the means of, contraceptives, or whoever attempts to propagandize these methods for the purpose of preventing pregnancy shall be punished by imprisonment from one month to one year and by a fine of 25 to 100 Lebanese pounds.

Article 538—The same punishment shall be inflicted upon whoever sells or offers to sell, or whoever stocks for the purpose of selling any means of contraceptives or whoever facilitates their use through whatever method.

Article 209 prohibits publicizing contraception by such means as "Talking or shouting whether made by people or transformed through mechanical machines in such a way as to be heard, in both cases, by those who have nothing to do with the act" and "writings, drawings, pictures made by hand, photographs, films, symbols, and all kinds of illustrations, if displayed in public places, or open places, or sold, or offered to be sold, or distributed to one person or more."

Since its inception the LFPA has on repeated occasions sought, through its workshops, seminars, lobbies, and other means of political and bureaucratic persuasion to bring about an amendment of the current legislation to legalize the full use and prescription of contraceptives. A special committee was formed by the Minister of Health in 1970 to recommend such amendments to the relevant articles of the Penal Code. It was not until September 16, 1983 (Legislative Decree No. 12), that the infamous articles were finally annulled.

The prohibitive nature of the law has not, however, prevented the government from offering a variety of supportive measures to assist the activities of the LFPA. Nor has it restricted the entry of contraceptives into the country. Rampant commercialism, and the proclivity of the Lebanese to circumvent bureaucratic and legal restrictions have guaranteed a steady flow of supplies. But the circumvention of the law did not really begin, at least on a large scale, until 1969. Until then contraception was limited to upper-class married couples and to women who secured medical reports certifying that further pregnancies would endanger their health. Early in the 1960s, contraception became more prevalent but continued to be provided mainly through doctors' clinics. The outpatient department of the American University Hospital started to offer contraceptive services, on a limited scale, in a private and semisecret manner.

In 1969 the LFPA received from the International Planned Parenthood Federation (IPPF) a donation of some 25,000 crates of Eugynon pills, obviously intended as a gift to assist in launching the LFPA's program. The gift, however, could not be cleared through customs on grounds that the law forbids the importation of such products. The presence of a sympathetic Minister of Health at the time allowed the LFPA to find a devious but ingenious way to get around the law. A request was made to release from customs the 25,000 boxes of "medicament" to be used for the regulation of menstrual cycle of women. All the boxes of Eugynon pills were relabeled as "medicament" and were duly cleared through customs. The approval of the Minister read as follows:

TO: The Family Planning Association in Lebanon
SUBJECT: Request to Import Medicaments.

With reference to your request mentioned above, this Ministry wishes to inform you that it approves, as an exception, your request to import 25 thousand boxes of the medicament, Eugynon, being a gift given to your Association by the International Planned Parenthood Federation, on the condition that it will be distributed *gratis* by the clinics of your Association, within the rules laid down by (Ministerial) Decree No. 340/1 dated 10/10/1968 which relates to this type of medicament.

Signed
Minister of Health

Fortunately, since then a succession of Ministers of Health have all been sympathetic to the idea of family planning, and have approved all such requests. Dr. Adnan Mroueh, president of the Association, has, in fact, served as Minister of Public Health and Social Affairs from October 7, 1982, till February 5, 1984, during the first cabinet formed under President Amin Gemayel's tenure in office.[3] They simply reissue the same reply, changing only the dates. Dealers in pharmaceutical products were quick to seize the opportunity. They too, started to import and clear their contraceptive supplies as "medicaments."

The survival of this curious anomaly in the law must, no doubt, account for the inaccessibility of contraceptives to some groups and might explain part of the reluctance of potential users to actually adopt forms of contraception. Much like the gap between ideal and actual family size, there is still a discrepancy between the proportion of wives who approve and desire further family planning information and those who actually use any form of contraception. For example, while three out of every four wives between the ages of 15 and 49 approve of the use of contraception and two-thirds expressed a desire for further information on the subject, only 53 percent are currently using any method. Of these, the largest proportion are using traditional methods such as coitus interruptus, rhythm, and douching. The use of tubal ligation, IUD, and vasectomy are hardly visible. In no instance do they exceed 1 percent (for further details see Chamie 1977a:56).

Such discrepancies between knowledge, attitude, and practices, and variations in the forms of contraception currently in use must, in part, reflect differential in access to contraception among various groups, let alone their preparedness to utilize already available means. This is one indication that to a significant portion of Lebanese wives, contraception, particularly the modern forms, are still inaccessible to them.

In areas like Tyre, almost four years after the establishment of the LFPA, slightly more than one-fourth of the males were not using any contraception, although 97 and 90 percent had knowledge of pills and condoms, and around 71 percent were favorably predisposed toward some form of birth control. More revealing, perhaps, only 25 percent had heard of family planning clinics. Nine percent knew about the services such clinics provide, and 7 percent were aware that family planning clinics are established in Lebanon (Tanas 1974:136).[4]

Even in Bourj-al-Brajneh, a suburb of Beirut that was the scene of the first family planning clinics, a large number of the wives interviewed indicated that the source of much of their information on family planning was derived from their informal network of friends and relatives. Only a few mentioned doctors. Physicians and other medical officials must have no doubt felt hesitant, because of the legal prohibitions, to talk about, let alone prescribe, birth control with their clients (Dib 1975:3).

There are other institutional barriers, unrelated to the legal inhibitions or the inaccessibility of contraception and family planning services, which continue to act as disincentives. Mention will be made here of a few that were noted by the fieldworkers as sources of resistance or obstacles they had to reckon with in their encounters with potential users.

Foremost among these is the dehumanizing and degrading experience women have had with hospitals, clinics, and other bureaucratic requirements of modern medicine. An appointment with a doctor, from the perspective of a village woman, is more than just a cumbersome encounter. It disrupts her daily routine and exacts other more taxing psychological and material demands. It involves, among other things, a special trip to the city, long hours of waiting, and often subjects relatively sheltered and timid women to intimidating and degrading encounters with hospital staff. The woman must submit herself to probing and embarrassing questions, and she must be willing to part with her deep-rooted reluctance to undress before a male doctor.

Rumors and fears as to alleged or real side effects of contraception—particularly pills, IUD's, and vaginal tablets—were also noted by the fieldworkers as a nagging source of resistance. Some of the women were inflexible in their attitudes and were not willing to cast aside some of their folk and traditional methods of birth control for what seemed to them to be more imperfect and hazardous alternatives. Most of the recipients needed to be reassured that side effects are not injurious to health and can be effectively and promptly controlled.

One final source of resistance, often observed in other similar experiences with family planning, should be noted. Rural and traditional women are often overwhelmed by a crushing sense of economic powerlessness and uncertainty. Partly because of their poverty and the excessive amount of energy, time, and resources they are forced to expend on managing their households and maintaining subsistence, they develop a rather resigned and fatalistic world view. This same defeatist and powerless attitude pervades their feelings toward pregnancy and fertility control (Mernissi 1975b:418–19).

Several of the fieldworkers noted similar manifestations: women who have resigned themselves to their fate and greet another pregnancy as part of "life's burdens." One fieldworker reported a familiar refrain she hears on her rounds and visits:

> Times are difficult. We must accept what is written to us with fortitude and resignation. There is little we can do about our fate as wives and mothers. We are the sacrificial lambs. We are candles destined to burn to give light to others.

These and other such defeatist attitudes, which accompany intense poverty, economic uncertainty, and the perception of a woman's role as one of resigned acceptance of adversity, will certainly be reflected in similar defeatist feelings with regard to family planning and fertility control.

Poignant as they may seem, however, such attitudes are not as resolute and inflexible as they outwardly appear. Fieldworkers, in fact, met little resistance in altering such perceptions or in persuading women to accept contraception as a normal and regular human activity. To a considerable extent, the same is also true about the other sources of institutional blockages and disincentives.

The Lebanese Family Planning Association

Given the legal prohibitions and some of the normative and institutional barriers to family planning, it is meaningful to explore how the LFPA perceived and formulated its goals and objectives. How did it rationalize its activities and implement its specific programs?[5]

The discussion will only touch on two aspects: First, an attempt is made to find out how the LFPA has coped with and adjusted to some of the cultural and institutional barriers and other possible sources of resistance to family planning. Second, we will also identify and account for the shift in its perspective from fertility control to community development. In both these efforts the role of the *wasita* as a cultural broker, a carrier of new modes of consciousness and life-styles, becomes quite pronounced.

Coping with Cultural and Institutional Barriers

The first task confronting the Association during its formative period was to secure official recognition. This seemingly simple and routine task proved to be a nagging source of irritable delays and a drain on its resources. It took two years of relentless effort before the Association was granted the status of a tax-exempt public utility agency on February 2, 1971. Judging by the initial resistance or reluctance they faced, the founding members resorted to every possible means, often employing their extensive personal networks and contacts with public figures and influential politicians to generate support and enthusiasm for their idea. Early in their endeavor, they also began to realize that soliciting and winning the support of individual politicians is not enough to guarantee the official approval of the Parliament. Furthermore, many of the government officials at that time did not, it seems, fully realize that family planning involved, among other things, birth control.

The struggle to amend the Penal Code was, as we have seen, even more problematic and demanding. It was not until September 1983 that the Association finally succeeded in annulling the prohibitive articles of the Criminal Code. This implied that for fourteen years (since 1969), and despite the nonenforcement of the law, the LFPA had to resort to various circuitous and cumbersome means to introduce contraceptives in the country. Often, this has meant that officials of the Association had to carry, as part of their personal effects, packages of contraceptives under the pretext of preservatives against venereal disease. Since many of the founding members were gynecologists and obstetricians, such alibis became more plausible and legitimate.

At the popular level, the LFPA did not meet any organized opposition. In implementing its programs and services, the Association, nonetheless, was highly sensitive to some of the possible sources of resistance.

Eager as they seem at times in forging ahead with their plans—a feature that characterizes other similar crusading movements—they have, nonetheless, moved cautiously.

All the officials of the LFPA we interviewed, executive officers, past presidents, staff, and volunteers, seemed fully aware that no matter how family planning is perceived, it implies major changes in some of the touchy and sensitive areas of traditional culture and society. To varying degrees they were all aware that one cannot possibly talk about the virtues of small families and spacing of children unless one invades the sanctuary of family relationships, kinship obligations, sexual morality, and religious values. They were also equally aware of the political and administrative constraints they are compelled to work under. In fact, at times they were inclined to dramatize these sources of resistance to imbue their tasks with a sense of unusual accomplishments.

Be that as it may, the Association has, on several occasions, been willing to temper its expectations to accommodate or circumvent possible sources of resistance, fear, and suspicion the public continues to harbor toward family planning. As such, it had to resort to various guises to introduce the topic. The most appropriate and salutary means was to sugar-coat the seemingly "bitter pill" of family planning within the context of primary health care and child and maternity welfare. A few such unobstrusive instances of sugar-coating can be sighted.

In March 1969 the Family and Child Welfare Society of Lebanon sponsored a seminar on the Lebanese family. The topics of the seminar had, in effect, dealt with various dimensions of family planning. This was, perhaps, the first time that the issue was discussed publicly, and spokesmen of the various religious communities and other civic leaders were invited to present the positions of their respective communities with regard to family planning. The organizers of the seminar, who incidentally were also the founders of the LFPA, chose deliberately to call their seminar "Responsible Parenthood" to avoid whatever objections or sensitivity the participants or the public might have toward family planning.

Similarly when the LFPA started to establish its family planning centers early in the 1970s, its activities and services were all introduced within the framework of public health and child and maternity welfare. Under such guises they were able to avoid much of the sensitivity and self-consciousness often associated with exclusive family planning clinics. A research assistant involved in one such center at the American University Hospital had this to say about her experience with women who came for assistance: "It is a health center so they do not feel too self conscious, and they often discuss the problem among themselves while I listen, which makes it more natural and less of a clinic (Sabet 1970)."

In other words family planning sneaked through the back door and has never become a public issue in its own right. It was introduced initially within the context of responsible parenthood and child and maternal welfare, and as of late it has been promoted through the broader concern of community development. This is not a cause for regret. Indeed, by acquiring a low profile, whether consciously or not, the LFPA has managed to avoid public controversy and debate over the objectives and means of their movement. In doing so, it has accomplished much more than it would have had the issue attained wider recognition.

In a similar vein, rather than talking about fertility control, prevention of births, and unwanted pregnancies, the LFPA has emphasized instead the detrimental effect of large family size and very closely spaced births on the health and welfare of individual family members. This is quite apparent in the various slogan and poster campaigns the LFPA has organized thus far. This epidemiological and gynecological bias is expected given the overwhelming medical background of LFPA's membership. It has, nonetheless, spared the Association an involvement in the ethical controversy over reproductive freedom and the right of individuals to determine the number and spacing of children, and allowed it to rationalize its activities on the relatively more neutral humanitarian and gynecological grounds.

This same concern is equally displayed in the lectures, panels, and workshops for training fieldworkers and the public campaigns the LFPA has organized. For example, the following undesirable side effects often associated with large families and closely spaced pregnancies are singled out: high fetal wastage, high infant mortality from communicable diseases and malnutrition, high frequency of diabetes and gynecological disorders in mothers, decreased maternal efficiency, and retarded physical growth and intellectual development of children. One of the documentary films the LFPA has repeatedly projected in its orientation workshops, and one that has been received favorably by the fieldworkers, deals with problems of side effects of repeated pregnancies.

One of the younger and more emancipated *wasitas* employs a similar but more persuasive argument to change women's attitudes toward conception and birth control. Realizing that many of the traditional women "manipulate" pregnancy to attract the sexual responsiveness and attention of their husbands, she points out to them that they can accomplish the same objective more effectively by limiting fertility:

> I tell them that too many pregnancies and too close together will destroy a woman's health and rob her of her beauty and charm. Rather than attracting your husband you become repulsive to him. Rather than looking after your body and preserving your figures, you spend your time nursing babies and sick children. You become distressed, ugly and nagging all the time. It is then that you invite your husband to walk out on you and seek other women.

The same fieldworker reported that most of her clients were equally receptive to common-sense matters of personal hygiene and cleanliness. She implores them to take daily baths, buy new clothes, and be well-groomed, because: "Your health, beauty and looks are your only resource. It is these, not an added child, which are your insurance against abandonment."

Aware of the possible religious opposition, particularly since traditional villagers are inclined to resist the adoption of any form of birth control on alleged fears that such intervention constitutes a violation of religious doctrine and the sanctified wish of God, the LFPA has recruited the support of religious leaders known for their sympathetic views on family planning. On virtually all the seminars, workshops, and round-table discussions they have organized, spokesmen of the various communities have always been present to reassure the public that there is nothing in religious dogma or belief that is antithetical to family planning. In some instances religious sheikhs have, in fact, accompanied family-planning officials and fieldworkers on their initial visits to villages where religious opposition was anticipated.

Fears as to the various side effects of pills, vaginal tablets, and other new forms of birth control have been, as we have seen, a barrier to the diffusion of family planning. Rumors, especially since potential users are prone to be highly suggestible and exaggerate possible side effects, could be quite pernicious. The LFPA, because of its predominantly medical orientation and background of its membership, has displayed considerable interest in these problems. In training fieldworkers, they place special stress on diagnosing and coping with such side effects. Much of the time of the fieldworkers and other volunteers is taken up in talking with, and allaying the fears of, potential users about such rumors. In one particular instance, a whole village was alarmed by unconfirmed reports that women in an adjacent village had suffered from excessive bleeding, nausea, and other disagreeable symptoms because of a new brand of pills they were using. The LFPA promptly assembled a bus-full of women from the "stricken" village and drove them over as tangible evidence to discredit the rumors. The effort was effective and has persuaded the LFPA to resort to such measures in combating barriers of this sort. More important, these and other such episodes have convinced the LFPA of the necessity of involving and enlisting other women, preferably on an informal and voluntary basis, in the design and distribution of family planning services.

By 1974, in less than five years of the LFPA's operation, eighteen family planning clinics in rural and urban areas of Lebanon were already established. Impressive as these are, the accomplishments of the LFPA should not be measured solely in terms of the number of family planning clinics it had established. More significant, perhaps, are the programs and activities it launched in related and auxiliary areas. Foremost among these is the National Fertility and Family Planning Survey it conducted in 1971. The survey, in the absence of official census figures, remains to this date one of the few reliable sources of information on demographic and manpower characteristics.

It is pertinent to note that the results of the survey were welcomed and exploited by the LFPA in support of its objectives. By disclosing a general need as well as a generally favorable attitude for family planning in the country, the LFPA has been able to rationalize and solicit support for its programs. The gap between the positive attitudes and the actual practice of family planning at the national level was attributed to the inaccessibility of contraceptives. Other findings of the survey, namely the relevance of the various socioeconomic indicators for fertility and family size, were also of assistance in this regard.

Armed with such realities, the LFPA has invested considerable effort in educational and public information programs to enhance social awareness for some of the adverse consequences of unplanned parenthood. Accordingly, it has been very active in generating and disseminating the appropriate messages in support of its activities. Initially, such efforts took the form of organized mass-media campaigns through public and private networks as part of a general outreach program. Gradually, however, because of budgetary constraints, the LFPA has restricted its efforts to holding annual conferences, symposia, and workshops to awaken and stimulate the interest of the public in population and population-related issues. These highly publicized sessions draw together a number of experts and scholars in various fields of specialization that touch on family planning, as well as representatives from various private and public institutions. They are also attended by Ministers, military officials, and various religious and civic leaders of the country, along with officials of private voluntary organizations, journalists, health and social workers, students, etc.

Through such sessions the LFPA has been able to reach and mobilize particular target groups, such as students, military personnel, social workers, and individuals active in voluntary and welfare organizations. They have also enabled the Association to sustain its lobbying efforts, which finally led to the formation of the National Population Council in 1983. (For further details regarding the composition, prerogatives, and objectives of the Council, see Iliyya 1984.)

In the area of training, the LFPA has been equally effective and perhaps more tangible and concrete in its results. A sizable number of training workshops is organized annually. Participants include both its own staff and public health and social workers of appropriate welfare associations. Sessions, on the whole, consist of lectures and film projections and cover, in addition to the major topic of family planning, contraceptive use and effects and a variety of other social and health-related issues. The intensive training administered to the *wasitas* is, naturally, much more comprehensive and technical in scope (for further details see, LFPA 1977).

By far, the most ambitious and vital accomplishment of the LFPA has been its community-based program. The program draws on the efforts of the largest number of staff (both employees and volunteers), has a separate budget, and purports to reach a much wider grass-roots participation. Like other community-based programs it is basically an effort to motivate community groups to marshal their own resources to solve their own problems. Basic as this premise is, it marks a significant shift in the philosophy and strategy of the Association.

From Fertility Control to Community Development

There is a clear effort on the part of the LFPA, at least in some of its activities during the past decade, to justify and introduce its programs within the context of social development and general welfare. This has also been accompanied by a gradual shift from the predominantly medical and professional orientation of its initial activities to a wider framework of community self-help through nonclinical and paramedical volunteers. This shift was, in part, a reflection of the changing perspective of the IPPF, the funding agency, which had undergone similar transformations and began, particularly after the 1974 World Population Conference in Bucharest, to emphasize the concept of self-reliance and community-based programs. In the post-Bucharest spirit, many governments and family planning organizations extended the scope of their population efforts to the incorporation of family planning within socioeconomic and health-development programs. Incidentally, the debate at Bucharest was essentially between the so-called "survivalists," who were more concerned with socioeconomic development. The 1974 conference made a vital contribution towards a convergence of these conflicting views and gave rise to the intermediate position of husbanding both development and fertility control (for further details, see Teitelbaum 1974; Korten 1975).

The shift in perspective was also abetted by the emergence of "volunteering" as a catalyst for grass-roots participation and for motivating community groups to enlist their own resources in voluntary self-help projects. The intention underlying such projects is to mute or tone down the "donor-receiver mentality" and the "charity syndrome" often perceived as obstacles to family planning programs and social development in general (Fullam 1978:4–5).

The IPPF was one of several international family planning organizations that adopted such views. Its member associations, of which the LFPA is one, welcomed this burgeoning interest in community development. Indeed, the LFPA was prompt in heeding its call, having established its own community-based program in the Zahrani district of Southern Lebanon in the fall of 1975. Justifications for such a shift are self-evident.

The relatively poor success of its previous clinical approach, along with the financial constraints it put on the Association, must have no doubt reinforced its enthusiasm for community-based family planning services. The degree of attendance in the medical clinics was not up to the desired or optimal level. The high cost of maintaining a clinic forced the Association to charge a fee, which only economically privileged women were willing to pay. Moreover, a contraceptive user, not suffering from health problems, was not in need of a doctor or clinic. The urban location of the clinics rendered such facilities virtually inaccessible to the rural population the Association was hoping to reach (LFPA 1979:33).

By far, however, the shift in the activities of the LFPA in the direction of community development and social welfare was also a by-product of the unusual circumstances associated with the protracted civil disturbances. In considerable respects, in fact, the war has helped in reinforcing and extending the scope of its activities. It must be recalled that the LFPA had just launched its community-based family planning service project in Southern Lebanon when the civil war broke out in 1975. Many of the people returning to their villages in the South to escape the heavy fighting in Beirut were already, it seems, using contraceptives. This doubtlessly helped in generating a favorable attitude in support of family planning already being promoted then through campaigns, lectures, village meetings, and the like. When fighting spread to the South in June 1975, the LFPA center in Saida was one of the few functioning welfare agencies, and it was inevitably drawn into relief and welfare assistance of every sort. People were facing shortages of food, supplies, and medicines. Access to medical personnel and doctors became extremely limited and hazardous. The paramedical staff and fieldworkers of the family planning centers stepped in to assist in such relief efforts. The car bearing the familiar family planning insignia, which used to distribute contraceptives to distributors, began transporting patients, ferrying supplies, and maintaining the flow of vital services.

More than any other activity of the LFPA, the community-based distribution program reflects the Association's sensitivity to some of the indigenous cultural values and institutions and the possibility of mobilizing such mediating structures in processes of development and social change. This expressed itself in concrete instances where the LFPA was able to enlist the support of seemingly "traditional" elements and networks to initiate and legitimize notions of family planning.

By resorting to such culturally meaningful forms of mediating change, the Association heightened the intensity of its persuasiveness and credibility while reducing anticipated sources of resistance. A few such concrete instances are worth noting.

For example, to avert possible religious or other conventional opposition to its activities, the LFPA began soliciting the support of religious leaders known for their sympathetic views on family planning. Initial contacts were established with the local leaders of every village the LFPA entered. In these traditional settings characterized by high religiosity, individuals who are recognized as shaping public opinion were consulted throughout the planning phase. When convinced of the program's worth, they can exert enormous positive influence on the attitude of their community.

Indeed in many villages it was the local religious leaders who called the inhabitants to attend public gatherings in which they introduced the topic of family planning. In some instances the announcements were made through the mosques of the villages. The use of such a persuasive symbol of authority has not only secured the attendance of a large audience, it also awakened its interest and receptivity. In effect, they were being reassured that there is nothing in religious dogma that was antithetical to family planning.

In another instance, when the LFPA was conducting its KAP survey of the Zahrani, its staff members took the time to get personally acquainted with the villagers. More than just assessing the number of married women in the reproductive age, the intention in making such home visits was to socialize with them and announce themselves as people who are genuinely concerned with their problems. These home visits, many of which were made in the evenings, took the form of informal social calls, which reinforced the receptivity of the Zahrani inhabitants to the LFPA. Having won the hospitality and trust of the people was doubtlessly invaluable in enhancing the public image of the Association and the legitimacy of its programs.

The *wasita* is clearly the most elaborate expression of the effort to mobilize indigenous and local resources in inducing change in some of the traditional values and behavioral patterns associated with fertility. The *wasita*'s success is due to her role as a dispenser of family planning information and services as well as an agent of community development and social change.

The *wasita*, to begin with, is a woman who is deeply embedded in her community and well acquainted with its needs, its cultural norms, and institutions. While interacting with her women peers by visiting them at home, she makes use of oral and informal means of communication that are pertinent to her nonliterate milieu. Being of the same gender as her clients has naturally enhanced her credibility as a source of vital information and services.

Her constant presence among the village women makes her readily accessible, at virtually all times, to attend to unforeseen but urgent problems. This is particularly the case in handling symptoms of side effects. In some instances the *wasita* is called late at night to the home of a woman to attend to emergencies involving cases of bleeding, vomiting, or nausea. Her readiness to cope with such chores has heightened her status and sense of self-esteem. More important, perhaps, it has also enabled her to offer her clients some of the elemental needs of dignity, privacy, and self-reliance, which a visit to a male doctor or more impersonal clinic or medical institution quite often violates.

War-generated problems and other circumstances associated with protracted civil disturbances have, as we have seen, given the *wasita* the opportunity to diversify and expand her role. This, too, has entailed a perceptible increase in her self-image and status in the community. She is no longer merely a dispenser of contraceptives or an agent for disseminating ideas on the virtues of family planning. She is now participating in a broader process of social development. To hear the *wasitas* talk about it, their social standing in the community was treated with more regard and deference. They became an enviable role model.

Several were elected by other villagers to be members of local emergency committees set up to deal with problems of relief and welfare. Others were sought more regularly and consulted on all sorts of personal and social problems. Their homes were no longer places women sought simply to replenish their supply of pills, but as one *wasita* put it, they also came to visit and socialize.

Another noted with pride how women in the village respect her opinions and how eager they are to be seen with her:

> They are so impressed by the fact that a car comes to pick me up and that I carry files and pamphlets under my arm. I have become a symbol of modernity. I am not only their avenue for new knowledge, facts; I represent a new life style they wish to identify with and emulate.

Peter Berger once made the observation that, in some Third World countries, the ball-point and the wristwatch as "structures of time and literacy express the mystique of modernity and its promise of a better life." (Berger et al., 1973:145). The *wasita* in southern Lebanon, as an agent for mediating norms of family planning (the ethos of rationality and control) and as an instrument of social welfare and community development, becomes part of that mystique of modernity. A packet of contraceptives and the agent who mediates them, not unlike the wristwatch and the ball-point, become in the words of Peter Berger "the outward, visible signs of an inward transformation of consciousness."

Many of the *wasita*s we interviewed had, in fact, an exaggerated sense of their self-esteem and prestige. The circumstances of the war and their involvement in relief and welfare services did, nonetheless, enhance their incentives and motivation. More important, it permitted them to carry on most of their family planning activities under the expedient guise of community development. In doing so, they avoided whatever sensitivity and self-consciousness people still have about birth control. It also allowed them to underplay the mercenary element of their activity; they retain half the price of every packet of pills they distribute. A packet is offered at the nominal price of one Lebanese pound, or about 20 cents.

Considerations of this kind—i.e., the proclivity of the *wasita* to reach and influence members of her own community and to extend her role— accounts for her effectiveness in generating favorable attitudes toward family planning and in making tangible contributions, modest as they are, to community development and cultural change.

This is not an idle or exaggerated claim. Follow-up studies appear to confirm some of the above assertions. In one such study (Deeb 1977:22– 23), the *wasita* was found to be the main source of information and education on matters of family planning and related concerns. Close to 35 percent of the women covered in the Zahrani project admitted that they continue to consult the *wasita* on a variety of personal problems. It is also estimated that the use of contraceptives in the same district increased from 40 to 60 percent; a rather substantial proportion after only two years of the establishment of the community-based program (Deeb 1977). A more recent study, which surveyed a sample of 200 women in the Zahrani area, revealed that 76 percent held positive attitudes towards the *wasita*'s personality and the role she plays in the community (LFPA 1982:318).

Concluding Inferences

Given the politicization of demographic variables in Lebanon and some of the entrenched institutional and cultural barriers to family planning, it is instructive to explore how a family planning association could emerge and become effective in such a controversial and highly sensitive context.

The story of the LFPA is, to a large extent, a success story, even more so when one considers the inadequacy and/or failure of voluntary associations in general to transcend their parochial and communal surroundings to address genuine public issues. Lebanon, as has been repeatedly suggested, has not been able to harbor or sustain civic sentiments or ties of any appreciable magnitude. Public life and secondary group relations have always suffered from a deficiency of civility. Voluntary associations, of the pure and secular variety, are not likely to prosper in such a milieu. Accordingly, much of the welfare and benevolent needs continue to be mediated through primordial and private networks.

Instances where publics have been aroused in support of some social issue are extremely rare, even when they involve vital concerns over matters of life and death, war and peace. It is in this sense that the experience of the LFPA is instructive. It has succeeded where many other comparable efforts have failed. Its success, I have maintained, is largely due to its ability to mobilize and harness indigenous and traditional elements in reinforcing its objectives and activities. By enlisting the support of traditional and religious figures and symbols, the LFPA bolstered its public image and the legitimacy of its programs without threatening the sense of social cohesion and psychic well-being of its constituency.

Several pertinent inferences can be drawn from such an experience. As a cultural broker, the *wasita* shares much with all the other agencies of adaptive modernization identified so far. Like the political *za'im*, patrimonial manager, family association, house union, and urban quarter, it is another concrete example of an institutional arrangement for achieving the appropriate synthesis between universal and particular interest; between the desire for change and the concern for balance and harmony. While remaining embedded into her own social fabric, the *wasita* was likewise successful in stretching herself to accommodate other purposive interests and rational concerns. In this sense she too became another form of "grafting" of new patterns of behavior on the existing normative structure.

Another self-evident inference stands out. Women are no longer treated as passive recipients of services but have become involved in decisions that have a direct impact on their lives. Studies on the dissemination of new ideas and modes of conduct suggest that recipients are normally more receptive to information emanating from within their own social circle or informal networks than through official and secondary sources. Results of a score of KAP surveys in Lebanon reveal that such informal networks, even in villages or towns where family planning clinics exist, continue to be a major source of information and support (Tanas 1974; Dib 1975; Van Dusen 1973). Through its community-based program, the LFPA is simply taking fuller advantage of such an accessible but often ignored resource. In other words, women and their traditional social circles are not treated as a constraint on development, a useless relic of old times, or a nuisance to be contained or eliminated. They have been utilized as a resource or levers for positive change and grass-roots development.

By involving women from within the community in providing family planning and other welfare services, the *wasitas* become much more responsive to the social, economic, and psychic needs of the women they live with. Comparative research in this area has demonstrated that even the most human, informal, and accessible clinical services remain alien to some of the basic needs of women for privacy and dignity. As we have seen, traditional women in southern Lebanon, as elsewhere, continue to display reluctance to expose themselves to the demands of modern medicine. A trip to a family planning clinic, particularly if it is part of a hospital compound or an outpatient department, involves a disruption of normal daily activities, considerable expenditure in terms of transportation and costs of medicaments, excessive waiting and delays, and often embarrassing encounters with medical personnel. The community-based program removes much of these restraints. A visit to the house of a *wasita* becomes almost like an ordinary social call. In some instances, the presence of the *wasita* is not even demanded. She usually instructs other members of the household to attend to the transaction in her absence. The recipient simply shows her card, and she is given the proper packet of pills. Some of the *wasitas* simplify the task even further. They assign their clients code numbers or specific colors by which their corresponding pills may be identified even by a child or any other member of the household.

The above observations prompt one to reemphasize the importance of small units and seemingly nonrational and informal organizations in coping with some of the population-related problems. Partly because of the bias in Western models and perspectives in favor of the more secular and rational dimensions of planning, there has been the tendency to denigrate traditional agencies as useless and nostalgic residues of the past. This, I feel, is a serious and costly error; one that is based on a misunderstanding of the adaptive role that so-called traditional and smaller organizations or systems have or can play in disseminating the necessary knowledge, attitudes, and practices relevant to a particular population policy. Accordingly, we are repeatedly told, by foreign and native experts alike, that the survival of kinship ties, communal attachments, and sectarian loyalties are impediments to an effective population policy and that the sooner we erode such values and institutions, the more successful we are in achieving desired objectives.

Historical and more recent evidence speaks otherwise. As we have seen, a variety of small and informal institutional arrangements, sustained by the survival of primordial attachments, have been quite effective in exposing the Lebanese to some of the requirements of modernization and rational planning without eroding cultural identity or threatening communal attachments. The sensitive area of population and family planning is no exception. Here, as well, informal networks and parochial voluntary associations have been far more effective in generating the proper attitudes regarding family planning and in coping with some of the demographic problems than some of the specific and purposively created family planning schemes.

For example, several of the outstanding demographic problems in Lebanon—particularly the relative youthfulness of the population, the high frequency of widows, and the rural exodus—can be more appropriately coped with through the adaptive mechanisms of these smaller social units. The pervasiveness of family networks and the supports widows, dependents, and recent migrants receive from extended kinship and communal ties no doubt mitigate the possible adverse effects of these unusual demographic features (for further details, see Khalaf 1978).

If such small and informal systems have been flexible and receptive to the socioeconomic and cultural transformations Lebanon has been undergoing, then it becomes illogical to conclude that one of the major preconditions for an effective population policy is the erosion of traditional ties, institutions, and values. Instead, we must learn to refrain from tampering with them unnecessarily and utilize them creatively in our planning. Problems such as maternity and child care, welfare, health, education, vocational training, incentives for reducing fertility, support for the young and the aged (social, psychological, and economic), and other benevolent and recreational functions can be handled appropriately and relatively efficiently by small units at the lower levels of the system.

These small agencies, as we have seen earlier, do not only mediate between the impersonal authority of the central government and the personal and communal aspects of special groups (familial, ethnic, religious, or otherwise), they fill a void left by an inefficient and often mistrustful bureaucracy.

Furthermore, such internal and informal forms of social control are more likely to inspire the allegiance and commitments of its subjects. More important, they eliminate the need for the sort of vast, formal costly measures that any system of external control must resort to.

Recognition of the interdependence between the multilevel systems (large and small units, local and national etc.) implies that one can never formulate a "whole plan." Indeed, one can set forth major objectives and then seek to identify pivotal "levers" of manipulation that can activate the forces necessary to approach the objectives. Janet Abu-Lughod has aptly labeled this the "Archimedean principle of planning." It essentially involves that we "locate the *pivotal lever outside and at a distance* from the system to be moved, and then utilize the forces set in motion by the lever to have the *system move itself.*" (Abu-Lughod 1972:12). This is reminiscent of Herbert Spencer's warning embodied in his often-quoted illustration of the bent iron plate. In trying to flatten the wrought-iron plate, it is futile, Spencer suggested, to hammer directly on the buckled-up part; we only make matters worse. To be effective, our hammering must be around, and not directly on, the projected part we wish to reduce.

The moral of all this is simple: indirect measures such as enforced secondary education for women, inhibition of early marriage, provision of well-paying jobs to increase the proportion of women in the labor force etc., may do much more to solve some of the problems generated by rapid population growth than all the activities designed to control fertility and migration.

CHAPTER TEN

Social Structure and Urban Planning

W HILE THE INTERPLAY between cultural values and family planning has been mutually reinforcing, the impact of such an interplay has not been equally supportive when one considers the plight of urban planning in Lebanon. By enlisting and mobilizing the support of some of the culturally rooted elements and symbols, the Lebanese Family Planning Association was able, as we have seen, to "sugar-coat" family planning, bolster its public image, and safeguard the legitimacy and credibility of its programs. In more explicit terms, both the social standing of the *wasita* and the effectiveness of the LFPA were reinforced as a result.

No such mutually supportive instances can be singled out in Lebanon's experience with urban planning. If anything, the relationship has been more subversive in character. To some extent this might well be due to the nature of urbanization and the scale and scope of the urban planning. Given its magnitude, urban planning cannot and should not, perhaps, be entrusted, as in the case with family planning, to one single voluntary association. The actors involved in the management of urban space are more likely to represent state and national agencies or be part of a team of foreign experts. Such individuals are known to serve the political and commercial interests of their client groups and are, consequently, less likely to display much concern for the aesthetic and rational qualities of urban strategies or zoning schemes.

Such considerations notwithstanding, it is still instructive, given the overriding thesis of this volume, to explore the nature and consequences of the dialectics between some of the persisting structural features of

This essay is a revised version of a chapter originally published in Ann Meyer, ed., *Property, Social Structure, and Law in the Modern Middle East* (Albany, N.Y.: State University of New York Press, 1985). Used by permission.

Lebanese society and urban planning. Several justifications can be advanced for carrying such a case study.

One justification for studying these dialectics is that no matter how planning is defined, whether in its narrow physical perspective or in a more broader social context, it connotes the injection of rationality into a particular area of human life. In its narrow sense, planning is predominantly concerned with issues surrounding the physical form of the city, the spatial arrangement of urban functions, and the control and the allocation of land. In its broader sense, urban planning represents "deliberate efforts to order the environment so as to realize certain common goals and values. As such, it is concerned not merely with the rational allocation of resources but, more importantly, with the selection of goals and values toward which these resources should be directed" (Weaver 1963:97).

In both senses, however, attempts are made to control the environment by eliminating such hazards to health and well-being as slums or traffic congestion and by adjusting future growth to a master plan. In this sense zoning, like other ordinances regulating traffic, urban renewal, and public amenities, becomes an integral part of urban master planning. They are all efforts to exert control over the distribution of land use and the allocation of other resources (Wilhelm 1962:2).

Implicit in all this are issues such as the ideal size of cities, the optimum ration of primate to other cities, and the impact of increasing urbanization on existing social institutions and value. These, and other such issues, involve the introduction of a certain degree of rationality, control, forecasting, cost-benefit analysis etc., into an area previously left to private initiative or to the chance combination of other societal changes.

Within such a context, it becomes meaningful to consider how a relatively "modern" notion of land-use planning and zoning has been introduced and incorporated into a sociocultural milieu in which seemingly "traditional" values and loyalties are expected to militate against such an introduction.

The dialectical nature of the relationship between urban planning as rational strategies for controlling and allocating resources and some of the persisting features of a pluralistic society like Lebanon discloses another poignant dilemma, one that is central to the dominant concern of this book. The very elements of that social structure that are sources of viability and solidarity—such as kinship and communal loyalties, patron-client networks, and other primordial attachments—are also sources of vulnerability. As we have seen, while the average Lebanese continues to derive social and psychic supports and some tangible benefits from cultivating such "traditional" ties, it is also these ties that impede or distort urban planning and zoning. Once again, in other words, norms that enable in some respects, disable in other respects.

A further feature worthy of study is Lebanon's unique laissez-faire and liberal tradition. In mobilizing and managing its human and economic resources, successive governments in Lebanon have continued to pursue policies that encourage free enterprise and private initiative in virtually all sectors of the society. Such rampant liberalism manifests itself in an excessive degree of individualism at the personal level and in the near absence of government intervention at the state level. Conscious perhaps of both its own limitations and the resourcefulness and enterprise of its subjects, the government has reduced its interference to a minimum. While such a liberal tradition might have served well the interests of private enterprise and is consistent with the political realities of a pluralistic society, it is certainly not compatible with the requirements of urban planning.

One of the basic tools of urban planning is, after all, the promulgation of orderly legislation dealing with the just and equitable conveyance of property from private to public use. By its very nature, such a process involves restrictions on certain freedoms. The Lebanese in general have always resisted such restrictions and have continued to perceive any plan as an unwarranted infringement on the private use of property.

Once again, it becomes pertinent within such a context to explore how such seemingly incompatible traditions—norms associated with laissez-faire, freedom, and nonintervention and those necessitated by the growing need for planning, coordination, and control—have been reconciled in Lebanon. As will be demonstrated, such a reconciliation has not as yet been effectively maintained. Consequently, much of the urban crisis Lebanon is facing is attributed to the failure of planning so far to curb or restrain some of the inauspicious consequences of individualism and laissez-faire.

In addition to the internal considerations of the persistence of communalism, the laissez-faire ethos, the rapid urbanization, there are economic and political forces external to Lebanon that also account for the failure of urban planning. Massive internal migration generated by Israel's unrelenting bombardment of Southern Lebanon, the successive influx of Palestinian and other refugees and their convergence on already congested urban districts, and the influx of Arabian capital and foreign remittances and the consequent speculation in real estate and soaring land values have all had a disruptive impact on the government's ability to implement general master plans or specific zoning schemes. In elucidating the nature of the interplay between planning and the social structure, it is vital to document the implications of such external sources.

Lebanon's urban crisis is a reflection of yet another unresolved problem: the persisting discrepancy between urban legislation and ordinances and actual concrete behavior and spatial patterns. In all human societies, even among the most civic-minded and orderly, the two rarely converge. In Lebanon, however, the gap between the two is clearly more visible than elsewhere. As will be seen, Lebanon has never been short on master plans and blueprints. As early as 1930, and long before the increasing scale and intensity of urbanization began to appear, the country had already experimented with several planning schemes. None of these schemes and master plans, however, were approved or implemented. This gap between audacious planning and executive ineffectiveness has continued to characterize all subsequent efforts at master planning and zoning. Even when adopted, certain dimensions of the plans were almost always transgressed and violated.

Given this persisting discrepancy, it is meaningful to shed further light on the nature of the relationship between social processes and spatial forms. More concretely, an attempt is made to demonstrate how the fashioning of spatial forms can influence social processes, and conversely how a particular spatial environment can reflect certain social and normative considerations. The interplay between these two forms of consciousness, the "geographic" and the "sociological," as they have been labeled by David Harvey (1973), continues to attract considerable controversy.

Early city planners such as Howard and Abercrombie and more recently architects such as Lynch (1960) and Doxiadis (1968), trained in a tradition of spatial consciousness, have sought to show how the modification of spatial forms can mold the social process. Others, particularly Jacobs (1961), Webber (1963), and Gans (1970), attack this form of "spatial environmental determinism" and support, instead, an alternative perspective in which a social process is viewed as possessing its own dynamic that often—in spite of the planner—will achieve its own particular spatial form.

Though in a different context, some of the earlier writings of Lévi-

Strauss (1963) reflect this same general perspective, particularly when he shows how the spatial layout of a whole village in a primitive culture may reflect the mythology of the people and their pattern of social interaction. Likewise, Lowenthal and Prince (1964) have also demonstrated how each age fashions its environment to reflect existing social norms.

While one should recognize the complementary and dialectical nature of this process, it is still more appropriate in the case of Lebanon to explore the impact of the social system on land-use patterns and other spatial arrangements. Given the nature of urbanization, the relative recency of planning, and the tenacity of certain social and normative elements, it becomes more meaningful to document how the social structure has affected planning and zoning ordinances rather than to consider the impact of such laws on the social structure. More specifically, an attempt is made to demonstrate how certain persisting features of the social and cultural structure shape, modify, and even distort existing laws and their application.

It is necessary, however, to consider first some of the striking features of urbanization and the nature of urban planning and zoning in Lebanon.

The Nature of Urbanization and Urbanism

Two general features of urbanization in Lebanon have concrete implications for understanding the nature of the dialectics between planning and the social structure, namely: the relatively swift and recent character of urbanization and the persistence of traditional ties and communal attachments.

Despite its compelling site and favorable geographic location, for centuries Beirut remained a curiously small and insignificant agglomeration. As recently as the late eighteenth century, its population was estimated at six thousand, and in 1848 not more than fifteen thousand. After 1860 the incessant flow of rural exodus began and has never ceased since. The first evidence, however, of the increasing scale of urbanization—as measured by the intensity of construction activity—did not really appear in Beirut until early in the 1950s. Until then, the city continued to assume its horizontal and even skyline with the traditional suburban villas overwhelming the urban scene. As in most European towns before industrialization, people in Beirut were at the turn of the century still living and working within the same place. Daily routines were carried out within clearly defined quarters, and the neighborhood survived as an almost self-sufficient community with which the individual identified. There was a strong sense of neighborliness, and patterns of behavior were largely regulated through kinship and religious ties. Physical and social space, in other words, were almost identical. Ethnic and religious affiliations created relatively homogeneous and compact neighborhoods (*hārāt* or *'ahya'*), which until recently continued to provide security and a deep sense of community. More important, these neighborhoods offered the urban dweller a human scale and types of social networks he could comprehend and in which he could find a uniquely individual space.

With rapid urbanization (the consequence of both internal migration and natural growth rates in the population) this pattern could not naturally sustain itself. Since nearly two-thirds of this rural exodus was directed towards Beirut, the capital grew by nearly tenfold since 1932 and trebled its residential population between 1932 and 1964. This rapid and almost instantaneous growth of Beirut was not only due to internal demographic factors; be they rates of natural increase or rural exodus. To a large extent, it was also a reflection of external pressures that generated added demand for urban space. The waves of Palestinian refugees after 1948 and the political instability in neighboring Arab countries intensified this demand. So did the subsequent inflow of capital from the Gulf states and foreign remittances that sought investment in the already lucrative real estate and construction sectors of the economy. The building boom of the 1950s and 1960s, with all its manifestations of mixed and intensive land-use patterns and vertical expansion of Beirut, was largely a by-product of such forces. The same uncontrolled and haphazard patterns of growth were maintained early during the 1970s. Shortly before the outbreak of civil disturbances in 1975, greater Beirut was probably absorbing 75 percent of Lebanon's urban population and close to 45 percent of the inhabitants of the country. In addition, its already choking 101 square kilometers had to accommodate an estimate of 120,000 daily commuters from adjoining suburbs (Ragheb 1969:110).

By the early 1970s, Beirut's annual rate of growth was estimated at 4.0 percent, which implied that the city was bound to double in less than twenty years. The magnitude of this change may still be expressed in more concrete terms: if the current rates of growth are maintained, Beirut has to accommodate and provide housing, schooling, medical services, and transportation etc. for at least 40,000 new residents every year.

It is in this sense that Beirut is associated with the phenomenon of primacy and over-urbanization. Insofar as the degree of urbanization is much more than would be expected from the level of industrialization, then Lebanon is among the few countries—along with Egypt, Greece, and Korea—that may be considered "over-urbanized" (Sovani 1969).

This is not the place to explore the various implications of primacy and over-urbanization. Suffice it to note that this is one of the most critical problems Lebanon faces, a problem with serious social, psychological, economic and, as recent events amply demonstrate, political implications. Urban congestion, blight, depletion of open spaces, disparities in income distribution, rising levels of unemployment and underemployment, housing shortages, exorbitant rent, problems generated by slums and shanty towns, and to a considerable extent urban violence . . . these are all a by-product of over-urbanization. In short, the scale and scope of urbanization has outstripped the city's resources to cope effectively with the continuously mounting demand for urban space and public amenities.

These problems have been compounded by another peculiar feature of Lebanese urbanization: the survival of communal and traditional loyalties. Repeated studies have shown that the swift and extensive urbanization Lebanon has been experiencing has not been associated, as is the case in most other societies, with the same degree of decline in kinship and communal loyalties (see, for example, Gulick 1967; Khalaf and Kongstad 1973; Khuri 1975). In other words, the intensity and increasing scale of "urbanization" as a physical phenomena has not been accompanied by a proportional degree of "urbanism" as a way of life.

What this suggests, among other things, is that a sizable proportion of the urban residents are, in an existential sense, *in* but not *of* the city. To both recent migrants and relatively more permanent urban settlers, city life is predominantly conceived as a transient encounter to be sustained by periodic visits to rural areas, or through the development of rural networks within urban areas. Accordingly, urbanization in Lebanon has not meant the erosion of kinship ties, communal loyalties, and confessional affinities and the emergence of impersonality, anonymity, and transitory social relations. As in other dimensions of social life, the network of urban social relations, visiting patterns, and the character of voluntary associations still sustain a large residue of traditional attachments despite increasing secularization and urbanization. In many respects Beirut—and this is also true of Tripoli, Saida, and other major cities—is more a "mosaic" of distinct urban communities than a "melting pot" of amorphous urban masses.

Inasmuch as the survival of such features has been a source of communal solidarity, providing much of the needed social and psychic supports, they also account, as we have seen, for much of the deficiency in civility and the erosion of public and national consciousness. More important, perhaps, they act as barriers to urban planning and zoning.

The protracted civil crisis of the past decade has not only compounded these problems, it has generated others of a far more critical and serious magnitude. Vast areas, in addition to the central business district, have been totally or partially destroyed. Massive population shifts have generated further disparities and imbalances between the various communities and intensified confessional hostility and urban violence. The virtual collapse of state agencies and legitimate institutions created further opportunities for the violation of zoning and construction ordinances.

Antipathy Toward Planning

One general observation can be inferred from the discussion thus far: the swift and extensive nature of urbanization and the survival of a large residue of traditional norms account, in part, for the failure of planning and zoning to curb the haphazard and unguided growth of Beirut. Urbanization, in other words, happened much too quickly; clearly outstripping whatever institutional agencies of social control existed at the time. Furthermore, because of the persistence of personal and communal loyalties, the few attempted planning schemes remained unrealized blueprints. This is not all that surprising. In a political culture like Lebanon where hierarchy, rank, patronage, and other particularistic considerations are recognized, zoning and planning norms are apt to be violated.

Planning schemes

In the early 1930s, public officials in Beirut began to display considerable concern for the physical development of the city. Lebanon, it must be recalled, was then under the French Mandate, and all the early "plans" were inspired and undertaken by French experts. Successive teams of such specialists were engaged to prepare the necessary guidelines to direct the future growth of Beirut. A brief survey of the salient features of these "plans" is necessary, particularly since they set the pattern for other town-planning schemes and developments.

The earliest city plan for Beirut was prepared by the French consultant Danger in 1932. This was the first attempt at comprehensive planning taking into account geographic, geological, demographic, and human features of Beirut and its adjacent communities. The plan established the three main traffic arteries (Beirut-Damascus, Beirut-Tripoli, and Beirut-Saida) and proposed other new roads and bypasses. More significantly, it outlined zoning coefficients and varying densities of various occupations and recommended residential developments along the lines of garden cities. Danger, almost fifty years ago, had the foresight to treat Beirut and its suburbs as one unit. He also demonstrated a judicious concern to conserve and promote some of the environmental and aesthetic features of the city. As such, the plan proposed measures for the protection of elevated areas, the development of public parks and gardens, the building of sanitary sewers, and the organization of refuse collection and slum clearance. Unfortunately, the Danger plan was never approved and hence its recommendations were never implemented. (For further details see Salam 1972; the Executive Board of Major Projects for the City of Beirut, 1968.)

The Ecochard Plan of 1944 did not fare any better. It, too, was based on exhaustive studies and maintained that the planning of Beirut should extend beyond its limited administrative boundaries to encompass the coastal stretch from Nahr el Maout in the North to Ouzai in the South. Like the Danger Plan, it outlined the major traffic arteries and highway network and displayed the same concern for the protection of natural sites, open spaces, and public gardens. It even went so far as to provide an inventory of the valuable trees that should be maintained in Beirut. It also went into greater detail in proposing zoning ordinances, the location of the airport and other civic centers, industrial zones, and popular housing. The city was divided into twelve zones—commercial, industrial, and residential—with varying densities. Like its predecessor, however, this plan was never approved, although many of its recommendations were incorporated in later plans.

The Egli Report or plan of 1950 was essentially a reappraisal of the earlier Ecochard Plan. It recommended the adoption of most of its proposals, particularly the layout of the highway system, but reduced the number of zones from twelve to five. Again, this plan was never approved although some of its recommendations formed the basis for further studies, which resulted in the General Master Plan of 1951–54.

But this General Master Plan—the only officially approved plan that has been responsible for the development of Beirut since—was nothing but a network of roads derived essentially from the Ecochard Plan. It provided no zoning. It did not consider any of the factors that could affect future developments; such as the location of industry, airports, harbor, tourism etc. Nor did it make any effort to preserve the natural sites and historic monuments of the city. More important, perhaps, it failed to consider Beirut within its broader metropolitan and regional context. The results became painfully obvious: commercial centers invaded residential districts, ground floors and front gardens were converted into shops and side-walk cafes, offices located themselves in apartment buildings, streets were over-congested with traffic, soaring land values made it impossible to provide for green areas and open spaces, and the lack of protection of natural sites and monuments eroded the little that remained of the national and architectural heritage. Conditions in the suburbs were even worse. Since there was no plan or zoning legislations for the outskirts, no limits whatsoever were imposed on built-up areas. Entire suburbs mushroomed overnight and started to close in on the city. Stretches of virgin land were converted into parcelization schemes for purposes of commercial speculation.

In short, at the very time that Beirut and its suburbs were experiencing their most intensive demographic pressure and urban expansion, planning schemes were either totally absent or deficient. At least until 1964, by the time that the first town planning legislations were formulated in Lebanon, the only control that existed was an obsolete building code. But by then it was too late to curb or redirect the chaotic growth.

Since the Building Code of 1932 and the town planning laws of 1963 are the two legislative documents responsible for planning and zoning in Lebanon, a word about each is in order.

The Building Code

The Lebanese Building Code, which has been subjected to four substantive amendments since its enactment in 1932 (1940, 1954, 1964, 1971), like all other official schemes in Lebanon, leaves little to be desired except its implementation. The Code was inspired by the French and is very explicit in its provisions. It covers specific requirements and regulations regarding matters such as construction and occupancy permits; the overall envelope within which a building must be contained; the unobstructed visual distance between the facade of the building and the limit of the land (this is usually a minimum of 4.5 meters to insure a "clear view," i.e., to permit the opening of a window for ventilation and lighting); setbacks, from both the road and neighbor; plot ratios specifying coefficients of surface and total exploitation; the appearance of buildings and their structural safety; parcelation or subdivision of land; parking space; and penalties etc. . . . .

Most of the provisions are very stringent in their requirements and if applied could have safeguarded the urban environment from further abuse, or at least contained some of the ugly manifestations of the dehumanization of living space Lebanon has been witnessing during the past two decades. In many respects the damage is irreparable. To permit the misuse of a parcel of land, insignificant as it may seem initially, is bound to have long-lasting and irreversible consequences. For example, Article 7 of the Code specifies that a newly constructed building cannot be supplied with electric power, water, and telephones unless the proprietor secures an "occupancy permit" verifying that the actual specifications of the final product are consistent with the approved original design of the building. If implemented this could impose effective controls on the rampant construction violations. Municipal authorities, however, have not been able to detect, let alone contain or prevent the ingenious strategies the Lebanese have developed to transgress this and other construction ordinances.

Quite often, for example, proprietors could, after securing the occupancy permit, add another floor, violate setback regulations, or convert the use of a floor space from residential to commercial. Most such clandestine constructions take place stealthily at night to avoid notice. Even if detected, penalties and fines are nominal and insubstantial compared to the benefits they derive from such transgressions. Often a modest bribe to a municipal clerk or inspector is sufficient to ensure that the infraction is ignored.

Article 18 of the Building Code, which is concerned with the outside appearance and aesthetic quality of buildings, requires proprietors to periodically restore, paint, and embellish the facades of their buildings, otherwise the appropriate authorities are empowered to undertake such beautification at the expense of the proprietors. This, too, is never enforced, generating as a result much of the ugly and blighted quality of the urban environment.

The lack of enforcement of such rules reflects the proclivity of proprietors to ignore these requirements, just as much as it reflects the reluctance of municipal authorities to enforce them. In both instances, however, they are doubtless an expression of deficient civility and the pervasive lack of concern citizens in general display for the quality of public space. Incidentally, while the exterior and facades of buildings are neglected, this is not necessarily true of their interior, which are generally more cared for.

No other area, perhaps, is subjected to as many violations as that regulating the coefficient of exploitation of land. The Code makes a distinction between zoned and unzoned areas and specifies the total and surface coefficients for each, along with the height of the building, number of floors, setbacks etc. Possibly because of soaring land values and the eagerness of the Lebanese to exploit every meter of space he is entitled to, here too the extent and nature of violations are staggering. This applies to large-scale entrepreneurs, contractors, and speculators just as it applies to the simple homeowner keen on maximizing his private interests. The strategies they have developed for circumventing the law are both subtle and ingenious.

For example, Article 14 of the Building Code specifies the areas that are normally excluded in calculating the coefficient of exploitation; such as open terraces and balconies that do not exceed 20 percent of the surface area of the floor; basements and pillar floors; attics; and projections and protrusions devoted for decorative and other purposes. In each of these instances, proprietors, particularly after securing their occupancy permits, manage ultimately to extend their construction to exploit such areas, thus exceeding the optimal coefficient required by the law.

The conversion of pillar and attic space into full-fledged floors is by far one of the most recurrent and visible violations. This is particularly the case in suburban and rural areas where zoning regulations restrict the number of floors to a maximum of three. By filling in the pillar floor, intended originally as structural support, and by rearranging slightly the attic space, a three-story building becomes in fact five.

The same is also true of the regulations governing parking space and garages in the basement of apartment buildings. The Code is equally stringent here, but most proprietors find their way around such restrictions and end up leasing such space for commercial use.

The alibis to which they resort are legion and quite accessible. All that is needed is proof that the passage leading to the basement is too steep or narrow to permit the entry of vehicles. In some instances proprietors actually contrive pillars or other structural barriers to obstruct such passage. They are then more than willing to pay the substitute fee to secure the release of the basement. In nearly all such instances, what should have been legitimate parking space for tenants is leased out as a warehouse, stereo-club, bar, or some other commercial space. More than any other factor, this has compounded the parking problems and traffic congestion Lebanese cities suffer from. Recent estimates reveal that there is one motor vehicle for every 4½ persons in Lebanon. Given the small size and high density of the country, this is a notoriously high ratio and is bound to have adverse implications for the quality of urban life. As it is, side-walks, alleyways, courtyards and other pedestrian and open spaces are being mindlessly eaten up and transformed into parking lots. Since municipal authorities are normally lax in detecting and penalizing such transgressions, their magnitude has increased considerably, particularly during the past five years.

Given widespread anarchy and disorder and the erosion of state sovereignty, agencies empowered to safeguard public safety and security, have been reluctant to exercise their legitimate responsibility. Municipal authorities, judges, and magistrates, in the absence of supportive judiciary institutions, harbor legitimate fears about initiating any legal or criminal proceedings. Even when violations are detected, proceedings for legal action are still virtually inoperative under present circumstances.

Town Planning Legislation

The town planning legislation of 1963 stands out as an important threshold in Lebanon's checkered history with urban planning. It marks the first serious attempt at comprehensive planning and legislation and was the product of a commission appointed by the government in 1961. The commission produced the so-called "Plan Directeur de Beyrouth et sa banlieue,"[1] which established all the densities for the various zones, particularly the outskirts of Beirut, set the location for industry and governmental centers and protected the coast, beaches, woods, and natural sites. More important, the commission also produced the first set of planning legislation, which was to apply to the whole of Lebanon and has been in operation since.

In brief, the 1963 legislation concentrated all matters related to town planning in one single authority, the Directorate General of Town Planning, attached to the Ministry of Public Works. It also established a Higher Council for Urban Planning (HCUP), a totally independent body formed of representatives of interested ministeries.[2] Both the Directorate and the Council are expected to follow priorities established by the Government, but they are nonetheless given the full right to decide on the areas that need planning.

On the whole, by tightening control over building permits, architectural aesthetics, and land parcelization, the new legislation has been so far moderately successful in controlling some of the earlier gaps inherent in the obsolete Building Code. For example, the HCUP has recently drafted a proposal to amend those articles of the Building Code dealing with violations to render them more stringent. If and when the proposed amendments are approved by the Parliament, it will become theoretically impossible for the violator to consider or retain his transgression unless he is willing to assume the full burden of the heavy fine. The proposed law calculates the fine as five times the required construction dues on all the built-up area in addition to the price of the imaginary land generated by the violation. To give a concrete instance, suppose a proprietor constructs unlawfully an additional floor and by so doing he increases his build-up area by 500 square meters beyond the coefficient required by the law. In certain areas of Beirut, where the land value is as high as $3000 per square meter, the fine might easily reach the neighborhood of $200,000.

Theoretically, such impositions could of course act as effective deterrents. In practice, however, they are likely to remain futile unless supplemented by executive powers to implement them. Given the erosion of state powers and rampant lawlessness with which Lebanon is currently beset, they are unlikely to be enforced.

The effectiveness of the legislation and the HCUP has also been seriously handicapped by some other persisting shortcomings. There is, first, the ubiquitous conflict of interest with other government agencies reluctant to relinquish prerogatives they had once enjoyed. More grievous, perhaps, is the failure to establish an adequate reform of existing land taxation or control over land speculation. Because of the usual collusion between private entrepreneurs and the political establishment, it is virtually impossible to impose any effective restraints on the abusive consequences of excessive speculation in real estate.

In most of these instances, it is naturally the substantial entrepreneurs and businessmen with political connections who stand to benefit from such circumstances. They are usually privy to some vital tips or hints as to the areas which are to be subjected to zoning in the near future. They venture then to purchase vast stretches of land in anticipation of such opportunities; particularly since zoning will almost always generate a sharp increase in land values.

The adverse effects of speculation has other equally abusive consequences. As we have seen, it was impossible under the old legislation, because of soaring land values, to expropriate land for any urban redevelopment on a large scale. To overcome this barrier, the new legislation stipulated the establishment of Mixed Real Estate Companies (public and private) in which the government will become shareholder to the amount to which it is normally entitled under the expropriation laws, i.e., 25 percent of the property. The private sector will receive the remaining 75 percent. The mixed company will undertake the planning of the entire zone and then proceed to sell property in accordance with the master plan developed for the zone, which must include open areas, parks, schools, and other collective facilities. Ideally such a system is supposed to protect individuals from being penalized by expropriation for the benefit of others. Also, the appreciation of land value, resulting from such projects, will be shared more equitably by every owner pro rata to his deed. Although the law has been in existence for sixteen years, it has been obstructed, almost paralyzed, by the interference of large property owners in districts where mixed companies were created. Such entrepreneurs are usually opposed to these schemes because they impose limits on their free and uncontrolled speculation in real estate. Unfortunately, only three such projects, all in the suburbs of Beirut, have been actually implemented. Studies for four other areas—Tripoli, Saida, and Hammanah and Sofar (the latter two being mountain resorts)—have been completed and await approval by proper authorities.

Finally, and perhaps most important, although the HCUP has been established as an independent and central authority to consider all matters pertaining to urban planning and zoning, it is only empowered to "express its opinion" (Article 4 of the Urban Planning Legislation), and hence can only act in an advisory capacity. Many of its decisions and deliberations are often overruled or ignored by the Council of Ministers or President of the Republic. Indeed, the President of the Republic has exceptional powers at his disposal enabling him to enact special decrees by which he can modify the zoning or land-use pattern of any area without reference to the HCUP. On several occasions successive Presidents

are known to have made opportune use of such extraordinary prerogatives. Needless to say, a mere reclassification of a zoned area from, say,
residential to industrial increases the coefficient of exploitation, and by
so doing generates a manifold increase in land value.

Familism, Patronage, and Commercialism

The bulk of the discussion thus far has been concerned with identifying some of the salient features of urbanization and the nature of urban
planning and zoning in Lebanon. An attempt was made to show how
urbanization as a physical phenomena had a disruptive impact on the
government's ability to control or regulate the unguided and haphazard
growth of urban districts. Urbanization, with its concomitant internal
and external pressures, generated by massive population shifts, capital
inflow, and speculation in real estate, occurred all too swiftly to permit
the development of effective plans and zoning schemes. The process of
urban planning itself was also handicapped by administrative pitfalls and
some deep-lying antipathies toward planning as rational strategies for
controlling and allocating land as a resource. The successive schemes and
master plans, many of which were nothing more than a network of roads,
remained unimplemented blueprints. The same is true of the Building
Code of 1932 and the Town Planning Legislation of 1963. Despite their
stringent provisions and restrictions, they too, as we have seen, failed to
impose any effective control on the abuse of the urban environment.

But this is only part of the story. The failure of urban planning in
Lebanon is also in part a reflection of certain persisting features of its
social structure. This final section explores the impact of three such features—familism, patronage, and commercialism—on the spatial structure. The discussion will necessarily be brief and sketchy. The intention
is simply to highlight some of the obvious implications of such traditional elements for urban planning and zoning.

The survival of family loyalty, with its associated norms and institutions, as repeated studies have demonstrated, continues to have a visible
impact on the spatial structure and physical layout of urban areas. The
family in Lebanon, despite the inevitable decline in the sense of kinship
generated by increasing urbanization, mobility, and secularization, continues to have a social and psychological reality that pervades virtually all
aspects of society. There is hardly a dimension of one's life that is un-

touched by it. To a considerable extent, a person's status, his occupation, political behavior, personal values, and various events in his life cycle are largely defined by his kinship affiliation. So intense and encompassing are kinship attachments that the average Lebanese, as we have seen, continues to seek and find refuge and identity with close family circles.

Incidentally, the disruptive and shattering events of the civil war have, in several respects, strengthened the family and reinforced kinship attachments. As the public world becomes more savage, menacing, and insecure, people have been more inclined to escape into the family to seek comfort in its domesticity and privacy.

Such pervasive familism does not only manifest itself in particular architectural features that survive in traditional urban quarters, such as the inward-looking house, the bent-doorway, the *dar, harat,* and courtyard, they also determine the location of residence, visiting and shopping patterns, and much of the associational behavior of persons even in highly mobile and modern urban districts. Patrilocal residence, extended family obligations, the desire to retain control of family homesteads and real estate, and the system of inheritance, which permits the divisibility of property into an infinite number of individual shareholders, make it extremely difficult to introduce a system of urban renewal or redevelopment of traditional urban quarters.

Indeed, much of the "confused look," irregularity, and anarchy of Lebanese cities, particularly as they manifest themselves in torturous streets, labyrinthian quarters, unusual lot shapes and sizes, are to a large extent a reflection of the persistence of such kinship norms and primordial loyalties. It should be remarked here that the layout of the traditional neighborhood is not by itself necessarily incompatible with urban planning standards. Despite their seemingly "confused look," many of the older neighborhoods would have survived as viable and colorful forms of human association had they been preserved by the new plans. Unfortunately, many of the new schemes display little sensitivity to such spatial arrangements. Hence, rather than re-routing expressways to protect some of the graceful and edifying features of such communities, the new expressways often disfigure their natural layout and destroy their communal and intimate character. It is then that the neighborhoods and quarters begin to assume some of the anomalous and dysfunctional features.

A pluralistic society like Lebanon, marked by persistent disparities in status and opportunity and sustained by highly personalized networks of reciprocal obligations and primordial loyalties, generates circumstances germane for the development of patronage and clientelistic politics. To a large measure, much of the sociopolitical history of Lebanon may be viewed as the history of various groups and communities seeking to se- cure patronage: client groups in search of protection, security, and vital benefits, and patrons seeking to extend the scope of their clientage.

Patronage, as we have seen, appears in many guises and is certainly not unique to Lebanon. In virtually all known societies, with or without diffuse and ascriptive loyalties, individuals and groups normally seek to advance their private ends particularistically. In Lebanon the most viable and visible form of patronage is the middleman, the *wasit,* and the bro- ker, who provide greater access to opportunity and needed benefits for their clients in return for their political support and loyalty. It is in this sense that patron-client ties involve the reciprocal exchange of extrinsic benefits. Both the patron and the client, in other words, have a vested interest in maintaining this kind of mutually beneficial transaction. As demonstrated earlier, clients in Lebanon have no other accessible avenue to secure some of their personal services and favored treatment than through their allegiance to a patron, and patrons can only maintain their power by extending the size of their clientage support.

This pervasive feature of Lebanon's social structure doubtlessly affects the process of zoning in some substantive and concrete ways. Patronage, it must be borne in mind, rarely appears alone. It carries with it a host of other disquieting features: endemic corruption, bribery, graft, nepo- tism, executive and administrative incompetence, private interference in public decisions and *quid pro quos* all suggest that private and particular- istic ends are being promoted at the expense of public and universalistic expectations. Government bureaucracy is overstaffed with incompetent and inept civil servants, most of whom owe their careers to the favoritism or *wasta* that a political or communal leader applied on their behalf. Now they are in a position to return the favor; and they do so in some tangi- ble ways.

Within such a context, virtually everyone within the government civil bureaucracy—from the simple municipal clerk who overlooks a minor transgression to a high government official who intervenes on behalf of either his "client" or "patron" to re-route a road network or re-zone a certain area—is placed in a strategic position to affect the redistribution of rewards and benefits in society. This is naturally more the case when it involves land or real estate, which is in Lebanon one of the most viable forms of commercial speculation. Examples of this sort are legion.

Finally, in a mercantile culture like Lebanon, excessive commercialism and its concomitant bourgeois values have always been given a free hand. Such rampant commercialism has become so rooted into the ethos of the average Lebanese that he is inclined to reduce every relationship and dimension of his life to a cash nexus. Practically everything and anything is for sale in Lebanon. Every entity and human capacity is conceived as a resource for the acquisition of profit or as a commodity to be exchanged, for the highest bidder, in a competitive market place. Land is certainly not spared. Indeed, with the staggering increase in land values, due to capital inflow and other inflationary tendencies, the commercial traffic in land (particularly since the 1950s) has become one of the most viable sources of private wealth. The inevitable result is a ruthless plunder of Lebanon's scenic natural habitat and the dehumanization of much of its living space. Hardly anything is spared: shore lines, green belts, public parks and private backyards, suburban villas, historic sites and monuments . . . they have all been giving way to a more intensive form of exploitation and land use.

In a more concrete sense, this has also meant that municipal and other civic authorities are no longer able to provide the necessary funds to expropriate vital areas for public use. Hence some of the choicest parcels of land, often earmarked as public parks and green areas, are ultimately converted into commercial use. Curiously, legislation in Lebanon permits such conversion. Urban planning regulations stipulate that after a lapse of ten years from the time a particular district has been zoned, all such green areas can be released and converted to private use. Indeed, this is what actually happens in most such instances. Since municipal councils cannot afford to pay the exorbitant expropriation compensation, they usually welcome such conversion.

Legislation also provides that 25 percent of a property can be acquired free if it is affected by planning, usually when a parcel of land is intersected by a proposed road network. But this too obstructs rather than facilitates comprehensive planning. On the whole, landowners are happy to part with such property, particularly since the financial rewards accruing therefrom more than compensate for the loss. An anticipated passage of a road almost always generates a manifold increase in the value of land.

The outcome of such excessive commercialism is painfully clear: by reducing every relationship to a cash nexus, the moral and aesthetic restraints that once controlled the growth of cities and shaped their human habitat are completely eroded and sacrificed. Once commercialization takes precedence in a society, then any concern for the aesthetic, human, or cultural dimension of living space is bound to be dismissed as superfluous and dispensable attributes. As a result, it is of little concern whether cities are ugly, whether they debase their inhabitants, whether they are aesthetically, spiritually, or physically tolerable, or whether they provide people with opportunities for authentic individuality, privacy, and edifying human encounters. What counts is that commercial transactions occur on a scale and with an effectiveness to meet the only criteria of bourgeois survival: economic growth and the insatiable appetite for profit.

As long as such materialistic values remain dominant in Lebanese society, zoning is more likely to be a reflective rather than an independent social force for controlling urban land use. Indeed, short of a fundamental change in the basic values underlying kinship, patronage, and commercialism, which could help transform Lebanon into a more civic and secular society, planning and zoning can do little to protect the urban environment from further abuse.

Concluding Remarks

What inferences can be made regarding the interplay between urban planning and the social structure in Lebanon? We clearly cannot generalize too much from the Lebanese experience. The nature and particular milieu within which urban planning has occured is too unique to permit any meaningful generalization beyond the Lebanese context.

For example, the deep-rooted weakness of state agencies and the consequent deficiency in civility and public consciousness—all of which have direct implications for urban planning—are a bit too pronounced in Lebanon. The state, compared to other forms of primordial loyalties and communal allegiances, has always been an enfeebled and residual institution. Likewise, as a fragmented political culture, Lebanon has experienced a comparatively high incidence of repeated episodes of civil unrest and social disorder. The rampant chaos and lawlessness generated by such protracted episodes renders any enforcement of law a vain and futile effort. Furthermore, when lawlessness becomes so widespread, offences like the expropriation of property and the violation of construction and zoning ordinances become legitimate and forgivable transgressions.

These and other such peculiarities notwithstanding, it is still possible to draw a few instructive lessons from the Lebanese experience that have some cross-cultural implications.

One such inference is that planned change is hard and rare virtually anywhere. To a large extent, the urban growth of Beirut, and this is certainly true of other cities, has been regulated more through the free play of market forces than through deliberate planning and zoning. As we have seen, some of the basic ingredients of urban planning, such as comprehensive zoning, equitable and balanced distribution of population density, proper traffic dispersion and flow, the interrelationships of land uses, landscape design, and more significantly anticipating some of the likely consequences of the increasing scale of urbanization on cultural ethos and traditional modes of behavior . . . are all left to chance and fortuitous circumstances. Indeed, many of the areas within Beirut, much like the unchecked and often chaotic suburban growth, have grown without the guidance of a comprehensive master plan.

Even today, it is estimated that not more than 7 percent of the total built-up area of Lebanon has been zoned or planned. In all these unplanned ares, construction is not controlled and maximum exploitation is authorized. Furthermore, in sizable portions of the planned areas, the plan simply confirms already existing trends. In other words, rather than anticipating and directing the course of future developments, planning has often meant the reinforcement of already established spatial patterns.

For example, the growth of the industrial belt around the suburbs of Beirut was largely the by-product of such forces. The heavy migration from rural areas to the cities of the fifties and sixties and the consequent availability of a large reserve of cheap labor in the suburban zones prompted many industrialists to locate their firms and establishments in the adjoining areas. The master plan of 1963 simply confirmed this reality by assigning a high coefficient of exploitation to such peri-urban areas.

Not only have certain areas grown without a master plan, but others have developed contrary to the specifications of rigid planning schemes. Hamra, the once fashionable and cosmopolitan middle-class urban district in West Beirut, is one such dramatic instance. It grew despite the general conception of the Master Plan to divert the urban development along the southern axis of metropolitan Beirut. Because of the absence of traditional patterns of land holding, the transfer of land was rendered possible through cadastral legislation. There is evidence that parcels, at least in the Hamra district, were individualized as early as 1928; a tendency that must have encouraged land transactions and speculations in real estate as a viable economic venture (for further details, see Khalaf and Kongstad 1973:30). This same pattern has repeated itself in a score of other districts and suburbs.

Another feature that Lebanon shares with other countries in the region, and possibly elsewhere in the Third World, is the disjunction between "over-urbanization" and "under-urbanism." As we have seen, the increasing scale and intensity of urbanization in Lebanon—apparent in the swift pace of urbanization, primacy, the high proportion of people living in urban agglomerations, high densities, mobility, and mixed land-use patterns—have not been accompanied by a corresponding degree of "urbanism" as a sociocultural and psychological phenomena. What this has meant, among other things, is the survival of a large residue of non-urban ties and loyalties and certain communal forms of spatial patterns. Some of these "traditional" survivals, particularly those which express themselves in functional neighborhoods, homogeneous quarters, and expedient pedestrian alleyways and courtyards, could be viable sources of communal solidarity and social and psychological reinforcement.

Partly because of the bias in Western models and perspectives, there has been the tendency to denigrate such traditional forms and spatial arrangements as useless and nostalgic residues of the past. We treat extended kinship networks, family associations, and parochial and communal organizations with nearly the same disregard. This is a serious and costly error; one based on a misunderstanding of the adaptive role that so-called traditional and smaller organizations or systems can play in alleviating some of the disquieting features of rapid urbanization.

The experience of other Arab cities with urban planning is equally shortsighted. Traditional neighborhoods and residential quarters, in the name of the urban zoning and master plans, have been either willfully bypassed and destroyed or allowed to atrophy as their functions diminish. Consequently, attempts are being made now to artificially re-create by fiat what could have been a more natural and viable alternative for coping with some of the unanticipated consequences of rapid urbanization.

Considerations of this sort prompt one to suggest that the failure of planning in Lebanon is only in part a reflection of communalism, laissez-faire ethos, or rampant commercialism. To a large extent it is also due to deficiencies in the plans themselves. The borrowed schemes that, as elsewhere in the Arab world, were designed and implemented by foreign experts, were often insensitive to the particular needs and interests of local groups and communities. Had the successive master plans evinced more receptivity to such local sentiments, they would have been more effective in adapting the rational schemes to some of the traditional elements rooted in society. By doing so they would have doubtlessly avoided some of the needless hostility and resistance to the plans. For no matter how planning is defined, it always involves a certain degree of congruence between planner and user. When this congruence is not observed, the user will violate the plans.

The experience of Lebanon with urban planning highlights another significant but often overlooked feature; namely, how the persistence of clientelistic politics and other forms of patronage allows strategically placed individuals to affect the redistribution of rewards and benefits in society. As we have seen, zoning laws and ordinances are manipulated to permit various interest groups wider and more intensive opportunities to exploit their property or to take advantage of speculative ventures generated by anticipated planning or re-zoning schemes. Obviously well-connected individuals with appropriate political backing are more likely to benefit from such opportunities. But then so do ordinary citizens of lesser socioeconomic standing, who likewise use their own patronage networks to secure favored treatment or protection from the law.

Finally, the Lebanese experience reveals a curious but poignant paradox: a dissonance between the rather orderly and viable regulation of private space in homes, neighborhoods, and quarters matched by mindless and almost total disregard for public space. This is clearly a symptom and a source of the deficiency in civility that pervades society. In other words, the average Lebanese is so preoccupied with the internal comforts of his family and private domain that he evinces little concern for public welfare and civic developments. He also becomes correspondingly more likely to violate zoning ordinances.

CHAPTER ELEVEN

On the Demoralization of Public Life

Things fall apart; the centre cannot hold;
Mere anarchy is loosed upon the world
The blood-dimmed tide is loosed, and everywhere
The ceremony of innocence is drowned;
The best lack all convictions, while the worst
Are full of passionate intensity.
—W.B. Yeats, "The Second Coming"

FOR OVER A DECADE, Lebanon has been victimized by some of the most barbaric and unrelenting forms of senseless violence and indiscriminate terror. Hundreds of thousands have already lost their lives, and many more have been permanently maimed and scarred. Entire towns, villages, and regions have been devastated; communities have perished and cities have been beseiged. Property and resources have been ransacked or laid to waste. During periods of intensive fighting, entire communities continue to face the horrors of sudden death and the indignities of uprootedness and dislocation.

Lebanon, in fact, has been besieged and beleaguered by every possible form of belligerency and collective terror known to human history: from the cruelties of factional and religious bigotry to the massive devastations wrought by militant organizations and state-sponsored armies. They have all generated an endless carnage of innocent victims and an immeasurable toll of human suffering and anguish. The sight of bereaved women wailing over the bodies of their slain kin, panicked refugees fleeing their stricken homes with their scant and disheveled belongings, or disfigured casualties being rescued from the debries and rubble of car bombs and explosions have become much too familiar spectacles of mass terror.

The media, both local and foreign, continue to cover such bestiality

This essay is a revised version of an essay originally published in *Studies in Comparative International Development* (Spring 1982), 17(1):49–72. Used by permission.

with shocking candor and realism. So much so, in fact, that Lebanon is no longer treated as a destabilized, fractured, and precarious republic. Its public image has now degenerated to a dispensable nuisance; an ugly metaphor beyond understanding and beyond cure.

Unlike other encounters with civil violence, which are often swift, decisive, and localized, and where a sizable part of the population could remain sheltered from its traumatizing impact, the Lebanese experience has been much more protracted and diffuse. The savagery of violence is also compounded by its randomness. In this sense, there is hardly a Lebanese today who is exempt from these atrocities either directly or vicariously as a mediated experience. Violence and terror have touched virtually everyone. It is everywhere and nowhere. It is everywhere because it could no longer be confined to one specific area or a few combatants. It is nowhere because it cannot not be identified or linked to one concrete cause. Recurring cycles or episodes of violence erupt, fade, and resurface again for no recognized or coherent reason.

In a tragic sense, the Lebanese have been homogenized by fear, terror, and grief. No one is less or more privileged than others. Despite their many differences, they have been rendered equal by a decade of protracted violence and endemic fear. It is the fear of being marginalized, assimilated, or banished that accentuates the intensity of hostility between the warring communities. The more threatened communities become, the more they resort to violence to preserve their endangered identities, and the more apprehensive they become about the prospects of resolving the conflict, lest they lose whatever minimal gains they have made thus far.

The warring communities have also locked themselves into a dependent relationship with violence and chronic conflict. It is in this sense that violence becomes both protracted and insoluble. It is a form of self-entrapment that blocks all avenues of creative peaceful change. It is sustained by a pervasive feeling of helplessness, demoralization and an almost obsessive dependency on external patrons and foreign brokers.

Some observers go so far as to suggest that in Lebanon protracted violence has become an intrinsic part of society's ethos and mythology (Azar and Cohen 1979; Azar 1985). This is apparent in the diffuse and overwhelming character of conflict. It pervades every aspect of social life. "In acute cases, every action, every statement, and every institution acquires value and meaning in relation to the conflict itself. . . . It has become an absorbing and full-time concern overshadowing, thereby, many other societal, communal and individual interests. It has frustrated intra-communal opportunities for social and political alliances" (Azar 1985:4).

This type of protracted, random, and impotent violence has little, if anything, to do with other forms of insurgency, protest, and civil unrest witnessed in post-revolutionary regimes and often condoned as legiti-mate, salutory, even therapeutic. In such instances, it is argued, civil un-rest arises as a necessary stage in the dialectic of self-discovery. In other words there are times when violence can be understood and condoned as a return to sanity, an experience through which society seeks to re-cover its lost integrity and virtue. Acts of savagery, even coarse and boor-ish behavior, become legitimate moral responses to the rampant immo-rality and hypocricy that pervade the social fabric of the body politic. People resort to violence, so to speak, in a desperate effort to expunge those evils. (For an elaboration of these and other related views see Rub-inoff 1971:3–7.)

I am, of course, advancing here a more pathological view of violence. The protracted disorder and anarchy, the impoverishment and demorali-zation of public life, and the erosion of civility and accepted standards of morality and decency have little to do with the rebirth and recovery of virtue and justice. As such, they are unlikely to rescue Lebanon from its deepening crisis and transform it into a more civil and edifying social order. Nor should they be dismissed as a transient phase that will even-tually be shaken off when impassioned and aroused masses return to their sensibilities. The vulgarization and impoverishment of public life are only the manifestations of a more menacing moral crisis. They are the out-come of years of consolidated animosity, widespread fear, chronic trauma, and the frenzy of hatred. The result is what Hazlitt calls the "'pleasure of hating' which eats into the heart of religion, and turns it into rankling spleen and bigotry; it makes patriotism an excuse for carrying fire . . . it leaves to virtue nothing but the spirit of censoriousness, and a narrow, jealous watchfulness over the actions and motives of others" (As quoted by Edward Said 1985:5).

Indeed, what Lebanon has been experiencing is not only the fragmen-tation of a political system, but the dismemberment of a society.[1] The most elementary social ties that normally hold a society together—ties of trust, loyalty, confidence, compassion, and decency—have been in many respects fatally eroded. And it is relatively easier to recreate a state than to rebuild a society. A state can be reconstituted by legislation, contracts, pacts, or covenants—as Lebanon has seen several times in her political history—but how does one reconstruct a society?

Pervasive Demoralization

The problem is compounded in Lebanon for two obvious but difficult reasons: first, it is a pluralistic society that has experienced a drastic breach of faith, mutual hostility, and bitterness among its various communities. Second, and perhaps more important, individuals and groups have not only been living outside society or civility, but they have discovered that continuing to do so is expedient and advantageous for them.

This occurs when both state and legitimate institutions have been discredited and conventional patterns of authority and deference are losing their grip.[2] Traditional political leaders, for example, can no longer command obedience, nor can they control dissident or recalcitrant elements within their own constituencies. Traditional values, not only deference and respect, but moderation, restraint, civility, and decency have eroded. All this generates a breakdown in norms and the disintegration of social bonds. A thirst develops for novelties, unfamiliar pleasures, and nameless sensations—all of which lose their savor as soon as they are gratified. It creates a world of boorish decadence, of rootless masses and unanchored social groups free from legal, moral, or social restraints, demanding instant gratification for their newly aroused impulses. In short, a world of graceless hedonists.

At no point in the recent history of Lebanon has the average citizen faced any sweeping or dramatic change that required a complete rearrangement of his beliefs and attitudes regarding the basic perceptions of his environment and the nature of his citizenship. The civil war and its aftermath offer such a momentous watershed. Periods of civil unrest, particularly those marked by diffuse and protracted violence, anarchy, and disorder, normally generate moods of introspection and rethinking. People are inclined to restrain their conventional impulses and become more sober and self-controlled in the interest of reappraising and redirecting their future options. Rather than freeing them from their prewar excesses, the war has paradoxically generated the opposite reaction: it has unleashed appetites and inflamed people with an insatiable desire for material satisfaction and acquisition.

Such acquisitiveness assumes pathological manifestations during holidays. Holiday seasons in Lebanon have always invited moods of compulsive, almost manic, shopping and extravagant spending. Celebrations of the past few years, possibly because of the sharp contrasts and incongruities in public life, have carried with them more grotesque and ludicrous manifestations. Department stores, shops, makeshift stalls, and street vendors displayed as dazzling an assortment of goods as they did before the war. While one cannot prove this empirically, there has been an increase in the number of shops selling frivolous and dispensable knickknacks, gadgets, decorative objects, cosmetics, jewelry, clothes, and other items which feed on the Lebanese proclivity for vain and indiscriminate buying. While the shops glitter with festoons and ornaments, the fetid streets and sidewalks are littered with rancid garbage and gushing sewers. Shoppers literally have to step over the slime of sewage and discarded refuse to heed their cravings for more material goods. Oddly enough, the littered streets and sidewalks, let alone anxiety over the political situation or soaring prices, do not seem to restrain such impulses. The compulsion to buy has become almost a national pastime, an outlet for traumatized individuals in their futile attempt to restore their damaged self-regard and personal worth.

In more conceptual terms, Lebanon at the moment is a textbook example of what sociologists call "anomie"; a social state in which society's norms can no longer impose effective control over people's impulses. In times of rapid social change, people face considerable confusion, uncertainty, and conflict in expectations. Not only do the norms themselves become ambiguous, but people's desires and expectations become extravagant and excessive. The limits between the possible and the impossible are unknown as are those between what is just and what is unjust, between what is moderate and immoderate, between legitimate claims and hopes and those which are illegitimate. Consequently, people become victims of a chronic condition of constant seeking without fulfillment. (For an elucidation of Durkheim's classical treatment of anomie see, among others, Clinard 1964:1–56.) The deprived and not-so-deprived feel cheated and denied, particularly when rampant commercialism, sustained by resourceful and aggressive mass media, constantly whets consumer appetites for limitless goods and creates expectations that are beyond reach. It is then that they acquire the belief that they are entitled to such items, by fair means when possible and foul means if necessary. And it is in this precise sense that demoralization has become endemic in Lebanon; namely, that foul and illegitimate means have become necessary to secure desired goals.

The average Lebanese today is not only being denied his natural claims to live in a decent and edifying environment, he is also beginning to realize that he cannot secure even his daily needs for food, shelter, security, safety, and public utilities unless he compromises himself and violates society's norms or his own moral principles. He is compelled, for example, to resort to devious and irregular means to guarantee his water, electricity, telephone, and fuel. Willingly or not, he contributes to all sorts of organizations, subscribes to a score of ideological periodicals and political pamphlets, keeps his neighborhood thugs contented, and maintains a political profile consistent with prevailing but shifting ideological currents. In short, he is a helpless victim of extortion and fraud.

The exorbitant prices he pays cannot be a by-product of natural inflationary market tendencies; they reflect the extortion and heavy exactions that agents and self-appointed guardians, patrons, and middlemen impose on him. For example, fuel oil, petrol, and gas prices have more than tripled during the past two years. Rents, medications, clothing, and schooling, and some food products have done the same. The yearly rent of a three-bedroom flat, in some urban districts of Beirut, is as high as L£75,000 ($20,000), excluding heating and hot water, which landlords arbitrarily refuse to provide. Native Lebanese have difficulty convincing a landlord to lease them an apartment even if they can pay the rent. The preference is for itinerant foreign tenants who can be replaced without payment of key money. Though a sizable proportion of the apartment houses completed since the war remain vacant, landlords demand excessively high rents far exceeding the market value of an apartment or the limits of propriety. Without price or rent controls, proprietors hike their rates and prices on any pretext.

By imposing a road block at strategic points of the North-South Highway, a few militia men, alone or with the support of their organizations, can generate critical fuel and power shortages. In these recurrent instances, prices have risen irretrievably, to say nothing of the nuisances, irritations, and intimidating encounters to which people are subjected as a consequence. As a result, the daily life of the average citizen has been trivialized. He spends much of his time and resources doing endless and futile chores simply to cope with the sheer exigencies of survival. If one could construct a time-budget for an average Lebanese to discover his time allocation and the activities on which he has been expending his efforts, the exercise would reveal considerable trivialization. Few of his daily activities are either creative or intellectually engaging enough to enrich or contribute to his own self-actualization or well-being.

Though not as obtrusive as some of the other ugly manifestations of the civil war, such trivialization in the long run might prove to be more debilitating and damaging. What this means, in effect, is that more people are withholding or withdrawing human energy, in the form of action, thought, or feeling, that could have gone into more meaningful and enriching social activities. A large residue of human energy, in other words, is being misspent and mismanaged. The result is not only a pervasive feeling of entropy and lifelessness but the perhaps more painful realization that one is less than what one could have been had circumstances been different.

In this sense, some of the trials and tribulations of the Lebanese are not markedly different from the harassment and intimidations experienced by prisoners of war. Survivors of such captivity all speak with horror about the physical torture and terror they endured, and the psychological damage and deprivation they suffered when they were compelled to participate in senseless and trivial activities that insulted their intelligence and injured their human dignity and worth. Any Lebanese of average intelligence feels equally crippled and intimidated by wasting hours lugging pails of water to his apartment, queuing for his gas or his turn at a check point, waiting for a telephone connection, and the score of other irritating encounters that leave him prostrate and embittered.

Nothing can be taken for granted any longer. Deficient telecommunication systems, congested traffic, and irregular mail services render all forms of social interaction fortuitous and unpredictable. After the early morning hours, for example, telephoning becomes virtually impossible. One is compelled to accomplish much of one's business and contacts at unexpected hours, even if this means rousing colleagues from sleep. The irregularity of all other forms of public utility has necessitated a restructuring of many of daily life's regular patterns. No one is spared such hazards. Bankers and entrepreneurs, housewives and charwomen, all are helpless victims of this fortuitousness. Appointments are rarely honored; contractual commitments are easily violated. Short-term expediency has replaced long-term planning. People live, so to speak, situationally. This is all they can do, after all, when social life becomes characterized by a high degree of unpredictability and contingency. The day-to-day routines that once structured their daily existence now play havoc with their lives.

Even the simplest domestic chores, once a source of effortless pleasure, have been transformed into cumbersome and loathsome activities. By the end of the day, one is left with a crushing sense of defeat and insignificance.

What is so unusual, one might easily ask, about such symptoms? Don't all civil wars, particularly those accompanied by protracted chaos and violence, generate moods of decadence, corruption, and demoralization in public life? Even without civil wars, there are moments in the history of all societies when inhibitionary rules are suspended. Sometimes the inhibitions are lifted for a day or so, as in Mardi Gras or other national festivities. In other instances inhibitions are removed temporarily and permissiveness becomes more diffuse in society and assumes forms of collective and mass hysteria characterized by the emergence of all sorts of irrational fads and crazes. In this sense, Lebanon is no exception. What is unique are the profound manifestations of such demoralization and their pervasive, deep-rooted character. The experience of other societies also tells us that no generation is ever really aware of the implicit dangers of demoralization and decadence until it is almost too late (see Rubinoff 1971:6). Lebanon already may have reached that critical point.

It is also not surprising that the country is experiencing such pervasive normlessness given its precarious pluralism, fragmented political culture, and deficient civility. Lebanon's remote and recent political history is replete with instances where local sentiments and parochial commitments have undermined civic consciousness and national loyalties. The dialectics and tension between these two allegiances have had grievous implications for the political management of the country. (For a fuller treatment and further historical documentation of this point see Khalaf 1979.) The tension between private interest and public welfare, rampant double standards (e.g., decency, civility, kindness, compassion, cleanliness, courteousness, and urbanity within one's private domain, but a lavish display of antithetical attributes when one ventures into the public sphere), the proclivity of the Lebanese not only to transgress but actually to take the law into his own hand, and the total disregard of public welfare if it happens to clash with private interest are all manifestations of this conflict.

Lebanon's political history demonstrates the paradoxical and often inconsistent implications of this tension. Though the average Lebanese derives much of this social support and psychological reinforcement from such local and communal allegiances, these forces are the same elements that create his deficient civility. The same forces that sustain his social identity prompt him on occasion to violate and betray his society's normative standards. The Lebanese is being demoralized, in other words, by the very forces that are supposed to make him a more human and sociable being. Expressed differently, the elements that account for the resourcefulness, prosperity, cultural awakening, and solidarity of certain communities, are also the elements that fragment the society and weaken its civic and national loyalties. The formation and deformation of Lebanon, so to speak, are rooted in the same forces. Much of the evidence in the preceding chapters substantiates this essentially dialectical relationship between the enabling and disabling factors inherent in Lebanese society.

Consequences of Rampant and Protracted Violence

As suggested earlier, the war and the concomitant demoralization and decadence in public life are to a large extent by-products of deficient civility. At the same time, the war itself has doubtless been a source of added demoralization. In other words, the war has not only accentuated already preexisting predispositions toward normlessness, but has generated circumstances that have rendered demoralization more intense and pervasive. Even if the average Lebanese were the most restrained, balanced, and law-abiding citizen, the spectacle of violent events he has witnessed during the past ten years is enough to disenchant and demoralize him. He has been exposed to the terror and brutality that accompanies naked violence and civil unrest: mass and indiscriminate murder, random shelling and explosions, sniping, torture, mutilation, kidnapping, looting, and reckless destruction of property and human life.

What this means in effect is that, voluntarily or not, more than one generation of Lebanese has been tutored or socialized into violence. The reader is invited to reexamine a sample of pronouncements, declarations, and assertions that leaders and spokesmen of the various warring factions continue to make. Basically, they are all appeals for the legitimization of violence in the name of autonomy, self-defense, liberation, or national sovereignty. Rival groups engage in mutual debasement. Their media have developed elaborate and effective strategies for such mutual devaluation. Each group depicts the "other" as the repository of all evil, wicked, and demonic attributes. The manifestations and consequences of such "demonization," to borrow a term identified and elucidated by John Mack (1979), have been poignant and damaging. All the unacknowledged and undesirable attributes of one's group are seen to reside in the "other." By evoking such imagery, the "other" is transformed into a public menace, a threat to security and national sovereignty. In this context, aggression against the "other" assumes a purgative value. It becomes an act of liberation, the only way to preserve or restore national integrity and dignity.[3] Terror and violence masquerade as virtue and patriotism. The so-called "national struggle" and "liberation" have become a congenial disguise for venality, egoism, and avarice.

Under such circumstances, when violence runs berserk and assumes the cruel manifestations of cold-blooded murder of innocent victims and hostages, leaders hasten to attribute these crimes to undisciplined elements, infiltrators, or mysterious third parties. Even more curious than this predisposition to rationalize and legitimize violence is the equal readiness to shift the targets of hostility. Any cursory review of the events and factions involved in the hostility reveals that human aggression is being transformed into what sociobiologists call an innate desire for destructiveness or a compulsion to kill. How else can one explain the confusing and inconsistent pattern of violence? Within days, yesterday's allies become tomorrow's enemies. Overnight, accursed and detestable "traitors" are transformed into public "heroes." Hardly a day passes by without incidences of bitter fighting occurring among rival factions within the same ideological groups or organizations. As innocent victims fall, the familiar but tragicomic pattern of events unfolds with its noted predictability: the morning press would carry statements by leaders of the warring factions, each accusing the proverbial mysterious or undisciplined elements, and vowing not to permit such pernicious infiltrators to plant seeds of discord and disunity among "brothers of the same cause or people of the same house."

Violence has not been confined to warring factions involved in the political struggle. It has spilled over to other segments of society. Ordinary acts of homicide, perhaps for the first time in the history of Lebanon, are beginning to assume some grotesque features. Victims of such crimes—often killed in pointless or petty thefts or larcenies—are tortured and abused. In at least three such instances recently, the victim's mutilated and disfigured corpses were dismembered and deposited in different parts of the city. Acts of vandalism, ranging from the willful and malicious destruction of public or private property to the desecration and abuse of the natural habitat, have also become more violent and pervasive.

The point is that in such an atmosphere of rampant anarchy and violence, other manifestations of demoralization and the decay of public life seem pardonable and trivial indiscretions by comparison. For groups who have witnessed such total disregard of human life and the desecration of its basic human values, offenses like the expropriation of public property, violation of construction and zoning ordinances, etc., become legitimate and forgivable, at least to the offenders.

If one could construct a composite empirical index to measure the proportion of people using illegitimate and unethical means to secure the ends or amenities of their everyday life, one would discover that a significant portion of society has been living unlawfully, and thus outside a civil order. The index would include items ranging from the most visible—expropriation of property, occupation of homes, violation of construction laws and zoning ordinances, pirating of public utilities (particularly water, electricity, and telephones), trespassing, littering, mutilation of public property, looting, vandalism—to the less visible, but equally objectionable, such as extortion, smuggling, graft, tax evasion, and cheating on national examinations.

Judging from earlier and more recent instances, the effects of most of these transgressions could be permanently and irretrievably damaging. Lebanon's experience during the 1958 crisis, although the scale and intensity of civil unrest and erosion of state institutions was more limited at the time, provides ample proof of the government's inability to contain or reverse the detrimental consequences of such violations. This is most visible in the expropriation of real estate property, the unlawful construction of houses, and other violations of construction laws and zoning regulations. Some of Beirut's choicest urban sites have been converted into squalid slums and squatter settlements. These makeshift and supposedly transient arrangements have slowly become permanent structures.

The magnitude of such violations has grown exponentially during the past ten years. They now assume ugly, defiant manifestations. For example, all shops and bazaars in the devastated central business district of Beirut have been relocated elsewhere with almost total disregard for their disruption of the surrounding environment. People can build almost anything anywhere. Noise and nuisance-generating industry and services invade residential areas while scenic side-walks and lush meadows are being displaced by warehouses and traffic terminals. National parks, public gardens, historic sites, and monuments are neglected and abused with impunity by squatters and street vendors. Vacant lots and unfinished construction sites become garbage dumps. Ground floors are converted into storage depots and work shops. The front yards and walled patios that once adorned the traditional suburban villas are giving way to a more intensive and chaotic pattern of land use. Likewise, the shrubs and trees that once lined the streets and alleyways shrivel and wither away from inattention or misuse. Much of the urban space, in fact, other than the vast areas damaged by the war, seems in a pitiful state of disarray.

Despite soaring land values, or perhaps because of them, land speculation goes on at unprecedented rates. In vogue at the moment are touristic beach resorts and exclusive swimming clubs. Taking advantage of a loophole in the special zoning laws regulating beach areas, speculators exploit every possible site. At the rate such projects are presently expanding, Lebanon's entire shoreline within a few decades will be dotted with "Summerlands," "Merrylands," "Marinas," and "Aqua-Marinas." In the process, what is supposed to be public space and open to all citizens is converted to private commercial ventures. Only those who can afford exorbitant membership fees or those with power connections enjoy such resorts. The less fortunate—the poor and not-so-well connected—are excluded.

This mindless exploitation of open space is not confined to beach areas. It takes place everywhere. Commercially minded politicians, oblivious of the fact that Lebanon already suffers from excessively high densities (about 250 inhabitants per square kilometer), perceive such speculation as a sign of economic vitality and resourcefulness in an otherwise sluggish postwar economy. To them, these features are to be encouraged, not decried. Parliament is currently discussing two proposals to introduce amendments to the urban planning laws that would permit Lebanese everywhere to increase the exploitation of their land very substantially. Such measures will further accentuate the damaging consequences of excessive commercialization and irrational real estate speculation. As was shown earlier, the inevitable result is a ruthless plunder of the natural habitat and the dehumanization of living space.

The dehumanization of living space is compounded and made more visible by other war-generated problems. Successive waves of displaced refugees had to seek shelter from their beleaguered villages and bombed districts to find alternative housing. Fashionable highrise apartments, temporarily abandoned by their occupants or others in the final stages of construction, became readily accessible targets. Sometimes within hours entire neighborhoods would be invaded. In some instances, residents who had stepped out of their homes on short errands would return to find them broken into and occupied. Proprietors and landlords have resorted to all sorts of measures—barricading doorways with thick iron gates and heavy bolts, elaborate alarm systems, bodyguards, and armed attendants (all new and viable forms of business ventures)—to avert such hazards and safeguard their property. In the absence of proper sanitation and regular amenities, the standard of housing in most such buildings and neighborhoods has deteriorated markedly. They are pockets of squalor and urban blight that will generate serious social and legal problems in the future. Already many refugees refuse to vacate their premises unless they are properly indemnified with key money or other compensations. Much like car theft, smuggling, bootlegging, and pirating, occupying houses has become a highly organized activity with accomplices, agents, and middlemen.

All these violations are no longer perceived as criminal offenses or forms of antisocial behavior. On the contrary, they are committed with a considerable display of machismo and bravado and hardly evoke any feelings of guilt or shame. In many instances, the perpetrators and their agents, who operate highly organized and successful rackets, are fully recognized (some in fact have acquired public notoriety), but nothing has been done thus far to arrest or prosecute them. Judges and magistrates, in the absence of supportive judicial institutions, have legitimate fears about initiating legal or criminal proceedings that might endanger their own lives. Even when suspects are arrested, which happens rarely, proceedings for legal action and eventual arraignment and conviction are virtually inoperative. Until very recently, state penitentiaries have been defunct.

Under such circumstances, one can understand why those who are nominally empowered to safeguard public safety and security are reluctant to exercise their legitimate responsibility. They, or their families, might become targets for retaliation or reprisals. This fear of retributive action pervades other dimensions of everyday life and, more than any other factor, has compelled furtive and anxious citizens to restructure their lives and confine their mobility to an ever-constricting circle or network of acquaintances. This is perhaps one of the most painful and disruptive by-products of the war.

Reversing the Natural Course of History

Social and intellectual historians remind us that a fascinating transformation in the historical evolution of most societies involves its passage from a relatively "closed" to a more "open" system: membership, entry or exit, and access to privileges and benefits are no longer denied by virtue of limitations of religion, kinship, or race. Such openness accounts for much of the spectacular growth in the philosophical, artistic, and political emancipation of contemporary societies (Nisbet 1970:97–100). What Lebanon has been experiencing during the past ten years is the reversal of this natural and usually inevitable historical transformation. We are, once again, creating closed communities. The boundaries and horizons within which people circulate and interact continue to shrink. A generation of children and adolescents has grown up thinking that their social world cannot extend beyond the confines of the small communities within which they have been compelled to live.

This same fear prompts many to forfeit legitimate claims or rights, lest they offend those who have usurped these rights. Sometimes a slight reprimand, an accusing glance, or a hint that might be perceived as incriminating or injurious, even when appropriate and justified, is enough to provoke outrage and hostility. Those who are arrogant, abrasive, or violent in temper get their own way. One's esteem and social standing, in fact, is in direct proportion to one's arrogance and abrasiveness. In Lebanon these days, the meek inherit nothing; they are more likely to be disinherited of the little they have. Manifestations of this are legion; from street encounters to the inner sanctum of schools and universities, the offended is at the mercy of the offender. The violator, through shameless impudence and assertiveness, gets away with his transgressions.

Since many have come to accept all such violations of private rights with resignation and passive submission, it is little wonder that they should meet the demoralization of public life with the same moral indifference. Instructors and university administrators, for example, accept the erosion of academic standards as a reality they have to reckon with, not resist. Professors admit they are reluctant to fail students or censure misconduct in the present political climate. Cheating, purchasing of exams and term papers, and tampering with grades are becoming more widespread. Students resort to intimidation to have their grades changed, and teachers are known to acquiesce. Disciplinary committees, which normally consider these cases of student misconduct, have been suspended. Hence much of the aberrant behavior of students goes undetected and undisciplined. Despite stringent controls in the preparation and administration of examinations, leakages are also more common.

The moral indifference with which the Lebanese are accepting the demoralization of public life assumes other disquieting forms. As noted, people cannot depend on public authority for security and safety or to secure their basic amenities. The average citizen has been reduced to a helpless victim of extortion. The more fortunate, those with proper political connections or some sense of daring, either take the law into their own hands or resort to their own ingenious, and often devious, means to safeguard their lives and interests. For example, because water and power supplies are getting scarce and erratic, private citizens have resorted to resourceful ways of securing them. Many apartment houses in Beirut (at the cost of not less than L£12,000 or U.S. $1,000) have been drilling their own artesian wells to guarantee, by internal hydrostatic pressure, an ample supply of brackish water. Almost all major apartment houses and commercial establishments have installed their own power generators. The adverse consequences of such indiscriminate abuse—both to the future level of water and its hygienic quality or noise pollution— is of no regard to those who undertake such projects. As in other instances, the government cannot impose limits on this flagrant abuse of natural resources and public welfare.

More despicable is the abandon with which the Lebanese litter and pollute the environment. Even garbage has been politicized. The multimillion dollar incinerator plant, recently constructed in the eastern part of Beirut, supposedly can accommodate seven hundred tons of garbage daily. It hardly receives one-tenth of its capacity. Christian militia groups have refused to permit garbage trucks from the city's western districts to unload their waste. Such garbage, they say, could easily contain time bombs or other explosives. Mounds of uncollected garbage get bigger, and the temporary garbage dump near the airport runways has become a nuisance to public health and a hazard to civil aviation. The government has yet to approve the site of an alternative incinerator, appropriate on both political and ecological grounds. Successive cleaning campaigns by various civic-minded groups have done little so far to render citizens less negligent in disposing their waste.

The recent wave of car explosions, yet another form of reckless violence that has generated a staggering increase in casualties and damage to property, has prompted furtive and panic-stricken citizens to resort to their own means of warding off such lethal hazards. Side-walks, streets, and sometimes entire blocks and neighborhoods are cordoned off or blocked by stones, barrels, and discarded furniture to prevent cars from parking. Others have resorted to more permanent means of implanting iron bars and chains in order to barricade areas adjoining their premises. This has not only meant the usurpation and abuse of public property, but has obstructed the flow of traffic and compounded the problems of urban congestion. It has also eroded that little which remains of the aesthetic quality of the urban environment.

The once attractive streets and side-walks of certain neighborhoods are littered with garish and gaudy products. Itinerant street vendors display their merchandise on cars, carriages, lamp posts, street railings, and trees. Makeshift eating stalls are flanked by vendors of cosmetics, perfumes, electronic products, pocket computers, ready-made clothes, household appliances, and lewd periodicals. The rhymed chants of vendors compete with the amplified blasts of cassettes and recorded music. Street walls and shop windows are defaced by layers of political graffiti, portraits of martyred fighters, and suggestive ads for the latest lascivious films.

The people one encounters on public streets have also changed. One no longer sees neighbors strolling casually. There is hardly a safe and edifying place for friends and families to meet, let alone where children can frolic and play. All one sees are shabby and fierce-looking strangers jostling each other as they heed their impetuous and fleeting impulses. The neighborhoods of West Beirut epitomize today all the demoralization that has impoverished public life and eroded traditional Lebanese civility and decency: vulgarity, greed, gaudy commercialism, and graceless hedonism.

Adapting to the Demoralization of Public Life

How have the Lebanese reacted to, or coped with, the demoralization that has impoverished and dehumanized the quality of their public life and damaged their sense of personal worth and dignity? The most striking and disquieting symptom is the general mood of indifference and entropy that has overwhelmed most people. The experience of traumatization, severe suffering, grief, affliction, and the perversion of the meaning of life, seem to have muted peoples' sensibilities and crippled their capacity to feel outraged. In itself, this is a measure of the corrosive and debilitating character of demoralization. People have been so dispirited that they have lost the nerve to express and mobilize their discontent. Obnoxious and disagreeable features of everyday life that once provoked their contempt and disdain—from the indiscriminate abuse of the natural habitat to travesties of justice and the violation of human life—are now accepted as normal appendages to a postwar society.

It is curious that with all the adversities that have beset the Lebanese, there has been no collective effort to mobilize public grievances against such abuses and violations. In all open and democratic societies, chronic victims of collective suffering often sense that their problems are invisible to many in society. They have consequently taken dramatic steps in the form of public demonstrations, civil disobedience, and acts of sedition, etc. to arouse public attention and transform problems into public issues. In Lebanon, outraged journalists, public figures, theologians, and indignant citizens do express their concern, but these have not developed into concerted or organized efforts. A genuine attempt to organize a peace march in the spring of 1984, part of a burgeoning peace movement, failed to materialize despite the public and media attention it inspired and attracted.

The ineffectiveness of this and other collective movements is caused partly by the absence of "publics" in the true meaning of the term. The country is splintered into all sorts of quasi-groups, communities, confessions, neighborhoods, fronts, and militias—even the street is recognized as a political entity. There are, however, no "publics" capable of transcending such parochial milieux to articulate common societal issues. Many problems are masked and unrecognized, and people continue to re-experience diffuse and impotent hostility. In this sense they remain powerless to express their resentment against groups or persons.

Like other forms of accumulated discontent, pent-up resentment and impotent hostility is bound to manifest itself in symptoms of psychic distress and personality disorders. It is difficult at this stage to substantiate empirically the extent and pattern of such symptoms, but it is clear that the Lebanese have already paid a high psychic toll. Diffuse anxiety, fear, and the uncertainty generated by the taxing problems of restructuring one's career and everyday life have produced a wide range of psychological disturbances. Heads of households have been compelled to relocate the place and form of their employment. This, among other things, has necessitated long periods of involuntary isolation from their families.

Others have suffered from the opposite condition: men unaccustomed to spending much of their time at home find the excessive intimacy and idleness they have been forced to endure intolerable and suffocating. The experience of emptiness, of an inability to feel, and a growing sense of despair and hopelessness have also been emotionally crippling. This has accentuated the sources of friction and tension within the family and added to the mood of despondency.

Psychiatrists and general practitioners report that, in addition to the expected increase in symptoms of hypertension and the gastrointestinal, cardiovascular, and other psychosomatic disorders that often accompany instances of extreme societal disruptions, there are other peculiar symptoms that a growing number of Lebanese exhibit. These particularly include phobias and acute anxiety reactions and depressions. For example, one university counselor reports that about 30 percent of his student clients report one of the following recurring phobias: being stopped or kidnapped by armed men, being stranded in a religious community other than one's own, or being stuck in an elevator due to erratic power failure.

These, and other symptoms, suggest that a fairly large portion of the Lebanese today feel embittered, anxious, and adrift without any firm moral guidance or political security. Many have come to question their cultural and political heritage and their own allegiance to it. They continue to be anxious about the present and uncertain about the future. The few who understand and could have foreseen the forces that are destroying and demoralizing their society feel impotent and powerless to do anything. It is little wonder that feelings of indifference, despair, and panic have become so common.

What is equally disheartening are the ways in which the various socioeconomic groups have reacted to this deepening moral crisis. At the risk of some oversimplified generalizations, one can discern three general patterns. First, many of the privileged classes and upper bourgeoisie take refuge in Europe's capital cities to indulge their need for conspicuous consumption and idle leisure. Those who stay behind heed those same hedonistic impulses in the exclusive resorts, marinas, boutiques, disco clubs, and shopping centers that have mushroomed since the war and appear to be thriving. Proprietors of such establishments speak with amazement about record-breaking sales and traffic in their business, even when compared to the boom of the prewar years. A growing number of both the most privileged groups and the upper bourgeoisie are pursuing much of their culture and leisure within their own living rooms. Recurrent instances of sporadic fighting, kidnapping, and remote-controlled explosives continue to generate moods of caution and fear. At night people are afraid to leave their homes and, when they do, they venture outside their neighborhoods only reluctantly. By late afternoon, streets in certain communities are deserted. As a result, home-centered entertainment and activities, particularly video clubs and bridge and dinner parties, have become very popular among these groups.

Second, middle-class and limited income groups—doubtless the groups that the war has hit the hardest—have little choice except to retreat grudgingly into the privacy of their own homes. The family in Lebanon has always been one of the most enduring and solid social institutions. Strong kinship ties and loyalties, even in times of relative stability and peace, have always been a source of psychic reinforcements and social supports. (For prewar evidence to support this, see Diab and Melikian 1974; Prothro and Diab 1974.) The war's disruptive and shattering events have, in many respects, strengthened the family and reinforced strong kinship and gregarious sentiments. Seeking refuge within the family is a reflection of a natural impulse to withdraw from a cruel and demoralizing world. As the outside world becomes more savage, menacing, and insecure, people have escaped into the family for comfort in its domesticity and privacy. Whether the family will be able to withstand such pressure remains to be seen. In the meantime it has extended itself and assumed added functions. For example, beyond absorbing a larger share of the leisure, welfare, and benevolent needs of its members, it is also serving as an economic base. Many, particularly lawyers, craftsmen, retailers, and agents have been forced to convert their homes into offices for their business operations.

Third, just as the upper and middle classes have withdrawn from public life, the lower classes have taken to the street. Uprooted masses and displaced refugees, largely unanchored in any stable social group, are asserting their presence in all sorts of ways. Like other rootless masses who have just been released from the shackles of poverty and oppressive traditional communities, they are eager to display, indeed flaunt, their newly acquired freedom and material possessions. Whether this "new class" will emerge as a permanent and stable social stratum in the society remains to be seen. In the meantime, they are certainly one of the most visible, assertive, and permissive social groups. They indulge their new whims unabashedly, almost like impulsive children fondling new toys. Many drive new cars for the first time. Others are exposed to all the temptations of city life. And they do so with all the recklessness and abandon of excitable initiates. The volume of noise and litter they generate in the process is stupendous.

In all three instances, civility is becoming more deficient and the quality of public life is further impoverished. Privileged social groups are so preoccupied with preserving their threatened social world and life-styles that they can contribute little to public life. Through their exclusive resorts, elite clubs, and other social sanctuaries, they are careful to avoid or exclude those of lesser or different status and shield themselves from the squalor and filth that is often only a few yards away.

The middle classes are also turning inward. Since they cannot afford to patronize such exclusive sanctuaries, and since other public outlets have become so threatening, more and more middle-class families are seeking shelter in their own homes. This too, is another form of stultifying self-absorption. In their preoccupation with their private troubles and insecurities, they are oblivious of their surrounding environment. By enriching their private domain, they have little left to offer publicly. Rather than enriching public life they seek to retreat from it.

The indulgent lower classes are engrossed with the novelties and thrills of public life. Even if they had the inclinations or resources, they are not likely to display (at least not for the time being) moderation in their behavior or civic concern for public welfare. They have taken to the street, after all, to demonstrate their contempt and disregard for those institutions that had denied them legitimate access to these benefits and amenities earlier.

Conclusions: The Need for a Restoration of Civility

Although Lebanon's protracted civil war has been raging now, with varying intensity, for over a decade, it is still extremely difficult to predict its impact with any certitude. Judging, however, by the little it has accomplished so far in the way of generating any fundamental structural transformations in the country's political and socioeconomic institutions, it has been a futile, costly exercise in violence. The only visible changes are the symptoms of demoralization and entropy I have outlined. If I have described these symptoms forcefully, it is because I wish to disclose the menacing nature of this deepening moral crisis Lebanon is facing.

The crisis is, at heart, a moral one. While it might not have started that way, it did nonetheless degenerate into one. In accounting for the crisis, one could easily, as several observers have already done, provide evidence to support one or more of the following causes: growing socioeconomic imbalances, disparities in power and privilege, relative deprivation, class conflict, confessional hostility, perpetual grievances of dominant groups within society, the armed Palestinian presence, inter-Arab rivalry, superpower politics, or the fragility of Lebanon's precarious democracy. It is doubtful, however, if all these forces could have created so much havoc in our society had we not been, in the first place,motivated by sentiments and loyalties that often betray or violate civic and national consciousness. Indeed, the intensity, scale, and duration of violence, along with the accompanying demoralization, reveals that the Lebanese are deficient in civility. If we accept this premise, then the task of reconstructing Lebanon requires more than rehabilitation, resettlement, or reorganization of the country's socioeconomic and political institutions. More pressing is the need to restructure the very basis of group loyalties and national identities. But how does one restore civility to a society that has experienced rampant normlessness and demoralization?

For the time being, the prospects are not very promising. Even if one were to accept the most optimistic of all possible scenarios (that inter-Arab rivalries are resolved, the Palestinians are repatriated to their national homeland, Israeli and Syrian troops are withdrawn, the adverse effects of superpower politics are contained, the internal socioeconomic disparities and political differences that have divided the Lebanese and fragmented their society disappear, and that, as a result, a modicum of consensus is reached regarding the coveted national accord), one still has to reckon with the problems of demoralization. The deep underlying causes and many manifestations of the crisis, it must be remembered, are spiritual and psychological. Civility cannot be legislated by fiat. Nor can it be restored overnight by political rhetoric and ideological slogans. Civility can only be cultivated when citizens begin to harbor genuine and undivided commitment to civic and national values and institutions, or, more important, when such commitments are not permitted to be eroded or superseded by private and communal interests.

For the first time throughout the crisis, recent political developments began to show a few, albeit fickle, signs in that direction. During the Independence celebrations of November 22, 1980, for example, a "flag day" was declared that inspired a spontaneous and exuberant reaction among virtually all segments of the population in support of their national symbol (which, for a while, had been bypassed in some communities in favor of other flags and emblems). The Lebanese flag was hoisted almost everywhere, often with open chauvinistic defiance. The instance of the flag was perhaps no more than a vacuous and possibly contrived gesture. It did, nonetheless, reflect a patriotic spirit rarely displayed before.

The Lebanese government has also recently taken some measures to extend its powers and enforce its legitimate authority. One sees more evidence of law-enforcement agencies. More efforts are made to arrest criminals and impose fines on those convicted. Special legislation has been enacted to control the violations of construction laws and zoning ordinances. Successive campaigns have been launched to warn the public against indiscriminate littering and pollution. Well-intentioned as they are, all these efforts have had little impact so far on controlling these problems, or alleviating some of their worst consequences.

More significant are the efforts to reorganize and expand the army and to initiate the process of formulating a national accord. The controversial army bill is yet to appear before the Parliament for approval. In the meantime, vast areas of the country continue to be beyond the control of the legitimate military forces of the sovereign powers of state agencies. Dialogue over Lebanon's political future, particularly the character and extent of restructuring existing institutions and constitutional reforms, has not fared any better.

It is too early to ascertain whether such a dialogue, diffuse as it is at the moment, will materialize in a viable covenant acceptable to all groups. If one were to judge, however, by the public pronouncements of politicians, parliamentarians, and spokesmen of the various factions, there appears to be little consensus on the critical and still unresolved issues that provoked the civil disturbances, let alone the immense new problems generated by them. Indeed, the polemics over these issues have become sharper and the cleavages more irreconcilable. The divisive forces that keep the communities apart have, as of late, become more acute. Open discord and bitter conflict have also infiltrated factions within the same communities. Political coalitions are being splintered into disparate groups. Lebanon today is clearly more dismembered and fractured than at any other period in its history. The only efforts toward reconsolidation are assuming, unfortunately, sectarian or communal ties.

Security conditions, after a brief respite, have also taken a sharp turn to the worse, with all the familiar but gruesome manifestations of yet another round of terror and violence. In addition to the usual toll of random and innocent victims, there have been assassination attempts on the lives of religious leaders, foreign diplomats, and journalists. All the major traffic links between East and West Beirut continue to be closed because of indiscriminate sniping and shelling. Once again, the political future of Lebanon seems shrouded with mystery and uncertainty. What is certain is that civility has been irreparably damaged, and the hopes of ever establishing a secular and civil order are all the more faint and distant.

CHAPTER TWELVE

Disinherited Liberals:
Ras-Beirut in Jeopardy

Exile is the unhealable rift forced between a human being and a native place, between the self and its true home: its essential sadness can never be surmounted.
—Edward Said, "Reflections on Exile"

R AS-BEIRUT, THIS ONCE VIBRANT, mixed, and open suburban community in West Beirut, is in the throes today of tumul-
tous transformations that if uncontained, will profoundly change its character, disfigure its cosmopolitan image, and cripple the role of the liberal
constituency it has hosted for over a century.

By virtue of its mixed ethnic and religious composition and permissive
political atmosphere, Ras-Beirut evolved as a safe refuge for dispossessed
and marginal groups periodically out of favor with the political regimes
in the adjacent Arab states. It also served as a critical gadfly and safety
valve for testing innovative ideas and modes of life, and for mobilizing
public dissent and collective grievances. More important, and because of
the presence of the American University of Beirut (AUB), it displayed
some of the typical features of a university town. It produced and attracted a relatively young, literate, and highly professional and mobile
population; unmistakably middle class in its occupational composition
and urban life-style.

As a cultural and intellectual sanctuary, it fostered, indeed licensed,
experimentation in nearly all domains of public and private life, from
serious ideological doctrines and political platforms to the more frivolous
manifestations of trendy fads and fashions. Repressed and inventive groups
were free to challenge and debunk conventional authority and orthodox
doctrine and to experiment with untested ideas and new recipes, away
from the tyranny of oppressive political regimes and mindless censor bur-
eaus.

In this sense, Ras-Beirut was, albeit on a much more modest scale, the closest the Arab World could ever get to having its own "Greenwich Village," "Latin Quarter," or perhaps a "Bloomsbury Group" or a "Vienna Circle." It, too, could boast of its own avant-garde literary circles, cliques, and colonies of artists, poets, popular writers, journalists, and coffee-house intellectuals. It also abounded in little magazines, eccentric and bizarre periodicals, publishing houses, experimental theaters, art galleries, fashionable boutiques, and side-walk cafes.

Unlike other comparable avant-garde and liberal communities, however, Ras-Beirut did more than shelter marginal groups and countercultural expressions and symbols. Itinerant groups in search of the urban rewards of anonymity, excitement, and vitality (literally those who came today and left tomorrow) and settled residents who harbored deep commitments and traditional attachments could feel equally at home. In a more fundamental sense, Ras-Beirut was also instrumental in shaping some of the consequential ideological movements in the entire region. Virtually all the crucial political and sociocultural changes in the Arab world—both those which ushered hope for national resurgence and those which became sources of disunity and discordance—were initiated or given vent in Ras-Beirut. Pan-Arabism, Arab Nationalism, Arab and/or Progressive Socialism, Regional and National Ba'thism, Lebanese secularism, Syrian Nationalism, resistance and liberation movements (Palestinian and otherwise), communism, and a score of other radical, reactionary, and reformist groups have all found to varying degrees a receptive and enthusiastic audience in the community.

Ras-Beirut was as vital in other, perhaps more mundane and tangible, dimensions of cultural and everyday life. The range and sweep of ideas and life-styles launched or hosted within or around Ras-Beirut were as dazzling in their variety as they were far-reaching in their impact. The so-called first generation of Lebanese secularists and successive groups of gifted scholars, writers and public figures—many of whom were associated with AUB—were instrumental in articulating and popularizing ideas and values that transformed the lives and visions of millions of Arabs.

Quite often this restless search for novel encounters, at virtually all levels—ideological, commercial, and in patterns of everyday life—became exuberant; often tempestuous. Individuals espoused and dismissed political platforms as readily as they did fads and fashions. The area, nonetheless, engendered a refreshing mood for eclecticism and experimentation unmatched elsewhere in the region. Furthermore, the intellectual and cultural dynamism of Ras-Beirut, long before the mass media began to partake in the rapid dissemination of ideas and life-styles, was visible in the ripples it was generating far beyond the limited confines of its community.

The central thesis of this essay is that because Ras-Beirut developed into such a "melting pot" of diverse religious, ethnic, and ideological groups, it was able to sustain its unique role and stature as the only genuinely "open" community in the entire Arab world. By virtue of such openness, it engendered sentiments of trust, mutual respect, and deference to pluralistic life-styles. A remarkable spirit of tolerance pervaded all social contacts. This nurtured a deep and sincere sense of caring for others, sustained by respect for differences. Such sentiments were visible in the pluralistic composition of the community just as much as in the diversity of outlooks and perspectives.

No one tried to oppress, tyrannize, defame, or malign the other. Just as the Sunni Muslim and Greek Orthodox, the Druze and Protestant lived together; so did groups drawn from discrepant socioeconomic backgrounds or those who professed divergent ideologies and life-styles. There was room for everyone: the devout and heathen, pious puritans and graceless hedonists, left-wing radicals and ardent conservatives, footloose and self-centered Bohemians and steadfast chauvinists and conventional patriots. They all had a stake in preserving this almost amorphous and permeable character of Ras-Beirut. Diversity animated and enriched life in the community. It was a source of vitality; not a cause for paranoia and hostility between groups.

More remarkable, it accomplished all this and remained, until very recently, a relatively peaceful, wholesome, and edifying social neighborhood. It enjoyed all the redeeming virtues of an open metropolis and an intimate social circle. It was both cosmopolitan and provincial, vibrant and sobering: almost akin to a "global village." As long as Ras-Beirut remained a subculture of its own, different from and marginal to the rest of the society, it was able to deprovincialize and upgrade the quality of cultural life in Lebanon and Arab society.

Another striking feature, one that also accounts for the distinctive character and unusual role Ras-Beirut has come to play, is its association with AUB. Since their inception, both AUB and Ras-Beirut have had a unique and mutually reinforcing relationship. In a fundamental sense, neither could have been possible without the other. Despite their exceptional legacy and rich heritage, perhaps because of them, both are in

264   RAS-BEIRUT IN JEOPARDY

jeopardy today. They are being threatened, in fact, by the very forces
they have harnessed and unleashed.

It is rather anomalous that AUB should now be at odds with those
very nationalist sentiments that it was the first to foster at the turn of the
century. Likewise, Ras-Beirut is being made vulnerable by the liberal and
republican virtues it had engendered. It was, after all, AUB's own liberal
and secular constituency that created Ras-Beirut as a distinct university
town. It was also this constituency that protected and enhanced AUB's
autonomy and integrity. In fact, the relationship between Ras-Beirut and
AUB—the "town" and "gown," so to speak—has been a remarkable
twinship. It is doubtful, as we shall see, whether Ras-Beirut could have
developed into the liberal and open community it became without AUB.
It is also equally doubtful whether AUB could have survived in any other
sociocultural and political setting.

Just as Ras-Beirut is not any ordinary neighborhood, AUB is not merely
an academic institution. Both, without undue exaggeration, are rare traditions and unique phenomena. No other single university or comparable urban district in the Third World has had such a compelling impact
on the public life of so wide a region. Both have been enormously successful. Both are endangered entities today; victims perhaps of their own
success. Any threat to one is bound to have grievous implications for the
other.

This is why what is at stake today is very ominous and could foretell
the unfolding of the final episodes of Lebanon's long agony. Indeed,
many other communities have perished in Lebanon. Hundreds of thousands have lost their lives, and many more have been permanently maimed
and scarred by a decade of senseless violence and indiscriminate terror.
Entire villages, towns, and regions have been devastated and property
and resources ransacked or laid to waste. Virtually no one in Lebanon
today has been spared the anguish of uprootedness, exile, or other forms
of banishment and spiritual homelessness.

Menacing as these cruelties and horrors are, and one cannot emphasize
them enough, what Ras-Beirut is witnessing might still embody more
crucial implications for the ultimate future and destiny of Lebanon. It is
in this sense that Ras-Beirut stands today at the edge of a historic watershed. The harbingers of these disquieting transformations have already
become much too imminent during the past two years. If uncontained,
and the recent escalation of chaos and violence in the area indicates that
they have already become both rampant and irreversible, then the entire

community might perish. Such an eclipse is grievous and lamentable. It heralds the end of the last bastion or oasis of liberalism in a region seething with dogmatism and intolerance. Lebanon will lose its one and only viable example of successful pluralism. The Arab world will also have to live without its coveted safety valve.

How and why did Ras-Beirut develop those features in the first place? What are the forces threatening it and what, if anything, can still be done to halt its further erosion? In short, this is an attempt to document the transformation and deformation of Ras-Beirut. It is also an impassioned outcry, feeble as it might be, to lament a dying legacy.

A brief historical overview is in order first, if only to elucidate the repetitive character of such dismaying episodes.

Beirut Decomposed: A Brief Overview

Alas, the Lebanese never seem to learn from their history. Otherwise, history would not be repeating itself; and with such menacing consequences. Much like the social fabric of Lebanese society, Beirut's eventful history has also been marked by periods of relative harmony and peace interspersed with episodes of intense communal hostility and sectarian strife. Beirut, in this sense, is a microcosm of Lebanon's fragmented political culture. The same divisive forces, which on occasion threaten the delicate balance of power and erode civility in society, have also reinforced the segmented and parochial character of Beirut.

In its early development, Beirut evinced some of the spatial and communal features (e.g., distinct quarters and relatively homogeneous and self-sufficient neighborhoods) so typical of preindustrial cities. This was inevitable, given its pluralistic composition and the role it played as a refuge for intermittent waves of political émigrés and minority groups. Beirut is also noted, however, albeit for brief interludes, for the uniformity in its urban ethos and the distinct identity it evolved as a maritime coastal city with persisting links with the mountain and the hinterland. The spectacular growth of Beirut during the nineteenth century might well be due to its proclivity to reconcile these two seemingly inconsistent attributes.

As a result, Beirut was "open" to new encounters; particularly foreign culture, European trade, and an incessant flow of goods, people, and borrowed ideologies. But it also sustained groups and communities who retained their nonurban ties and primordial networks and sentiments. To Albert Hourani (1981), this is, after all, what distinguishes the ideology of the city from that of the mountain; so crucial for understanding the political development of Lebanon since 1920. "The urban idea of Lebanon was neither of a society closed against the outside world, nor of a unitary society in which smaller communities were dissolved, but something between the two: a plural society in which communities, still different on the level of inherited religious loyalties and intimate family ties, coexisted within a common framework" (Hourani 1981:175).

As a result, while the various communities displayed some of the expected and visible differences in everyday life, they also shared much. This was apparent in common social values and patterns of social interaction and popular culture. Leila Fawaz (1983), by amassing evidence from a variety of sources, both local and foreign, provides vivid and persuasive proof of such homogeneity and coexistence.

This is clearly true of the first half of the nineteenth century. Partly because of Beirut's compact size and predominantly commercial character, intermingling and collaboration between the various communities was both inevitable and vital for their mutual coexistence and survival. Intercommunal mixing, at least in the center of the town, was greater than is usually assumed. Merchants of various communities were partners in private business ventures. They collaborated and assisted each other in times of austerity and financial need. More important, they perceived themselves as members of an urban merchant community, resisting the hostile elements that threatened their common economic interests (Fawaz 1983:106).

In the old souks and bazaars, artisans and traders worked side by side. Spatial segregation and location of shops was occupational and not religious in character. Much like the spatial layout of residential quarters, the bazaars were strikingly uniform in their architectural features. On the whole, social interaction was characterized by sentiments of goodwill and mutual tolerance and personal ties of intimacy, familiarity, and trust. Such mutual cooperation was not confined to domestic and commercial relations. It spilled over into other spheres of public life. Christians and Muslims continued to meet together at official functions and served on the same committees, courts, and mixed tribunals (for further evidence see, Fawaz 1983:112).

This almost idyllic interlude in Beirut's history did not survive for too long. By the 1840s, as Ottoman power began to decline and European influence was becoming more ascendant, there was a marked shift in the relative position of the various communities (for further details see, Chevallier 1968; Salibi 1965; Khalaf 1979; Fawaz 1983). As a result, religious identification became sharper. Denominational and sectarian tension and hostilities increased in number and intensity. In some instances, denominational antagonisms were, in fact, more acute than the purely sectarian ones (Jessup 1910; Ma'oz 1968; Tibawi 1969; Salibi 1965).

The middle decades were not only marked by increasing tension, but it was the period during which Beirut was beginning to witness the first symptoms of rapid urbanization. It is then that Beirut's population began to swell and spill beyond its medieval walls. Estimated at about 6,000 in the 1820s, Beirut's population leaped to 120,000 by the end of the century. More unsettling, perhaps, Christians were becoming much more numerous, thus upsetting the demographic sectarian balance that had characterized the earlier decades. For example, while the religious composition of Beirut was roughly equal during the 1830s and 1840s, by the 1890s the proportion of Christians became two-thirds compared to nearly one-third for Muslims. Much of this change was, of course, due to the influx of Christians (mostly Maronites) fleeing their persecuted village communities. In the 1840s, Maronites made up only 10 percent of Beirut's population. Shortly after the massacres of 1860, the proportion of Maronites more than doubled, while that of other Christian sects remained roughly the same. (For these and other related estimates, see Fawaz 1983:131–32.)

Concomitant with these striking demographic changes, or perhaps because of them, the spatial structure of Beirut began to assume some of the features associated with confessional segregation. Confessional residential quarters started to appear, in an almost concentric pattern, around the old historic center of the city. On the whole, Christians—initially Greek Orthodox and then Maronites—settled mostly on the eastern flanks around es-Saife and Remeil. Eventually these developments expanded further in the direction of Achrafieh. Muslims drifted southward in the direction of Zokak el Blat, Bachoura, Mazraa, and Moussaytbeh. Generically, these became part of what is popularly labeled as lower and upper Basta. The western suburbs of the city—Ain Mraisse, Hamra, and Ras-Beirut—remained fairly open and started to attract, early in their development, a heterogeneous and mixed group of residents.

As peace returned to Lebanon after the 1860 civil hostilities, Beirut consolidated its economic, political, and cultural supremacy. Disparities, however, between the two dominant religious communities became sharper, particularly as the newly emergent Christian bourgeoisie began to enjoy a greater share of power and privilege. Denominational hostility receded and, once again, sectarian and communal conflict became more visible. At the turn of the century, in fact, Christian-Muslim clashes had become so recurrent that hardly a day went by without an incident involving some violent confrontation between confessional groups, particularly as individuals ventured into neighborhoods other than their own (see Jessup 1910; Khalaf 1979; Fawaz 1983).

It is then that the spatial configurations of the new residential quarters began to display even sharper and more explicit confessional undertones. Gradually, Beirut started to lose its unifying character as a city. No sooner, in other words, had Beirut assumed the proportions of a sizable urban agglomeration than it was decomposed into separate and distinct communities, each with its own schools, charitable and benevolent societies, hospitals, and political and social clubs. Even daily newspapers and other periodicals and popular publications, which at the turn of the century had already become numerous, reflected the distinctive segmental character of each of the three communities (see chapters by Rashid Khalidi, Marwan Buheiry, and Hisham Nashabi in Buheiry 1981).

There were, no doubt, a few notable instances when Christians and Muslims transcended their communal differences and participated collectively in underground political movements and secret societies. This was particularly true during the period of national struggle against Ottoman repression and centralization of the Young Turks at the turn of the century (i.e., between 1880 and 1908). On the whole, however, the initiative and nature of voluntary associations were communal and local in character.

In this sense, Beirutis were never given the chance to experience full urbanity for any substantial period of time to permit the development and appreciation of civic ties and secular interests. Primordial affinities, particularly those sustained by family, village, and communal loyalties, found ample opportunity to reinforce their identities in the newly emerging urban localities. Ras-Beirut, like Basta and Achrafieh, sustained many of these traditional affinities. Early in its development, however, it also displayed a greater tolerance for differences and inventive experimentation. Hence, it was able to evolve into the open, mixed, and cosmopolitan community it became. These attributes reinforced its image as an animated sanctuary for liberal ethos and life styles.

The Transformation and Deformation of Ras-Beirut

Ironically, and not unlike a few of Lebanon's other edifying features, Ras-Beirut is largely a historical accident; more the result of fortuitous circumstances than deliberate planning. What could have happened, one might ask, had not Daniel Bliss first laid eyes on this deserted stretch of sand dunes and wild cactus and persuaded the American Board of Commission for Foreign Missions to transform the "city's garbage dump" into the site of what has become the most distinguished American academic institution in the Middle East? No other single factor has been as persistent and instrumental in shaping the growth of Ras-Beirut as the compelling presence of AUB. Both the spatial and sociocultural attributes of the community are, perhaps unwittingly, an unintended consequence of this historic accident. I say unwittingly, because if one reexamines the recorded accounts of the early missionaries and founding fathers of the "Syrian Protestant College," as it was called then, it was not their intention to generate all the secular and liberalizing forces Ras-Beirut came to host (for further details, see Jessup 1910; Bliss 1920; Penrose 1941).

What is unmistakable is that the founding of AUB in 1866 can be clearly singled out as the first instance of institutional invasion of a garden farming area. An indigenous population (roughly not more than 30 households), mostly Sunni Muslims, Greek Orthodox, and Druze landowners and tenants, was already in residence in the sparsely settled neighborhood. Despite sectarian differences, these groups evinced relatively common life-styles, similar folkways, and a distinct Ras-Beirut dialect. They emerged as a homogeneous group and developed a strong sense of loyalty and attachment to their neighborhood. Though they had an extended residence in an urban and literate setting, the first few generations of this original population remained the least educated and, at least initially, resisted the Western and secular incursions. Whatever socioeconomic mobility or elevation in economic status they enjoyed was largely a by-product of their landownership and the subsequent appreciation of land values and speculation in real estate. We have here, in other words, the nucleus of a truly urban bourgeoisie.

Around the turn of the century, AUB's presence began to attract another group that slowly contributed to the growth of the indigeneous community. Though no doubt a composite group of varied backgrounds, these initial waves of migrants had much in common: they were mostly Christian families from rural areas who were drawn into Ras-Beirut by the cultural facilities and employment opportunities AUB was beginning to generate. Initially, the influx of new families was very slow; roughly about four to five families every year (for these and other such details, see Khalaf and Kongstad 1973). Soon after World War I, however, their number increased appreciably. A cursory review of real estate transactions shows that a sizable portion of these families had already become land holders in the 1920s. Along with some of the prominent Druze families (e.g. Rawdah and Talhuq), Greek Orthodox (e.g. Bassoul, Sourati, Tarazi, Rubeiz, Bikhazi) and Sunni Muslims (e.g., Itani, Taqoush, Yamout, Zantout, Nsouli, Naja etc.), property was being transferred to a growing number of newcomers. Names like Khauli, Dumit, Makdisi, Rasi, Baroudi, Nassar, Nassif, Cortas, Jurdak, Kurani, Hajjar, Khuri, and Haddad—to mention a few—began to appear in the cadastral register. They were all Protestants—or more appropriately converted Protestants—who were attached to the University and the burgeoning activities of its affiliated missions.

Numerically, they may not have been much. They did, though, constitute a socially significant group; one that was to mold the character of the area for at least the subsequent fifty years. While the early indigenous groups resisted the Western and missionary incursions and for some time managed to remain untouched by them, the new Protestant community was understandably receptive and perhaps too eager to absorb some of the Calvinistic virtues and modes of conduct. They were not only converted to the faith; they also acquired some of the concomitant Puritan and Protestant life-styles. The so-called "Protestants of Ras-Beirut," in fact, became an euphemism to define the identity and social character of this new urban community. And it was a community in almost every sense of the term: an orderly, cohesive, God-fearing group, sparked by the frugal habits of work and accountability and a strong sense of neighborhood—the Protestants promptly left their impact on the community. They maintained close family ties and acquired a civic-minded concern in the affairs and welfare of their community. Voluntary associations of all varieties—ranging from serious political and cultural societies to more mundane organizations such as Boy Scouts, Sunday school meetings, and women's auxiliary gatherings in support of charitable causes—began to attract wider participation.

Education and exemplary behavior were the keys to social mobility. Despite their modest socioeconomic background, the "Protestants of Ras-Beirut" soon emerged as a highly literate and mobile social group. Members of this generation, take pride in recounting their success stories.

Two recent autobiographical accounts by Anis Makdisi (1983) and Anis Frayha (1978)—two exemplary prototypes of this earlier generation —provide vivid and colorful anecdotes to substantiate such impressions. Both came from humble village origins, were converted to Protestantism and received their college education at AUB. It is there that they were exposed to the Calvinistic ethics and Puritanism of the American founding fathers and successive generations of devoted scholars and teachers. To Makdisi and Frayha, like countless other graduates of the period, being at AUB was a total experience. It embraced not only the acquisition of skills, but opportunities for students to try various life-styles, to learn from each other, to have their unexamined belief-systems challenged, and, above all, to have association with men who demonstrated in their lives the values of liberal education and free inquiry.

The exposure left an indelible mark on their personalities and future career. Both earned their Ph.D.'s in the United States and returned to AUB to become resourceful and reputable professors of Arabic: Makdisi as a literary critic and poet, and Frayha as a linguist and folklorist. Both were deeply immersed in the communal life of Ras-Beirut and participated in civic and church activities, but both had an impact that extended beyond the narrow confines of their small community. Their successful careers as scholars also served them well in more than just the symbolic rewards of status and self-esteem. Like many of their colleagues, they were able to enjoy some of the modest comforts of elevated standards of living. Most of them, for example, were able to amass considerable wealth, invest in real estate, build commodious houses in Ras-Beirut and their mountain villages. They are clearly bequeathing their children much more than they ever inherited from their parents.

The Protestants' elevation in social status and their swift assimilation into the urban community of Ras-Beirut was clearly apparent in the slow but persistent increase in construction activity. The period between the wars (between 1920 to 1940) witnessed an intensification of development particularly along the main streets radiating from AUB. Cheap land values encouraged further construction. Suburban villas with red-tiled roofs, walled gardens, and well-tended patios emerged as landmarks to stamp the urban character of the whole community.

One remarkable feature about these developments is that despite the spatial and social transformations the area was undergoing, for over eighty years Ras-Beirut retained its communal and village character. On the whole, the "Protestants" remained a timid and cautious social group despite their receptivity to secular and Western styles of life. The typically middle-class morality they were imbued with proved effective in generating an achievement ethic, community consciousness and some of the moral dictates of Puritanism, but these were hardly sufficient to create the more venturesome attributes necessary to cope with the increasing scale of urbanization and commercialization the area was to witness during the fifties and sixties.

One should not, however, misread the nature or magnitude of the other social and cultural changes that were slowly being entrenched or sparked off around Ras-Beirut. Spatially, the area retained its suburban character, but the cultural and ideological changes it hosted and reinforced were both vital and far-reaching in their impact. In fact, something akin to a "Silent Revolution" was slowly taking place. This was most apparent in the type of questions and issues the burgeoning intelligentsia were beginning to probe and address publically at the time. (For further details, see papers by Rashid Khalidi, Marwan Buheiry, and Hisham Nashabi in Buheiry, 1981.) It was also visible in some of the unobtrusive but fundamental changes in everyday life.

Clearly many of these novel ideas and attitudes originated elsewhere. Other parts of Beirut, no doubt, contributed to this cultural and literary awakening. Those articulated around Ras-Beirut, however, were comparatively richer in variety and scope. By virtue of its openness and proclivity for experimentation, the area served, in fact, as a testing ground for many of the controversial and polemical issues, conflicting ideologies, and permissive life-styles that the other more cloistered communities hesitated to adopt.

Much of the credit goes, of course, to the first generation of so-called Lebanese secularists—towering figures like Nasif al-Yaziji, Butrus al-Bustani, Faris al-Shidyaq, Jurji Zaydan, Ya'qub Sarruf, Faris Nimr, Salim and Bishara Taqla, Yusuf al-Asir, Shibli al-Shumayyil, and Farah Antun—who had laid the groundwork and stimulated much of the popular enthusiasm for change. Through the popular journals and periodicals they had established (e.g. *Al-Muqtataf, Al-Muqattam, Al-Hilal, Al-Ahram, Al-Jawaib, Al-Jinan, Al-Junayna, Nafir Suriyya*) they were instrumental in disseminating ideas and values that transformed the lives and visions of millions of Arabs (for further details regarding the origin and content of these ideas, see Hourani 1962; Salibi 1965; Sharabi 1970).

This cultural awakening was no doubt heightened by the critical political transformations overwhelming the region at the time. This was, after all, the period of national struggle marked by growing hostility towards Ottoman, French, British, Zionist and other colonial and occupying forces. It was a time of upheaval and bafflement, fraught with the fearsome specter of Ottoman oppression, ravages of famine, the cruelties of two world wars, and the hopes and frustrations of the struggle for independence and self-determination.

It was during this period that Arab thinkers were grappling with the nagging question regarding the nature of nationalist sentiments, political identity and cultural heritage and how to forge autonomous political states without alienating themselves from Pan-Arabist sentiments.

The traffic in ideas and personages Beirut witnessed during the period between the wars was prodigious, even stupendous; both in number and diversity. Three recent autobiographical accounts—'Anbara Salam al-Khalidi (1978), Wadad Cortas (1983), and Munah al-Solh (1984)—recall nostalgically the incessant stream of Arab and other dignitaries who visited Beirut at the time they were growing up, roughly between the two world wars. The diversity of books, periodicals, daily newspapers, opinions, and world views they were exposed to were as dazzling in their variety as they were far-reaching in their impact. They were equally impressed by the new cultural activities (e.g., public lectures and debates, organized sports, concerts, youth clubs), awakened national sentiments (participation in political parties, protest movements and street demonstrations and mass rallies), and subtle changes in mannerisms and social behavior (opportunities for the sexes to mix freely and the appearance of new styles of conduct, etiquettes, and conventions). Ras-Beirut, in particular, because it was able to accommodate waves of intinerant groups and immigrants, was comparatively more receptive to such diversity than the other two communities (i.e., Basta, and Ashrafieh).

This was particularly visible in virtually all the manifestations of popular cultural expressions, just as much as in the more serious scholarly output of local scholars. To a large extent, all the intelligentsia at the time were essentially asking the same questions: Who are we? Who is to blame for our fragmentation? Who are our friends and enemies? Where do we go from here? The answers they gave, however, depending on their own particular sociopolitical milieu, were strikingly different.

For example, members of the French-educated Maronite intelligentsia living mostly in the eastern suburbs of Beirut, who were frequent contributors to *La Revue Phénicienne,* had different perceptions of Lebanon's identity and its future than the Sunni Muslim intelligentsia. The latter were more inclined to espouse Islamic, Pro-Ottoman, and ultimately Pan-Arab and Arab Nationalist causes consistent with their political constituency and readership.

Furthermore, what readers in the Christian suburbs found appealing in *Al-Bashir,* their counterparts in the Muslim quarters sought in *Thamarat al-Funun, Al-Mufid, Al-Nida', Nabras, Al-Haqiqah* etc. The journals and periodicals around Ras-Beirut—earlier ones like *Kawkab al-Subh al-Munir, Al-Nashra al-Usbu'iyya, Al-Junayna,* and eventually *Al-Abhath* and *Al-Kuliyyah*— were considerably more open to a diversity of viewpoints and world views, more moderate in their opinions and more receptive to secular and liberal ideas. Incidentally, this is not too unlike the readership and orientations of the three current leading dailies of Beirut: *Al-'Amal, Al-Safir,* and *Al-Nahar.* They continue to represent the distinct political subcultures that pervade the three broad communities in Beirut.

The period between the two wars marks also a significant watershed in the cultural and intellectual history of Ras-Beirut. AUB had just survived the economic and political adversities of the past two decades and emerged strengthened by the new opportunities and genuine public support for the type of education it was offering. By the early 40s its graduates were already placed in key positions throughout the region (particularly Sudan, Egypt, Palestine, Trans-Jordan, Syria, Iraq, Iran, and Ethiopia) and were eagerly sought by the new governments bent on new programs of reform and modernization (Penrose 1941:219–21). In response to the burgeoning nationalist sentiments and changing political climate in the region, AUB was secularized in 1920 and succeeded in reorganizing and extending its curriculum to meet the growing demand for applied and professional training. Its local faculty and staff achieved rights and privileges (particularly in regard to rank, promotion, and voting privileges etc.) that ended the earlier distinctions between so-called Anglo-Saxon and non-Anglo-Saxon teachers and administrators.

It was also in this period that the first generation of Western-trained local scholars started to return to Lebanon. In virtually every discipline or program within AUB—initially in Arabic, history, education, and then gradually in the social, physical, and medical sciences—a critical mass of resourceful and spirited scholars was emerging to assume a more prominent role in the intellectual life of the community.[1] The small nucleus of local scholars (Ya-qub Sarruf, Faris Nimr, Jabr Dumit, and Bulus Khauli) who had accompanied the University since its inception, was joined by another handful (Mansur Jurdak, Jurjus and Anis Makdisi, and Philip Hitti) at the turn of the century. It was not, however, until the twenties and thirties that the first sizable group of local scholars returned to AUB after receiving their advanced training in the United States. The intellectual and cultural life of the community, let alone the enhanced stature of the University, have not been the same since.

The limited scope of this essay does not permit an adequate recognition of the collective or individual legacy of this generation of scholars. They clearly merit a fuller tribute and a more probing inquiry. A methodical intellectual history will, one day, reveal the seminal and vital character of their contributions and how deeply they have influenced the subsequent course of teaching and research in the region.[2] I can only name a few in passing here: Asad Rustum, Constantine Zurayk, Zeine Zeine, and Nabih Faris in history; Jibrail Jabbur, Anis Frayha, Kamal Yazigi in Arabic; Charles Malik in philosophy; Said Himadeh, Husni Sawwaf in Business Administration; Albert Badre and George Hakim in Economics; Habib Kurani, George Shahla, and Jibrail Katul in Education; Nikula Shahine in Physics; Aziz Abdul-Karim and Adib Sarkis in Chemistry, Philip Ashkar, Henry Badeer, Dikran Berberian, Hrant Chaglassian, George Fawaz, Sami Haddad, Amin Khairallah, Mustafa Khalidi, George Khayat, Nimeh Nucho, Philip Sahyoun, and Hovsep Yenikomeshian in Medicine, and Charles Abou-Chaar and Amin Haddad in Pharmacy.

Just as successive generations of dedicated American scholars were able to inspire and patronize local talent, so did this resourceful and spirited nucleus of local scholars. Much like their American mentors, they too devoted the most productive years of their career to the University, immersing themselves in the life of the community, and many of them did not leave AUB until their retirement. Their presence served as a source of inspiration to successive generations of younger scholars. More distinctive perhaps, they had a broad and public conception of their role; a feature that extended and deepened the sphere of their influence and public image. Partly because of their exceptional gifts and the unusual circumstances of the time, they did not confine their intellectual concerns within the narrow walls of the campus. They were sparked by a spirit of public service and a longing to participate in debating and resolving the critical problems and public issues the Arab world was facing at the time.

This is quite apparent in both the nature of their scholarly output and extent of public involvement. While the earlier generations excelled in establishing local periodicals and popularizing issues (e.g., *Al-Kuliyyah, Al-Muqtataf*) and addressed predominantly Arab audiences, this "middle generation" extended and internationalized the scope of their intellectual and professional interests without ignoring the cultural needs of their local and regional constituency. They launched scientific research projects, published in professional foreign journals, and produced what were to become standard references for years to come. A cursory review of their bibliography reveals the impressive range and diversity of their intellectual concerns (see Tamim 1967).

What was particularly rewarding—and surviving members of this generation continue to reflect on those years with considerable nostalgia—is the spirit of open dialogue that pervaded and animated their lives. Intellectuals, like the rest of the community, rarely remained in solitude. There were intimate circles and personal networks to provide the sense of fellowship, camaraderie, and solidarity. The circles brought together individuals with diverse backgrounds, ideological leanings, and religious denominations. The search for knowledge and devotion to free inquiry helped them in transcending their parochial differences. So did the opportunities to participate in several of the publications, cultural and scientific organizations, and voluntary associations they helped establish.

Incidentally, it was out of such small cliques that some of the most resourceful endeavors, distinguished scholars, and public figures emerged. One such striking instance is the handful of scholars drawn from a variety of disciplines—Said Himadeh, Charles Malik, Constantine Zurayk, George Hakim, Charles Issawi, Husni Sawwaf, Halim Najjar, Anis Frayha, and Zeine Zeine—who collaborated together in editing volumes and publishing *Sisilat al-Abhath al-Ijtimaʿiyyah (Series of Social Studies)* in the midforties. Similar such collaborative efforts, often sparked by little more than the enthusiasm of like-minded colleagues, produced other impressive landmarks in the form of journals *(Al-Abhath, Middle East Forum, Middle East Economic Papers, Berytus)*, research centers (Economic Research Institute, Middle East Area Program, Arab Chronology and Documents), international conventions (The Middle East Medical Assembly), and associations (The Alumni Association, *Al-Urwa Al-Wuthqa*, Civic Welfare League).

Incidentally, many of these outstanding scholars had occasion to distinguish themselves in the more public and international spheres of their careers. Some served as ambassadors and ministers, or assumed the responsibilities of high office in the United Nations and other international organizations. Others were instrumental in establishing crucial organizations like the Arab Office in Washington or served as special advisors to various heads of state (see Hourani 1984 for further details).

It was during the period between the wars that participation in such activities—along with the burgeoning facilities for competitive sports, public performances, music, art, and theatre—began to attract wider appeal. As in the other more serious endeavors of research, political activism, welfare, and civic-minded concerns, the seemingly more frivolous and playful pursuits—which often underlie competitive athletics and expressive artistic events—also allowed individuals and groups to transcend their parochial identities and melt into a common cosmopolitan subculture.

Actually, many of these activities (beginning in the late forties), even the benign recreational and cultural clubs on campus, became highly politicized. Most prominent among these were *Al-Urwa Al-Wuthqa* (The Close Bond) and the Civic Welfare League. The former was formed in 1918 to promote and encourage the study of Arab culture. The latter, established in 1933, was likewise part of a rural development program where both faculty and students participated in establishing summer camps in rural communities and offered assistance in agriculture, home economics, public health, and literacy campaigns (for further details, see Penrose 1941; Munro 1977). Both became notorious in subsequent decades for their controversial and highly charged political activities. They offered political tutelage to successive generations of nationalists and left-leaning political activists.

It is within such student organizations that the likes of George Habash, Wadi Haddad, and Hani al-Hindi, among many others, initiated their political careers, developed their Pan-Arabist sentiments and espoused their hatred for Zionism, imperialism, and the superpowers. For those who could not find enough within the campus, other "voices" were beginning to beckon in the surrounding neighborhoods. In the early 1930s, Antoun Sa'adeh had just established the Parti Populaire Syrien (PPS), and was propounding his views for a united "Greater Syria" as a secular, modern, and nationalist state. First, as a clandestine organization and gradually as an open but tightly organized party, the *Zaʿim*, as he was fondly called by his followers, attracted a sizable part of the liberal intelligentsia of the time (see Sharabi 1978, for a personal account of Saʾadeh's charismatic presence and influence).

The subsequent decades ushered in other more compelling "voices," and many of the same liberal groups were predisposed to shift their ideological commitments in support of Pan-Arabist, Socialist, leftist, Baʾthist and ultimately Palestinian liberation movements. Those who were not so politicized were left alone and were free to remain disengaged from any of the dominant ideological groups. In fact, a rather large portion of the liberal community remained neutral and uncommitted and were involved in the apolitical cultural and intellectual expressions Ras-Beirut was beginning to host. Once again, in other words, there was room for everyone.

It was precisely this open and cosmopolitan milieu that enhanced Ras-Beirut's appeal and stature. Liberals from other communities in Lebanon and elsewhere in the Arab world converged on it in successive waves and larger numbers. Munah al-Solh (1984), a prominent Sunni Muslim liberal and political analyst, singles out this same feature in accounting for his own political socialization. He pays tribute to his teachers at the Islamic Maqassed of Beirut (e.g., Zaki Naccache, Omar Farroukh, Ibrahim Abdel ʾAl) for sharpening his awareness of Arab heritage. He also notes with pride the influence of popular journalists and political activists (e.g. ʿAbd al-Qadir al-Qabbani, ʿAbd al-Ghani al-Uraisi, Ahmad Tabbarah, Ahmad ʿAbbas etc. . . .) in intensifying his nationalist sentiments. But then he goes on to admit that it was at AUB, at Faysal's restaurant, at the Arab Cultural Club, and in the private homes of his Protestant friends that he became cognizant of other "voices" and novel modes of conduct.

The sweeping sociocultural, political, and commercial transformations the area witnessed during the fifties and sixties reinforced and complemented, at least initially, the cosmopolitan and pluralistic character of Ras-Beirut. To a large extent, this is the point when Ras-Beirut ceases to be synonymous, culturally and intellectually, with AUB. Beginning in 1948, waves of Palestinian migrants started taking residence in the area. Political events in both Syria and Egypt, particularly after the Suez crisis of 1956, generated another influx. Armenian refugees, particularly professionals and semiprofessional groups that had settled elsewhere in

Lebanon (after the Massacres of 1914), also started to converge on Ras-Beirut.

Despite their divergent backgrounds and the varying circumstances underlying their uprootedness, all these groups had much in common: they were drawn predominantly from highly literate, urban, and middle-class families with marked Anglo-Saxon traditions and a predisposition for socioeconomic mobility. Though they were all "displaced" groups, they retained little of the attributes of refugee and marginal communities. They evinced, from the very beginning, a noticeable readiness to be assimilated into Ras-Beirut. They were also instrumental in accelerating the pace of change by adding to and enriching the cultural and economic vitality of the area. The upper and middle-class Palestinians, many of whom managed eventually to acquire Lebanese citizenship, brought with them professional skills and a comparatively high proportion of professors and university graduates. A mere listing of a few of the names who joined the University during the fifties indicates how vital this generation of Palestinians has been in upgrading the quality of professional and intellectual life of the area.[3]

Not only AUB, but other colleges, schools, and cultural centers were going through a period of growth and expansion. The inflow of capital from the Gulf and the concomitant speculation in real estate provided other employment opportunities. In addition to providing a handy reservoir of professional talent, Palestinians (and this is also true of Egyptians and Syrians who left the UAR after episodes of nationalization of private enterprise), ventured into profitable and enterprising sectors of the economy. This was particularly visible in banking, insurance, business services, and retail. The Intra Bank, Arabia Insurance Co., and other consulting and contracting firms (such as Dar al-Handasa and ACE) come to mind. Armenians were equally resourceful. They, too, contributed their own ethnic and occupational skills, particularly in professional and semi-professional vocations like pharmacy, dentistry, nursing, photography, electronics, etc.

By the late fifties, Ras-Beirut was already displaying all the characteristic features of increasing commercialization and rapid growth. Urbanization was so swift, in fact, that in less than two decades the spatial character of Ras-Beirut was almost totally transformed. Mounting pressure for urban space, the invasion of commercial establishments and the sharp rise in land values and speculation in real estate resulted in large-scale construction and corporate financing. The attractive red-tiled villas, which one graced the suburban landscape, soon gave way to a more intensive form of land utilization. Towering structures in reinforced concrete with glittering glass facades and prefabricated aluminum frames began to overwhelm the urban scene.

The sense of neighborhood and the homogeneous residential quarters that housed regular and stable families were also threatened by a more impersonal form of residence, such as single men's apartments, furnished flats, and rooming houses to accommodate a growing itinerant population. It was not uncommon, for example, to have the basement of a building utilized as a stereo-club, bar or nightclub, or possibly a garage or warehouse; the ground floor as a movie house, side-walk cafe, restaurant or display parlors; the first few floors as bank and financial premises, executive and administrative branch offices of foreign companies, marketing research outfits, insurance companies, transportation and airline agencies, single or collective doctor's clinics, or offices of other professionals. These offices existed side by side with beauty shops, Swedish massage institutes, and haute couture and fashion shops. The upper floor might be residential units, penthouse apartments, and roof gardens. (For further details see Khalaf and Kongstad 1973.)

Gradually, Ras-Beirut started to lose its cohesive and wholesome character as a residential neighborhood and became a tempting ground for attracting sightseers, shoppers, tourists, and other transient groups that sought refuge in its anonymity and permissive outlets for casual and titillating forms of entertainment. In turn these changes carried with them some of the concomitant by-products of rapid urbanization; a higher incidence of personal deviance and social disorganization and a relaxation in sexual norms and standards of public morality.

Despite these inevitable transformations, the area remained, until the early seventies, the most dominant and arresting urban center in the Arab world. It retained its mixed composition and displayed, because of rampant consumerism, an even greater propensity to experiment with novel forms of cultural expressions. The commercialization of popular culture as profitable ventures, reinforced by a permissive political climate and free and uncensored media, encouraged further eclecticism and sensationalism. The highbrow exclusive periodicals of the early sixties (e.g. *Hiwar, Mawaqif, Sh'ir, Al-Adab, Al-Adib, Al-Fikr*) were supplemented by a plethora of new tabloids and glossy magazines. Even daily newspapers broadened their coverage to reach the growing intellectual interests of its readership. Many, for example, started publishing literary and cultural supplements.

Art, theatre, music, and dance displayed a variety of genres; ranging from serious surrealistic expressions to mediocre appeals to taste and aesthetic standards. Traditional folklore, arts, and crafts were not spared. They too, were victimized by the ethos of cash nexus and excessive commercialization. Publishing houses, with an eye on quick returns, were also eager to publish almost anything. Book exhibits became celebrated events, and book stores continued to sell, despite the inevitable debasement of literary standards, perhaps the richest possible variety of books and periodicals found anywhere in the Arab world.

AUB was no longer the exclusive cultural sanctuary. Other centers and outlets emerged to satisfy this aroused appetite for popular culture, ideas, and ideological discourse. Politically motivated cultural and information centers, sponsored by adjacent Arab regimes and ideological groups, established their own programs and publications, or subsidized particular newspapers (e.g. *Dirasat 'Arabiyya, Journal of Palestine Studies, Shou'un Falastiniyya, Al-Hawadith* etc.). Many of the foreign embassies and their affiliated cultural missions, including the Kennedy Center, British Council, Goethe Institute, University Christian Center, Italian, Spanish, and Russian cultural centers, Arab Cultural Club, and Islamic Cultural Center, contributed to the diversity of "voices" and "scripts." More important, one was at liberty to listen and incorporate what one heard.

As scholars could pursue their research and teaching in an atmosphere of intellectual freedom, so did the growing ranks of free-lance writers, editorialists, columnists, and opinion makers. Caustic political humor became a popular pastime. Ziad Rahbani's gifted sketches and musical comedies, portraying the deepening pathologies of Lebanon's pluralism and the futility of sectarian violence, were reminiscent of Omar al-Ze'inny's biting poetic ditties of the thirties and forties.

Such popular and other pseudo-intellectual "voices" became more audible and appealing. Some, in fact, were beginning to mute and overwhelm those of the more serious and dispassionate scholars. The restless and baffled among the young read the musings of Onsi al-Hajj and Adonis with the same intensity that earlier generations approached Constantine Zurayk's essays on Arab Nationalism or Rene Habachi's discourses on existential philosophy. It was intellectually fashionable to be engaged. There was an air of chic about it. The avant-garde, of all shades, flaunted their causes célèbres with considerable abandon and self-indulgence. They, too, had their own networks and social circles. Side-walk cafes, snack bars, and restaurants, much like the formal headquarters of other explicit groups, became identified with particular kinds of intellectual and ideological clients and subcultures.

In short, despite the inevitable commercialization and politicization of cultural and intellectual expressions, Ras-Beirut remained an exuberant place to be in. Diversity, once again, animated and enriched life in the community. It allowed groups to lead divergent lives yet live side by side.

War-Generated Dislocations

The deformations associated with the outbreak of civil hostilities in 1975 are far too complex and profound in their manifestations and consequences to be adequately discussed here. For over a decade, Ras-Beirut, like the rest of the country, has been subjected to some of the most bizarre and barbaric forms of reckless violence, protracted chaos, and decadence. The preceding chapter chronicled some of these disquieting features, particularly those which have exacerbated the already enfeebled civility and the impoverishment and demoralization of public life. The most I can do here is to disclose the new sources of such deformations and to identify how segments of the intelligentsia are reacting to and coping with the forces that wreaked havoc in their private lives and usurped their liberalizing roles.

It is actually a credit to Ras-Beirut's resilience and tenacity that it has been able to resist such relentless punishment for so long. The assault on Ras-Beirut and the consequent demoralization of public life, it must be emphasized, have been more the result of exogenous forces than inherent contradictions or hostility between endogenous groups rooted in the community. In fact, Ras-Beirut is perhaps the only community in Lebanon that did not experience any direct violent confrontation between coexisting groups. Once again, in other words, Ras-Beirut became a victim of its openness, moderation, and tolerance. Refugees and displaced groups from other warring areas, in progressively large numbers, are converging on it and expediting its demise.

The inflow of Palestinian refugees (strikingly different in both educational level and political orientation from the highly literate and urbanized groups who came in 1948) began in 1970 after the Black September incidents led to the eviction of the PLO from Jordan. Virtually all the successive major events associated with the civil strife of the past decade[4] have generated massive demographic shifts, aroused communal hostilities, and led to the decentralization and reconcentration of population groups and urban functions along sectarian lines, much as they did in the nineteenth century. Displaced Christian groups rushed in the direction of the eastern suburbs, and Sunni Muslims, Shi'ites, Kurds, Palestinians, and Syrians drifted into West Beirut and the southern suburbs (for further details, see Nasr 1982).

The groups who converged on Ras-Beirut, more so than those who settled elsewhere, were much more alien to the patterns of life and cultural norms prevalent in the area. On the whole, they were dislodged, dispossessed and unanchored groups, traumatized by fear and violence and raging with bitterness and pent-up frustrations. More disquieting, they had no attachments to, or appreciation of the community they found themselves in. To many, in fact, Ras-Beirut was simply an urban space to be occupied and amenities to be exploited. Such encroachment was occurring at a time when both state and legitimate institutions were being discredited and conventional patterns of authority and deference were losing their grip.[5]

Some of these deformations—pervasive anomie, normlessness, and transgression of public and private property—were so instantaneous and devastating that one could actually see the change happening; not from year to year, month to month; but from day to day. Sometimes, within hours entire neighborhoods would be invaded and converted into pockets of squalor and urban blight.

More damaging was the assault on the pluralistic way of life and the liberal norms that encouraged coexistence and harmony between the various groups. Quite often, in reaction to confessional hostility elsewhere, the fears and apprehensions of Christians are provoked. Already a large number of Christian families have left the area. Others who used to seek it for its educational, cultural, recreational, or employment opportunities, have stopped doing so, or have taken temporary measures to seek them elsewhere. The demographic preponderance of Shi'ites, compounded by the often assertive and intimidating behavior associated with dislodged groups, is also beginning to provoke similar apprehensions among Sunnis and other threatened minorities.

In short, the genuine coexistence and feelings of mutual trust and tolerance, which for over a century enriched and edified life in the community, is slowly being eroded. The open defiance and arrogance of one group is met with grudging timidity and acquiescence of others. As a result, all social relations have become guarded and furtive.

Wadad Cortas (1983) recalls that when she was growing up in Ras-Beirut in the thirties, their Sunni Muslim landlord used to instruct the drummer man who roused the believers before dawn during the month of Ramadan, to muffle his drum lest he disturb his Christian neighbors. A touching gesture! A Muslim believer could observe his religious duties without offending his Protestant neighbor. During the past few years, the exact opposite has been taking place. As the *mu'azins'* calls for prayer were getting louder and religious festivities more vociferous, Christians became furtive about decorating their own Christmas trees.

The assault has been extended to include other symbols and manifestations of liberalism and permissive life-styles. Foreign subjects and institutions—university presidents, diplomats, journalists, professors, priests etc.—are indiscriminately eliminated, kidnapped, or blown up. Stereo-clubs, bars, supermarkets, and liquor stores, have likewise become symbols of blasphemous and satanic decadence. The same minds, academic institutions, cultural centers, edifying streets and neighborhoods—which once animated the world around them—have now become despised targets of hostility or are allowed to waste and atrophy.

Entropy and Estrangement

What is more poignant is the mood of entropy, futility, and defeat that now overwhelms the liberals. Of course, initially they were outraged and did all they could to fend off the forces that were disfiguring their community and damaging their sense of personal worth and dignity. In fact, as warring factions in other parts of Lebanon and Beirut were getting more belligerent, some of the few sobering and moderating voices were those emanating from Ras-Beirut.

One very expressive example, other than the isolated efforts of a score of other thinkers and activists, was the "group for Unified Lebanon," founded in 1975, as part of an Institute for Lebanese Studies. The group, a rather loose association of professionals, intellectuals, and political activists, sought to enlighten the public about the confessional and aberrant character of civic strife and to propose appropriate strategies of social and political reform. They experimented with every conceivable means of mobilizing discontent: debates, round-table discussions, public demonstrations, published monographs, position papers, and pamphlets calling for a secular and more democratic state. Their weekly, pungent, and caustic editorials—particularly those of Najib Abu-Haydar, Munir Shamma'a, Hasan Musharafiyeh, Joseph Mugheizel, Layla Kadi etc. . . . — were ardently read. Bit by bit, however, the overwhelming and devastating character of the war dissipated and dwarfed their impassioned concerns.

This same cycle—outrage, disillusionment, resignation, withdrawal, and entropy—has characterized other segments of the intelligentsia. Scholars, writers, journalists, poets, even political activists display similar disquieting and debilitating symptoms: outrage, accompanied first by frantic and impetuous expressions of disbelief and protest, then grudging recognition of the irrationality and often mysterious nature of the corrosive forces (both internal and external) destroying Lebanon, bitter disillusionment with the impotence and futility of their own actions, and finally resignation and withdrawal. As a result, large segments of the intelligentsia, particularly those who refuse to join or support any of the warring factions or suffer the indignities of diaspora and expatriation, are now demoralized by crippling feelings of impotence and futility. This is, after all, what entropy is all about: a progressive withholding of energy and creative thought that could have gone into more constructive and meaningful effort.

This is particularly painful because it is this liberal community, it must be recalled, that was sparked by an expansive and optimistic view of its mission and espoused global and liberal ideas during the latter part of the nineteenth century. Since then, successive generations of this once-recalcitrant and outspoken community are now muted and diminished. They are consumed, instead, by obsessive and minimal concerns of personal survival in a cruel and menacing world. Today they are a living embodiment of Yeats' admonition:" The best lack all conviction, while the worst are full of passionate intensity."

It is not very reassuring, nor flattering, to heap public praise, as many of us continue to do, on the proverbial resilience, elasticity, and resourcefulness of the Lebanese. Even professional psychiatrists, attuned as they are to depict latent and unrecognized sources of pathology, have been prone to misread such symptoms. After a visit of only ten days in January

1983, as part of an assessment team to survey the health needs of Lebanon, Mansell Pattison (1984:35) came back with this glowing impression:

> In the past decade it is estimated that 100,000 Lebanese were killed
> and 2,000 severely crippled. During periods of intermittent shell-
> ing, as much as one-third of the population were dislocated from
> their homes. Thus I fully expected to find a war-devastated popu-
> lation, with obvious evidence of war trauma. Much to my surprise,
> this was not the case. The Lebanese population, both Christian and
> Moslem, were relieved, cheerful, energetic, enthusiastic, basically
> rebuilding their country. It was like a country of buzzing worker
> bees."

In accounting for what he terms this "excellent psychological survival
of the Lebanese people," Dr. Pattison (1984:35–36) cites, among other
things, the cultural tradition of tough endurance of occupation and war
. . . and the strong psychological supports they continue to receive from
family, kin, and community.

Yes, certain segments of the society have shown this ability to adapt
and endure the trauma of war. They have, however, paid dearly for it.
The general quality of their lives, both emotionally and intellectually, has
been grossly diminished and trivialized. There is, as a result, much less
of the Lebanese, in both quantitative and qualitative terms. Rather than
inviting praise, this is in fact the worst indictment one can have against
any society: that people are less than they could have been had circumstances been different. Among intellectuals, in particular, this is visible in
pervasive symptoms of demoralization, banality, and shrinking intellectual horizons.

Though not peculiar to any particular society (see, for example, some
of the recent publications of Christopher Lasch 1977, 1979, 1984), Lebanese intellectuals are plagued by a heavier and more nagging dose of
such features than their counterparts elsewhere. Indeed, the life-histories
of many Lebanese intellectuals display unmistakable instances of such unrelenting erosion in the scope of their creative and public concerns.

For example, the same persons who had launched their careers during
the thirties by elucidating universal issues such as freedom, democracy,
emancipation, the meaning of culture, and the impact of Western civili-
zation etc. . . , shifted their concerns during the forties and fifties to

considerations of Arab nationalism, ideological struggle, and self-determination. By the sixties, when Palestine became the overriding issue, the same groups diverted their energies almost exclusively in that direction. The scholarly output of a score of distinguished intellectuals (Constantine Zurayk, Nabih Faris, Fayez Sayegh, Walid Khalidi, among others) provide vivid examples.

With the outbreak of civil hostilities, when the Lebanese crises began to assume grievous manifestations, many became convinced that problems such as the political reorganization of Lebanon and prospects for secular reform were more legitimate and compelling areas of concern. By the late seventies, however, Lebanon itself became unmanageable as the country was dismembered further by factional struggle and foreign occupations. Intellectuals could no longer understand, much less predict and control, the forces disintegrating their society. Trapped in their own dwarfed and endangered little worlds, disillusioned by the disregard and indifference of their Arab and Palestinian "brothers," many turned further inward and sought shelter in their cloistered neighborhoods. In desperate attempts to ward off such threatening incursions, they resorted to community action, organized cleaning campaigns, and took measures to ensure the release of kidnapped victims, stolen property, and illegally occupied houses. In short, they became glorified Boy Scouts; self-appointed guardians of the dwindling virtues of decency and civility.

By the summer of 1982, they also started to lose control over Ras-Beirut. The Israeli invasion and repeated episodes of fighting in the southern suburbs and the Biqa ushered in massive waves of dislodged and embittered Shi'ite were already beginning to be splintered, much like other confessional groups, by factional rivalries. Their leaders, both old and new, could no longer command obedience, nor could they control militant elements within their constituencies. It became also apparent that the Shi'ites were not simply competing for urban space. Nor were they content with correcting the imbalances and injustices they suffered. A growing number were bent—at least those who were heralding the advent of a new "Islamic Republic"—on changing the entire character of Ras-Beirut. Israeli atrocities in the South, reinforced by America's indifference and their own ethos of martyrdom and militancy, legitimized their nascent radicalization.

Threatened and voiceless, liberals had little choice other than seeking refuge in one of their last remaining sanctuaries: AUB. Until then the campus managed to remain, at least physically, the only strip of inviting landscape in an otherwise devastated and blighted environment. The appointment of Malcolm Kerr as president had heartened many of them. They renewed their interest in the affairs of the University and revived their flagging enthusiasm for teaching and research. For a while they harbored dreams that as long as AUB could be preserved, hopes for restoring its endangered legacy might be rekindled. The dreams were promptly and brutally shattered. David Dodge, then acting-president, was kidnapped before Kerr could assume his official duties. Dodge suffered the horrors of captivity for a year. Kerr's fate was even more tragic. He was assassinated just as he had completed his first year in office.

Both Dodge and Kerr, it must be remarked, are not ordinary American citizens. Both are descendents of early "missionary" families. Both were born in Lebanon, adopted its language, and devoted the best part of their lives championing Arab causes; much like their illustrious parents. It is ironical that they, along with other members of the University community, should have become targets of such ruthless and indiscriminate violence.

To survive such assaults, AUB has been compelled to make increasing concessions to the "town." At times such concessions became so extensive that the University reversed its traditional role and became a mere extension of the "town." When one enters or takes a casual stroll on campus, it is difficult to discern town from gown. The same graffiti, slogans, posters, banners, and other such symbols of the prevalent political culture, disfigure and mutilate its walls and trees. The same intolerant mood is beginning to overwhelm the campus and is displayed in the often graceless and assertive manner in which student activities are organized and launched. It is doubtful whether AUB can resist such incursions any further without risking its autonomy and stature as a distinguished institution of higher learning. In fact, the whole future of the University, let alone its growing financial deficit, is today in serious jeopardy.

The last form of disinheritance, by far the most pitiful and tragic, is that many Lebanese cannot even seek refuge in their families. Literally, homes have degenerated into houses. As spouses, children, and other dependents are sent away to more peaceful and edifying places, husbands often brave the hazards of civil violence alone. Many, in fact, are trapped by their depleting assets and resources. Flimsy as these are, they are the last tenuous bonds sustaining their ties to a dying social order. Dispirited members of this group can still be seen strolling on AUB campus, almost

ritualistically, at dusk. The sobering company of their dwindling colleagues is their only respite from the heartless world outside. Their nostalgia for the past has all but vanished. They are plagued, instead, by the
forebodings of a bleak and uncertain future.

Exile and Homelessness

It is in this sense that the exile of the liberals of Ras-Beirut is an acute
and total experience. They are disinherited in the full meaning of the
term: intellectually, spiritually, and emotionally. They have also become
homeless in a more explicit sense. They suffer the anguish of solitude
isolated from their most intimate and enduring family ties. If one accepts
Edward Said's (1984:159) poignant treatment of exile as the "unhealable
rift forced between a human being and a native place, between self and
its true home," then what some Lebanese have been suffering is indeed
a forbidding form of such experience.

Like the true exiles, they are being denied an identity, a home, and a
heritage. They, too, suffer banishment and the stigma of becoming outsiders. They have also witnessed the horrors of indiscriminate violence,
deportation, and mass extermination. They are, likewise, impelled by an
urge to reassemble a damaged identity and broken history. Edward Said
is, of course, correct to argue that the Palestinians' suffering is compounded because "they have been turned into exiles by the proverbial
people of exile, the Jews . . . and that they are reliving the actual process
of uprootedness at the hands of the exiles" (Said 1984:164). If that is
so, then the exile of the Lebanese is compounded even further because
Israelis and Palestinians, among others of course, have had their share in
intensifying and prolonging Lebanese agonies.

The Lebanese—at least those who have not as yet opted to leave their
country—do not suffer some of the usual problems associated with immigrants, refugees, and other exiles: the angst of breaking away from
one's familiar surroundings and adjusting to a new and strange culture
(see Lewis Coser 1984 on Jewish intellectual refugees and Edward Said
1984 on Palestinians). But those who stay behind suffer a worse predicament: they are banished and have become spiritually homeless in their
own backyards. They are also denied the exposure to new sensations,
world views, and visions that elevate the appreciative sympathies Said
talks about.

Finally, they are gripped by a more crushing sense of impotence and defeat. Palestinians, Jews, and Armenians can at least identify and mobilize their outrage against those who banished them. They are all equally aroused by an "exaggerated sense of group solidarity, and a passionate hostility to outsiders" (Said 1984:164). The Lebanese cannot even vindicate their collective grievances. As intellectuals, they suffer added indignities and insults to their intelligence: persistent mystification and distortion of their own history. Many of the contemporary intellectuals have had both cognitive and conceptual difficulties in accepting the orthodox view prevalent at the time they were growing up; namely, that there were mysterious and unidentified forces that accounted for the so-called "Lebanese miracle," and that had transformed its precarious pluralism into a "valiant little democracy," a "privileged creation" and a "bold cultural experiment." Now that this myth is being shattered, we turn back and mystify Lebanon's descent into anomie. Hence, much of the tension and violence is attributed to "mysterious forces," "borrowed ideologies," and "shadowy organizations." In other words, both the forces responsible for Lebanon's formation and those associated with its deformation have been mystified. Little wonder that intellectuals are baffled by this nagging predicament. They are trapped in an enigmatic and decaying social order they can neither understand nor reform.

Can this happen? Will it be allowed to happen? Can communities just atrophy and wither away while significant others watch the assault? Communities, like particular cultures, are slow to die. In some respects this is even a more painful fate than sudden death. They could, however, as Ibn Khaldun cautioned us, become corrupt and deformed. Or, less likely in the case of Lebanon, they could be transplanted elsewhere. There are hardly any "open" communities left that could host such a salubrious subculture. Many of the groups involved in the hostility—both internal and external—have not been idle and disinterested observers. They have, wittingly or otherwise, exacerbated the magnitude and intensity of conflict.

Ras-Beirut, with all its liberal and republican virtues, modest as they are, epitomized what Lebanon could have become. Perhaps neither Lebanon nor the rest of the Arab world could have ever lived with such an open and cosmopolitan community. It is the last outpost of resistance to all forms of dominance and subjugation to totalitarian doctrines or ways of life. Marginal and other itinerant groups sought refuge in Ras-Beirut. It was not, however, the insulated kind of refuge that entrapped or sheltered individuals from broader or higher forms of consciousness. It was not an enclosure but an open space; perhaps a window to other open places.

Over twenty years ago Charles Issawi (1966:80–81) observed prophetically that

> Lebanon is too conspicuous and successful an example of political democracy and economic liberalism to be tolerated in a region that has turned its back on both systems. It may be answered that such fears are unfounded, that the conscience of the world would not allow any harm to befall such a harmless country as Lebanon, that the neighboring world would not want to have a recalcitrant minority on their hands, and that it is in their interests to preserve Lebanon as "a window on the West." But to anyone who has followed the course of national and international politics in the last fifty years, such arguments are sheer nonsense. Minorities have been effectively liquidated, windows have been violently slammed and hardly a ripple has stirred in the conscience of the world.

Concluding Remarks

For the first time in Ras-Beirut's history, a disproportionate number of dispossessed and uprooted masses, with no ties to the area or appreciation of cosmopolitan urban ethos or tolerance to other ways of life, are beginning to deform its mixed and open character. Such massive demographic shifts have, of course, happened elsewhere in Lebanon and in other communities of Beirut. In nearly all such instances, as we have seen, they upset the sectarian balance, precipitated further hostilities, and created cloistered and sealed communities. The hegemony of Maronites over the eastern suburbs, the Sunni Muslims over Basta and Moussaytbeh and, more recently, the Druze over the Shuf have not been felicitous examples of peaceful coexistence. Nor are they likely to usher Lebanon into a more secular and liberal era.

One would not decry or lament the eclipse of community, any community, if the commitment to subcultural values and parochial attachments are being weakened by the prospect of broader national or civic identities. This is after all the natural course of evolution of all liberal social orders. Social and intellectual historians remind us that a fascinating transformation in the historical evolution of most societies involves its passage from a relatively "closed" to a more "open" system: membership, entry or exit, and access to privileges and benefits are no longer denied by virtue of limitations of religion, kinship, or race. Such openness accounts for much of the spectacular growth in the philosophical, artistic, and political emancipation of contemporary societies (Nisbet 1970:97–100).

Lebanon has been inverting and reversing the natural course of history. Indeed, what we have been witnessing is the substitution of one viable form of pluralism for a more regressive and pathological kind. We are destroying a community that permitted people with multitudinous and sometimes utterly different backgrounds, conflicting moral codes and divergent expectations to live side by side. What is emerging is a monolithic archetype that is hostile to any such coexistence or free experimentation.

The Shiʿites, by dint of circumstances beyond their control, are in the throes today of a historic watershed, a great divide; a threshold in the literal and precise meaning of the term: Ras-Beirut, and to a large extent Lebanon, is about to cross over into a direction that it did not have before. If the Shiʿites can learn from the pitfalls of other groups, they could rescue Ras-Beirut from its demise and possibly emerge as the architects of a new secular order in the rest of the society. They are in a position, in other words, either to reform Lebanon or to exacerbate its deformation.

Ras-Beirut's predicament is instructive because it carries a faint hope, perhaps the last, that reasonable solutions are still possible in a predominantly unreasonable country. Given the horrors and anguish of the past decade, one is inclined to entertain—out of sheer exhaustion if not faith in the innate goodness of human nature—that there is still hope for a miraculous regeneration and return to sanity.

Are the Shiʿites likely to heed the earthy wisdom of Robert Frost and choose the "Road Not Taken," the road less traveled by and, by doing so, make all the difference? Or are they more likely to lapse into the grievous errors of the past? As the price of folly gets more ominous and menacing, the Lebanese are yet to learn from the ravages of their blood-stained history. Reluctantly, I am prone to conclude, just as Charles Issawi did twenty years ago, with H. G. Wells' story, *The Country of the Blind*. You may recall that the two-eyed man who strayed into that country was not made king!!

Notes

1. ON THE DIALECTICS OF TRADITION AND MODERNITY

1. Of the many criticisms of the earlier paradigms, particularly the tradition-modernity dichotomy, the following are worth noting: Levy (1953:161–97); Apter (1968:113–35); Hoselitz (1961:83–113); Shils (1971:122–59); Riggs (1964); Bendix (1967:292–346); Frank (1971); Omvedt (1971:119–37); Mazrui (1968:68–83); Wertheim (1971:76–94); Gellner (1964:138–48); Sinai, (1971:53–75); Eisenstadt (1974:225–52); Eisenstadt (1968:35–61); Tipps (1973:199–226); Desai (1971:474–548).

2. John Lewis (1969), Clifford Geertz (1968), Rustow and Ward (1964), S. N. Eisenstadt (1974), Ernest Gellner (1973), to mention a few, are instances of the kind we have in mind.

3. For added substantiation of the notion that traditional institutions may be adaptive to modern society and politics, see: Gusfield (1967:351–62); Singer (1972); Rudolph and Rudolph (1967); Willner (1964); Bellah (1971:377–404).

4. S. N. Eisenstadt, among others, has in several of his earlier writings emphasized the discontinuities and breakdowns inherent in the process of modernization. See Eisenstadt (1964:345–67); and Eisenstadt (1966).

5. A noted exception in this regard is Samuel Huntington (1968).

6. For a clarification of this point see Robert A. Nisbet (1967:132–41). This conception comes close to the "sacred-collectivity" model outlined in David Apter (1965:31–33).

7. For an elaboration of this view point see Chandler Morse (1969:238–382).

8. For an excellent and lucid survey of the political and social thought inherent in this ideal of authenticity and its implications for a general theory of the structure of personal, social, and political life in the modern world, see Marshall Berman (1970).

4. CHANGING FORMS OF POLITICAL PATRONAGE

1. The often-invoked Article 95 of the Constitution states: In order to promote harmony and justice, the communities will be equitably represented in government employment and in the composition of the Ministry without jeopardizing the good of the State." Translated into quantitative and operational terms, this system of apportionment has meant that the Chamber must always include

a number of Deputies divisible by 11 (i.e., 33, 44, 77, or 99) so that for every 6 Christian Deputies there would be 5 non-Christians (Sunnis, Shiʿites, and Druze).

2. For example in 1951 there were a small number of relatively large districts, 9 altogether for 77 Deputies; in 1953, 33 districts for 44 Deputies; in 1957, 28 districts for 88 Deputies; and since 1960 the number has stabilized at 26 districts for 99 Deputies.

3. The text quoted in Bahige B. Tabbarah (1954:167) was reproduced from *Al-Jarida* (Beirut:September 7, 1953).

4. Initially conceived as a loosely organized alliance to defend the national integrity of Lebanon against the emergent socialist and revolutionary trends sweeping Arab countries at the time, the Hilf evolved into a rather cohesive political coalition with a unifying ideological base and concern for national priorities. It struck a receptive note among the electorate and managed to secure 23 seats in the 1968 elections; nearly one-fourth of the entire Chamber. For further details, see Entelis (1974:161–72).

5. For a sociohistorical analysis of the modernizing impact of both these seemingly "traditional" organizations, see Schatkowski (1969) and Early (1971).

5. PRIMORDIAL TIES AND POLITICS

1. Saadeh was founder and leader of the Syrian Social Nationalist Party (PPS). Founded in 1932, it was perhaps one of the first secular and doctrinal parties that transcended confessional and regional allegiances. After its abortive coup of 1949, Saadeh was tried and executed. Aris, a Moscow-trained labor union leader and member of the Communist Party, ran for Parliament unsuccessfully a score of times.

2. The forthcoming chapter will provide more extensive evidence in support of the relationship between family background and political succession.

3. In opposition to the political attitude of the National Bloc of the Eddes who were inclined to maintain some ties with France, Bishara al-Khuri and his Constitutional Bloc insisted on the complete independence of Lebanon while still part of the Arab world. This found some appeal among Muslim leaders particularly the Solh family who too spoke of an Arab but independent Lebanon.

4. The three main criteria identified by Arnold Hottinger (1966:104) in delimiting the category of *zaʿim* are implied here, namely: "local limitation of the group; tendency towards heredity of function; exchange of economic support given to the clients against political loyalty coming from the clients."

5. The often-quoted Article 95 of the Constitution states: "As a provisional measure and for the sake of justice and amity, the sects (religious communities) shall be equitably represented in public employment and in the composition of the Ministry."

6. THE PARLIAMENTARY ELITE

1. The estimates of Harik and Messarra differ slightly, but both, nonetheless, point out to the same directions.

2. Michael Hudson (1968:240) has arbitrarily chosen the birth date of 1910

as a dividing line between Deputies raised in a traditional as opposed to a post-Ottoman or modern era.

3. In instances of multiple or dual occupations, the one the Deputy lists in his biographical sketch is considered by Harik (1975:209) as basic occupation.

4. Hudson and Harik estimate the average turnover rate at 42 percent. My calculations were based on Messarra's official list of Deputies and the terms they served.

5. In two of his publications, Iliya Harik (1972:15–29; 1975:210–11) has questioned the importance of kinship ties in the recruitment of parliamentary elite.

6. Some sort of political elections were held in Lebanon for a brief period after 1900. Historians, however, agree that given the severity of Ottoman rule such elections could have hardly been free or voluntary. In 1922 the Mandatory powers instituted by decree the so-called "Representative Council" to be elected by universal male suffrage. It was not, however, until Lebanon won its independence in 1943 that the whole Chamber was elected. Prior to that a varying number of Senators—ranging from 12 to 21—were appointed by the French. If we include the first "Commission Administrative" of 1920–22, then the Lebanese would have gone to the polls sixteen times. For further details see Messarra (1974:340–63); Saʿadeh (1964).

7. The incidence of close kinship ties among the parliamentarians is both complex and numerous and deserves fuller treatment. One instance of such interrelationship among five prominent political families (Khuri, Chiha, Firʿawn, as-Saʿd, and Issa al-Khuri) is sufficient to illustrate the intensity and pervasiveness of family networks in Lebanese politics: Bishara al-Khuri is the brother-in-law of Michael Chiha, who in turn is the paternal cousin of Henry Firʿawn. Habib Pasha asʿ-Saʿd is the maternal cousin of Bishara al-Khuri's father, who in turn is a distant relative of Nadra Issa al-Khuri.

8. It was my intention to document such an inference by a systematic analysis of how various parliamentarians voted on particular issues and bills. Because of the protracted civil crisis, it was impossible to gain access to the files or archives of the Chamber to undertake such an exploration.

9. Mr. Kamel al-Asʿad, Speaker of the current Chamber, speaks of the total absence of the Parliament during the crises of 1958 and 1969. See *An-Nahar,* December 20, 1975, Issue No. 12694, p. 3.

10. A parliamentary "Initiative Committee" composed of eleven Deputies was formed in December 1975 and submitted a set of socioeconomic, political, and administrative proposals for reform. Sensible as some of the proposals were, they were neither presented before the Parliament nor were they expressed in the form of specific legislative bills. For a full text of the proposals see *An-Nahar* (1975:3).

11. The Official Parliament House is located in the center of the city, an unsafe district. It has also been ransacked and partially destroyed.

7. FAMILY FIRMS AND INDUSTRIAL DEVELOPMENTS

1. Bert Hoselitz (1961) insists, and perhaps rightly so, on making such a distinction. He advances the notion that adherence to traditional norms or practices

should not be conceived as an effort to venerate the sacred traditions of the past for tradition's sake (something that is implied in traditionalism as an ideology), but rather in terms of their usefulness for the present.

2. The term is used here as defined by Harbison and Myers (1959:69): "Patrimonial management is business management in which ownership, major policy-making positions, and a significant proportion of other jobs in the hierarchy are held by members of an extended family."

3. For a detailed analysis of the degree of consultation and delegation of authority among a sample of Lebanese industrialists, see Khalaf (1963:159–67).

4. Harbison and Myers (1959:67) define constitutional management as follows: "When government intervenes in the labor-management relationship to regulate terms and conditions of employment and to protect or encourage the growth of labor organizations which themselves challenge management's authority, we find that the rule-making power of employers is shared in a 'constitutional' manner with other agencies."

8. FAMILY ASSOCIATIONS

1. In two companion papers, Eugene Litwak (1960) has successfully demonstrated the need and capacity for extended families to exist in modern societies.

2. Some of the entries prior to 1927 are inconsistent and not systematically recorded. Though it has been possible to survey the broad rural-urban distribution of some of the early entries, the specific analysis of the organizational and functional aspects is confined to 1927 and on. The same is true of the religious identity of the associations.

3. Unfortunately, the early entries in the Ministries of the Interior and Social Affairs were not adequately recorded. Consequently, the specific identity of some of the earlier associations could not be identified in any precise manner.

4. For purposes of classification, Beirut and its suburbs along with the following major cities are considered urban: Zahle, Tripoli, Saida, and Sour. The urban-rural category refers to those associations which indicated that they have branches or meet in Beirut in winter but move to their respective villages in summer.

5. I am fully aware that formal expectations and actual practice quite often diverge. Their professed objectives, nonetheless, provide some measure of their awareness and concern. It is quite clear that this awareness was not confined to formal and verbal assertions. Interviews with a sample of executive officers and more direct observations of the actual operation of a few of these associations confirmed these impressions.

9. CULTURAL VALUES AND FAMILY PLANNING

1. The survey was based on a sample of 30,000 households, roughly one-fifteenth of all households in Lebanon, and was intended to provide information on the economically active population and to describe the demographic, social, and economic characteristics of the resident population.

2. Mention to fieldworkers, here and elsewhere in the chapter, refers to personal interviews held with about twelve wasitas ("mediators") who were involved in the community-based distribution program in the Zahrani district of Southern Lebanon. I wish to acknowledge here the assistance of Mr. Towfic Osseiran, secretary general of the LFPA, and his staff for rendering such interviews possible.

3. Prime Minister Shafik al-Wazzan has, on a score of public occasions, admitted that it was Dr. Mroveh's interest and involvement in family planning which, after all, enhanced his qualifications and appeal to assume that office.

4. This survey was completed before the LFPA introduced its community-based services and programs, hence the low proportion of respondents who were neither aware of the existence of family planning clinics or the type of services they provide.

5. The reader interested in further details concerning the emergence of the LFPA, its organizational structure, objectives, activities, and programs, can consult a recent comprehensive dissertation on the subject (see Iliyya 1984).

10. Social Structure and Urban Planning

1. Studies for the Plan were directed by Mr. Ecochard with the cooperation of a team of local professional architects. Although the Plan continues to bear his name, Mr. Ecochard had at the time publicly dissociated himself from the officially approved plan.

2. The composition of the HCUP was modified in June 1977 to include the following: the general director of Town Planning, a representative of the Ministry of Interior, a representative of the Ministry of Public Works, a representative of the Council for Reconstruction and Development, the president of the Syndicate of Engineers, and a university sociologist. The council holds regular weekly meetings.

11. On the Demoralization of Public Life

1. Since I have, throughout the period of war, been living in the so-called western part of Beirut, many of my remarks and direct observations are more likely to apply to this rather than other regions of Lebanon.

2. For an account and analysis of the events and circumstances associated with civil strife and the erosion of state institutions in Lebanon, the interested reader can consult any of the score of books that have already appeared. The following are particularly helpful: Salibi (1976); Gordon (1979); Khalidi (1979); Deeb (1980).

3. One can easily provide ample documentation of this process of "demonization" from other comparative instances of inter-group conflict. Two such persisting instances, Greeks and Turks in Cyprus and Arabs and Israelis in Palestine, have been recently explored by psychiatrists. See Group for the Advancement of Psychiatry (1978); and Volkan (1979).

12. DISINHERITED LIBERALS: RAS-BEIRUT IN JEOPRADY

1. I am currently completing a paper that explores more fully the impact of the earlier generation of American missionaries and other scholars associated with AUB on the intellectual and cultural awakening in Lebanon.

2. The interested reader should consult the invaluable bibliography of AUB faculty publications (1866–1966) prepared by Suha Tamim (1967) in celebration of the University's centenary in 1966.

3. No listing can be exhaustive, but the following is sufficient to delineate the magnitude of this group: Abbas, Afifi, Alami, Ali, Asfour, Attallah, Awad, Azzam, Baramki, Bulos, Butros, Dabbagh, Dajani, Durr, Fakhri, Farah, Faris, Fouleihan, Halasa, Hanania, Hanna, Hijab, Hussayni, Inglessis, Jouzy, Katul, Kawar, Khalidi, Khamis, Kurban, Malak, Muwafi, Najm, Nasr, Rizk, Salti, Sayegh, Shibre, Siksek, Suidan, Tarazi, Tuqan, Umar, Yaqub, Yashruti, Zahlan, Zayid, Ziadeh, Zuwiyyah.

4. In addition to daily episodic incidences that have had a cumulative impact on the intensity and pattern of population movements, the following major events must be singled out: The outbreak of fighting between rival factions in the old business center of Beirut in April 1975; followed by those which drove Palestinians, Kurds, Syrians, and other marginal groups out of the eastern suburbs; repeated confrontations between the Syrian army and the Lebanese Front, first in the Eastern suburbs in 1978, and then again in 1981 in Zahle and the mountains of Matn and Kisrwan; the Israeli invasions of 1978 and 1982; the war between Druze and Christian militias in September 1982 in the Shuf and Aley; recurrent hostilities between Shi'ites and other groups in the southern suburbs.

5. For an account and analysis of the events and circumstances associated with various phases of the war in Lebanon and the erosion of state institutions, the following books among a score of others, are particularly helpful: Salibi (1976); Gordon (1979); Khalidi (1979); Deeb (1980).

Bibliography

Abu Jawdeh, Boulos. 1973. *Al-Abu Jawdeh: Tarikhahum wa-Salalatahum* (The Abu Jawdeh Family: Their History and Genealogy). Adonis Press.

Abu-Lughod, Janet. 1972. "Problems and Policy Implications of Middle Eastern Urbanization." Beirut: UNESOB.

Aouad, Ibrahim. 1933. *Le droit prive des maronites au temps des emirs chihab (1607–1841)*. Paris: Librarie Orientaliste.

Apter, David. 1965. *The Politics of Modernization*. Chicago: University of Chicago Press).

——1968. "The Role of Traditionalism in the Political Modernization of Ghana and Uganda." In David Apter, ed., *Some Conceptual Approaches to the Study of Modernization*, pp. 113–35 Englewood Cliffs, N.J.: Prentice-Hall.

Attallah Association. 1965. *Jami'at al Attallah* (The Attallah Association). Beirut: n.p.

Azar, Edward, ed. 1983. *Lebanon and the World in the 1980's*. College Park, Md.: University of Maryland Press.

——1985. "Protracted Social Conflict in Lebanon." Center for International Development, University of Maryland.

Azar, Edward and Stephen Cohen. 1979. "Peace as Crisis and War as Status-quo: The Arab-Israeli War Environment." *International Interactions* 6(2):159–84.

Batatu, Hanna. 1979. "Class Analysis and Iraqi Society." *Arab Studies Quarterly* 1(3):222–44.

Bell, N. W. and E. F. Vogel. 1968. "Toward a Framework for Functional Analysis of Family Behavior." In Bell and Vogel, eds., *A Modern Introduction to the Family*, pp. 1–34. New York: Free Press.

Bellah, Robert N. 1971. "Continuity and Change in Japanese Society." In B. Barber and A. Inkeles, eds., *Stability and Change*, pp. 377–404. Boston: Little, Brown.

Bendix, Reinhard. 1964. *Nation-Building and Citizenship.* New York: Wiley.

——1967. "Tradition and Modernity Reconsidered." *Comparative Studies in Society and History* (April) 9(3):292–346.

Berger, B. M. 1966. "Suburbs, Subcultures, and the Urban Future." In S. B. Warner, Jr., ed., *Planning for a Nation of Cities,* pp. 143–62. Cambridge: MIT Press.

Berger, P., B. Berger, and H. Kellner. 1973. *The Homeless Mind.* New York: Random House.

Berman, Marshall. 1970. *The Politics of Authenticity* New York: Atheneum.

Bettelheim, B. 1960. *The Informed Heart.* Glencoe: Free Press.

Bill, James and Carl Leiden. 1984. *Politics in the Middle East.* 2d ed. Boston: Little, Brown.

Binder, Leonard. 1966. "Political Change in Lebanon." In L. Binder, ed., *Politics in Lebanon,* pp. 283–327. New York: Wiley.

Blau, Peter M. 1964. *Exchange and Power in Social Life.* New York: Wiley.

Bliss, Frederick. 1920. *The Reminiscences of Daniel Bliss.* New York: Fleming Revell.

Bowring, John. 1840. *Report on the Commercial Statistics of Syria.* London: Clowes.

Braude, Benjamin and Bernard Lewis, eds. 1982. *Christians and Jews in the Ottoman Empire,* vols. 1 and 2. New York: Holmes and Meier.

Buheiry, Marwan. 1981. "Bulus Nujaym and the Grand Liban Ideal 1908–1919." In Marwan Buheiry, ed., *Intellectual Life in the Arab East,* pp. 62–83. Beirut: American University.

Bullough, Vern. 1967. *Sexual Variance in Society and History.* New York: Wiley.

Burckhardt, John L. 1822. *Travels in Syria and the Holy Land.* London: J. Murray.

Cardoso, and Faletto, 1979. *Dependency and Development in Latin America.* Berkeley: University of California Press.

Cernea, Michael. 1981. "Modernization and Development Potential of Traditional Grass Roots Peasant Organizations." In M. Attir, B. Holzner, and Z. Suder, eds., *Directions of Change: Modernization Theory Research and Realities,* pp. 121–39. Boulder, Colo.: Westview Press.

Chamie, Joseph. 1977a. *Religion and Population Dynamics in Lebanon.*

Ann Arbor, Mich.: Population Studies Center, University of Michigan.

——1977b. "Religious Fertility Differentials: Lebanon, 1971." *Population Studies,* vol. 31, no. 2.

Chamie, Mary. 1977. "Sexuality and Birth Control Decisions Among Lebanese Couples." *Signs* (Autumn), 3(1):294–314.

Chevallier, Dominique. 1968. "Western Development and Eastern Crisis in the Mid-Nineteenth Century: Syria Confronted with the European Economy." In Polk and Chambers, eds., *Beginning of Modernization in the Middle East,* pp. 205–22. Chicago: University of Chicago Press.

——1971. *La societe du Mont Liban a l'epoque de la revolution industrielle en Europe.* Paris: Librairie Orientaliste.

Chilcote, Ronald, 1981. *Dependency and Marxism: Toward a Resolution of the Debate.* Boulder, Colo.: Westview Press.

Churchill, Charles, H. 1853. *Mount Lebanon: A Ten-Year Residence from 1842–1852,* vol. 3. London: Saunders and Otley.

——1862. *The Druzes and Maronites under the Turkish Rule.* London: Spottiswoods.

Clarke, J. I. 1972. Introduction to *Population of the Middle East and North Africa,* J. I. Clarke and W. B. Fisher, eds. London: University of London Press.

Clinard, Marshall. 1964. *Anomie and Deviant Behavior.* New York: Free Press.

Colletta, N. J. 1975. "The Use of Indigenous Culture as a Medium for Development: The Indonesian Case." *Prisma* (November), 1(2):61–62.

Cortas, Wadad. 1983. *Dhikrayat* (Reminiscences). Beirut: Institute of Arab Studies.

Coser, Lewis. 1984. "Refugee Intellectuals." *Society* (November/December), 22(1):61–68.

Courbages, Y. and P. Fargues. 1973. *La Situation Démographique au Liban.* Beirut: Publications del l'Universite Libanaise, Librairie Orientale.

Crow, Ralph E. 1966. "Confessionalism, Public Administration and Efficiency." In Leonard Binder, *Politics in Lebanon,* pp. 167–86. New York: Wiley.

——1970. "Parliament in the Lebanese Political System." In A. Kornberg and L. Musoff, eds., *Legislatures in Developmental Perspectives,* pp. 273–302. Durham, N.C.: Duke University Press.

Davison, R. H. 1954. "Turkish Attitudes Concerning Christian Muslim Equality in the 19th Century." *American Historical Review* (July), 59(4):848.

Davison, Roderic. 1963. *Reform in the Ottoman Empire, 1856–1876.* Princeton, N.J.: Princeton University Press.

Deeb, Marius. 1980. *The Lebanese Civil War.* New York: Praeger.

Deeb, Mary. 1977. "The Impact and Effectiveness of the Community Based Family Planning Services Program in the Zahrani Area" (Southern Lebanon). Beirut: American University.

de Lamartine, Alphonse. 1835. *Souvenirs, impressions, pensees et paysages pendant un voyage en Orient, 1832–1833,* vol. 2. Paris: Mackette-Farne.

Desai, A. R. 1971. "Need for Revaluation of the Concept." In A. R. Desai, ed., *Essays on Modernization of Underdeveloped Societies,* 2:474–548. Bombay: Thacker.

Deutsch, Karl. 1961. "Social Mobilization and Political Development." *American Political Science Review* (September), 55(3):493–514.

Dib, George. 1975. *Law and Population in Lebanon.* Law and Population Monograph Series Number 29. Medford, Mass. Fletcher School of Law and Diplomacy.

Doxiadis, K. 1968. *Ekistics.* London: Hutchinson.

Dubar, Claude and Salim Nasr. 1976. *Les classes sociales au Liban.* Paris: Presses de Pa Foundation Nationale des Sciences Politiques.

Durkheim, Emile. 1964. *The Division of Labor in Society.* Glencoe, Ill.: Free Press.

Early, Evelyn A. 1971. "The Amiliyya Society of Beirut: A Case Study of an Emerging Urban Za'im." M.A. thesis, American University of Beirut.

Eisenstadt, S. N. 1963. "Modernization: Growth and Diversity." Bloomington: Department of Government, Indiana University.

——1964. "Breakdowns of Modernization." *Economic Development and Cultural Change* (July), 12(4):345–67.

——1966. *Modernization Protest and Change.* Englewood Cliffs, N.J.: Prentice-Hall.

——1968. "Reflections on a Theory of Modernization." In A. Rivkin, ed., *Nations by Design,* pp. 36–61. New York: Anchor Books.

——1973. *Traditional Patrimonialism and Modern Neopatrimonialism*. Beverly Hills: Sage Publications.

——1974. "Studies of Modernization and Sociological Theory." *History and Theory* 13(3):225–52.

Entelis, John P. 1974. *Pluralism and Party Transformation in Lebanon: al-Kata'ib 1936–1970*. Leiden: Brill.

Ericksen, E. Gordon. 1954. *Urban Behavior*. New York: Macmillan.

Etzioni, Amitai. 1958. "Human Relations and the Foreman." *Pacific Sociological Review* (Spring), 1(1):33–38.

Executive Board of Major Projects for the City of Beirut. 1968. *Comprehensive Plan Studies for the City of Beirut*. Beirut: J. S. Saikali Press.

Farley, J. Lewis. 1859. *Two Years in Syria*. London: Saunders.

Fawaz, Leila Tarazi. 1983. *Merchants and Migrants in Nineteenth Century Beirut*. Cambridge: Harvard University Press.

Fernea, Elizabeth Warnock. 1985. *Women and the Family in the Middle East*. Austin: University of Texas Press.

Ferrarotti, Franco. 1959. "Management in Italy." In Harbison and Myers, *Management in the Industrial World*, pp. 232–48. New York: McGraw-Hill.

Frank. Andre G. 1971. *Sociology and Development and Underdevelopment of Sociology*. London: Pluto.

Frayha, Anis. 1978. *Qabl An Ansa* (Before I Forget). Beirut: Al-Nahar Press.

Frey, F. 1965. *The Turkish Political Elite*. Cambridge: MIT Press.

Friedland, William. 1969. "A Sociological Approach to Modernization." In Morse, Ashford et al., eds., *Modernization by Design*, pp. 34–84. Ithaca, N.Y.: Cornell University Press.

Froman, L. 1967. *The Congressional Process: Strategies, Roles and Procedures*. Boston: Little, Brown.

Fullam, Maryellen. 1978. "Volunteering a Developing Way of Life." *People* 5:4–5.

Gans, H. 1970. *People and Plans*. New York: Basic Books.

Gebara, M. 1964. "The Social Background of the Lebanese Parliamentary Elite 1960–1964." M.A. thesis, American University of Beirut.

Geertz, Clifford, ed. 1963. *Old Societies and New States*. New York: Free Press.

——1968. *Agricultural Involution: The Process of Ecological Change in Indonesia*. Berkeley: University of California Press.

——1971. "After the Revolution: The Fate of Nationalism in the New States." In B. Barber and A. Inkeles, eds., *Stability and Change*, pp. 357–76. Boston: Little, Brown.

Gellner, Ernest. 1964. *Thought and Change* London: Weidenfeld and Nicolson.

——1973. "Post-Traditional Forms in Islam: The Turf and Trade, and Votes and Peanuts." *Daedalus* (Winter), 102(1):191–206.

Gibb, H. A. R. and H. Bowen. 1957. *Islamic Society and the West*, vol. 3, part 2. London: Oxford University Press.

Goode, W. J. 1963. *World Revolution and Family Patterns*. New York: Free Press.

Gordon, David. 1980. *Lebanon the Fragmented Nation*. London: Croom Helm.

——1983. *The Republic of Lebanon: Nation in Jeopardy*. Boulder, Colo.: Westview Press.

Group for the Advancement of Psychiatry. 1978. *Self-Involvement in the Middle East*. New York.

Gubser, P. 1973. "The Zu'ama of Zahlah: The Current Situation in a Lebanese Town." *Middle East Journal* (Spring), 27(2):73–90.

Gulick, J. 1967. *Tripoli: A Modern Arab City*. Cambridge: Harvard University Press.

Gusfield, Joseph. 1967. "Tradition and Modernity: Misplaced Polarities in the Study of Social Change." *American Journal of Sociology* (January), 72:351–62.

Guys, Henri. 1850. *Beyrouth et le Liban*, vol. 2. Paris: Ramquet.

Hagen, Everett. 1957. "The Process of Economic Development." *Economic Development and Cultural Change* (April), 5(3):193–215.

Halpern, Manfred. 1963. *The Politics of Social Change in the Middle East and North Africa*. Princeton, N.J.: Princeton University Press.

——1964. "Toward Further Modernization of the Study of New Nations." *World Politics* (October), 17:158–81.

al-Hamamsy, Leila Shukry. 1972. "Belief Systems and Family Planning in Peasant Societies." In Brown and Hutchings, eds., *Are Our Descendants Doomed?*, pp. 335–57. New York: Viking.

Harbison, Frederick. 1959. "Management in Japan." In Harbison and Myers, *Management in the Industrial World*, pp. 249–64. New York: McGraw-Hill.

Harbison, F. and E. Burgess. 1954. "Modern Management in Western Europe." *The American Journal of Sociology*, (July), 60(1):15–23.

Harbison, F., and C. A. Myers. 1959. *Management in the Industrial World.* New York: McGraw-Hill.

Harik, Iliya. 1965. "The Iqta' System in Lebanon: A Comparative Political View." *The Middle East Journal* (Autumn), 19(4):405–21.

——1968. *Politics and Change in a Traditional Society, Lebanon, 1711–1845.* Princeton, N.J.: Princeton University Press.

——1972. *Man Yahkum Lubnan.* Beirut: Dar an-Nahar.

——1975. "Political Elites of Lebanon." In G. Lenczowski, ed., *Political Elites in the Middle East.* Washington: American Enterprise Institute for Public Policy Research.

Hartmann, Heinz. 1959. *Authority and Organization in German Management.* Princeton, N.J.: Princeton University Press.

Harvey, D. 1973. *Social Justice and the City.* London: Edward Arnold.

Hirschman, Albert. 1970. "The Search for Paradigms as a Hindrance to Understanding." *World Politics* (April), 22:329–43.

Hitti, Philip. 1957. *Lebanon in History.* London: Macmillan.

Hoselitz, B. F. 1961. "Tradition and Economic Growth." In R. Braibanti and J. J. Spengler, eds., *Traditions, Values, and Economic Development,* pp. 83–113. Durham, N.C.: Duke University Press.

Hottinger, Arnold. 1966. "Zu'ama in Historical Perspective." In L. Binder, ed., *Politics in Lebanon,* pp. 85–105. New York: Wiley.

Hourani, Albert. 1961. *Arabic Thought in a Liberal Age.* London: Oxford University Press.

——1962. "Historians of Lebanon." In B. Lewis and P. M. Holt, eds., *Historians of the Middle East.* London: Oxford University Press.

——1968. "Ottoman Reforms and the Politics of Notables." In W. Polk and R. Chambers, eds., *The Beginnings of Modernization in the Middle East,* pp. 41–68. Chicago: Chicago University Press.

——1981. *The Emergence of the Middle East.* Berkeley: University of California Press.

Hourani, Cecil. 1984. *Unfinished Odyssey.* London: Weidenfeld and Nicholson.

Hubeiysh, Khalil. 1978. *Al-Hubeiysh fi al Tarikh* (The Hubeiysh Family in History). n.p.

Hudson, M. 1966. "The Electoral Process and Political Development in Lebanon." *The Middle East Journal* (Spring), 20(2):173–86.

——1968. *The Precarious Republic.* New York: Random House.

Huntington, Samuel P. 1966. "The Political Modernization of Traditional Monarchies." *Daedalus* (Summer), 39(3):763–88.

——1968. *Political Order in Changing Societies.* New Haven: Yale University Press.

Hurewitz, J. C. 1956. *Diplomacy in the Near and Middle East,* vol. 1. Princeton, N.J.: Van Nostrand.

Iliyya, Samar. 1984. "Family Planning; The Lebanese Experience: A Study of the Lebanese Family Planning Association. M.A. thesis, American University of Beirut.

Imad, Yusef. 1973. *Al-Jami'ah al-Qarqmaziah wa-Tarikhihah* (The Qarqmaziah Association and Its History). n.p.

Inkeles, Alex. 1966. "The Modernization of Man." In Myron Weiner, ed., *Modernization: Dynamics of Growth,* pp. 151–66. New York: Basic Books.

Issawi, Charles. 1966. "Economic Development and Political Liberalism in Lebanon." In Leonard Binder, ed., *Politics in Lebanon.* New York: Wiley.

——1966. *The Economic History of the Middle East, 1800–1914.* Chicago: Chicago University Press.

——1967. "British Consular Views on Syria's Economy in the 1850's–1860's." *American University of Beirut Festival Book* (Festschrift), pp. 103–20. Beirut: Centennial Publications.

——1973. *Issawi's Laws of Social Motion.* New York: Hawthorn.

——1982. *An Economic History of the Middle East and North Africa.* New York: Columbia University Press.

Jacobs, J. 1961. *The Death and Life of Great American Cities.* New York: Random House.

al-Jaridah. 1953. *Beirut Daily.* September 7.

Jessup, Henry H. 1910. *Fifty-Three Years in Syria,* vol. 1. New York: Fleming Revell.

Jouplain, M. [Bulus Noujaim]. 1908. *La question du Liban, etude d'histoire diplomatique et de droit international.* Paris: A. Rousseau.

Karpat, Kamal. 1977. "Some Historical and Methodological Considerations Concerning Social Stratification in the Middle East." In C. A.. Van Nieuwenhuijze, ed., *Commoners, Climbers and Notables,* pp. 83–101. Leiden: Brill.

Kerr, Clark, et al. 1960. *Industrialism and Industrial Man.* Cambridge: Harvard University Press.

Kerr, Malcolm. 1959. *Lebanon in the Last Years of Feudalism, 1840–1866.* Beirut: Catholic Press.

——1966. "Political Decision Making in a Confessional Democracy." In

L. Binder, ed., *Politics in Lebanon*, pp. 187–212. New York: Wiley.

Khalaf, Samir. 1963. "Managerial Ideology and Industrial Conflict." Ph.D. diss., Princeton University.

———1965. *Prostitution in a Changing Society*. Beirut: Khayats Publishers.

———1967. "Lebanese Labor Unions: Some Comparative Structural Features." *Middle East Economic Papers*, pp. 111–38.

———1969. "Basic Social Trends in Lebanon." In Beirut College for Women, ed., *Cultural Resources of Lebanon*, pp. 147–159. Beirut: Lebanon Bookshop.

———1975. "The Americanization of the World: Western Perspectives on Modernization in Developing Societies." In *The Centrality of Science and Absolute Values*, 2:1071–95. New York: International Cultural Foundation.

———1978. "Population and Family Planning in Lebanon." Research and Training Project on Cultural Values and Population Policy. Hastings Center, N.Y.: Institute of Society, Ethics, and the Life Sciences.

———1979. *Persistence and Change in 19th Century Lebanon: A Sociological Essay*. Beirut: American University of Beirut and Syracuse University Press.

Khalaf, Samir and Per Kongstad. 1973. *Hamura of Beirut: A Case of Rapid Urbanization*. Leiden: Brill.

al-Khalidi, 'Anbara Salam. 1978. *Jawla fil-Dhikhrayat bayna Lubnan wa Filastin* (A Trip Through Memories Between Lebanon and Palestine). Beirut: Dar al-Nahar.

Khalidi, Rashid. 1981. " 'Abd al-Ghani al-'Uraisi and *al-Mufid:* The Press and Arab Nationalism before 1914." In Marwan Buheiry, ed., *Intellectual Life in the Arab East (1890–1939)*, pp. 38–61. Beirut: American University.

Khalidi, Walid. 1979. *Conflict and Violence in Lebanon: Confrontation in the Middle East*. Cambridge, Mass.: Center for International Affairs.

al-Khuri, Bishara. 1960. *Haqa' iq Lubnaniya*, vol. 1. Harissa, Lebanon.

Khuri, Fuad. 1969. "The Changing Class Structure in Lebanon." *Middle East Journal* (Winter), 23(1):29–44.

———1975. *From Village to Suburbs*. Chicago: University of Chicago Press.

Kirk, D. 1967. "Factors Affecting Modern Natality." In *Proceedings of the World Population Conference, Belgrade, 1965*. New York: United Nations.

Kooy, G. A. 1963/64. "Urbanization and Nuclear Family Individualization: A Causal Connection?" *Current Sociology* 12(1):13–24.

Korten, David. 1975. "Population Programs 1985: A Growing Management Challenge." *Studies in Family Planning* 6(7):178–87.

Landau, J. 1961. "Elections in Lebanon." *The Western Political Quarterly* 14(1):120–47.

Lande, Carl H. 1973. "Networks and Groups in Southeast Asia: Some Observations on the Group Theory of Politics." *The American Political Science Review* 67:103–127.

Landes, David S. 1957. "Observations on France: Economy, Society, and Polity." *World Politics* (April), 9(3):329–50.

LaPalombara, Joseph and Myron Weiner. 1966. "Political Parties and Political Development: Observations for a Comparative Survey." *Items,* Social Science Research Council (March), 20(1):1–7.

Lapham, Robert. 1978. "Some Ethical Considerations in Family Planning Programs." In Bermant, Kelman, and Warwick, eds., *The Ethics of Social Intervention.* Washington, D.C.: Hemisphere Publishing Corporation.

Lasch, Christopher. 1977. *Haven in a Heartless World.* New York: W. W. Norton.

——1979. *The Culture of Narcissism.* New York: W. W. Norton.

——1984. The Minimal Self. New York: W. W. Norton.

Lebanese Family Planning Association. 1974. *The Family in Lebanon* (in Arabic). Beirut: Lebanese Family Planning Association.

Lebanese Family Planning Association (LFPA). 1977. *The Community Based Family Planning Services Program.* Beirut: LFPA.

Lebanese Family Planning Association. 1979. *Min Ajl Ghadin Akthar Ishraqan ila al-Usra wal Mujtama* (For a Brighter Future to the Family and Society). Beirut: LFPA Publications.

Lebanese Family Planning Association (LFPA). 1982. *Al-Siyasat al Sukkaniyah fi Lubnan* (Population Policy in Lebanon). Beirut: Research Center, Institute of Social Sciences, Lebanese University.

Lebanese Republic, Direction Centrale de la Statistique. 1972. *L'enquete par sondage sur la population active an Liban.*

Lebanese Republic, Ministry of Planning. 1965. *Social Welfare in Lebanon.* Beirut.

Lemarchand, Rene. 1972. "Political Clientalism and Ethnicity in Tropical Africa: Competing Solidarities in Nation-Building." *The American Political Science Review* (March), 55(1):68–90.

Lemarchand, Rene and Keith Legg. 1972. "Political Clientelism and Development: a Preliminary Analysis." *Comparative Politics* (January), vol. 4, no. 2.

Lerner, Daniel. 1964. *The Passing of Traditional Society*. Glencoe: Ill.: Free Press.

Lévi-Strauss, C. 1963. *Structural Anthropology*. New York: Basic Books.

Levy, Marion J. 1952. *The Structure of Society*. Princeton, N.J.: Princeton University Press.

—— 1953. "Contrasting Factors in the Modernization of China and Japan." *Economic Development and Cultural Change*, pp. 161–97.

Lewis, Archibald R. 1969. "The Midi, Buwayhid Iraq, and Japan: Some Aspects of Comparative Feudalism, A.D. 469–1055." *Comparative Studies in Society and History* 11(1):47–53.

Lewis, Bernard. 1968. *The Emergence of Modern Turkey*. London: Oxford University Press.

Lewis, John. 1969. "The Social Limits of Politically Induced Change." In Morse, Ashford et al., eds., *Modernization by Design*, pp. 1–33. Ithaca, N.Y.: Cornell University Press.

Litwak, Eugene. 1960. "Occupational Mobility and Extended Family Cohesion." *American Sociological Review* (February), 25:9–21.

—— 1960. "Geographic Mobility and Extended Family Cohesion." *American Sociological Review* (June), 25:385–94.

Lowenthal, D. and H. Prince. "The English Landscape." *Geographical Review* 54:304–46.

Lynch, K. 1960. *The Image of the City*. Cambridge: MIT Press.

Makdisi, Anis Khoury. 1980. *Ma' al-Zaman* (With the Times). Compiled and Edited by Yusuf Ibish and Yusuf Khoury. Beirut.

Maksoud, Clovis. 1966. "Lebanon and Arab Nationalism." In Leonard Binder, ed., *Politics in Lebanon*, pp. 239–54. New York: Wiley.

Ma'oz, Moshe. 1968. "The Impact of Modernization on Syrian Politics and Society during the Early *Tanzimat* Period." In Polk and Chambers, eds., *Beginnings of Modernization in the Middle East*, pp. 333–50. Chicago: University of Chicago Press.

—— 1968. *Ottoman Reform in Syria and Palestine, 1840–1861*. New York: Oxford University Press.

Mardin, Serif. 1962. *The Genesis of Young Ottoman Thought*. Princeton, N.J.: Princeton University Press.

Matthews, D. 1960. *U.S. Senators and Their World*. Chapel Hill: University of North Carolina Press.

Mazrui, Ali. 1968. "From Social Darwinism to Current Theories of Modernization." *World Politics* 21:68–83.

Melikian, Levon and Lutfi Diab. 1959. "Group Affiliation of University Students in the Arab Middle East." *Journal of Social Psychology* 49:145–49.

———1974. "Change in Group Affiliation of University Students in the Arab Middle East." *Journal of Social Psychology* 93:13–21.

Melikian, L. and L. Diab. 1974. "Stability and Change in Group Affiliation of University Students in the Arab Middle East." *Journal of Social Psychology* 93:13–21.

Mernissi, Fatima. 1975a. *Beyond the Veil: Male-Female Dynamics in a Modern Muslim Society.* New York: Wiley.

———1975b. "Obstacles to Family Planning Practice in Urban Morocco." *Studies in Family Planning* 6(12):418–25.

Messarra, A. 1974. "La structure sociale du Parlement libanais." Thesis, Université de Strasbourg.

———1983. "The Organization of Accommodation in Lebanon: Parliament and Paraparliaments in a Plural Society." Paper read at the conference, "Violence and Conflict Management in Divided Societies." European Consortium for Political Research—West Germany, March 20–25, 1983.

Mills, Arthur. 1956. "Economic Change in Lebanon." *Middle East Economic Papers,* pp. 75–97. Economic Research Institute: American University of Beirut.

Morse, Chandler. 1969. "Becoming vs. Being Modern: An Essay on Institutional Change and Economic Development." In Morse, Ashford et al., eds., *Modernization by Design,* pp. 238–382. Ithaca, N.Y.: Cornell University Press.

Munro, John. 1977. *A Mutual Concern: The Story of the American University of Beirut.* New York: Caravan.

Musallam, B. F. 1983. *Sex and Society in Islam.* Cambridge: Cambridge University Press.

Myers, Charles. 1959a. "Management in India." In Harbison and Myers, *Management in the Industrial World,* pp. 137–53. New York: McGraw-Hill.

———1959b. "Management in Chile." In F. Harbison and C. Myers, *Management in the Industrial World,* pp. 169–84. New York: McGraw-Hill.

An-Nahar. 1972. *Al-Intikhabat* (Elections). Beirut: Dar an-Nahar.

——1972. *Beirut Daily*. December.

Nash, J., J. Dandler, and N. Hopkins, eds. 1976. *Popular Participation in Social Change*. The Hague: Morton.

Nash, Manning. 1960. "Kinship and Voluntary Associations." In W. E. Moore and A. Feldman, eds., *Labor Commitment and Social Change in Developing Areas*, pp. 313–25. New York: Social Science Research Council.

Nashabi, Hisham. 1981. "Shaykh 'Abd al-Qadir al-Qabbani and *Thamarat al-Funun*." In Marwan Buheiry, ed., *Intellectual Life in the Arab East*. Beirut: American University.

Nasr, Salim. 1982. "The War, Urban Networks and Population Movement in Greater Beirut." *Al-Waqi'* (Fall), no. 5/6, pp. 317–32.

Neale, F. A. 1852. *Eight Years in Syria, Palestine and Asia Minor*, vol. 1. 2d ed. London: Colburn.

Nisbet, Robert A. 1967. *The Sociological Tradition*, pp. 132–41. New York: Basic Books.

——1970. *The Social Bond*. New York: Knopf.

Omvedt, Gail. 1971. "Modernization Theories: The Ideology of Empires," In A. R. Desai, ed., *Essays on Modernization of Underdeveloped Societies*, 1:119–37. Bombay: Thacker.

Pappenheim, Fritz, 1959. *The Alienation of Modern Man*. New York: Monthly Review Press.

Parsons, Talcott. 1957. "The Social Structure of the Family." In Ruth Anshen, ed., *The Family: Its Functions and Destiny*, pp. 241–74. New York: Harper.

——1963. "Christianity and Modern Industrial Society." In Edward A. Tiryakian, ed., *Sociological Theory Values and Socio-Cultural Change*, pp. 33–77. New York: Free Press.

Pattison, E. Mansell. 1984. "War and Mental Health in Lebanon." *Journal of Operational Psychiatry* 15:31–38.

Penrose, Stephen. 1941. *That They May Have Life*. (Princeton, N.J.: Princeton University Press.

Peters, Emrys. 1963. "Aspects of Rank and Status Among Muslims in a Lebanese Village." In J. Pitt-Rivers, ed., *Mediterranean Countrymen*. The Hague: Mouton.

Poliak, A. N. 1939. *Feudalism: Egypt, Syria, Palestine, and the Lebanon, 1250–1900*. London: The Royal Asiatic Society.

Polk, William, ed. 1962. "Document: Rural Syria in 1845." *Middle East Journal*, 16:508–14.

——1963. *The Opening of South Lebanon, 1788–1840.* Cambridge: Harvard University Press.

Polk, William and Richard Chambers. 1968. Editor's Introduction to *Beginnings of Modernization in the Middle East,* pp. 1–25. Chicago: University of Chicago Press.

Porath, Yehoshua. 1966. "The Peasant Revolt of 1851–61 in Kisrawan." *Asian and African Studies* 2:77–157.

Poujade, Eugene. 1867. *Le Liban et la Syrie, 1845–1860.* Paris: Librairie Nouvelle.

Prothro, E. T. and L. N. Diab. 1974. *Changing Family Patterns in the Arab East.* Beirut: American University of Beirut.

Radcliffe-Brown, A. R. 1968. "Introduction to the Analysis of Kinship Systems." In N. W. Bell and E. I. Vogel, eds., *A Modern Introduction to the Family,* pp. 242–71. New York: Free Press.

Ragheb (Southall), I. 1969. "Patterns of Urban Growth in the Middle East." In G. Breese, ed., *The City in Newly Developing Countries,* pp. 104–26. Englewood Cliffs, N.J.: Prentice-Hall.

Riggs, Fred V. 1964. *Administration in Developing Countries: The Theory of Prismatic Society.* Boston: Houghton Mifflin.

Rondot, P. 1966. "The Political Institutions of Lebanese Democracy." In L. Binder, ed., *Politics in Lebanon.,* pp. 127–42. New York: Wiley.

Ross, J. 1949. *Parliamentary Representation.* New Haven: Yale University Press.

Rostow, Walt W. 1960. *The Stages of Economic Growth: A Non-Communist Manifesto.* Cambridge: Cambridge University Press.

Rubinoff, Lionel. 1971. "The Crisis of Modernity: The Implicit Barbarism of Technology." In Lionel Rubinoff, ed., *Tradition and Revolution.* Toronto: Macmillan.

Rudolph, Lloyd and Suzanne Rudolph. 1967. *The Modernity of Traditions.* Chicago: University of Chicago Press.

Rustow, Dankwart A. and Robert A. Ward. 1964. Introduction to D. A. Rustow and R. A. Ward, eds., *Political Modernization in Japan and Turkey,* pp. 3–14. Princeton, N.J.: Princeton University Press.

Rustum, Asad, ed. 1934. *Al Usul Al-Arabiyyah Li Tarikh Suriyyah Fi 'Ahd Muhammad 'Ali Pasha,* vol. 5. Beirut: American University.

——1937. "Safhah Jadidah fi Tarikh al Thawrah and Durziyah: 1834–1838." *Al-Mashriq,* vol. 35.

Saab, Hassan. 1966. "The Rationalist School in Lebanese Politics." In Leonard Binder, ed., *Politics in Lebanon*, pp. 271–82. New York: Wiley.

Sa'adeh, G. A. 1964. *Tarikh at-Intikhabat fi Lubnan*. Junieh: Arab Publishing Agency.

Saba, Paul. 1976. "The Creation of the Lebanese Economy: Economic Growth in the Nineteenth and Early Twentieth Centuries." In Roger Owen, ed., *Essay on the Crisis in Lebanon*, pp. 1–22. London: Ithaca Press.

Sabet, Magda. 1970. "Family Planning in Lebanon Was Only Discovered When We Started to Work on It." *Daily Star*, January 25.

as-Safa. 1964. Beirut, March 10.

Said, Edward. 1984. "Reflections on Exile." *Granta* (Autumn), 13:159–72.

———1985. "Edward Said Reflects on the Fall of Beirut." *London Review of Books*, July 4, pp. 3–4.

Salam, A. 1972. "Town Planning in Beirut and Its Outskirts." In John Taylor, ed., *Planning for Urban Growth*, pp. 109–20. New York: Praeger.

Salem, Elie. 1965. "Local Elections in Lebanon: A Case Study." *Midwest Journal of Political Science* (November), 9(4):367–87.

———1966. "Cabinet Politics in Lebanon." American University of Beirut. Mimeographed.

Salibi, Kamal. 1959. *Maronite Historians of Medieval Lebanon*. Beirut: Catholic Press.

———1965. *The Modern History of Lebanon*. London: Weidenfeld and Nicolson.

———1976. *Crossroads to Civil War*, New York: Caravan Books.

Sayigh, Y. 1962. *Entrepreneurs of Lebanon*. Cambridge: Harvard University Press.

Schatkowski, Linda. 1969. "The Islamic Maqased of Beirut". M.A. thesis, American University of Beirut.

Scott, James C. 1972. "Patron-Client Politics and Political Change in Southeast Asia." *The American Political Science Review* (March), 66(1):91–113.

Sharabi, Hisham. 1970. *Arab Intellectuals and the West: The Formative Years, 1875–1914*. Baltimore: Johns Hopkins University Press.

———1978. *Al-Jamr wal Ramad* (Coal and Ashes). Beirut: Dar al-Tali'at.

Shaw, Stanford. 1968. "Some Aspects of the Aims and Achievements of the 19th Century Ottoman Reformers." In Polk and Chambers, eds., *Beginnings of Modernization in the Middle East*, pp. 32–33. Chicago: University of Chicago Press.

al-Shidyaq, Tannus. 1970. *Akhbar al-'Ayan fi Jabal Lubnan*. F. E. Bustani, ed. Beirut: Universite Libanaise.

Shihab, Haydar. 1933. *Lubnan fi Ahd al Umara' al Shihabiyyin*. A. S. Rustum and F. E. Bustani, eds. Beirut: Catholic Press.

Shils, Edward. 1957. 'Primordial, Personal, Sacred and Civil Ties." *British Journal of Sociology* (June), 8:130–45.

——1961. "Further Thought on Tradition and Modernity." *The Problems of Afro-Asian States*. London: Congress for Cultural Freedom.

——1962. *Political Development in the New States*. The Hague: Mouton.

——1971. "Tradition." *Comparative Studies in Society and History* 13:122–59.

Shuayb, Diana. 1984. "Family Loyalty and Career Preferences in Lebanon," M.A. thesis, American University of Beirut.

Shwayri, Emilie. 1964. "Family Firms as a Factor in Lebanon's Industrial Growth." M.A.thesis, American University of Beirut.

Siebel, H. D. and A. Massing. 1976. *Traditional Organization and Economic Development*. New York: Praeger.

Siegel, Bernard. 1955. "Social Structure and Economic Change in Brazil." In S. Kuznets, W. E. Moore, and J. Spengler, eds., *Economic Growth: Brazil, India, Japan*, pp. 388–411. Durham, N.C.: Duke University Press.

Sinai, R. 1971. "Modernization and the Poverty of Social Science." In A. R. Desai, ed., *Essays on Modernization of Underdeveloped Societies*, 1:53–75. Bombay: Thacker.

Singer, Milton. 1972. *When a Great Tradition Modernizes*. New York: Praeger.

Sinnu, Baha al Din Rashid. 1984. *A'ilat Sinnu* (The Sinnu Family). Beirut: n.p.

Smelser, Neil. 1963. *The Sociology of Economic Life*. Englewood Cliffs, N.J.: Prentice-Hall.

——1964. "Toward a Theory of Modernization." In A. Etzioni and E. Etzioni, eds., *Social Change*, pp. 258–74. New York: Basic Books.

Smilianskaya, I. M. 1966. "The Disintegration of Feudal Relations in Syria and Lebanon in the Middle of the 19th Century." In Charles Issawi, ed., *The Economic History of the Middle East 1800–1914*, pp. 226–47. Chicago: University of Chicago Press.

———1972. *Al Harakat al-Fillahiya fi Lubnan.* Translated by Adnan Jamous. Beirut: Dar al-Farabi Press.

Smith, Tony. 1985. "Requiem or New Agenda for Third World Studies?" *World Politics* (July), 37(4):532–56.

Smock, David and Audry Smock. 1975. *The Politics of Pluralism: A Comparative Study of Lebanon and Ghana.* New York: Elsevier.

al-Solh, Sami. 1960. *Mudhakkirat* (Memoirs). Beirut: n.p.

al-Solh, Munah. 1984. "Kiyan Mu'allaq bayna Thaqafatayn Siyasiyyatayn" (Suspended Entity Between Two Political Cultures). Beirut: *al-Safeer,* May 14.

Sovani, N. V. 1969. "The Analysis of Over-Urbanization." In G. Breese, ed., *The City in Newly Developing Countries,* pp. 322–30. Englewood Cliffs, N.J.: Prentice-Hall.

Srinivas, M. N. 1971. "Modernization: A Few Queries." In A. R. Desai, ed., *Essays on Modernization of Underdeveloped Societies,* 1:138–48. Bombay: Thacker.

Stanhope, Lady Hester. 1846. *Memoirs of the Lady Hester Stanhope,* vol. 1. 2d ed. London: Henry Colburn.

Starr, Paul. 1977. "Lebanon." In C. A. O. Van Nieuwenhuijze, ed., *Commoners, Climbers and Notables,* pp. 203–25. Leiden: Brill.

Suleiman, M. 1967. *Political Parties in Lebanon.* Ithaca, N.Y.: Cornell University Press.

Tabbarah, Bahige B. 1954. "Les forces politiques actuelles an Lidan." Thesis, Université de Grenoble, April.

Tamim, Suha, ed. 1967. *A Bibliography of A.U.B. Faculty Publications, 1866–1966.* Beirut: American University.

Tanas, Raja. 1974. "Family Planning: Knowledge, Attitude, and Practice in Tyre, Lebanon." M.A. thesis, in Sociology, American University of Beirut.

Tarabey, Bardalian. 1983. *Al-Tarbey fi al-Tarikh* (The Tarabeys in History). Lahd Khatir Publishing House.

Teitelbaum, Michael. 1974. "Population and Development: Is a Consensus Possible?" *Foreign Affairs* (July), 52(4):742–60.

Tibawi, A. L. 1969. *A Modern History of Syria.* Edinburgh: Macmillan; New York: St. Martin's Press.

Tipps, Dean C. 1973. "Modernization Theory and the Comparative Study of Societies: A Critical Perspective." *Comparative Studies in Society and History* (March), 15:199–226.

Van Dusen, Roxan. 1973. "Social Changes and Decision Making: Family Planning in Lebanon." Ph.D. thesis, John Hopkins University.

Volkan, Vamik. 1979. *Cyprus, War, and Adaptation: A Psychoanalytic History of Two Ethnic Groups in Conflict*. Charlottesville: University Press of Virginia.

Volney, Constantin Francois. 1788. *Travels Through Syria and Egypt in the Years 1783, 1784, 1785*, vol. 2. London: C. G. J. and Y. Robinson.

Wallerstein, Immanuel. 1974. *The Modern World System: Capitalist Agriculture and the Origin of the European World Economy in the 16th Century*. New York: Academic Press.

——1980. *The Modern World System II: Mercantilism and the Consolidation of the European World-Economy, 1600–1750*. New York: Academic Press.

Warwick, Donald. 1982. *Bitter Pills: Population Policies and Their Implementation in Eight Developing Countries*. New York: Cambridge University Press.

Weaver, R. 1963. "Major Factors in Urban Planning." In Leonard Duhl, ed., *The Urban Condition*, pp. 97–112. New York: Basic Books.

Webber, M. 1963. "Order in Diversity: Community Without Propinquity." In L. Wingo, ed., *Cities and Space: The Future Use of Urban Land*. Baltimore: Johns Hopkins University Press.

Welch, C. E. 1967. "The Comparative Study of Political Modernization." In C. E. Welch, ed., *Political Modernization*, pp. 8–14. Belmont, Calif.: Wadsworth.

Wertheim, W. F. 1971. "The Way Towards 'Modernity.'" In A. R. Desai, ed., *Essays on Modernization of Underdeveloped Societies*, 1:76–94. Bombay: Thacker.

Whyte, W. F. 1943. *Street Corner Society*. Chicago: University of Chicago Press.

Wiarda, Howard, ed., 1985. *New Directions in Comparative Politics*. Boulder, Colo.: Westview Press.

Wilhelm, S. M. 1962. *Urban Planning and Land-Use Theory*. Glencoe: Free Press.

Willner, Ann. 1964. "The Underdeveloped Study of Political Development." *World Politics* (April), pp. 468–82.

Winder, B. 1962. "Syrian Deputies and Cabinet Ministers, 1919–1959." *The Middle East Journal* 16(4):407–29.

——1963. "Syrian Deputies and Cabinet Ministers, 1919–1959." *The Middle East Journal* 17(1):35–54.

Yamak, L. Z. 1966. "Party Politics in the Lebanese Political System." In L. Binder, ed., *Politics in Lebanon*, pp. 143–66. New York: Wiley.

Yaukey, David. 1961. *Fertility Differences in a Modernizing Society*. Princeton, N.J.: Princeton University Press.

Zuwiyya, J. 1972. *The Parliamentary Elections of Lebanon, 1968*. Leiden: Brill.

Zimmerman, C. C. and M. E. Frampton. 1935. *Family and Society: A Study of the Sociology of Reconstruction*. New York: Van Nostrand.

Index